Historic Zuni Architecture and Society

An Archaeological Application of Space Syntax

ANTHROPOLOGICAL PAPERS OF
THE UNIVERSITY OF ARIZONA
NUMBER 60

Historic Zuni Architecture and Society

An Archaeological Application of Space Syntax

T. J. Ferguson

THE UNIVERSITY OF ARIZONA PRESS
TUCSON
1996

About the Author

T. J. FERGUSON has been engaged in archaeological and ethnohistoric research in the southwestern United States for twenty years. He completed his undergraduate education at the University of Hawaii at Hilo (1973), and received a master's degree in anthropology from the University of Arizona (1976), a Master of Community and Regional Planning from the University of New Mexico (1985), and a doctoral degree in anthropology from the University of New Mexico (1993). Dr. Ferguson worked for the Zuni Archaeology Program from 1976 to 1981 and from 1984 to 1985. His subsequent research at Zuni Pueblo has been undertaken as a Research Associate of the Zuni Archaeology Program (now the Zuni Heritage and Historic Preservation Office). From 1988 to 1995, Dr. Ferguson served as Director of Southwest Programs for the Institute of the NorthAmerican West, conducting anthropological research for land and water rights litigation and tribal cultural resources management. Since 1991 he has been an adjunct curator of archaeology at the Arizona State Museum, Tucson. In addition to continuing research in Pueblo architecture and society, Dr. Ferguson is investigating the history of Zuni and Hopi land use, focusing on the role that archaeological sites and natural resources play in the transmission and maintenance of Puebloan culture.

Cover: Ojo Caliente, about 1920. Photograph is by Jesse L. Nusbaum. (Courtesy of the Denver Public Library, Western History Division, Negative N329.)

THE UNIVERSITY OF ARIZONA PRESS

This book was set in 10.7/12 CG Times
∞ This book is printed on acid-free, archival-quality paper.
Manufactured in the United States of America.

99 98 97 96 9 8 7 6

Library of Congress Cataloging-in-Publication Data

Ferguson, T. J. (Thomas John), 1950–
Historic Zuni architecture and society : an archaeological application of space syntax / T. J. Ferguson.
p. cm. -- (Anthropological papers of the University of Arizona ; no. 60)
Includes bibliographic references and index.
ISBN 0–8165–1608–1 (acid-free paper)
1. Zuni architecture. 2. Zuni Indians--Social life and customs. 3. Zuni Indians--Antiquities. 4. Architecture and society--New Mexico. 5. Symbolism in architecture--New Mexico. 6. Spatial behavior--New Mexico. 7. Social structure--New Mexico. 8. Social archaeology--New Mexico. 9. New Mexico--Antiquities. I. Title. II. Series.
E99.Z9F47 1996
307.3'212'089974--dc20 95–50245
CIP

Contents

FIGURES

TABLES

Foreword

Andrew L. Othole
Pueblo of Zuni

Countless centuries ago the first Zuni (A:shiwi) People emerged from the depths of the four worlds beneath the bottom of the Grand Canyon. In an attempt to reach the surface, various species of vegetation and conifer were utilized to scale the steep walls. Once the surface was reached, the A:shiwi People were greeted by Sun Father. Oral narratives tell us that our ancestors had web palms and tails. Supernatural beings that accompanied Sun Father repositioned or corrected these irregular figurations. It was there that the A:shiwi People were given instructions to seek and locate the center of the universe, present-day Zuni. Physical evidence of their search dots the landscape throughout the Southwest; scattered habitation sites and associated burials recount their advancement.

Between the early eleventh century and the late 1800s, a dramatic change occurred in the Southwest. Architectural styles became more intricate and refined. Modern-day Pueblo people continue to be influenced by these techniques and styles. The Zuni (A:shiwi) People witnessed and participated in this change through evolution in their respective satellite communities rather than abandoning their homeland. Like an umbilical cord, our traditions and customs remain continual from the Archaic period through the Basketmaker to the contemporary Pueblos.

Dr. Ferguson's study of space and structure describes population estimates, temporal placement, and architectural arrangements of the historic Zuni settlements. His analysis of the 1885 farming villages compared with early seventeenth-century villages indicates little or no significant change in these sites. Early anthropologists of the late 1800s such as Mindeleff, Bandelier, Fewkes, and Cushing developed archaeological methodology and techniques. In the 1900s, individual researchers such as Spier, Hodge, Kroeber, Smith, Kintigh, Mills, and Ferguson, just to name a few, have improved on the earlier observations by constantly comparing and consulting site plans, site descriptions, and maps. In the end, they have verified similar conclusions. Many different techniques have been applied using different variables and archaeological procedures. Dr. Ferguson's research techniques were based on a sensitive approach that did not involve destruction of archaeological sites by excavation or collection of artifacts.

Dr. Ferguson, as a Research Associate of the Zuni Archaeology Program, was given permission by the Zuni Tribal Council to undertake his research to fulfill the requirements of his doctoral dissertation, in cooperation and coordination with the A:shiwi People. My association with Dr. Ferguson goes back to the early 1980s. Since then I have had the opportunity to work with him on various projects in the field, and he gave me the encouragement to pursue a discipline in archaeology. My understanding of anthropology and its scientific application and my holistic views prepared me to better grasp the subject matter. I later served as the Cultural Preservation Coordinator with the Zuni Heritage and Historic Preservation Office.

The experience that I gained in assisting Dr. Ferguson with the mapping of our ancestral architectural units on Dowa Yalanne and Heshoda Łuwal'a further inspired my interest in the prehistory and history of our ancestors. Dr. Ferguson's contribution and research was undertaken with a professional attitude and with an understanding of our lifeways that enabled him to maintain the highest respect and honor with the Zuni (A:shiwi) People.

Preface

The strategy of archaeology is to observe material objects in the present to understand the past. In this report, the structural relationship between the architecture of historic Zuni settlements and Zuni society is analyzed using archaeological information to learn something new about the changes that have occurred in historic Zuni society. A methodological basis is established to make inferences about the nonmaterial units of analysis that figure in the theoretical formulations used to describe the structure of society. In developing this methodology, an interdisciplinary approach is applied that draws on general theory from the fields of anthropology, sociology, architecture, and planning. The specific techniques of a new theory of space syntax developed by architects form the basis for analyzing Zuni settlements occupied between the Spanish Entrada of 1540 and the 1980s. It is through the analysis of a series of settlements that changes in the structure of architecture and society are charted.

The term architecture as used herein refers to both the method of planning and building structures and the structures themselves. The buildings that are the material products of architecture are arranged into settlements that physically house society. These settlements comprise a built environment that entails modification of extensive landscapes. It is the concept of space and how it is partitioned within and between the architectural units of the built environment that is the theoretical key to this research. Space as defined by architecture is appropriate for archaeological study because it entails a materialization that is often preserved in the archaeological record. The excavation of archaeological sites is a time consuming and expensive procedure. This work demonstrates a way to analyze information collected from surface surveys of archaeological sites, thus providing an opportunity to include a large number of sites in the analysis.

Although explicitly archaeological, this study crosscuts a number of disciplines. The information analyzed is derived from archaeological sites and contemporary standing architecture. The theory, method, and techniques of space syntax are adapted from architecture and planning. The results of the analysis are evaluated using ethnographic and historical data. The fundamental approach applied in the research is a form of structuralism, although this structuralism is specifically related to the planning of settlements and not to mentalistic or cultural variables. The goal is not to understand how architecture structures space as perceived or conceptualized by the Zuni Indians, but to develop a more abstract and analytical approach to systematically link the structure of Zuni society to the structure of the architectural forms that house it.

The time interval covered is a crucial one for understanding Southwestern prehistory and history. Considering the continuity between the prehistoric and historic Pueblos in the southwestern United States, many archaeologists have traditionally interpreted the prehistoric record using arguments based on analogy with contemporary Pueblos as known ethnographically. The theoretical and methodological validity of this interpretive strategy has come under criticism in recent years by archaeologists who assert that the changes that have occurred in the historic period make historic Pueblos an inappropriate analogy for prehistoric pueblos. They argue that a substantial decline in population, the entry of Athabaskans and Euro-Americans into the region, the introduction of new technologies and sociopolitical organizations, and the changing physical environment have all altered the historic Pueblos to such an extent that they are no longer analogous to their prehistoric predecessors.

The type and degree of change the historic Pueblos have undergone, therefore, is of some theoretical importance in Southwestern archaeology. The way to determine the validity of analogical arguments entailing comparison of prehistoric and historic Pueblos is through analysis of their structural and organizational properties and not through historical contingencies. Unfortunately, the relative lack of historical archaeology and the dearth of detailed historical information from written records make it hard to evaluate how exactly the Pueblos have changed. This fact adds significance to an archaeological investigation of change in historic Zuni society. Although this work does not explicitly address how the historic Pueblos differ from their predecessors, it does provide information pertinent to this topic.

Acknowledgments

This report is based on research that was funded in part through a National Science Foundation Dissertation Improvement Grant (BNS-8720491) supervised by Dr. Wirt H. Wills at the University of New Mexico. Dr. Jeremy Sabloff, Dr. Robert D. Leonard, Dr. Alfonso Ortiz, and Dr. Theodore Jojola provided many helpful comments that improved the original work.

The research was undertaken with the written permission of the Zuni Tribal Council. All fieldwork on the Zuni Indian Reservation was conducted between 1988 and 1991 under the auspices of the Zuni Archaeology Program (now the Zuni Heritage and Historic Preservation Office), directed by Roger Anyon. At the time, I was a Research Associate of the Zuni Archaeology Program.

Many people assisted me in mapping architecture at Dowa Yalanne, Wimaya:wa, and Heshoda Łuwal'a, and their help in completing the fieldwork in a timely manner is especially appreciated: Giani Baratta, Aleosandra Cazzaniga, Tom Chatterton, Sue Converse, Vernee Day, James Enloe, Cindy Herhahn, Barbara Holmes, Martha Graham, Dennis Gilpin, Renee Johnson, Brian Patrick Keane, Christina Koizumi, Ed Kotyk, Karen Kupnitzky, Laura Leach-Palm, Robert D. Leonard, Arthur Mason, Barbara J. Mills, Randy Nathan, Amy Nevitt, Andrew Othole, Julie Polk, Heidi Reed, Mark B. Sant, Ronald Stauber, Zachary Stauber, Wirt H. Wills, and Kate Wilson.

Through the years E. Richard Hart graciously shared valuable historical knowledge and many stimulating ideas about Zuni history and historiography. Ronald Stauber, Andrew Othole, and Robert D. Leonard deserve particular credit for their helpful advice and skill with field cartography. Special thanks are extended to Roger Anyon for his unflagging hospitality during numerous visits to his home in Zuni Pueblo. On these occasions, I benefited from untold hours of stimulating conversation about archaeological method and theory and from the food and shelter he provided to yet one more anthropologist who recurrently appeared at his door. Roger Anyon was instrumental in obtaining the information about Zuni vernacular and HUD homes analyzed in Chapter 6. Nan Rothschild, Barnard College, Columbia University, offered useful comments, and the manuscript has been improved through the editorial work of Carol Gifford. Photographers are identified in the captions. The Institute of the NorthAmerican West provided financial support for publication.

My parents, Doris and Thomas J. Ferguson, helped to support the field research. My wife, Barbara J. Mills, provided advice about quantitative techniques, and her enthusiasm and high standards for scientific research provided an endless source of inspiration and motivation.

CHAPTER ONE

Architecture and Society

There is an increasing appreciation by archaeologists that spatial patterns of behavior are related to social factors as well as to environmental concerns dealing with resource distribution (Agorsah 1988, 1993; Holl 1993). People locate themselves in space and design settlements to serve their social needs. In the southwestern United States, archaeological research directed toward investigating social organization has generally taken the form of "paleoethnography" in that it attempts to identify and explain changes in social organization in terms of the social units defined by ethnographers. This is an old and venerable research strategy, with its genesis in Cushing's (1890: 160) conceptualization of archaeology as simply ethnology projected into the past.

THE ARCHAEOLOGICAL STUDY OF SOCIETY IN THE SOUTHWEST

Since Cushing's time, archaeological research into prehistoric and historic social organization in the Southwest has entailed an attempt to determine the material analogs of the social units of the kin and clan descent groups made famous through the classic ethnographic work of Kroeber (1917), Lowie (1929), Eggan (1950), and others. Archaeologists have sought to identify households, lineages, clans, and moieties in the archaeological record (for example, Mindeleff 1900; Dean 1969: 191–192, 1970; Hill 1970a, 1970b; Lipe 1970; Rohn 1971: 31–41; Reid and Whittlesey 1982; Adams 1983; Vivian 1990: 421–448) and then frame subsequent interpretation of social change in these terms (Dozier 1970). Archaeologists thus remain dependent on the ethnographic record (Aberle 1970: 217–218). The derivation of purely archaeological (that is, material) units of social organization has not received the attention such units deserve, even though the explicitly archaeological units offer a perspective better suited to understanding the long-term social processes that result in the deposition of the archaeological record than does the ethnographic record.

Ironically, as paleoethnographic research has proceeded, the ethnographic and structural validity of many classic social units in kinship and descent theory are increasingly being called into question by ethnographers themselves (Allen and Richardson 1971). Whiteley (1985, 1986), for instance, has recently argued that Hopi clans, a mainstay of archaeological notions about Puebloan social organization, do not function as the ritual, jural, or economic corporate descent groups they are often imputed to be in structural-functionalist descriptions (compare Levy 1992, who articulates the conventional interpretation). As Whiteley (1986: 78) states:

> The division of Hopi social structure into households, lineages, clans, and phratries and the insistence that lineages and clans constitute distinct groups centered upon corporate estates have obscured the realities of Hopi society. That these descent-group levels are potentially *observable* is not denied. That they appear in isomorphic forms with parallel functions in the total social structure is quite simply not the case. . . . Descent theory provides a template for describing some elements of Hopi organization. However, its use is limited in scope, for Hopi society is more complex than the parameters of the theory allow [emphasis in original].

Cameron's (1992) investigation of the reorganization of settlement architecture and residential patterns following the factional dispute and social split at the Hopi village of Oraibi in 1906 supports Whiteley to the extent that it documents that the establishment of new settlements on Third Mesa was not by clan groups but by households.

It is time to move beyond the archaeological analysis of settlements using ethnographic terms. New concepts of social organization grounded in the material expressions of social life are needed. Inasmuch as some of these new concepts relate to the architectural remains that comprise such a prominent part of the archaeological record, we need new ways to describe and analyze architecture that move beyond the simple and all too common descriptions of settlement forms using terms such as "dispersed," "nucleated," and "aggregated." Although these terms serve to differentiate major types of settlement forms, they offer little with respect to describing or understanding the variation that exists within and among the societies that occupied the settlements.

SOCIAL STRUCTURE

A society comprises a set of individuals in which any two members of the set share relations of mutual interests, common culture, and institutional organization (Friedman 1975: 142). Every society has a structure that organizes the forms of social interaction that enable the individual members of that society to carry out the activities needed to sustain their lives and meet other needs. Social structure can and does change through time, so a structuralist approach is pertinent to the study of the development of particular societies.

The archaeological study of social structure, however, presents major theoretical and methodological problems. Archaeologists study tangible artifacts to learn about past human behavior, yet social structure is commonly perceived as intangible. As Sears (1961: 225) points out, "A prehistoric social system cannot be excavated like a house. . . . " Similarly, Redman and his colleagues (1978: 5) observe that "No social anthropologist or archeologist has ever seen a social structure," noting, however, that both may make inferences about social structure based on controlled observations. Whereas ethnographers can watch humans engaged in social interaction and make inferences about social structure based on the behavior they have observed, archaeologists must base their inferences on some objective connection between the structure of society and the material remains of the archaeological record. To begin this study of Zuni society, I draw together anthropological, sociological, and architectural theory to develop an archaeological approach to the study of social structure and its change through time.

Much of the anthropological research into social organization has concentrated on the structure of society as determined by the organization and functioning of kinship and descent groups, with emphasis on patterns of residence and inheritance (Lowie 1948; Murdock 1949; Eggan 1950). Social structure in this research is an analytical conceptualization of the ordered relations of parts to a whole. It describes the arrangement that links the elements of social life together, and explains how these elements function as a cohesive unit. Social structure is not perceived as static, however, for it is dependent on the persistence or repetition of behavior that can and does change through time in response to alterations in the social and technological context in which behavior occurs (Firth 1963: 30–40).

As Eggan (1950: 4–6) notes, the primary source of information for the study of social organization is the behavior of individuals in social situations. Society and culture are more general concepts, the content and organization of which are inferred from the primary data. Individuals, society, and culture are viewed as being interrelated in one ongoing process. In Eggan's (1950: 4) formulation, "A society is a group of individuals who have adjusted their interests sufficiently to co-operate in satisfying their various needs." Social structure is seen as the network of relations that binds the individuals of a social group together for certain purposes. Although the units of social behavior in any society are social usages, that is, behavior patterns between different individuals or groups under given conditions, the units of social structure are the social relations that develop through recurring expressions of social usages. Social structure, as the network of social relations between individuals and groups, is thus the organizational or configurational aspect through which society functions.

If a theoretical framework is to include social change, it must be built in a way that accommodates the alterations made to social structures through time. Firth (1963: 82–84) indicates that to be truly dynamic such analysis must make room for individual action, which entails a temporal dimension that ethnographers are rarely privileged to witness. In contrast, the real time depth embedded in the archaeological record is, in many respects, better suited for the investigation of social change than are relatively short-term ethnographic observations (Aberle 1970: 223).

One convention to deal with the shallow time depth of ethnographic information resorts to the conversion of space to time by comparing contemporary social groups ordered in a pseudo-temporal sequence. The resulting repression of time in social theory, however pragmatic, unfortunately entails a corresponding repression of history wherein social change becomes assimilated within functionalism. It is from this element of social theory that the sobriquet "structural-functionalism" derives. In the structural-functional approach, structure is reified and given an existence prior to and outside of social interaction. Rather than locating the source of change in the actions of individuals, change is explained in terms of the putative functional needs of the social groups arranged in a social structure. A fundamental problem with this conceptualization is that the focus is on social groups rather than individuals, and social groups and their perceived structure have no objective reality. Social organization is not a self-regulating biological organism that adapts to perpetuate itself. It is only through the actions of their constituent members that social groups function, persist, and change.

Eggan (1950: 7) notes that the role of an individual in relation to society and culture is an ambiguous one in anthropological theory. Individuals are necessary to the maintenance and perpetuation of a society, yet societies continue long beyond the lifetime of any particular individual or generation. This ambiguity is further compounded by the fact that individuals are tangible but societies are not. Thus, although we are interested in society, we have to study individuals to collect primary information about it. Archaeologists who want to study society must therefore approach the archaeological record in relation to the way it was formed through the actions and activities of individuals. The prehistoric aggregation of individuals into groups is an analytical problem, not an observational procedure. The roles of individuals and the relations of individuals to society thus pose a central problem in a structuralist approach to social organization.

Structuralism in anthropology, especially as epitomized by Lévi-Strauss and other European anthropologists, has traditionally sought to explain the great variation in social and cultural forms by demonstrating the shared relationships of these phenomena with a few, simple underlying principles (binary opposition, for example). Ultimately, the structures discerned beneath society and culture are theorized to be grounded in the structure of the mind (Ortner 1984: 135–138). Some archaeologists and other students of the built environment have adopted this type of structural approach to the study of the archaeological record (Glassie 1975; Deetz 1982; Small 1987), but these studies are more concerned with ideational behavior than with social interaction and thus address cultural rather than social issues. Classic structuralist studies are appropriate for some types of cultural investigations, but they have less utility for archaeological studies of social organization because this type of structuralism fails to incorporate society by giving material form to the individuals that comprise social groups. The theoretical hinge in classic structuralism is on what people think, not on what they do, and the relation between ideology and the material remains of the archaeological record is embedded in a "deep structure" of the mind that is mentalistic rather than behavioral.

In the 1980s, anthropologists developed a new type of structural theory, often termed praxis theory, to explain the genesis, reproduction, and change of form and meaning within particular sociocultural systems in terms of the intended and unintended actions of individual actors (Karp 1983; Ortner 1984: 144–160; Merrill 1988: 53–58). Analyses in this theoretical perspective are phrased in a set of terms denoting practice, praxis, action, interaction, activity, experience, and performance and in a related set of terms denoting agent, actor, person, self, individual, and subject. At the core of praxis theory is the postulate that practice reproduces the system, and that the system can be changed by practice. Much of systemic reproduction is viewed as taking place in the routine activities and intimate interactions of domestic life. One of the primary ways change occurs is through the application of strategies of human behavior based on traditional patterns of relations in the context of novel phenomena that respond in unanticipated ways. The change of context entails a refractoriness of the real world to traditional expectations that results in failed reproduction, that is, the production of new forms. Although the intentions of actors are accorded a central place in praxis theory, major social change does not generally come about as an intended consequence of action but as a by-product or unintended consequence of action. The inspiration in much of the development of praxis theory in anthropology stems from the work of the English sociologist Anthony Giddens, and it is important to review in some detail what Giddens terms structuration theory.

STRUCTURATION THEORY

Giddens's structuration theory is useful in analyzing the built environment because it articulates the essential theoretical position that the space defined by architecture does more than simply *represent* society. Architectural space is one of the primary means through which society is directly *constituted*. The spaces created by architecture incorporate society by physically enabling and constraining social interaction. Architecture arranges social interaction in recurrent patterns and thus gives form to social structure.

The Role of Individual Actors

Giddens's formulation of structuration theory incorporates many of the theoretical elements needed by archaeologists, namely a way to recognize the role of individuals in the formation of society and a clear conception of how time and space relate to social structure. In analyzing social science, Giddens (1979a: 202) came to the conclusion that:

> Most forms of social theory have failed to take seriously enough *not only the temporality of social conduct but also its spatial attributes*. At first sight, nothing seems more banal and uninstructive than to assert that social activity occurs in time and space. But neither time nor space have been incorporated into the centre of social theory; rather they are ordinarily treated more as "environments" in which social conduct is enacted [italics in original].

Following this realization, Giddens spent 15 years on a singular project to formulate a theory of structuration that incorporates space and time in explaining how the actions of individuals constitute society (Giddens 1989: 250). The fullest explication of this theory is in *The Constitution of Society* (Giddens 1984).

In his theory building, Giddens (1989: 253–256) has striven to avoid terms in which structure appears as something outside of or external to human action. In his conceptualization, structure is what gives *form* and *shape* to social life, but it is not *itself* that form or shape. In articulating structuration theory, Giddens (1990: 302) distinguishes social *relations* from social *interaction*. Social relations are ties that establish some kind of a bond between individuals or groups (for example, kinship relations). Social interaction comprises direct interchanges between people, whether face-to-face or mediated by other forms of communication. Social structure is defined as the rules and resources that are recursively drawn upon and reconstituted in processes of *interaction* (Giddens 1984: 19).

Rules specify procedures or conventions that guide the actions of agents (Giddens 1984: 17–25, 1989: 255). As Giddens conceives them, rules are more analogous to formulae than rigid and fixed prescriptions. He gives as an example the rules governing styles of dress in our own society, which range from specific uniforms in the military to less rigid prescriptions for civilians. Most people have considerable latitude in how they meet an almost universal rule to dress themselves in some fashion during social interaction. Rules have two distinct aspects: the constitution of meaning and the sanctioning of modes of social conduct. Rules are variable in their specificity and run the gamut from informal procedures that regulate common, everyday interaction to the more abstract and highly formalized codified law that governs social conduct.

Table 1.1. Types of Resources Used in the Production of Social Practices

Allocative Resources	*Authoritative Resources*
1. Material features of the environment (raw materials, material power sources).	1. Organization of social time and space (temporal-spatial constitution of paths and regions).
2. Means of material production and reproduction (instruments of production, technology).	2. Production and reproduction of the group (organization and relation of human beings in mutual association).
3. Produced goods (artifacts created by the interaction of 1 and 2).	3. Organization of life chances (constitution of chances of self-development and self-expression).

SOURCE: Giddens 1984: 258–262.

The Role of Rules and Resources

In structuration theory, rules are not conceptualized apart from the resources incorporated into the production and reproduction of social practices. Giddens (1984: 258–262) defines two classes of resources (Table 1.1). Allocative resources are material assets employed in adaptation to the environment, and their manipulation is integral in maintaining the continuity of societies across time and space. Authoritative resources are those used in organizing the temporal and spatial boundaries of social groups and regulating the opportunities available for individual development. Although valuing the influence of the natural environment on the patterns of social life, Giddens posits that authoritative resources play an equally important role in social interaction. All coordination of social systems across time and space necessarily involve a combination of both types of resources.

Giddens maintains that it is a fallacy to conceptualize structure as something outside of the activities of social agents. Structure has no objective reality and therefore no descriptive qualities of its own as a feature of social life, because structure exists only in a virtual way as rules and resources are manifested in the activities of people (Giddens 1989: 256). "The structural properties of social systems exist only insofar as the forms of social conduct are reproduced chronically across time and space" (Giddens 1984: xxi). Because structure exists only in and through the activities of people, structuration theory concentrates attention on the *reproduction of practices* (Giddens 1990: 313).

One of the central tenets of structuration theory is that social systems are not created by actors. Actors only reproduce or transform social systems, remaking what is already made in the continuity of praxis (Giddens 1984: 171). As Giddens (1984: 2) states, human social activities "are not brought into being by social actors but continually recreated by them via the very means whereby they express themselves *as* actors. In and through their activities agents reproduce the conditions that make these activities possible." The framework of structuration theory depends on understanding the recursive nature of social systems. In this recursiveness, the flow of action occurs in time and space, and this action instantiates rules and resources that otherwise have no time-space existence. In other words, it is through their recursive application that rules and resources become represented by concrete examples (Giddens 1989: 275). As Karp (1983: 134) observes, Giddens's concept of structure as being virtual rather than actual makes structuration a process of becoming rather than a state of being. This is important because structure thus becomes situated in time and among spaces.

Storper (1985: 416–418), in a sympathetic critique of structuration theory, argues that Giddens places instantiated rules in a position of primacy over the material world, that is, resources. Storper notes that Giddens aptly observes that material resources may serve simultaneously as the foundation for the purposeful activities of society and as a container for interaction in time and space. Storper thinks, however, that resources have a duration of existence that can provide continuity or impede change. Storper argues that structures thus have more "reality" than Giddens recognizes in his characterization of rules as "instantiated." Storper points out that this does not mean there is more or less of a role for human agency, only that there is a "differentiated (and thus limited) topography for the exercise of that agency, rather than an endlessly recursive plain."

In reconciling the views of Storper and Giddens, it becomes clear that although the entirety of structure has only a virtual reality, structure takes a material form through the reoccurring use of allocative resources. It is this fact that gives structuration theory a material basis that can be transferred to the interpretation of the archaeological record. The structure of the archaeological record is a fossilized trace of the instantiated rules and resources that comprise social structure (Binford 1968: 20–23). This idea is elaborated further in the following chapter, which describes how architecture and its remnants in the archaeological record are particularly amenable to the application of structuration theory.

The rules and resources drawn on in the production and reproduction of social action are at one and the same time the means of system reproduction. Giddens (1984: 25, 162) considers this to be a crucial idea in structuration theory, and he refers to this notion as the "duality" of structure. This "duality" is contrasted with the "dualism" of structure inherent in earlier theories of social organization, where agents and structures are conceived as two independent sets of phenomena. Viewed independently in a "dualism," structure is reified and assumed to have an objective reality that it does not have in real social life. In contrast, the concept of the "duality" of structure postulates that the structural properties of social systems are both the medium and outcome of the practices they recursively organize. Structure is thus not external to individuals and has no reality outside of their actions. In this sense, Giddens views structure much in the same way as does Durkheim (1965: 252–253). As traces of memory and as instantiated social practices, structure is internal rather than external to the actions of individuals.

Karp (1983: 136) observes that Giddens's theoretical formulation of agency and structure thus overcomes a number of the "two-headed monsters" that social science faces. Giddens's theory provides the means to obliterate the distinctions between the ideal and the real, structure and action, and statics and dynamics (Binford and Sabloff 1982). Furthermore, structuration theory does this in a way that respects the empirical data resulting from the diversity of activities and patterns that social agents generate, reproduce, and alter in different socio-historical circumstances (Cohen 1990: 33–36). By stressing structured modes of action rather than historically specific acts, structuration theory resists an individualist reduction of order, and by emphasizing that social systems only exist inasmuch as they are continually reproduced, Giddens's theory avoids reducing order to the enduring properties of collectivities.

Analyzing the structuration of social systems entails studying the modes in which those systems are materialized by actors who draw on rules and resources in diverse contexts to produce and reproduce that social system in interaction (Giddens 1984: 25). Consequently, analyzing a social system does not mean specifying the rules and resources that "compose" it, because social systems are not made up in such a way. Structure is implicated in the fragmentary, overlapping, and sometimes contradictory practices whereby day-to-day life is carried on. Analysis of social systems thus proceeds by investigating the forms of social interaction and their overlap with social relations as they are expressed in a given cluster of practices. Analytically, structure is always viewed as both constraining and enabling social interaction (Giddens 1984: 169, 1990: 313).

SPACE AS A COMPONENT OF SOCIETY

Classical theorists such as Spencer and Durkheim often viewed the morphological patterns of societies in geographical terms (Cohen 1990: 38–39). Subsequent social scientists, however, often explicitly dismissed all concern for time and space and consequently conceptualized order as comprising formal configurations of positions and relations. This led functionalists and system theorists to concentrate on the synchronous organization and regulation of social systems rather than on the spatial organization of society through time. This situation has changed, and many contemporary social scientists once again acknowledge in theory that social practices are spatially and temporally patterned and that these patterns substantially affect social praxis (Thrift 1983: 49, 1987; Urry 1987: 436).

In Giddens's theory of structuration, structure is always conceived of as a property of social systems that is carried in reproduced practices embedded in space and time (Giddens 1984: 86, 170). The regular or routine features of encounters constitute institutionalized features of social systems. No matter how firmly institutionalized, all social practices remain contextual, because social systems are predicated on the interaction of individuals in contexts of co-presence (Giddens 1990: 301–302).

Giddens (1984: 145–158) draws on Foucault's (1979) investigation of institutionalized disciplinary space to exemplify how spatial and social forms are unified. As Foucault observes, the character of disciplinary space in schools, asylums, and prisons derives primarily not from the association of an organization with a specific piece of territory but from the partitioning of space. It is the overall relational pattern rather than any particular part of the building that gives form to the social institutions that occupy it. For instance, beginning in the eighteenth century, buildings housing school classrooms in France were constructed with internal rows of clearly delineated classrooms separated by a connecting system of corridors. In regard to this, Foucault (1979: 148) comments:

> In organizing "cells," "places," and "ranks" the disciplines create complex spaces that are at once architectural, functional and hierarchical. It is spaces that provide fixed positions and permit circulation; they carve out individual segments and establish operational links; they mark places and indicate values; they guarantee the obedience of individuals, but also a better economy of time and gesture.

Giddens (1984: 143–144) observes that similar sociospatial processes pertain to settlements as well as to buildings.

Critics of structuration theory question the assertion that space is central to theories of society (Saunders 1989). These critics, however, often confuse location with space itself. Giddens (1989: 277) agrees with critics who point out that it is impossible and incorrect to develop a general science of space, because space per se has no *general* effects. The significance of spatial relations depends on the character of the social objects in question. What is needed is an examination of how different sociophysical properties of environments are brought into being in conjunction with specific forms of social development. Space itself cannot be invested with meaning, because space as such has no content (Giddens 1989: 280).

As he does with all elements of structuration theory, Giddens (1984: xvii) elucidates the relations of space and society to provide conceptions of human social activity that can be placed in the service of empirical work. Because the construction of buildings is one of the major resource consuming activities of any society (Markus 1987: 467–468), and because buildings and the settlements composed by buildings both incorporate space, structuration theory can be productively applied to the empirical analysis and interpretation of the built environment.

ARCHITECTURAL AND ANTHROPOLOGICAL THEORIES OF THE BUILT ENVIRONMENT

Among architects and scholars who study the built environment there is little agreement on many fundamental issues, including the nature of the medium itself, the basic units of organization, the meanings and functions of architectonic objects, and the relationships of built environments with symbol systems. Within the profession of architecture, Preziosi (1979: 4) observes, "What has passed for architectural theory has commonly consisted of little more than semantic maneuvering to gain maximal congruence of idiosyncratic classification in the service of academic and professional ambition, and architectural theory has tended to be a fragile ship open to the cross-currents of fashion."

Much of architectural theory consists of nothing more than reflexive, literary criticism in which buildings are treated as a type of metalanguage for discussing images, cultural values, or cultural history (Gloag 1975; Tafuri 1980; Lynch 1981). Consequently architectural discourse frequently focuses on aesthetic concerns relating to surfaces rather than on the spatial context of social activities. An increasing number of architects recognize that there is a disturbing and widening gulf between architectural practice and social science research (Baum and Valins 1977: 2; Stea 1987: xiv). This is distressing to those architects who think the chief obstacle to better architectural design is a lack of understanding of the precise relations between social behavior and spatial organization (Hillier and Hanson 1984: x).

A few recent treatises on architectural theory have incorporated perspectives from the behavioral sciences to elucidate environmental design (Lang 1987: 157–177). Lang (1987: 177), for instance, recognizes that:

> at any given time, the built environment reflects past and present concepts of normative patterns of behavior. We thus have a circular relationship in which social organization leads to patterns of built form and then social organizations, as they change, have to adapt to the affordances of the built environment and in their efforts to adapt they change the built world.

Lang does not provide, however, an explicit description of the mechanisms involved in this process or a method to quantify relevant variables. Social organization is thus considered only in normative terms and discursively evaluated.

Considering the importance of architecture as a type of evidence in various anthropological and archaeological descriptions of human society, it is surprising how little explicit theory anthropologists have generated pertaining to the built environment. In one of the few examples of anthropological theory building, McGuire and Schiffer (1983) present a general, and admittedly preliminary, theory to explain the design of vernacular architecture. They define architectural design as a "process whereby social groups make choices concerning recurrent sets of activities" and focus their theorizing on the compromises made in decisions concerning the activity sets of production, use, and maintenance of the built environment (McGuire and Schiffer 1983: 278). McGuire and Schiffer think that the aspects of architecture that "facilitate the workings of ideology and social structure are symbolic" and that these are less "concrete" than utilitarian functions (McGuire and Schiffer 1983: 281). They make some useful generalizations about how and why people make compromises in design decisions concerning the size, shape, and construction materials used in architecture, but they do not deal directly with how architecture constitutes society. They pay attention to social structure only inasmuch as it is a factor of a social inequality that results in a differential access to the resources used in the construction of architecture. McGuire and Schiffer do not address the fact that after construction architecture itself becomes a resource used in the structuring of the social interaction that reproduces society. Although they consider the effect social structure has on architecture and how architecture is used to represent symbols, McGuire and Schiffer do not deal directly with the more fundamental issue of how architecture effects society in an objective, material sense.

Hunter-Anderson (1977) builds an archaeological theory that explains architectural *form* in relation to the social and economic activities housed by buildings. Her primary interest is in explaining why some houses are circular and others are rectangular. Hunter-Anderson models architectural form in terms of three variables: volume of associated materials and activities, heterogeneity and simultaneity of living activities and social roles, and number of living activities and social roles. She postulates that as the values of these variables increase, there is a greater propensity for rectangular rather than circular housing. As the number of housed people increases, rectangular houses are arranged in rows to facilitate communication. As the heterogeneity of social roles and living activities increases, the internal space of houses is partitioned into rooms to prevent mutual interference and disturbance of the various activities and roles. Hunter-Anderson's theory provides insight into several of the factors that produce particular forms of architecture. It does not address, however, how individual buildings are situated to form settlements.

One of the most developed theoretical areas pertaining to architecture concerns the relationship between environment and behavior (Zeisel 1975: 3–12; Altman and Chemers 1980; Lawrence and Lowe 1990; Rapoport 1990). Environmental-behavioral relations include how physical surroundings fulfill needs for privacy and territory, the way people understand their surroundings, and how the built environment is perceived. Studies of environmental-behavioral relations demonstrate that people's responses to environments differ dramatically among cultures and among people with different social and physical characteristics within the same culture. Although generating interesting case studies, environmental-behavioral research has not produced the nomothetic theory needed for that research to be of use in archaeological studies.

Some architects subscribe to a theoretical perspective in which the built environment *reflects* rather than constitutes society, forming in essence a cultural cipher (Lang 1987: 166–177). Rapoport (1980: 287–289) calls this a "cognitive congruence model," suggesting that environments and lifestyles both reflect and are shaped by "cultural templates" that approximate the schemata held by people in a society. The built environment is viewed as a form of nonverbal communication that is decoded by the users. Anthropologists who subscribe to this theory consider architecture to be a form of communication in which the primary meaning of architecture is cultural rather than behavioral. In this perspective, buildings serve as a metaphor for experiencing the ancient past of myth in the present (Leach 1983; Hieb 1990). Within the physical constraints of functional and adaptational requirements, buildings are theorized as imprinting thought onto the landscape. Meaning is thus attributed to architecture and not inherent in it.

Closely related to this theoretical perspective, but somewhat more rigorous, are semiotic analyses of architecture in which the built environment is viewed as a vehicle or channel through which a culture transmits a symbolic message. Material structure is a complexly ordered series of mappings that intercede between a core set of formal or geometric orderings and the physical environment. Preziosi (1979: 13–14) points out that in order to measure variation in this approach, analysts need to array some constant measure or frame within which that variation can be highlighted and classified. He notes that all architectonic systems share at least one thing in common: they are made up of "space-cells." These space-cells vary widely in geometric configurations and size, but they all serve to bound portions of the spatial continuum by enclosing spaces in which human activities are localized in relatively habitual ways. Preziosi (1979: 13) thus views settlements as complex space-time frameworks for human interaction. Behavioral episodes are spatially embedded in the structure of buildings and open areas, and time is entailed in movement through architectural spaces. Preziosi (1979: 77) considers the material structure of the built environment as partly architectonic in origin and partly cultural, and he suggests that the architectonic system metaphorically mediates between the cognitive environment and the physical environment.

Ankerl (1981) voices a slightly different semiotic approach, one more closely related to structuration theory. He posits that the sociological meaning of architecture is what the space system denotes for the structuring of face-to-face communication. In conceptualizing architecture as an artifact, Ankerl's theory focuses on how architectural space conditions, stimulates, and affects the network of communications. Although not suggesting that architecture can be fully classed with language, Ankerl borrows terms from linguistics such as syntax and applies them analogically to model how the construction of architecture follows a strict system of rules. For Ankerl, space is the "word" of architecture, and architectural morphology and syntax create a space system that can be "read" like a "text." Unlike the linear connections between words in a spoken or written language, the "reading" of space is multilinear in that there are a number of discrete and alternative ways to experience space by taking different routes through a building. In Ankerl's way of thinking, the architectural opus as text is defined not by physical adjacency, nor by how spaces are packed into a building, but by the network of accessibility within a set of spaces. In the scope of a sociology of architecture, space has to be studied in terms of the framework it provides for social activities.

The propensity for architects to conceptualize architecture in linguistic terms includes the development of shape grammars used to formally define the relations between architectural "vocabularies" (sets of shapes), spatial relations, and rules used to create design "languages" (Stiny and Gips 1978; Stiny 1980a, 1980b; Stiny and Mitchell 1980). Shape grammars are thus concerned with the abstract generative principles of spatial patterns in highly refined mathematical terms. In some respects, however, shape grammars are too refined to model the real world of buildings and settlements that have often undergone a complex history of accretional development. The concept of shape in some ways obscures the more elemental relations that underpin human social and spatial orders. Rapoport (1980: 293) notes that the organization of space is a more fundamental property of environments than the shape of rooms or buildings. For this reason, space in architecture must be viewed at a higher level of abstraction than is present in the development of shape grammars.

Using a theoretical perspective closely related to shape grammars, Chippendale (1986) investigated design grammars in an archaeological study of megalithic monuments in England. Chippendale's interest was in ideational culture rather than in social behavior, and the ultimate aim of his anthropological-historical reconstruction thus required the reproduction of the methods of the prehistoric design process as well as the results. He concluded that design grammars in and of themselves were limited, because they elucidated the formal evidence of what was produced but did not indicate what people had in mind when they designed artifacts. Chippendale's review of analyses of megalithic monuments suggests that the formal geometric structure of these architectural artifacts could be reproduced either through the exact application of Pythagorean geometry oriented to celestial observations *or* through misjudged visual sightings during construction (Chippendale 1986: 456–465). Both design methods produced the same results. As a guide to human action and social behavior, therefore, design grammars are too limited in and of themselves to be of use in implementing structuration theory.

Some architects have commented on the growth characteristics of "traditional" towns, noting a coherent wholeness that grows piecemeal, bit by bit (Alexander 1966; Alexander and others 1987: 14). Alexander and his colleagues (1977) have developed a "pattern language" to describe this growth. This pattern language is closely bound to the contingent, historical, and functional properties of configurations, however, and is more concerned with hierarchical forms of spatial arrangement than with the more abstract forms of human spatial organization that characterize much of the built environment. The pattern language deals in an interesting manner with the components of settlements, but gives less consideration to how these components are globally assembled in settlements. As a result, although elements of the pattern language are often easily discernible in real settlements, the approach has only limited theoretical value in describing how the built environment constitutes society.

King (1980: 8) asserts that what is really needed is a cross-cultural frame of reference that describes the characteristics of built form relating to society. Ideally, this frame of reference would be equally valid in New York or New Guinea. In the last 25 years, several morphological investigations of the organization of building plans using graph analysis have provided just such a systematic method for the analysis of diverse buildings. A number of architectural treatises (March and Steadman 1971; Scott 1971; Friedman 1975; Tabor 1976; Steadman 1976, 1983; Kruger 1979a, 1979b, 1979c, 1981a, 1981b; Baybars and Eastman 1980; Earl 1980; Baglivo and Graver 1983; and Mitchell 1990) and a few archaeological analyses (for example, Hopkins 1987) have pioneered the rigorous investigation of the geometry of space using graph analysis as a universal frame of reference.

In Lawrence's (1987: 51) description, a graph comprises a set of points called nodes that are connected by lines. In an architectural analysis, each architectural space is represented by a node and the routes of movement between spaces are represented by lines. A planar graph can thus represent all interior spaces of a building and also the surrounding external spaces. Baybars and Eastman (1980: 289) point out that the human preference to live and work on horizontal planes allows significant relations to be investigated by means of abstractions involving the partitioning of the plane as abstracted in graph analysis. Through graph analysis, a number of buildings that appear to have very different configurations can be observed to share an underlying pattern. Graph analysis thus provides a means of visual representation and a method of structuring spatial organization for the comparative analysis of architecture from historically and culturally varying contexts.

However rich most graph analyses are as intellectual exercises, however, few of them attempt to incorporate a theory that explicitly relates the spatial structure of architecture to human behavior or society. Two prominent exceptions to this are the development of an experimental sociology of architecture (Ankerl 1981) and the theory of space syntax presented by Hillier and Hanson (1984). Ankerl's work is important in its use of graph analytical techniques to represent what he terms "architectural texts," but, like Edward T. Hall (1966), Ankerl incorporates into his research a wide range of sensory variables that are culturally determined and not particularly applicable to archaeology (for example, psychological aspects of the visual and auditory perception of architectural space). Ultimately, Ankerl's approach is more oriented toward semiotics than toward social interaction. As discussed in the next chapter, by analyzing the spatial contexts of social interaction used to reproduce society, Hillier's development of space syntax presents the best way to use Giddens's structuration theory in archaeology.

ARCHAEOLOGICAL CONSIDERATIONS

The application of structuration theory to the archaeological analysis of architecture raises a number of theoretical and methodological issues. Two key aspects of the archaeological record must be accepted and continually exploited to achieve a successful analysis. One aspect is that the archaeological record contains tangible resources (objects) that are produced by and used in social interaction. The other aspect is that the archaeological record is only a remnant of the past behavioral and social systems that resulted in its deposition and subsequent transformation. The archaeological record exists in the present, and, as fragmentary as it seems from an ethnographic perspective, it still holds a key to understanding the past.

The mute objectivity of the archaeological record, if used correctly, is actually beneficial from a theoretical perspective. Ankerl (1981: 387–388) warns that words labeling the systemic context of architecture can be a tyrannical pitfall rather than an analytical boon. Labels for room functions and particular architectural styles, and other kinds of nomenclature, can distract the analyst from directly grappling with the objective spatial relationships that exist. Ankerl actually recommends that architectural analysts adopt the approach of the "structural archaeologist," who, by nature of the archaeological record, must describe the space systems of societies for which no written documents, and therefore no labels, remain. As Ankerl (1981: 406) observes, "This is a tool not only for description but for proper architectural design; that is, a well-written architectural program must indicate the requirements in objective spatial terms." He notes that an archaeological approach to architecture tries to understand the subject by intentionally disregarding, and consequently leaving in parentheses, aspects of architecture debated in the conventional histories of architecture that often are the subject of passionate ideological controversies. Through archaeological structuralism, the analyst must find the essential characteristics and boundaries of styles, epochs, and regions of architectural history as they are revealed by their objective aspects *without* considering functional denominations. Thus description remains independent of labeling and concentrates on the architectural space system. As Ankerl concludes, the advantage of an archaeological approach to architecture is that it will handle with ease the architecture of various periods and regions. The archaeology of architecture thus comprehends the structural characteristics of architectural styles in an *intrinsic* manner instead of interpreting them within the framework of a cultural history.

At the same time that the archaeological record offers objective strengths, its fragmentary nature presents a corresponding interpretive challenge. It is clear, for instance, that the analysis of the archaeological record can get at social interaction much more readily than at social relations. The architecture found in an archaeological context constituted the means by which past social interaction was structured in the constitution of society and is thus particularly informative about social integration. Yet, for the reasons detailed by Allen and Richardson (1971), interpretation of the corresponding social relations of kinship using archaeological data is more intractable and less certain. Therefore, whole social systems cannot be dealt with easily through analyses of archaeological records. Whereas this limits archaeological analysis, it also opens up new ways to look at society in purely archaeological rather than ethnographic terms, moving beyond paleoethnography into a new type of social archaeology. Dohm's (1990) analysis of the effect of population nucleation on house size as measured by the area of architectural space and the number of contiguous rooms per village for historic Pueblo sites breaks new and important ground with respect to this issue. She dealt with architectural and archaeological units of analysis rather than ethnographic ones, and her study demonstrates the effect population size and density have on proximity in architecture.

The conceptualization of structure as the rules and resources recursively implicated in the reproduction of social systems entails a related methodological issue for archaeologists. We cannot directly observe rules or authoritative resources, which therefore must be inferred from the residue of allocative resources as we find them in the archaeological record. The nature of the archaeological record in this regard is mitigated by the precept of structuration theory that binds rules and resources together in social activity. One cannot be separated from the other, so that observing one provides a means to infer the other. The additional theory needed to postulate such inferences and a methodology that connects theory to the material record are discussed next to provide a framework in which to assess Zuni settlement.

CHAPTER TWO

Theory, Method, and Techniques of Space Syntax

Bill Hillier and his colleagues at the Unit for Architectural Studies, University College, London, have developed a set of techniques for representing, quantifying, and interpreting the spatial arrangement of buildings and settlements (Hillier and Leaman 1973, 1976; Hillier and others 1976). This set of techniques is termed space syntax, and it receives its fullest explication in *The Social Logic of Space* (Hillier and Hanson 1984). The theory of space syntax is that social relations and processes are structured in spatial configurations that shape the forms of social interaction. The formal analysis of spatial arrangements therefore provides information about the structure of society (Hillier and others 1987: 363). Space syntax constitutes a theory in that it provides a coherent group of general propositions used as principles in the explanation of a class of phenomena, in this case, architectural arrangements.

Hillier and Hanson (1984: x) identify two problems with previous spatial and social theories. First, there was no consistent descriptive account of the morphological features of architecture that could be related to human action and social structures. Second, there was no descriptive account of the morphological features of societies that could determine one kind of spatial embodiment rather than another. Hillier and Hanson think that this theoretical deficiency is related to a paradigm that conceptualizes society as an abstract and aspatial domain that happens to be situated in a separate, purely physical domain of space. As a result, space is viewed as being without social content and society without spatial form. Hillier and Hanson, in thinking that parallels Giddens's (1984) theory of structuration, reject this paradigm in favor of a theoretical position based on the premise that the spatial form of the built environment is one of the ways by which societies are constituted and reproduced.

Space syntax meets the three criteria that Hillier and Hanson (1984: 5) consider essential for a theory of space and society. First, space syntax has descriptive autonomy. Spatial patterns are described and analyzed in their own terms prior to any assumption of a determinative subservience to other variables. Second, the theory embodies the wide and fundamental variations that exist in architectural morphology, including, but not limited to, closed and open patterns, hierarchical and nonhierarchical organizations, and dispersed and aggregated forms. Third, space syntax accommodates the basic differences in the ways that space fits into the rest of the social system in terms of the amount of order and meaning invested in architecture.

THE SOCIAL LOGIC OF SPACE

The basic theoretical premise of space syntax is that space has a social logic that is intelligible if it is understood as being defined by two relationships: the relations among the occupants, and the relations between the occupants and other people. This idea is not unique to Hillier and Hanson's formulation of space syntax. Urry (1987: 443), for instance, also points out that there is a fundamental opposition between those who are local ("people like us") and those who are nonlocal ("outsiders"), and that this binary opposition may be set up and reproduced in various ways. What is unique to space syntax is the development of a robust set of analytical techniques to methodologically link theory to the empirical record. The method and techniques of space syntax derive from the theoretical conceptualization of architecture and the space it encloses, and the relation of both of these to society.

Buildings are viewed as artifacts that assemble elements into a physical object with a certain form and that order the empty volumes of space contained within those objects (Hillier and Hanson 1984: 1–2; Hillier 1985). The primary purpose of a building is the ordering of space, not the physical object itself. For instance, the primary purpose of a barn is not the edifice, but the ordered spaces that the building provides for the storage of tools, resources, and livestock. Because the ordering of space influences modes of social interaction, buildings have sociological meaning.

As described by Hillier and Hanson (1984: 19):

> The simplest building . . . [consists] of a boundary, a space within the boundary, an entrance, and a space outside the boundary defined by the entrance, all of these spaces being part of a system which was placed in a larger space which "carried" it. All these elements . . . have some kind of sociological reference: the space within the boundary established a category associated with some kind of inhabitant; the boundary formed a control on that category, and maintained its discreteness as a category; the world outside the system was the domain of potential strangers, in contradistinction to the domain of inhabitants; the space outside the entrance constituted a potential interface between the inhabitant and the stranger; and the entrance was a means of establishing not only the identity of the inhabitant, but also a means of converting a stranger into a visitor.

As a bounded space, the simplest building can thus be viewed as a cell. The most important distinction between the inside and the outside of a cell is the distinction between building interiors and their collective exteriors (Hillier and Hanson 1984: 18–20). There are two pathways of growth from the elementary cell: (1) subdividing or accumulating cells so that their internal permeability is maintained, and (2) aggregating cells independently so that the continuous permeability is maintained externally. The first pathway produces a building, the second a settlement. Compared with external spaces, building interiors usually have more categorical differences between spaces, more well-defined differences in the relations of spaces, and more deterministic encounters. External space is more generalized than internal space, with more access by a greater number of people, with fewer controls, and with more probabilistic encounters.

Buildings participate in a sociospatial system in two ways (Hillier and Hanson 1984: 20). First, they are spatially related to other buildings, and, second, they separate categorical social groups from the outside world. By using spatial separation to define and control a system of social categories, buildings define the relation of their occupants to other people in a settlement by conceptual analogy as well as by spatial relation. The occupants of a building are thus related to their neighbors both spatially and conceptually in that their interior system of spatialized categories is similar to or different from their neighbors.

Settlements are composed of primary cells (houses and other buildings), but there is also a continuous structure of open space that is not easily decomposed into elements for analysis. Hillier and Hanson (1984: 16–17) observe that the problem of analyzing settlements is the problem of analyzing the continuous open space and how it is related to other elements. The public space of a settlement is treated as an interface between the dwellings and the world outside the settlement, that is, the domain of inhabitants and the domain of outsiders. This interface determines how easy it is for outsiders to gain access to the inside of a settlement, and, once inside, how their movement is facilitated or controlled among spaces within the settlement.

A SYNTAX MODEL OF SPACE AS A MORPHIC LANGUAGE

Space in archaeology is usually conceived of in terms of distances measured in a plane or in three dimensions relative to a datum point (Plimpton and Hassan 1987: 439). In space syntax, however, space is analyzed primarily in terms of its formal and relational properties rather than its dimensional attributes. Space and society are both conceptualized as morphic languages, that is, as sets of entities ordered into different arrangements by a syntax. Syntax is defined as a set of related rule structures formed out of combinations of elementary objects, relations, and operations (Hillier and others (1976: 151–153).

Structure is realized in the physical world through morphic languages (Hillier and others 1976: 152–153). Morphic languages convey sociological meaning not by representing something else but by physically enabling and constraining patterns of social interaction. Architecture is sometimes used to represent symbols or other meanings, but this representational significance is secondary to the more fundamental structuring of space for social purposes. The morphic language of architecture includes an open space that "carries" buildings and other architectural structures; a growth process by which architectural cells are added to buildings and settlements; and a syntax comprising a set of elementary objects, relations, and operations capable of restricting how those cells are added. Complex spatial order is created out of elementary relational ideas, applied singly or in combination, as restrictions on an otherwise random process.

Hillier and Hanson (1984: 52–53) specify that the syntax model must: (1) find irreducible objects and relations, the elementary structures of human spatial organization; (2) represent these elementary structures in some kind of notation or ideography to compress the verbal descriptions of repetitive ideas; (3) demonstrate how the elementary structures are related to each other to make a coherent system; and (4) demonstrate how the elementary structures are combined to form more complex structures. The notational ideography used to compress descriptions of space uses morphological patterns rather than functional descriptions of space: cells and open spaces rather than kitchens, living rooms, or ceremonial chambers.

Compressed descriptions are based on two premises (Hillier and Hanson 1984: 54–55). First, spatial organization is created in buildings and settlements by various kinds of boundaries and permeability. Second, although there is an infinite number of different complexes of spatial relationships possible in the real world, there is only a limited number of underlying sets of organizing principles for these patterns. Essentially, if a cell is added to a growing collection it is either: (1) outside of others, in which case it has no relation; (2) in a contiguous neighbor relation; (3) in a relation of jointly defining space; or (4) in a jointly defining ring. If the cell is added inside another cell, it is either located: (5) concentrically by itself; (6) plurally within an outer boundary parallel to others; or (7) between an outer and an inner boundary. Human spatial organization is circumscribed by these possibilities (Hillier and Hanson 1984: 80).

The notational ideography rigorously represents the structure of space and its internal complexity using only the initial objects of open spaces and closed cells, and two basic syntactic relations, symmetry and distributedness (Hillier and Hanson 1984: 93–97). Spaces are symmetrical when the relations between them are equivalent and direct, and asymmetrical when there is an intervening space that one has to pass through in order to get from one to the other (Fig. 2.1). Asymmetry thus entails a notion of depth. Distributedness is characterized by the presence of more than one nonintersecting route between spaces, whereas nondistributedness is characterized by a branching, treelike structure with only a single nonintersecting route.

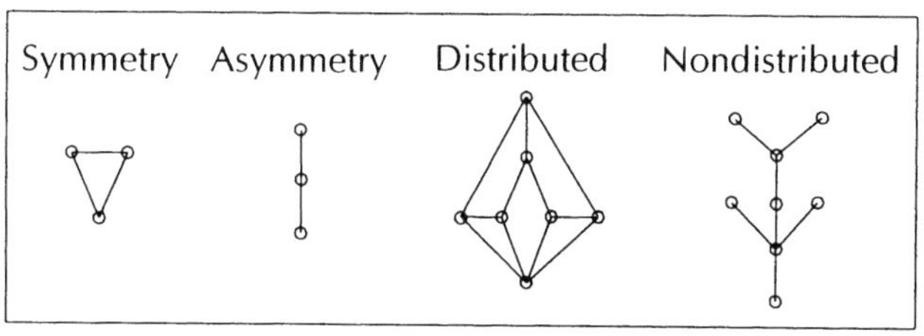

Figure 2.1. Basic syntatic relations.

In notational terms, every settlement is made up of: (1) a grouping of primary cells or buildings called X; (2) a surrounding space outside the settlement, the carrier of the spatial system, called Y; (3) in some cases secondary boundaries (gardens, courtyards and the like) superimposed on some or all of the buildings and intervening between those buildings and the unbounded space of the settlement, called x; (4) a continuous system of open space defined by X or x, called y, and (5) an interface between the closed and open parts of the system, identified by its constituent parts (for example, an X–y or an x–y interface). An X–Y interface would be a fully dispersed set of buildings. In an ideographic formula, "o" is used to signify that a building or open space contains the term following it.

Hillier and Hanson identify eight elementary formulae that describe the fundamental ways that space can be arranged (Table 2.1). The settlement patterns these formulae generate in elementary and recursive forms are illustrated in Figure 2.2 and classified with respect to the basic dimensions of the syntax model: the relations of distributedness and symmetry. In Figure 2.2, y space is denoted by a closed circle with a short bar connecting it to the architectural boundary where it serves as a threshold. In this figure, distributed space can be analogously thought of as glue that joins cells together by virtue of what they have between them, and nondistributed space can be thought of as using X to bind cells together by virtue of what is added around both (Hillier and Hanson 1984: 76–78).

The recursive processes in the generation of space entail the application of a set of ordering principles to an indefinite number of cells added one at time. For instance, recursion in the central space syntax is the process of adding cells to a central space defined in relation to the initial pair constituted by the elementary generator.

Table 2.1. List of Elementary Formulae

Settlement Form	Formulae
cluster	y
closed cell	X
clump	(Xy)
concentric	(X o X)
central space	(XX o y)
block	(X o XX)
ring - street	(XX o XX o y)
kraal	(X o X o XX)

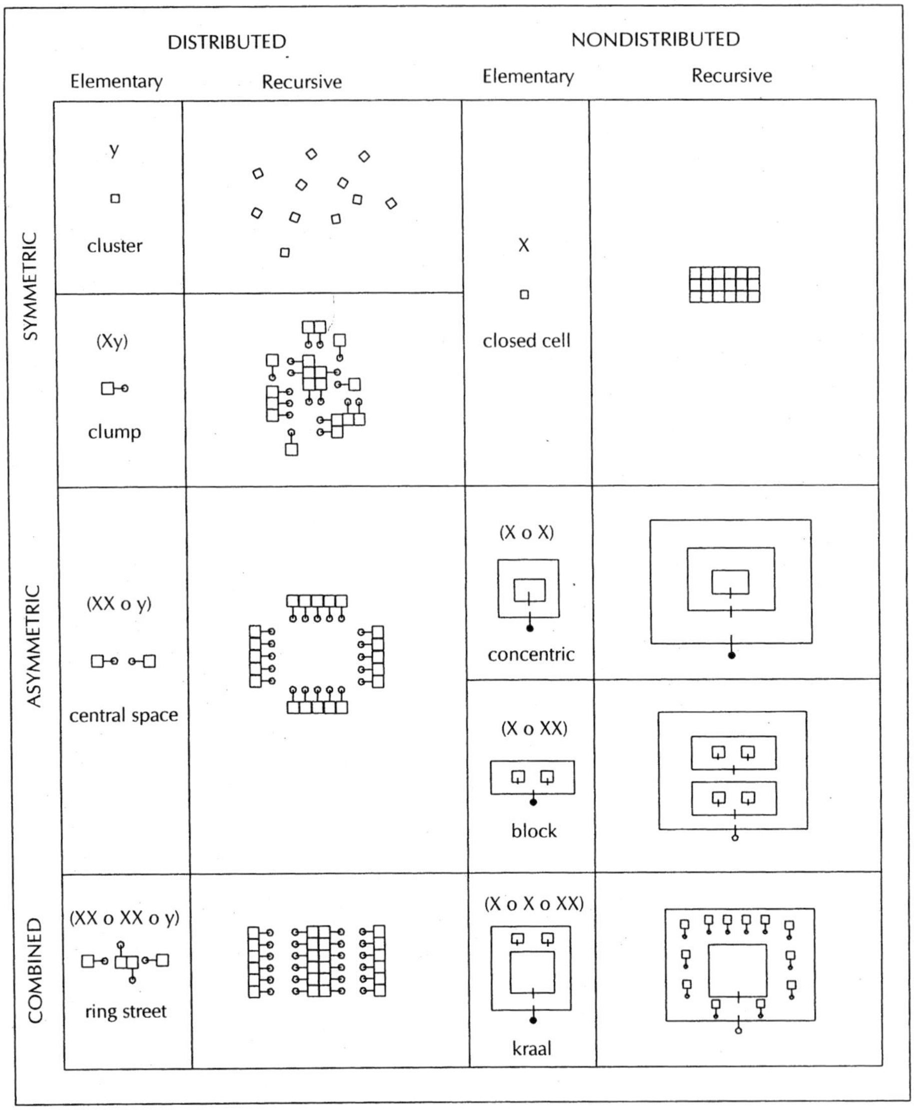

Figure 2.2. Elementary formulae and recursions, adapted from Hillier and Hanson (1984: 78).

In all of the elementary formulae, order in space is conceptualized as restrictions on an otherwise random process. More complex restrictions on the random process give rise to more complex and different forms of order. The notion of a random background growth process is the foundation of the syntactic argument, and it is a critical concept. Hillier and Hanson (1984: 205) suggest that random growth in architectural forms is theoretically equivalent to the concept of inertia for the physicist. Instead of trying to base the systematic analysis of human spatial arrangements on individual motivations, it is assumed that human beings will deploy themselves in space in some way, either randomly or with an interconnection to other people. The analytical imperative, therefore, is to determine how far individuals have related their spatial actions to the actions of others in a manner that yields pattern and form in space.

Space syntax thus entails the notion that a global or comprehensive architectural structure can come into being through the actions of individual people who operate without a centralized planning authority. This is an important idea. Some *prehistoric* pueblo villages in the Southwest were constructed as highly planned communities with a unified architectural structure, but many *historic* Pueblos exhibit a different type of growth sequence involving architectural agglomeration by individual households. Many of the historic Pueblos that expanded through accretion rather than centralized planning nonetheless maintained a strong spatial orientation toward plazas and sacred spaces. The conceptualization of space syntax by Hillier and Hanson provides a useful explanation of how the process of growth in these "unplanned" settlements occurred to produce architectural arrangements that functioned so well to support Pueblo community life.

The elementary formulae derived by Hillier and Hanson describe a variety of settlement forms, but the morphic language by itself is limited in its analytical utility. The application of the simple generative syntax to increasingly complex spatial arrangements yields increasingly general relational structures and tenuous descriptions (Hillier and Hanson 1984: 80). The analysis of real settlements in terms of the ideographic language entails long descriptive formulae that are cumbersome. Therefore, additional techniques are needed to productively analyze the complexity of real cases.

METHODOLOGY FOR AN ANALYSIS OF SETTLEMENT LAYOUTS

Every human settlement is an instantiated product of the recursive application of rules and resources. As such, every settlement is both a member of a broad equivalence class defined by elementary syntactic generators and a discrete entity with unique characteristics that differentiate it from other members of the same class (Hillier and Hanson 1984: 82–90; G. Mills 1989: 71). The goal of the syntactic analysis of settlements, however, is not typological; it is not the assignment of sites to classes in terms of the elementary generators. The goal instead is to describe and quantify the unique arrangements of space related to social interaction. The focus of the analysis, then, is on the variation in spatial arrangements within and between settlements rather than on the normative similarities they exhibit.

Settlements are viewed as spatial systems arranged between the primary cells (buildings) and the carrier space (the world outside the settlement). Space between these two domains governs the relations among the inhabitants of the system and between the inhabitants and outsiders. The central technical problem in the syntactic analysis of settlements is the graphic representation of the continuous open space that surrounds buildings (Hillier and Hanson 1984: 94–97).

As described in ideographic notation, the spatial system has two dimensions. The X dimension comprises all the buildings and the Y dimension comprises the carrier space. The two dimensions of the system correspond to a fundamental sociological difference between two types of people who use the settlement: X is the domain of the inhabitants; Y is the domain of noninhabitants who may occasionally appear in the system from outside. The y space of a settlement is the structure of public open space within settlements. There is a spatial interface for interaction among inhabitants and for interaction between inhabitants and outsiders. Application of the theory of space syntax depends on comparing the spatial interface relating to both types of interaction.

The open space structure of settlements is quantified using measures of symmetry-asymmetry and distributedness-nondistributedness. Values for these measures indicate (1) the degree of integration or segregation of space (the extent to which a space renders the rest of the settlement shallow and immediately accessible) and (2) the degree of diffusion in the control of space (the extent to which the arrangement participates in a system of ringy routes).

The techniques of syntactic analysis provide a way to investigate the global organization of a settlement without losing sight of its local structure and to describe space so as to make its social origins and consequences a part of that description. However, and this is a critically important point, the theoretical links Hillier and Hanson (1984: 82) propose between space and society are assumed rather than demonstrated. Hillier and Hanson (1984: 97) postulate that symmetry in spatial arrangements is correlated with social integration and asymmetry is correlated with social segregation. Distributed spatial arrangements are correlated with the diffusion of social control and nondistributed arrangements are correlated with unitary, superordinate control.

Hillier and Hanson (1984: 97–123) have developed a set of techniques to describe the open space structure of settlements by analyzing the system in terms of one-dimensional and two-dimensional organizations and then comparing the two. Two-dimensional organization is identified by delineating convex spaces with respect to maximal area-perimeter ratios. One-dimensional organization is identified by drawing straight or "axial" lines through convex spaces until all convex spaces are intersected and all axial links are made. Both of these spatial arrangements are represented by graphs with quantifiable elements used in statistical measures of syntactic variables.

Accurate maps or settlement plans are required for syntactic analysis. The open spaces at the thresholds of buildings are an important syntactic variable, so if the

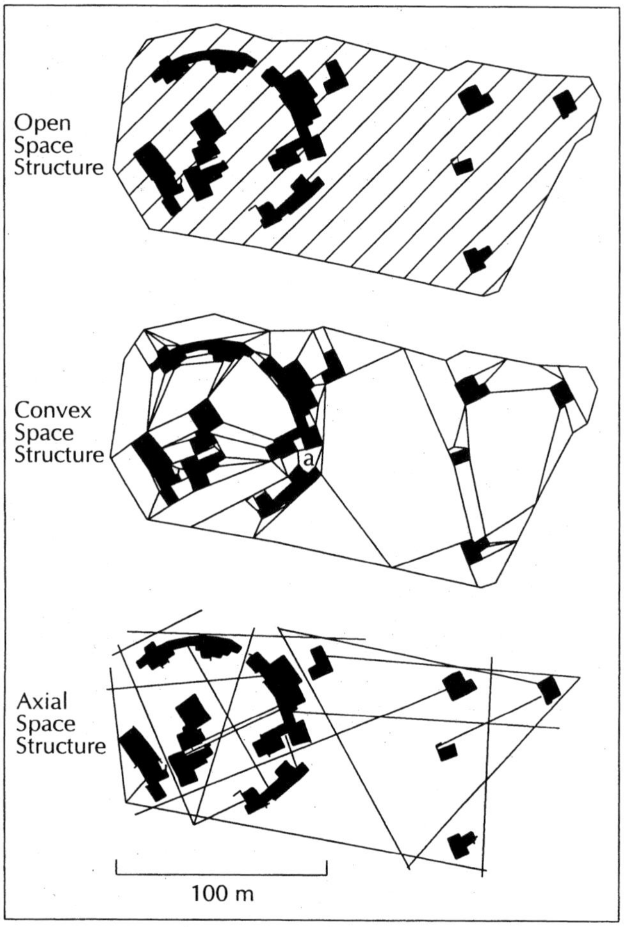

Figure 2.3. Three steps in the analysis of open space structure as applied to the plan of the Zuni settlement of Upper Nutria mapped in 1885 by Mindeleff (1891).

entrances of buildings are not precisely located on maps used for analysis only a portion of the entire set of key syntactic properties can be analyzed. The procedure to break apart settlement plans into graphs for quantitative analysis entails three steps. These steps are illustrated in Figure 2.3, as applied to Mindeleff's (1891, Plate 67) plan of the Zuni farming village of Upper Nutria in 1885.

The first step is to bound the area of continuous space between the buildings. In Figure 2.3, the open space structure is depicted with diagonal hatching. Hillier and Hanson (1984: 97–98) do not provide explicit instructions on how the exterior boundary of open space should be determined, perhaps because the exterior boundaries of the open space structure of the street-oriented European villages they use as exemplars of the techniques are self-evident. In the Puebloan architecture analyzed in this study, however, the boundaries of the open space structure are not so clearly defined. The presence of roof entryways in addition to doors, the portability of ladders that provided access from the ground surface to the roof entryways, and the absence of streets designed for vehicular traffic in pre-twentieth-century Zuni settlements all combine to make the boundaries of settlements more tenuous than those of European towns. After examining nineteenth-century photographs of Zuni settlements (Mindeleff 1891), I decided to arbitrarily bound settlements for analysis by drawing a line at a distance of 10 m from the edges of the buildings that make up the settlement. This boundary respects the relatively open access around the buildings in settlements like Upper Nutria, which could be approached and entered from all directions. Although arbitrary, this rule for bounding the open space structure for analysis was uniformly applied to all settlements, thus providing comparability in the analysis.

The second analytical step is to break apart the open space structure of settlements into a least set of convex spaces (Hillier and Hanson 1984: 97). The formal definition of a convex space is that no tangent drawn on the perimeter passes through the space at any point. This means that any straight line drawn between two points within a convex space will be entirely within that space (Fig. 2.4). A straight line drawn in concave space, in contrast, may fall partially outside that space. Concave spaces are divided into convex spaces by drawing dividing lines to create convex polygons.

The procedure for producing convex maps is essentially a visual one. First the boundary of the largest convex space in the settlement is delineated, then the next largest, and so on until all spaces have been subdivided into convex spaces. The property of convexity translated into human behavior means that in a flat convex space any two people that can be seen by a third person can also see each other (Hillier and Penn 1992: 48). Convex space maps can be reduced to graphs of

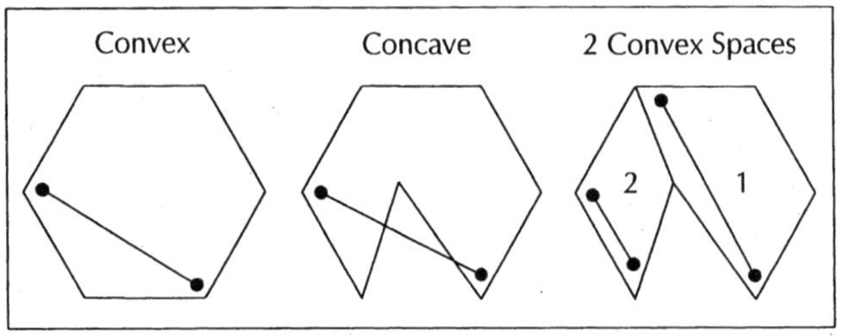

Figure 2.4. Visual definition of convex and concave spaces, with subdivision of a concave space into two convex spaces for analysis.

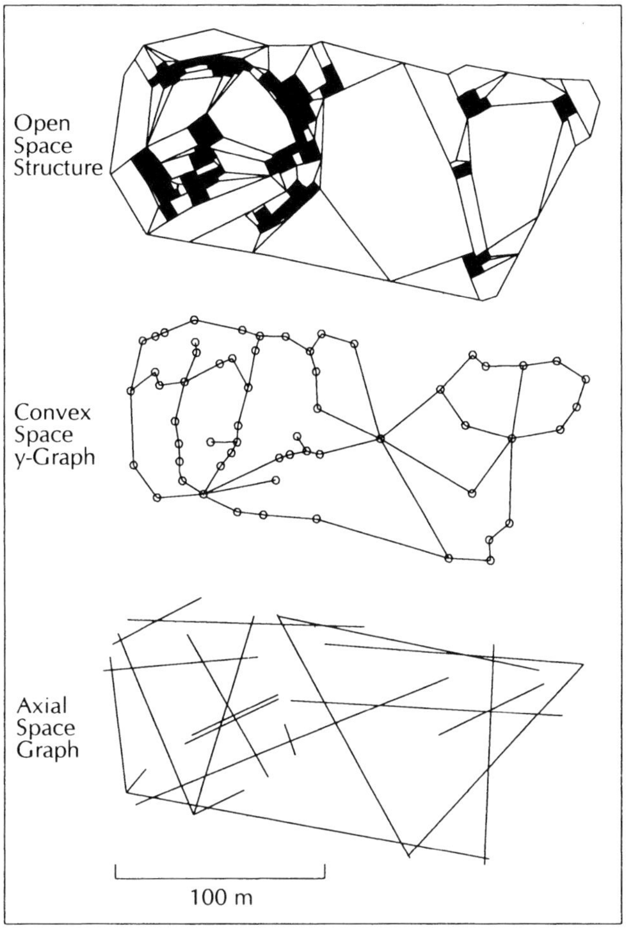

Figure 2.5. Reduction of the convex space map of Upper Nutria to a y-graph and an axial graph.

y-space by reducing each convex space to a dot and connecting each dot with lines depicting the relation of permeable adjacency to other convex spaces (Fig. 2.5). Convex maps and their y-graphs represent the two-dimensional structure of settlements in a form that can be quantified in a variety of ways.

The third step in the syntactic analysis of settlements is the creation of axial space maps. Axial space maps are produced by delineating the longest straight line that can be drawn through the open space structure, then the next longest and so on until all convex spaces are crossed and all axial lines that can be linked to other axial lines without repetition are so linked (Hillier and Hanson 1984: 99). Axial maps thus represent the open space structure of a settlement with a least set of straight lines that pass through all of the y-space. The axial map produced by this procedure is a graph (Fig. 2.5) that can be further analyzed to quantify a number of syntactic relations.

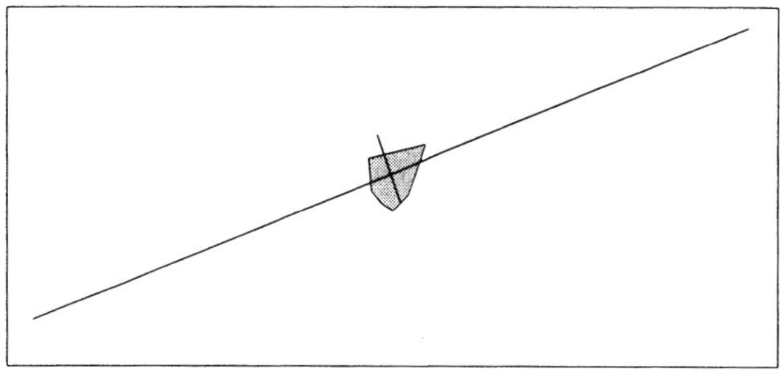

Figure 2.6. Point "a" in Upper Nutria (*see* Fig. 2.3) viewed as convex and axial space.

The basic concepts of syntactic relations support the quantitative analysis of different spatial patterns, that is, the measurement of the degree to which any configuration is symmetric or asymmetric and distributed or nondistributed. These spatial patterns can be determined for any point viewed as either convex or axial space. A space between two room blocks in the central section of Upper Nutria village, for instance, labeled as point "a" in the convex space structure of Figure 2.3, can be viewed as a discrete area (a convex space) or as the intersection of two axial spaces (Fig. 2.6). The statistical description of a space defines the set of syntactic relations of buildings in relation to other spaces and thus provides insight into the dynamics of the growth process. The linear dimensions (or area) of a space invested in particular syntactic relations represent the statics of architectural arrangement at a particular point in time.

Like network analysis (Hopkins 1987), several key statistics of space syntax address the degree to which a graph is dendritic or connected. A dendritic graph branches repeatedly without rejoining, entailing clear hierarchies of access and allowing minimum ease of movement and maximum privacy. A completely connected graph, containing all possible routes, allows greater ease of movement because any space can be reached from many alternative directions; there is no hierarchy of accessibility. Other key statistics, derived from graph theory, measure how the structure of convex and axial space approximates a grid. It is this grid, however deformed, that is the prime determinant of patterns of movement, especially pedestrian movement, in settlements (Hillier and Penn 1992: 50).

Hillier and Hanson (1984: 98–99) formulate several measures based on the convex space map or its derived y-graph. Three of these measures are used in this study. The first is the measure of convex articulation, calculated by dividing the number of convex spaces by the number of buildings in a settlement, as shown in the formula:

$$\text{convex articulation} = \frac{\text{number of spaces}}{\text{number of buildings}}$$

Lower values of convex articulation indicate less break-up of y–space and therefore more synchrony, and vice versa.

A second measure of convexity is grid convexity. It measures the degree of convex deformation of a grid by comparing the convex map to an orthogonal grid in which convex spaces extend across the system in one direction, whereas in the other direction the convex spaces fit into the interstices. Grid convexity thus compares the actual number of convex spaces with the minimum number that could exist for a regular grid with the same number of room blocks. Grid convexity is calculated with the formula:

$$\text{grid convexity} = \frac{(\sqrt{I} + 1)^2}{C}$$

Where: I is the number of room blocks surrounded by y
C is the number of convex spaces.

The formula for grid convexity yields measures that vary between values of 0 and 1; the lower the value the more deformed is the grid.

The third measure, derived from the y–graph, is convex ringiness. This statistic provides information about the distributedness of a spatial arrangement by measuring the number of rings in the spatial arrangement as a proportion of the maximum number of planar rings for that number of spaces. Convex ringiness is calculated with the formula:

$$\text{convex ringiness} = \frac{I}{2C-5}$$

Where: I is the number of room blocks
C is the number of convex spaces in the system.

Convex ringiness measures the distributedness of the y system with respect to itself, as opposed to X or Y.

Seven syntactic measures are derived from the axial map (Hillier and Hanson 1984: 99–114). The first of these is axial articulation, calculated by dividing the number of axial lines by the number of buildings in a settlement, as shown in the formula:

$$\text{axial articulation} = \frac{\text{number of axial lines}}{\text{number of buildings}}$$

Low values in this measure indicate a higher degree of "axiality," and high values indicate a greater breakup of axial space.

Another measure derived from the axial graph is axial integration of convex spaces, as calculated by the formula:

$$\text{axial integration of convex spaces} = \frac{\text{number of axial lines}}{\text{number of convex spaces}}$$

Low values for this measure indicate a higher degree of axial integration of convex spaces, and vice versa.

The comparison of axial spaces to an orthogonal grid with the same number of islands is measured by grid axiality, as calculated in the formula:

$$\text{grid axiality} = \frac{(\sqrt{I} \times 2) + 2}{L}$$

Where: I is the number of room blocks
L is the number of axial lines.

The formula for grid axiality yields values between zero and 1. High values for the measure of grid axiality indicate stronger approximation to a grid. Hillier and Hanson (1984: 100) note that, in general, values above 0.25 indicate a "griddy system" and those below 0.15 denote a more axially deformed system.

The distributedness of the arrangement of axial space in a settlement is measured through the axial ringiness statistic, calculated with the formula:

$$\text{axial ringiness} = \frac{I}{2L-5}$$

Where: L is the number of axial lines
I is the number of room blocks.

The formula for this variable as presented in Hillier and Hanson (1984: 104) contains a typographical error in which the dividend and divisor were inverted. By correcting the formula as presented here, the values provided in the example Hillier and Hanson work through to illustrate the formula are derived, and the formula has a parallel construction to the related formula for convex ringiness. The values for axial ringiness can exceed one because the map it is based on is nonplanar, although Hillier and Hanson (1984: 104) point out that high values are unusual.

One goal of quantitative analysis of syntactic relations is to concisely express the complex relational properties of individual spaces in terms of the whole system. In this regard, there are three primary statistics derived from the axial graph (Hillier and Hanson 1984: 108–123). The first of these is relative asymmetry, which measures the integration of individual axial spaces and the whole system of axial space arrangement. Relative asymmetry entails the relations of depth (the number of steps a space is away from the carrier), because spaces can only be deep from other spaces if it is necessary to pass through intervening spaces to arrive at them. The measure of relative asymmetry generalizes this syntactic relation by comparing how deep the system is from a particular point with how deep or shallow it could theoretically be, with the least depth being when all spaces are directly connected to the original space and the most depth when all spaces are arranged in a unilinear sequence away from the original space. Relative asymmetry is calculated with the formula:

$$\text{relative asymmetry} = \frac{2(\text{MD}-1)}{\text{k}-2}$$

Where: MD is the mean depth
k is the number of spaces in the system.

The mean depth of the system is figured by assigning a value to each space according to how many spaces it is away from the original space, summing those values, and dividing by the number of spaces in the system less one, that is, the original space. Values of relative asymmetry vary between zero and 1, with low values indicating a space from which the system is shallow (a space that tends to integrate the system) and high values a space that tends to be segregated from the system. The mean value of relative asymmetry provides a general measure of integration for the system as a whole.

A list of relative asymmetry values for axial spaces gives a true account of the distribution of integration and can be used to compare systems of the same size (those having the same number of spaces). A transformation is necessary, however, to compare systems of different sizes to eliminate the considerable effect that size has on the level, though not the distribution, of relative asymmetry values. This transformation is performed by comparing the relative asymmetry value of any space with the relative asymmetry value for the "root" space at the bottom of a graph that has a "diamond-shaped pattern." This is not a geometric shape; it is a justified map in which there are k spaces at mean depth level, k/2 at one level above and below, k/4 at two levels above and below, and so on until there is one space at the shallowest and the deepest points. The transformed statistic, real relative asymmetry, is calculated with the formula:

$$\text{real relative asymmetry} = \frac{\text{RA}}{\text{D}_\text{k}}$$

Hillier and Hanson (1984: 112) tabulate the D_k values needed to compare systems of different sizes varying between 5 and 300 spaces. Real relative asymmetry values will be both above and below 1. Low values indicate strongly integrated systems, whereas high values (above 1) indicate more segregated spatial arrangements.

A final statistic is the measure of control. Each space has a certain number of immediate neighbors. Each space therefore gives to each of its immediate neighbors 1/n, and these are then summed for each receiving space to give the control value of that space. Spaces with a control value greater than 1 will be strong control spaces; those below 1 are weak control spaces. Control is a local measure, because it only takes into account relations between a space and its immediate neighbors, whereas integration is a global measure that takes into account the relations of a space to every other space in the system.

Interpretation of the syntactic relations of the open space structure of settlements is based on a combination of visual and quantitative analysis using the postulates of the social logic of space as variables (Hillier and Hanson 1984: 122–123). Once integration and control values are derived, maps showing the core distribution of these values (for example, the top 10%, 25%, or 50% of the most integrating or controlling spaces) are produced for use in visual pattern recognition. Various permutations of integration and control maps can be generated for different purposes. The analytical goal is to determine how space is invested and structured in relation to global and local organization and how these syntactic relations structured the interaction of inhabitants and outsiders. A general picture is thus built of how the structure of the open space interface generates and controls social interaction.

PERMEABILITY ANALYSIS OF BUILDING INTERIORS

To develop a unified model applicable for all architectural space, Hillier and Hanson (1984: 143–175) extend the theoretical and syntactic arguments applied to settlements to buildings. Buildings are distinguishable from settlements by their tendency to embody a much higher degree of social information in their spatial form. Building interiors are different from settlement structure; they are not simply the same type of structure on a smaller scale. A building is a domain of knowledge in that it spatially orders social categories (such as households, sodalities, administrative bodies, disciplinary groupings) and a domain of control in that it orders boundaries. The boundary-forming walls of buildings are what spatially distinguishes these structures from the continuous open space that forms settlements. Every building, even a single cell, identifies at least one "inhabitant" who has special access to and control of the category of space created by the boundary. There is a dual nature to a boundary because it simultaneously creates a category of space (the interior) and a form of control (the boundary itself). In terms of the syntactic measures described in the preceding section, relative asymmetry articulates the relations of the category embodied in space, and distributedness articulates the relations of the boundary (the control on that category).

The analysis of buildings is formally similar to the analysis of settlements, but with interpretation for permeability rather than connectivity. The relation of contiguity in settlement analysis is replaced by the relation of direct permeability in building analysis, and the relation of containment in settlement analysis becomes the relation of controlling permeability in building analysis.

The translation of buildings into graphs is more straightforward in building analysis than in the analysis of settlements, because every interior of a cell or subdivision of a cell can be conceptualized as a point and represented by lines linking it to other cells. The carrier is the space outside the cell and it, too, is represented as a point. From these graphic elements, the configurational generators of symmetry and asymmetry, distributedness and nondistributedness can be derived to construct statistical patterns.

The spatial patterns revealed by permeability graphs of buildings are most evident when they are justified by placing the carrier space at the bottom of the graph. Every space in the building is assigned a depth value according to the minimum number of steps that must be taken to arrive at that space starting from the carrier, a step being defined as a movement from one space to another. Spaces are represented by circles and permeabilities by lines, and all spaces at the same depth are arranged horizontally above the carrier and connected with lines representing direct permeabilities. Figure 2.7 illustrates three building plans with the same adjacency of spaces, but with very different permeability graphs. Justified graphs permit relatively easy measurement of syntactic properties, so they lend themselves to a form of analysis that combines the visual decipherment of pattern with procedures for quantification.

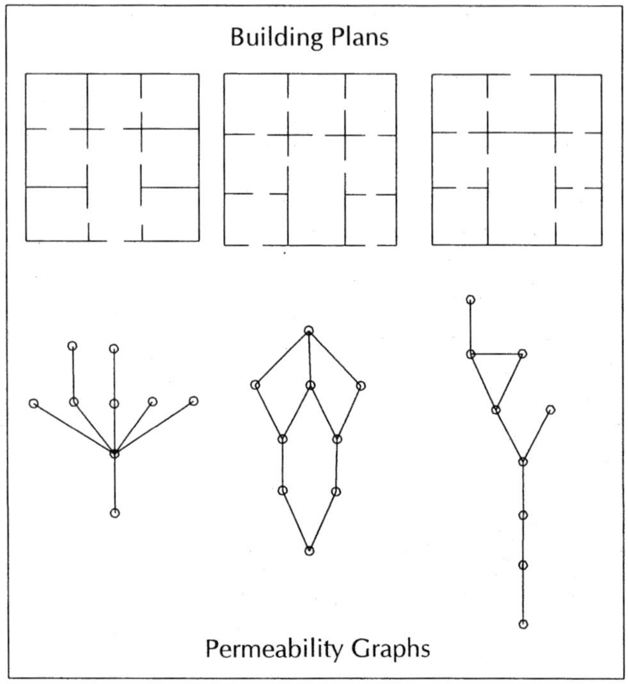

Figure 2.7. Examples of three buildings with identical room adjacency but different permeability graphs. (Adapted from Hillier and Hanson 1984: 150–151.)

The syntactic measures developed for settlement analysis can also be applied to building analysis. The relative asymmetry of a complex from any point can be figured by taking the point as the carrier of the system and calculating from that point as though it were the carrier. Variation will indicate the degree to which a particular space is integrated into or segregated from the complex as a whole. The relative asymmetry statistic is transformed with the same formula used in settlement analysis in order to compare buildings containing varying numbers of rooms or space cells. The measure of relative asymmetry in its raw and transformed states represents the symmetry-asymmetry dimension of the syntax model.

The measure of relative ringiness describes the distributed-nondistributed dimension of the syntactic model. The number of lines that connect a system of "k" points is k–1. This arrangement can only yield a ringless tree graph, so it follows that any increase in the number of lines in the arrangement will result in the formation of rings. The relative ringiness of building interiors can thus be determined as the number of distinct rings in a complex over the maximum possible number of planar rings given a particular number of points. This measure is calculated with the formula:

$$\text{relative ringiness} = 2p\text{–}5$$

Where: p is the number of points in the complex.

The relative ringiness of a point in the complex is determined by the number of independent rings that pass through that point over the maximum number that can pass through it (p–1 for p points), because any additional lines from any particular point will only repeat a link that has already been made.

The essential proposition of building analysis is that space within architectural complexes may be defined in terms of how the complex is arranged syntactically in relation to particular spaces within it. The richness in this differentiation is why interior structures carry more social information than exterior relations. In most but not all cases, the distributed system (the set of rings) is the set of spaces through which the visitor, subject to more or less control, may pass; the nondistributed system (the set of dendritic spaces connected to each other only through the distributed system) is the domain of inhabitants, with stronger sanctions against penetration by visitors.

DURKHEIMIAN NOTIONS OF INTEGRATION

As Bock (1964: 401) observed, a formal analysis that lacks content is as meaningless as a grammar without an accompanying lexicon. Hillier and Hanson interject social content into their formal analysis of architectural structure by entailing Durkheimian notions of social integration. Although the historical role of Durkheim in the development of structural and structural-functionalist anthropology is recognized by many anthropologists (Harris 1968: 465–480, 515–517), his work is held in low esteem by many contemporary scholars (Collins 1988: 107). Durkheim is rarely cited today by anthropologists concerned with social structure and integration. A perusal of recent social science journals indicates Durkheim's theoretical ideas about the topics of suicide and religion still have currency, albeit with more citations by sociologists than anthropologists, but his ideas about social structure are less popular. The theoretical value of ideas is not a question of popularity, however, but a matter of how those ideas figure into an explanatory framework. In this regard, the incorporation of Durkheim's concepts of mechanical and organic solidarity into the theory of spatial syntax warrants discussion.

As formulated by Durkheim (1964), mechanical solidarity is a form of social integration forged through similarities of group belief and structure, and organic solidarity is a form of social integration forged though an interdependence based on differences, such as the division of labor. Much of Durkheim's explication of the concepts of mechanical and organic solidarity is expressed in a quasi-evolutionary or developmental framework (Giddens 1979b: 27–38; Rueschemeyer 1982; Jones 1986: 34–38), such that tribal organizations were thought to be organized around mechanical solidarity and contemporary industrial societies to be organized on the basis of organic solidarity. In this perspective, societies characterized by mechanical solidarity were hierarchically organized in terms of inequalities deriving from the social circumstances of birth, aristocratic prerogatives, and hereditary transmission of property, whereas societies incorporating fully developed organic solidarity were characterized by inequalities deriving from talent and capacity. However, Durkheim (1964) states that all societies always exhibit both kinds of solidarity. Ultimately, then, the distinction between the two forms of solidarity has more heuristic than explanatory value.

Hillier and Hanson (1984: 142) state that the principle axiom of syntax theory is that spatial organization is a function of the form of social solidarity. Mechanical solidarity requires a segregated and dispersed space that separates the constituent social groups and helps maintain their individual identity as discrete social entities. Organic solidarity, in contrast, requires an integrated and dense space to facilitate the numerous social encounters needed for the exchange of information and material that ties together the mutually interdependent social entities. In interpreting the syntactic measures of spatial arrangements, Hillier and Hanson (1984: 96–97) postulate that asymmetry equates to social segregation and symmetry equates to social integration. Similarly, distributedness equates to the diffusion of social groups and nondistributedness equates to the unitary and superordinate control of social interaction.

Some social groups are defined by spatial proximity, such as a household. Other social groups, however, are "transpatial" in the sense that their membership is defined by criteria other than spatial proximity. Examples of transpatial groups include sodalities, social classes, and other groups whose memberships crosscut spatial groups. People can belong to both spatial and transpatial groups simultaneously. University professors, for instance, are members of a spatially discrete faculty at a particular institution and also belong to an academic discipline whose members are distributed widely in space. Transpatial groups generally manifest themselves spatially on occasion in some regular or ritualized form of social interaction, for example, at annual meetings of scholars (Hillier 1989: 17).

Building on the notions of mechanical and organic solidarity, Hillier and Hanson (1984: 256–261) make a distinction between what they term correspondence and noncorrespondence sociospatial systems. A correspondence system is one where spaces and social groups correspond to each other. A noncorrespondence system is one where spaces and social groups do not correspond; the social groups are transpatial in that they are distributed among the various spatial groups. These two types of systems have different internal logic by which they are reproduced spatially.

In correspondence systems, encounters result from physical proximity through membership in a spatial group and these encounters will reinforce each other at the expense of relations with members of other spatial and transpatial groups. Logically, then, the system will tend to become locally very strong and will require not only restrictions on encounters, but also strongly defined spatial boundaries. The logic of the correspondence principle is territorial, and the strength of the system is a function of its ability to maintain correspondence.

The logic of noncorrespondence systems is related to the split between spatial groups and other types of social associations not defined by residence, such as transpatial groups. Whereas spatial groups interact locally, transpatial groups operate across space to relate individuals in different spatial groups to each other and promote interaction between them. The noncorrespondence system must maximize encounters across space if it is to reproduce itself, because the transpatial social groups depend on interaction between members of different spatial groups to retain an identity as the system is reproduced. A noncorrespondence system, therefore, tends to be globally rather than locally strong, with weaker rules, weak boundaries, and a lack of hierarchy. Noncorrespondence systems depend spatially on openness in the interaction of both inhabitants and noninhabitants, coupled with a relatively weak and diffused local organization that orients the system toward the global level.

Although Hillier (1989) emphasizes the role of Durkheimian concepts of social integration in the social logic of space, the application of the method and techniques of space syntax is not entirely contingent on this aspect of the theory. Many applications of space syntax empirically explore social interaction using the methods and techniques of graph analysis, but do not make reference to Durkheimian sociology (Hanson 1989; Peponis and others 1989).

LIMITATIONS OF THE ANALYTICAL TECHNIQUE

Lawrence (1986: 331, 1987: 53) recognizes the ability of Hillier and Hanson's techniques to highlight the similarities and differences between buildings, but he criticizes space syntax because it does not yield any information about the meaning and use of specific spaces. Lawrence points out that "socio-psychological" approaches have provided a useful discussion for the comprehension and definition of boundaries, and he decries Hillier and Hanson for ignoring how individuals perceive space and social encounters. Furthermore, Lawrence notes that boundaries are not just created physically, but are also ordered by symbolic and juridic parameters that are transient in kind. Lawrence suggests that limiting the analysis of domestic architecture to a study of its configuration is misleading, because the meaning and use of domestic space is not solely dependent on its form. Lawrence thinks the fact that architecture can be transformed by reconstruction or remodeling during use limits the utility of Hillier and Hanson's approach.

Lawrence's criticism is flawed in that it perpetuates the erroneous notions that architecture and society are separate entities and that architecture is nothing more than a crucible for carrying meaning that exists independently in the minds of its occupants. In the context of Giddens's structuration theory, the transformation of architecture during use does not constitute a limitation because the design, occupation, and remodeling of architecture provides one of the means by which society is continually recreated. The fact that the social logic of space method ignores the "socio-psychological" aspects of architecture is a strength rather than a weakness for the archaeological application of this theory, because the psychological aspects of human behavior are contingent on cultural variables that are difficult to control with contemporary archaeological methods and data.

Leach (1978) criticizes space syntax because of what he characterizes as its "extreme" belief that spatial organization is a function of the form of social structure. He argues that the chasm between basic space syntax and real life sociology is wider than Hillier and his colleagues think. Leach asserts that the techniques of space syntax (Hillier and others 1976) cannot fully work unless something is already known of the relevant social structure, and the observed patterns in spatial arrangement can be related to known social structure in retrospect.

Leach is correct in his assessment that the space syntax techniques cannot fully work unless something is already known about the relevant social structure. This limitation is due more to the nascent character of space syntax at this stage of its development than to inherent limitations in the theory itself. Empirical work evaluated by existing knowledge may eventually overcome this limitation, resulting in a research program where new information can be created rather than in a program that simply verifies existing information. It should also be noted that Leach is well known for his views concerning the symbolic role architecture plays in culture (Leach 1983). In this regard, he undervalues the potential for archaeology to be something more than simply paleoethnography. The application of space syntax to the archaeological record offers the potential for the development of new archaeological (explicitly material) concepts of social organization that complement existing ethnographic concepts.

Batty (1989: 162) observes that Hillier and Hanson analyze the growth of spatial patterns, but neglect decline and decay. In terms of archaeological concerns, this is a major oversight that needs correction. Although extending the theoretical perspective and analytical techniques to incorporate the role that entropy plays in the formation of spatial patterns is beyond the scope of this study, this limitation needs to be borne in mind as the analysis proceeds.

Susan Ball and Wendy Bustard at the University of New Mexico have identified interanalyst bias as a problem in the consistent application of the techniques of space syntax (S. Ball and W. Bustard letter to T. J. Ferguson, May 4, 1992). For instance, in independent analyses of the same archaeological site, Ball and Bustard obtained statistically different results based on the predominant shape of the convex spaces each perceived; one analyst created maps primarily using triangles and the other used rectilinear shapes. This exercise reveals that although the definitions of the basic space syntax concepts are unambiguous, their application varies depending on a number of factors and on decisions made by individual analysts. In this regard, space syntax is like many other kinds of archaeological analyses subject to interanalyst variability (for instance, ceramic typology). Because this Zuni analysis was conducted by a single investigator using a consistent set of decision criteria, interanalyst bias is not an issue.

ARCHAEOLOGICAL CONSIDERATIONS

By combining Giddens's structuration theory with Hillier and Hanson's syntax theory, architecture can be viewed as the material by-product of the dynamic social processes that led to the recursive application of socio-spatial constructs by individuals. As such, the spatial structure of architecture found in archaeological contexts can be investigated to provide information about the social structure of the society that architecture housed. An archaeological application of a conjoined theory of space syntax as it relates to the structuration of society has several strengths and weaknesses that are briefly discussed here.

Stripped to its barest elements, the space syntax of the social logic of space model only requires the recognition of closed and open architectural spaces. Functional labels of spaces can be incorporated into the analysis, but such functional attributions are not a requirement of the method. The simplicity of the basic observational units is critical to an archaeological application of the model, because the identification of both the function of architecture and the occupancy by particular social groups (lineages, clans, kivas, medicine societies) is in and of itself a difficult archaeological procedure. By treating architecture as the basic observational and analytical unit, the space syntax model offers archaeologists an opportunity to develop new concepts of social organization that transcend ethnographic conceptualization. Rather than being reduced to paleoethnography, archaeology has the opportunity to use materially based concepts of social organization that contribute new kinds of information.

However, the resolution of the archaeological record is such that some critical attributes of architecture become obscured through time or cannot be determined using information from the surficial recording of archaeological sites. The process of architectural deterioration that creates ruins, including but not limited to roof collapse, wall fall, and the disintegration of wooden building elements, often obscures the entrances into rooms and buildings. Without precise knowledge of the location of these entrances, only a subset of the key syntactic properties can be analyzed. Be this as it may, the residual architectural structure evident in the archaeological record still provides a relatively robust set of data to which space syntax may be applied. Even though entrances are often obscured, the fundamental arrangement of rooms and buildings in historic Zuni settlements can be discerned from the remains of stone masonry walls still visible on the surface.

Settlements are dynamic entities that undergo continual change as they are used in relation to the developmental cycles of the social groups that occupy them (Goody 1971; Rock 1974). Archaeologists, however, essentially study archaeological sites as static artifacts, reducing what is actually a dynamic process to a state (Binford and Sabloff 1982; Kramer 1982: 671). The analysis of bonding and abutment patterns (Wilcox 1975; Reid and Shimada 1982), of closed fenestration, and of other architectural attributes provides a way to consider social dynamics in the analysis of the archaeological record, which is static at the time of investigation. All of these analyses require extensive observations, however, that generally can be derived only from standing architecture or from excavation of well-preserved sites. With regard to this problem, the syntactic variables in the social logic of space model represent dynamics, and the actual quantities and amounts of each represent statics. To some degree, then, the problem of statics and dynamics is partially resolved by space syntax, even though the archaeological sites are analyzed as instantiated entities.

A closely related issue in an archaeological application of space syntax concerns the contemporaneity of architectural cells. This attribute is particularly important in the analysis of building interiors, because in Puebloan architecture individual rooms may be abandoned and filled while adjacent rooms are still occupied. Prior to the analysis of the syntactic relations of space, independent lines of evidence must be used to isolate contemporaneous room sets. Determining the precise contemporaneity of buildings in settlement analysis is less critical than determining the contemporaneity of rooms for the analysis of building interiors, because buildings generally constitute impediments to access even after they are no longer occupied. Nevertheless, the various components of archaeological sites should be analytically separated when possible.

Finally, as Hillier and Hanson (1984: 197) caution, the social logic of space model cannot be applied in full without examining the very social relations that are the target of archaeological analysis. There is an inherent contradiction here in terms of archaeological analysis, because the full interpretation of the archaeological record thus requires knowledge that is not present in the archaeological record itself. The middle range theory building of ethnoarchaeology that relates social processes to the archaeological record would seem, therefore, to be an essential step in the full development of syntactic analysis. This study draws on some ethnographic data to evaluate the social logic of space variables, but the full ethnoarchaeological investigation that would be optimal has yet to be made. In this initial application of a syntactic analysis to a wide range of settlements and a more limited range of building interiors, I present an objective methodology that can be productively pursued in certain archaeological situations. In so doing, the residual weaknesses of the method in terms of archaeological analysis are identified as areas for additional research in the further promising development of the theory and method of space syntax in archaeology.

CHAPTER THREE

Perspectives on Zuni Settlement and Social Organization

To understand the changes that have occurred in Zuni settlement patterns and society, it is necessary to review the temporal placement and geographical location of Zuni settlements in relation to broad patterns of social organization, economy, demography, and land use. Because the Zuni villages occupied at the beginning of the historic period were the culmination of a long sequence of prehistoric development, the general patterns of settlement during the prehistoric era are summarized first. The subsequent discussion of settlement patterns during the historic era is divided into the conventional time periods used to order Southwestern history: the Contact, Spanish, Mexican, and American periods.

THE PREHISTORIC ERA

The Zuni Indians and their ancestors have lived in the Zuni River valley and the surrounding region for more than 1,500 years. Despite a number of major changes in house form, in settlement layout, and in locations of settlements during the prehistoric period, there is a remarkable continuity in the developmental sequence of Zuni culture. There is still much to be learned about Zuni prehistory (Kintigh 1990: 271–274), but the broad outlines of Zuni settlement patterns have been well known since the seminal work of Leslie Spier (1917) in the early twentieth century. Based on ceramics, architecture, and other attributes of the archaeological record, virtually all archaeologists who have worked in the Zuni area have come to the conclusion that the contemporary Zuni Indians are the direct descendants of the prehistoric Pueblo people who settled the region sometime prior to A.D. 400. Many archaeologists think that modern Zuni culture emerged as an amalgam that was created when the initial prehistoric Pueblo population on the Colorado Plateau merged with another group of people with a different cultural tradition, perhaps immigrants from the Mogollon area (Cushing 1896: 404–426; Woodbury 1979; Watson and others 1980; Ferguson 1981b).

The broad patterns of prehistoric Zuni settlement mirror the developments that took place throughout the region occupied by the prehistoric Pueblo people. The first settlements in the area were comprised of agriculturists living in pit houses of various types (Spier 1917: 300–301; Roberts 1939; Anyon and Robertson 1983: 413–423; Varien 1990: 204–206). These people later developed above-ground masonry structures, commonly called pueblos in the Southwest. At first the pueblos in the Zuni region were comprised of small, dispersed room blocks associated with subterranean pit structures or kivas. By A.D. 1000, the population in the Zuni area began to construct larger settlements oriented around Chacoan great houses with associated circular great kivas (Roberts 1931, 1932; Leonard 1991). After A.D. 1150, there were a number of post-Chacoan settlements in the Zuni area with aggregated room blocks and unroofed forms of great kivas (Kintigh 1991). Throughout this period, the occupation spans of most settlements were relatively brief, and many new villages were constructed over a wide area, perhaps in response to variability in climate and the gradually decreasing productivity of agricultural strategies.

As the prehistoric population of the Zuni region gradually increased in size through internal population growth and immigration, the mobility of communities became constrained (Anyon and Ferguson 1983; Ferguson 1985: 16–18). Each community required an agricultural area, presumably near its habitation, and an increasingly larger sustaining area for resource procurement. As the number of communities increased, the amount of available agricultural land decreased, and new settlements adversely impacted the ecology of the sustaining areas used by previously established communities. Regional packing of population into a finite area greatly diminished the ability to expand or maintain the settlement system, leading to a major change in the form and distribution of settlements.

In the mid-thirteenth century, a major shift occurred in the settlement patterns of the Zuni area. The occupation of virtually all small pueblos was relinquished and fewer, much larger, plaza-oriented settlements were founded in areas where more intensive agriculture was possible. These highly planned, late prehistoric communities were often surrounded by external walls that defined their exterior boundaries. In the drainage of the Zuni River alone, more than 37 of these large villages were occupied between A.D. 1250 and 1540 (Kintigh 1985: 73; Anyon 1992), incorporating an estimated 10,000 rooms. Similar settlements were occupied in adjacent drainages at the same time. Initially, many of the large pueblos in the Zuni area were only inhabited for relatively brief intervals, as short as 20 to 30 years. As the occupation of one pueblo was relinquished, another was founded somewhere else in the drainage of Zuni River. The settlement pattern in the late prehistoric era thus entailed the occupation of 8 to 12 large pueblo villages at any one time.

Several archaeologists have suggested that the relatively brief occupation spans of these large settlements was due in part to the processes of social fissioning and recombining of communities that resulted from the development of the new forms of social organization needed to integrate large numbers of people living in dense settlements (Woodbury 1956: 562; Kintigh 1985: 115–117). Other scholars think the increasing size of villages was due to climatic fluctuations in the late thirteenth century that made the concentration of labor in larger villages advantageous with respect to more intensive agriculture (LeBlanc 1978; Kintigh 1985: 112–113; Leonard 1991). Some of these scholars attribute the concurrent shift in the location of settlements to lower elevations to an increased risk of agricultural failure at higher elevations because of climatic changes. Still other archaeologists think the shifts in settlement pattern were related to prehistoric warfare (Woodbury 1959; Watson and others 1980). It is likely that all of these factors played a role in the settlement changes that occurred.

Although the precise set of causes that led to the development of prehistoric Zuni settlement patterns is not known, the patterns themselves are clear. Through time, there was a trend toward the occupation of fewer, much larger villages located in the lower elevations of the Zuni River. There was also a concurrent shift toward increased residential stability. By about A.D. 1450, a series of communities was established in the lower Zuni River valley that continued to be occupied into the historic period. These developments were accompanied by a relinquishment of habitation in other areas in the drainage of the Upper Little Colorado River. By the end of the prehistoric era, a Zuni settlement system had emerged that entailed the occupation of a few, very large villages in a core area of habitation that contained the best agricultural land in the region. This core area of settlement was surrounded by a much larger uninhabited region used for resource procurement. A similar development of settlement patterns occurred in the neighboring Acoma and Hopi areas (Adams 1978; Brew 1979; Garcia-Mason 1979), and by the onset of the historic period the only occupied villages in the Western Pueblo region were the Zuni, Acoma, and Hopi pueblos.

CONTACT PERIOD

In A.D. 1540, the year of the first Spanish Entrada in the Southwest, the Zuni Indians lived in six or seven large pueblos along a 24-km (14.3-mile) stretch of the Zuni River valley (Spier 1917: 216; Kintigh 1985: 114; Anyon 1992). From east to west, these villages were Kyaki:ma, Mats'a:kya, Halona:wa, Kwa'kin'a, Kechiba:wa, Hawikku, and, possibly, Chalo:wa (Fig. 3.1). These villages were situated on elevated landforms above the floodplain, such as low hills, ridges, or mesa tops. They were also located on or adjacent to the most fertile agricultural soils in the Zuni area, in positions to take advantage of abundant water resources at springs or at confluences of major drainages. Conservative estimates for the population of the Zuni area at this time are between 4,100 and 7,000 (Kintigh 1985: 86; Hart 1991a: 53).

The villages occupied in 1540 were comprised of massive terraced room blocks arranged to form streets and plazas. They ranged in size from an estimated 186 to 901 rooms (Kintigh 1985: 75). The initial settlements at these locations were probably large, planned pueblos similar to those occupied in the thirteenth and fourteenth centuries, but it is difficult to verify this observation because these pueblos were occupied for a long time and later room blocks were built on top of earlier ones. Excavations at Hawikku (Smith and others 1966) and Kechiba:wa (Lothrop 1919, 1923) show that the large room blocks at these two pueblos grew by slow accretion and gradual architectural modification over several centuries, and similar accretion probably took place at the other villages as well. The early occupation of all of the contact settlements has been obscured by two centuries or more of subsequent habitation. The earliest architecture at Hawikku, for instance, was buried under 4.5 m of cultural debris topped by the latest room blocks (Hodge 1918: 370).

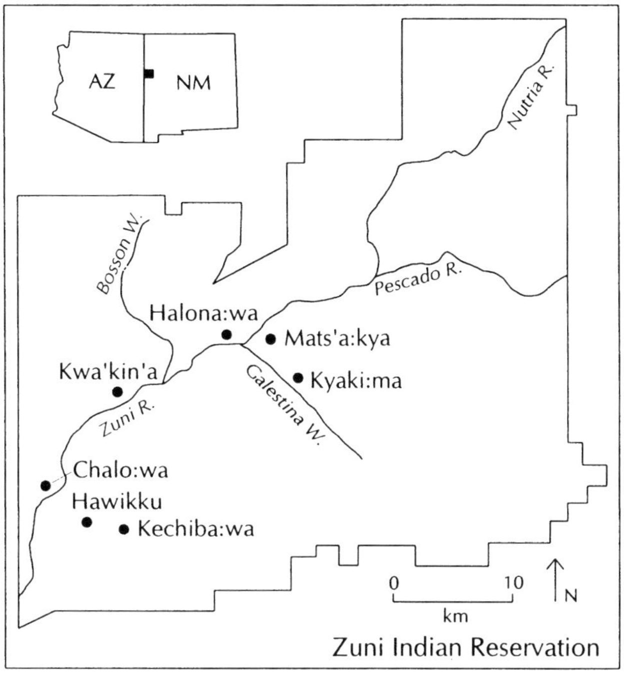

Figure 3.1. Zuni villages occupied in 1540.

The documentary record attests that the Zuni had a successful and well-established agricultural economy in 1540, but little is known about Zuni social and political organization at this time. Archaeologists drawing on the same archaeological and historical information have variously argued that the Zuni who occupied the contact villages were organized in a noncoercive, "egalitarian" society analogous to nineteenth-century Zuni Pueblo (Ferguson 1981b: 342) or, alternately, that they were organized into a "complex society" with a coercive, hierarchically organized structure of elites that is not analogous to later developments (Upham 1982). The fact that both arguments are made using the same data is indicative of the need for more research into late prehistoric and early historic social organization.

However archaeologists choose to characterize Zuni society in 1540 in terms of anthropological classifications, it is clear that the Zuni were well-organized with strong leaders. Estevan, the first emissary of European culture, was executed after his arrival at the Zuni villages in 1539 (Hodge 1937: 6–27). Coronado's arrival at Hawikku in 1540 was met with an effective and organized resistance based on a well-developed strategy involving spies, smoke signals, an armed force of 250 Zuni warriors, and stockpiled weapons at key areas of access into the pueblo (Bolton 1949: 119–125). The Zuni defended their village in a fierce battle before they retreated and let the Spaniards enter the pueblo. The military capability of the Zuni who lived at Hawikku is further documented by archaeological excavations at the site that exposed graves with funerary objects interpreted by Zuni as the ritual offerings buried with Bow Priests, also called War Chiefs (Smith and others 1966: 174, 225). Additional grave offerings at Hawikku have been interpreted as belonging to other types of community leaders, such as those of the medicine societies (Hodge 1966: 288–293). The most recent archaeological analysis of the distribution of funerary objects at Hawikku demonstrates that there were community leaders who exercised decision-making authority, but it does not attempt to label these leaders in ethnographic terms (Howell 1994).

The documentary history of the Coronado Expedition suggests, however, that there was no concentration of power in one political office. Casteñeda, a chronicler of the Coronado Expedition, commented, "They have no rulers, as in New Spain, but are governed by the counsel of their oldest men" (Hammond and Rey 1940: 253). Coronado added that based on what he could see and find out none of the Zuni villages had a central leader or "lord," for he had not seen any principal house "by which superiority over others might be manifested" (Bolton 1949: 127). Ladd (1979a: 488–489) notes that some Zuni people believe the contact period villages were governed by a supreme council of War Chiefs, whose members were distributed in each of the villages. Ladd suggests that rain priests and other religious leaders who attended to spiritual affairs also played an important role.

Although clearly there were differences in wealth, authority, and power among individuals, the Zuni contact villages were apparently incorporated into a single cohesive society through shared religion and ceremony. The multiple Zuni villages may have been organized in a political confederacy in which decisions were reached through a consensus involving leaders from all the villages. In a confederacy, the individual villages may have been ranked by criteria of ceremonial power or authority, but the representatives of all the villages would have participated in and contributed to discussions leading to executive action. This type of organization would have created political autonomy for individual people and villages and at the same time would have provided a way for all the Zuni villages to act in concert at a regional level when it was advantageous.

Analysis of ceramics from sites dating to the contact period indicates that pottery was exchanged among the villages and that some types of ceramics may have been produced by a small number of specialists (B. Mills 1991, 1995). The Zuni were also engaged in a widespread regional trade network, helping to redistribute products that moved along an east-west axis from the Great Plains to the Colorado River and a north-south axis that led into northern Mexico (Riley 1975). The arrival of the Spaniards initiated a long sequence of events that eventually disrupted the Zuni's trading patterns, land use, and settlement system.

When Coronado stormed and occupied Hawikku in 1540, the Zuni responded by temporarily retreating to the top of Dowa Yalanne, a steep-sided mesa rising 250 m (820 feet) above the Zuni River valley. This mesa provided an effective means of defense, because its sheer walls could be mounted using only a few, easily protected trails. Coronado is reported to have visited this "rock," where he was told that the Indians of the province had "fortified themselves" (Hodge 1937: 38–40). Nothing else is recorded about Coronado's visit to Dowa Yalanne, and the historical record gives no indication of the nature or extent of the settlement the Zuni established there. It is not known whether the Zuni simply camped on the mesa, or whether they constructed more substantial housing during the 1540 occupation. After a truce was achieved with Coronado, the Zuni on Dowa Yalanne returned to and reoccupied their villages in the Zuni River valley.

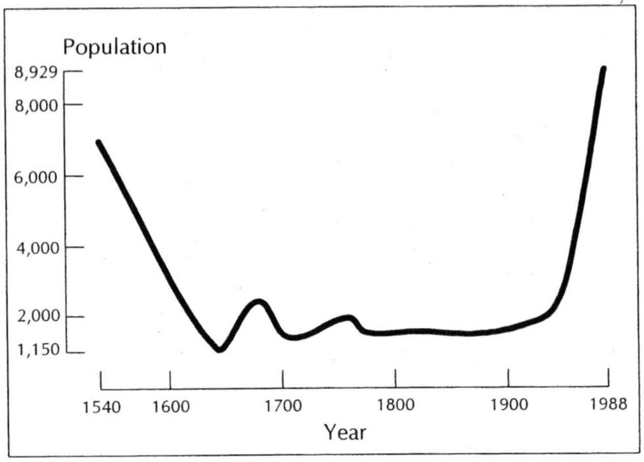

Figure 3.2. Zuni population from A.D. 1540 to 1988. (Information derived from Hart 1991a.)

SPANISH PERIOD

Coronado attacked and occupied Hawikku for several months in 1540, but his expedition soon moved on to the Rio Grande and this area became the focus for the first hundred years of Spanish exploration and colonization in the Southwest. Except for brief visits by Chamuscado in 1581, Espejo in 1583, and Oñate in 1604 (Hammond and Rey 1953, 1966), the Spaniards left the Zuni relatively alone until 1629 when Catholic missions were established at Hawikku and Halona:wa. Later mission *visitas* were added at Mats'a:kya, Kyaki:ma, and Kechiba:wa (Hodge 1937: 96). The greatest initial impact of the Spanish invasion of Zuni was a dramatic decline in the Zuni population. The Zuni had no immunity to the new diseases introduced by the Europeans, and epidemics took a devastating toll. Population estimates for the early historic period vary widely among different sources (Hart 1991a), but the overall trend is clear. This trend is illustrated in Figure 3.2, which plots a smoothed curve derived from 101 of the most reliable population estimates from the period A.D. 1540 to 1988. Scholars estimate that the Zuni population decreased by 66 percent in the first 64 years following contact with the Europeans (Holmes and Fowler 1980: 154–160). This population decline, along with other factors, required a reorganization of Zuni society and land use.

After the Spaniards established Catholic missions and visitas at several Zuni villages, the Zuni people came into regular contact with Europeans (Ferguson and Mills 1982: 44–66). The Spaniards introduced new items of material culture to the Zuni, including important new cultigens like wheat and peaches and domesticated livestock, most notably sheep, horses, burros, and cattle. The Zuni rapidly assimilated these innovations into their subsistence system, along with useful technology such as metal implements. As a result, the Zuni were able to exploit the environment in new ways to adjust to the changing sociopolitical conditions in the Southwest.

The introduction of livestock into the Zuni economy resulted in a new adaptive use of the Zuni environment. The grazing of sheep and cattle on distant ranges provided the Zuni with a new way to harvest the biomass of the sustaining area, converting grass into useful products (meat, wool, hides) that could be herded on the hoof back to the Zuni villages for use and consumption. Horses and burros increased mobility and made it easier to transport crops and other items. The incorporation of livestock into the Zuni economy made it feasible to undertake agriculture and other subsistence activities at a greater distance from residential settlements. Corrals and other architectural facilities were developed to support the livestock industry.

After 1630, attempts by the Spaniards to promote Catholicism and repress the Zuni religion were met with strong resistance, and violence soon followed. In February of 1632, the Zuni burned the Catholic missions at Hawikku and Halona:wa, martyring two Catholic priests in the process. After killing these two priests, the Zuni fled to the top of the "Peñol de Caiquima," an early name for Dowa Yalanne derived from the contact period village of Kyaki:ma located at the southwest edge of the mesa (Bandelier 1892a: 97–99; Hodge 1937: 91–93; Hackett 1942a: 181). The Zuni anticipated that the Spaniards would avenge the deaths of the priests, and Dowa Yalanne was once again used as a place of refuge in a time of danger. Within a month, a small party of Spanish soldiers was dispatched to punish the Zuni for killing the Catholic priests. When the Spaniards arrived at Dowa Yalanne, they were admitted to the mesa top where they obtained a promise that the Zuni would be "good" thereafter (Hodge 1937: 92). After a month-long occupation of Dowa Yalanne, the Zuni returned to their multiple settlements in the Zuni River valley. The Spaniards repaired the missions that had been destroyed and returned them to use.

During the seventeenth century, there was a decline in the number of occupied villages. The reduction of population, political pressure from the Spaniards, and raiding from the Navajo and Apache all contributed to attrition in the number of occupied settlements. Documentary evidence on the precise sequence of relinquishment of occupation of the contact period Zuni villages is meager. Bandelier's (1892a: 108) analysis of historical documents suggests that two pueblos were permanently abandoned prior to 1680, but there is insufficient archaeological and historical evidence to corroborate this observation. Violence became a regular part of the social environment in the seventeenth century as the Zuni defended their land and resources from encroachment from other groups and resisted Spanish attempts to suppress their culture and religion (Hackett 1942b: 289; Ferguson and Hart 1985: 58–61). Retrenchment of the Zuni population into fewer pueblos certainly would have facilitated defense.

One particularly devastating raid occurred at Hawikku in 1672 when the Apache sacked and burned *La Purísima Concepción de Háwikuh*, the Catholic mission. The Apache did not raid the native pueblo at Hawikku during this attack, however, and some historians regard this as evidence that the Apache and Zuni were engaged in a conspiracy against the Spaniards at this time (Hodge 1937: 98). Following the 1672 raid, the Zuni moved into and rehabilitated the rectory at the Catholic mission, subdividing large rooms into smaller enclosures and using the nave, cemetery, and patio for sheep corrals (Smith and others 1966: 121–125).

The Spanish oppression of pueblo life culminated in August of 1680 in the historic Pueblo Revolt, when the Zuni joined with all the other Pueblos in driving the Spaniards out of New Mexico. The Pueblo Indians were successful in obliterating almost all the physical evidence of Spanish occupation, including the destruction of historical records, and little is known from documentary sources about Zuni participation in the revolt. Spanish reports only record the fact that the Catholic missions were burned again and all the Spaniards stationed in the Zuni pueblos were killed, including two priests and possibly a small detachment of soldiers (Hodge 1937: 100, 127; Hackett 1942a: lii).

As they had done during two previous insurrections, the Zuni fled to the top of Dowa Yalanne during the Pueblo Revolt. One Zuni account of the revolt describes how, "When the Pueblo Indians as a body planned the revolt, the Zunis went to the mesa called by them To'wa yallanne . . . and prepared for defense. On their way they poisoned a number of springs. They also deposited stones near the brink of the mesa for use as missiles" (Stevenson 1904: 286–289). The documentary evidence indicates that between 1680 and 1692 the Zuni built and maintained a large settlement that incorporated many pueblo room blocks on the mesa top. The top of Dowa Yalanne is less than 250 ha (617 acres), and it does not contain enough arable land to have supported the entire Zuni population in 1680 (Kroeber 1916: 28–30). Consequently there can be no doubt that the Zuni continued to farm and graze livestock in the valleys surrounding Dowa Yalanne throughout the period of the Pueblo Revolt.

The occupation of Dowa Yalanne was pivotal in the development of historic Zuni settlement patterns. It is the first village in which the whole Zuni population gathered into a single settlement. Apparently every Zuni family maintained a residence on top of Dowa Yalanne that could be used for refuge when the Spaniards returned. Whether or not the contact period villages in the Zuni River valley continued to be used or intermittently occupied during the Pueblo Revolt is not known, but it is unlikely that they were totally abandoned. Nonetheless, the amount of trash in the form of potsherds, ash, and animal bones found in the middens at the Pueblo Revolt village on Dowa Yalanne demonstrates there was intensive use of the settlement during the 12 years of its primary occupation.

A valuable description of the Pueblo Revolt village in November of 1692 was written during an expedition led by Diego de Vargas, the Spanish General in charge of the "reconquest." The Zuni were forewarned of the impending arrival of the Spaniards by men from Laguna Pueblo and by the Spaniards themselves. Twelve Zuni emissaries with gifts of food were dispatched on horseback to meet Diego de Vargas and his soldiers at the springs at Pescado, 19 km (11.8 miles) east of Dowa Yalanne (Stevenson 1904: 287–288; Vargas 1914: 302). The next day, Diego de Vargas arrived at Dowa Yalanne, described in a contemporary account by Sigüenza y Góngora (Hodge 1954: 2) as the "no less impregnable rock of Caquima to which the apostate Zunis living in the vicinity had retired as a place safe from the hostile attacks of the Apaches, thus reducing their five pueblos to one only." The Zuni instructed the Spaniards to camp by the river below the mesa where, during a storm that night, the Spaniards were attacked by "clever and unfriendly Apaches" who made off with 16 head of livestock.

On November 11, 1692, Diego de Vargas and five squadrons of soldiers marched back to the base of Dowa Yalanne, where the Zuni had improved the trail to the mesa top to facilitate the Spaniards' ascent. As Diego de Vargas (1914: 304–305) recorded:

> I reached the said Rock, its front being crowded with the multitude of the said village, and the only way up being so difficult and long, I was forced, on account of its bad places, to mount it on foot and, although it cost considerable effort, I succeeded, and . . . being up there, saw the said table land to be very broad and spacious, extending apparently two Leagues, and I mounted my horse to go and enter the said Village where the natives received me with all its inhabitants whom I saw to be numerous; and having dismounted, I saluted them all, giving them Greeting . . . and being in their Square which contains three estufas, I ordered first that a great Cross be placed in it.

After bestowing absolution, Diego de Vargas (1914: 305) reported that the Zuni asked him to enter a room on the second story of the pueblo, where he was shown Catholic religious paraphernalia arranged on an altar with lit candles. Although these religious articles were remarkable in that no other pueblos Diego de Vargas visited in 1692 had retained any similar Spanish relics, what is of interest in a study of Zuni architecture is the description of the crowded village, with two-story buildings and a square or plaza.

When the Zuni relinquished the occupation of Dowa Yalanne following the absolution granted by Diego de Vargas, they did not reoccupy their multiple pueblos. Instead, the entire tribe coalesced settlement into a single, permanently occupied village at Halona:wa on the north bank of the Zuni River. Following this event, Halona:wa became known as Zuni Pueblo. Zuni Pueblo was greatly expanded at this time, and new room blocks were constructed to the south and east of the original pueblo, enclosing in a large plaza the restored Catholic church, *Nuestra Señora de Guadalupe de Zuni*. The church that had originally been constructed outside the pueblo on a trash mound thus came to occupy a central position in the settlement plan (Ferguson and Mills 1987: 245–247).

The consolidation of what had been six villages into one permanent settlement had to have been accompanied by a major reorganization of Zuni society in order to accommodate a unification of clans, medicine societies, and a multiplicity of religious priesthoods. This unification resulted in an intricate and complex social organization. As a result of the consolidation into a single settlement, Eggan (1950: 210–222) suggests the Zuni developed a strong, centralized social structure that emphasized household and village organization more than a strong clan system. By the early eighteenth century, the Zuni integrated a number of Spanish political offices into the authority structure of the tribe, the most important of which were the governor, lieutenant governor, and tribal council of *tenientes*. These tribal officials were charged with representing the Zuni people in political dealings with non-Indian authorities.

Political strife with the Spaniards continued at Zuni Pueblo after the Pueblo Revolt, and in 1702 Spanish officials conducted an investigation of Indians from Acoma, Laguna, and Zuni who had been urged to rebel by the Apache. The next year, in 1703, three Spaniards illegally residing in Zuni Pueblo were executed by the Zuni, who refused to tolerate the Spaniards' aggressive and overbearing behavior. These three "exiles" from Santa Fe had accompanied the priests and soldiers sent to reestablish the Catholic mission after 1692. During this incident, part of the Zuni population once again sought refuge on Dowa Yalanne, and another part of the tribe fled to the Hopi Pueblos. How long the Zuni remained on top of Dowa Yalanne during this occupation is not known, but the sojourn was probably brief (Hodge 1954: 3; Woodbury 1979: 472; Minge 1980: 51). The 1703 incident was the last documented occupation of Dowa Yalanne as a refuge. Even though habitation of the mesa ceased, Dowa Yalanne continues to be of ceremonial and ritual importance, and it is the location of a number of shrines and sacred areas still used by the Zuni people (Stevenson 1904: 61, 234; Culin 1907: 5; Parsons 1918).

In the eighteenth century, the Zuni developed a new land-use system that entailed the seasonal occupation of a variety of small settlements in satellite relationship to the single, permanently occupied village at Zuni Pueblo (Ferguson 1985: 25–29). These seasonally occupied settlements were used to support grazing and agricultural activities distributed throughout the area formerly occupied with full-time residential villages. By using seasonally occupied settlements, the reduced Zuni population was able to maintain a large community with a complex social organization at Zuni Pueblo and still benefit from the most fertile farmland and copious springs during the growing season. The settlement patterns of the eighteenth century were influenced by Navajo and Apache raids. Zuni Pueblo was built into a multistoried fortress, and the outlying, seasonally occupied settlements were located on elevated landforms that could be more easily defended than villages on the valley bottom.

During the eighteenth century, the villages that had been abandoned as residential locations were reused as "sheep camps," facilities used by herders who camped on the range while they tended livestock. The presence of deep dung deposits in the patio adjacent to the Catholic mission at Hawikku indicates this area was used to corral sheep long after occupation ceased (Hodge 1937: 107; Smith and others 1966: 119). Corrals in the plaza at Kechiba:wa provide evidence for similar use there (Mindeleff 1891: 81–82, 85). Sheep camps functioned in the livestock industry as basic support stations that supplied provisions to herders grazing livestock on grasslands far from Zuni Pueblo. The importance of livestock in the eighteenth-century Zuni economy is emphasized by the fact that in 1779 the Zuni were grazing 15,736 sheep (Minge 1980: 67), a sizable livestock industry by New Mexico standards of that period.

Some eighteenth-century sheep camps were located in areas of difficult access and were associated with hidden corrals and small room blocks. These areas were situated along ridges and on the benches of canyons throughout the Zuni River valley and tributary drainages. Although relatively numerous, few of these sites have been recorded by archaeologists. Many scholars refer to these fortified sheep camps as "refuge sites," because they provided safe places into which sheep could be driven and protected during Apache and Navajo raids (Spier 1917: 239–233).

Other "refuge sites" were established in part for peach orchard farming in areas of sandy soil that occurred at the bases and on the sides of mesas in the Zuni River valley. These agricultural spots were generally located in defensive positions on the tops of elevated landforms like knolls and benches, and they consisted of aggregated complexes of rooms, plazas, and corrals (Ferguson 1981b: 9–10). These settlements, sometimes referred to as "peach orchard villages," represented the exploitation of a new topographic setting for agriculture in the Zuni area, one made possible by the assimilation of new cultigens in the subsistence system. The presence of both peach orchards and corrals at these locations indicates they were used as multifunctional settlements, important in both agricultural and livestock activities. Cushing (1896: 332) considered these peach orchard villages to be refuge sites for ceremonial practices, built away from Zuni Pueblo where the Zuni could practice their religion freely without oppression from the Spanish authorities. The peach orchard villages were the largest of the seasonally occupied settlements in the eighteenth-century land-use system.

A 1790 census of Zuni conducted by Juan Pedro Sisneros documents five major outlying settlements that were seasonally occupied that year, in addition to Zuni Pueblo and smaller sheep camps (Minge 1980: 51, 56). These five settlements included Rancho Colorado with 96 occupants, Rancho de Piedras Negras with 28, Rancho de Galisteo with 105, Rancho del Cañon with 160, and Rancho del Señora Santa Ana with 15 people. Zuni Pueblo, referred to in the census by the mission name of *Nuestra Señora de Guadalupe*, had 717 recorded occupants, including 5 Spaniards. In total, the census enumerated 1,116 Zunis. The reliability of this census as a count of the total Zuni population is questionable, because it is not clear whether all Zuni were enumerated or only those Zuni nominally converted to Catholicism. The census does, however, indicate the importance of seasonally occupied settlements at the time.

Five other *ranchos* or farming settlements in the Zuni area are named in eighteenth-century church records in addition to the five settlements enumerated in the 1790 census. Three of them are located at Hawikku, Quihuaná, and Pinahua. The other two are named Rancho de la Laguna and Rancho de Moqui. The population of these ranchos is not enumerated, but Catholic priests at Zuni recorded numerous births, deaths, and marriages of people associated with the settlements (Hart 1991b: 78–79).

Some, but not all, of the settlements enumerated in the 1790 census and eighteenth-century church records can be correlated with the archaeological sites known to have been occupied in the eighteenth century (Fig. 3.3). Rancho de Piedras Negras is probably located near the

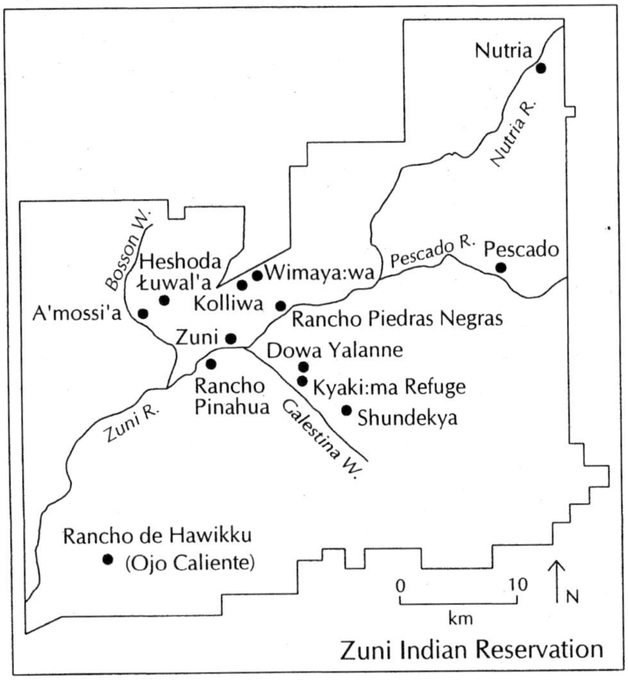

Figure 3.3. Spanish period Zuni settlements occupied during and after the Pueblo Revolt.

present-day community of Blackrock, where archaeological remains are visible on the north bank of the Zuni River on a basalt-topped mesa. Rancho de Galisteo presumably refers to a settlement or group of settlements in the vicinity of Galestina Canyon, southeast of Dowa Yalanne. Sites of this period are located on a bench of Dowa Yalanne adjacent to the contact period site of Kyaki:ma and at a location known as Shundekya. None of the individual settlements along Galestina Wash is large enough to house the population enumerated in the 1790 census, but taken as a group they might encompass enough rooms to house 105 people.

The locations of Rancho Colorado and Rancho del Cañon are more difficult to infer from their names, but the size of the enumerated population at those settlements suggests one of them was the large peach orchard village known to the Zuni as "Heshoda Łuwal'a." It comprises a cluster of aggregated room blocks situated northwest of Zuni Pueblo, set on a bench at the head of a deep canyon against cliffs of spectacular red and white Zuni sandstone (Spier 1979: 230–232). Heshoda Łuwal'a is known to have been occupied in the early nineteenth century when a youthful Lai-iu-ah-tsai-lu (alias Pedro Pino) resided there for several years prior to 1821 to evade the Catholic missionary at Zuni Pueblo (Cushing, Item 36). Lai-iu-ah-tsai-lu later became a prominent governor of Zuni Pueblo.

The rancho at Pinahua is probably a farming area in the vicinity of the late prehistoric site of Binna:wa, located 2 km (1.2 miles) west of Zuni Pueblo in the rich farming lands of the Zuni River valley. There was a nineteenth-century farmhouse located at Binna:wa, and there were other early historic settlements associated with farmlands located nearby at Hattsinawa and Hampassawa (Mindeleff 1891: 82–88; Fewkes 1891: 112; Spier 1917: 225–226). Probably the occupation of these sites or similar ones in the area formed the rancho referred to in the eighteenth-century records.

Rancho de Quihuaná, Rancho de la Laguna, and Rancho de Moqui have not been identified. Hart (1991b: 79) suggests that Quiahuaná is a Spanish spelling of a Zuni word that denotes the presence of water, which would imply this locality was near a spring. The name of Rancho de Laguna suggests it was located near a small body of water. Since the late prehistoric era, the Zuni have had the technology needed to construct small earthen dams and reservoirs, and Rancho de Laguna may refer to one such reservoir at an outlying farming settlement. Rancho de Moqui may have been a settlement farmed by Hopi people temporarily residing at Zuni or by the Zuni offspring of a Hopi progenitor.

The rancho at Hawikku undoubtedly refers to a farming area near the Contact period village whose residential occupation was relinquished after the Pueblo Revolt of 1680. The archaeological sites of Mumpalowa and Ky'actcekwa (Spier 1917: 225–226) may be associated with this rancho. Tree-ring dates from the farming village of Ojo Caliente demonstrate there was an occupation in this locality in the eighteenth century (Mills and Ferguson 1980; Ferguson and Mills 1988). A similar distribution of tree-ring dates at the farming village of Nutria records an eighteenth-century occupation there; it may be one of the ranchos documented in the Spanish records. Although no confirming tree-ring dates are available from Pescado, it is probably one of the ranchos named in the eighteenth-century Spanish records.

Other archaeological sites from the eighteenth century include A'mossi'a, located near Heshoda Łuwal'a on a bench overlooking the Zuni River valley, and Kolliwa and Wimaya:wa located on hills in Oak Wash north of Zuni Pueblo (Spier 1917: 233–234). Fortified sheep camps of the eighteenth century occur near the confluence of the Rio Pescado and Rio Nutria, in the canyons flanking Bosson Wash, and in the Nutria and Ojo Caliente areas on the Zuni Reservation (Ferguson 1985: 28–30).

By the end of the eighteenth century, the Zuni had totally reorganized their settlement system, taking full advantage of the new cultigens and technology introduced by the Spaniards. The basic settlement pattern entailing occupation of a single permanent residential village at Zuni Pueblo with use of a number of seasonally occupied satellite settlements continued into the next two historical periods.

MEXICAN PERIOD

In 1821 Spain ceded sovereignty over New Mexico to the newly created nation of Mexico. The interval from 1821 until Mexico ceded control of New Mexico to the United States in 1848 is known as the Mexican period. Zuni Pueblo was virtually left on its own during this time and was in large part responsible for its own defense. During this politically volatile period, the Zuni allied themselves variously with the Mexican government, with other Pueblos, and with several different bands of Navajo. The relations with the Navajo were not always friendly, however, and there were a number of Navajo raids on Zuni Pueblo and its satellite settlements during this period (Minge 1980: 84–103).

Historical information about Zuni settlements for these 27 years is meager. Few Spanish records document the period. Several Americans trapping fur in the Southwest visited the Zuni, but their accounts are not particularly informative regarding Zuni settlement and social organization (*St. Louis Globe-Democrat* 1911; Camp 1966: 37–38, 62; Voelker 1971: 374).

Support for the Catholic mission at Zuni Pueblo was curtailed and the resident priest was withdrawn. The mission buildings at Zuni Pueblo fell into disrepair and the roof of the church collapsed. Archaeological evidence in the form of tree-ring dates from the farming villages of Nutria and Ojo Caliente indicates there was increased construction at these settlements during the Mexican period (Mills and Ferguson 1980; Ferguson and Mills 1988). At Ojo Caliente much of this construction occurred on the bench above the valley bottom in a location that was more defensible than subsequent construction at the settlement (Mindeleff 1891: 96). Zuni Pueblo was maintained as a multistoried fortress with highly restricted access into the interior of the community.

AMERICAN PERIOD

The United States assumed control over the Southwest in 1846 when Kearney's Army of the West marched into and occupied New Mexico (Connelley 1907; Hart 1980: 27–33). In 1848 the sovereignty of the United States over New Mexico was formalized with ratification of the Treaty of Guadalupe Hidalgo, and New Mexico became a territory of the United States. The subsequent interval is thus known as the American period.

During the initial American exploration of the Southwest between 1846 and 1879, Zuni Pueblo became well known as an important provisioning station along the new trails and roads that were under development. Many brief descriptions of Zuni are documented in reports and publications produced by officials of the United States who participated in military expeditions and survey parties. The governmental expeditions were organized for a number of purposes, including scouting the route for a transcontinental railroad. Later, Mormon and Protestant missionaries, pioneers traveling the road to California, and American adventurers produced similar brief reports about Zuni. In 1879 the first anthropologists arrived at Zuni, and from that date to the present day a voluminous amount of detailed, technical reports on all aspects of Zuni settlement and society have been produced by scholars.

The initial accounts from the American period (Bell 1870: 164–165; Wheeler 1889: 60–62, 134; Sitgreaves 1962: 7) describe the Zuni's productive agriculture, including the peach orchards along the edges of the Zuni valley. Several of these reports also describe the defensive Zuni watchtowers that were constructed in or near dispersed farm fields for use during Navajo raids (Bieber 1974: 203–204; Green 1990: 253). The watchtowers were two-story buildings constructed on large boulders or elevated landforms, with narrow slit openings that could be used to fire arrows or rifles at the raiding party while protecting the occupant.

There are numerous descriptions of the farming village of Pescado dating from the period between 1846 and 1879, including those of Beale (Lesley 1929: 277–278), Cozzens (1876: 308–315), Edwards (Bieber 1974: 203–205), Kern (Hart 1980: 39), Klett (1874: 580), Mollhausen (1858: 83), Rice (Dillon 1970: 64–65), Simpson (McNitt 1964: 112–119), and Whipple (Foreman 1941: 135). Pescado was located on the major trail between Zuni Pueblo and Acoma Pueblo and was near several major springs. Most travelers thus either passed the village or camped in its vicinity. All the mid-nineteenth-century descriptions of Pescado are similar, commenting on the substantial "summer pueblo" surrounded by irrigated fields of wheat and corn. Several accounts describe Pescado as "abandoned," but these were observations made during the late fall or winter when the occupants of Pescado were in residence at the mother village of Zuni Pueblo.

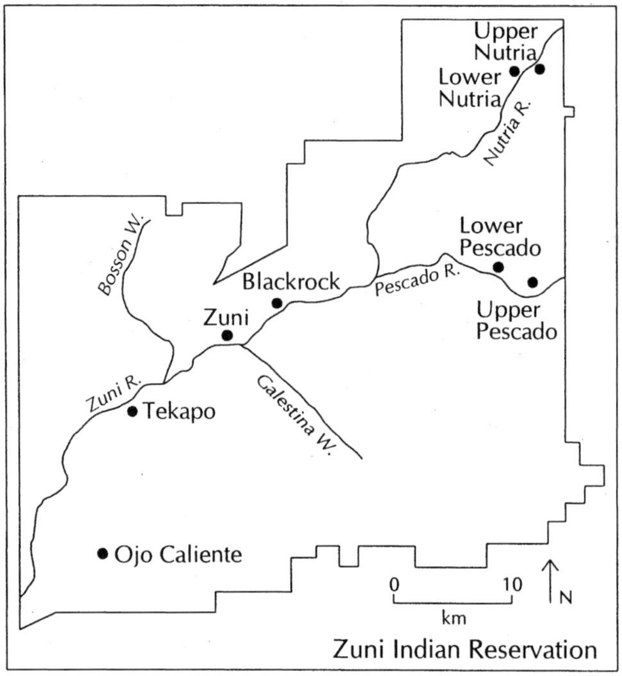

Figure 3.4. Major Zuni settlements occupied during the American period.

Not surprisingly, fewer mid-nineteenth-century observers wrote about the farming villages of Nutria and Ojo Caliente (Secretary of the Interior 1875: 586; Tenney 1876; Wheeler 1889: 60–62), which were located away from the major routes of travel. In addition to the three major farming villages occupied in the mid-nineteenth century, another farming area at Blackrock, located 6.4 km (about 4 miles) east of Zuni Pueblo (Fig. 3.4), was described by several people. This area, formerly known as Ranchos de Piedras Negras, was called Ranchos de Zuni by the nineteenth-century observers (Mollhausen (1856: 87). Whipple describes how the spring at the base of the mesa on which Ranchos de Zuni was situated was used to irrigate adjacent farm fields (U. S. Senate 1854: 65–68).

From 1846 to 1881 the Zuni experienced an economic boom as they increased agricultural production to supply a new market for the corn and forage needed by the United States to support military installations at Fort Defiance and Fort Wingate (Hart 1980: 25–85). As a result, the use of the farming villages located near farmlands that could be cultivated using ditch irrigation was intensified (Nutria, Pescado, and Ojo Caliente; Ferguson 1985: 40–71). The new source of income enabled the Zuni to purchase many new tools and construction materials, which they used to reconstruct Zuni settlements. The rate of this reconstruction accelerated as the need for defense diminished with the pacification of the Navajo and Apache that accompanied the establishment of military forts in the region. In 1881 a railroad was constructed through Gallup, New Mexico, 40 miles north of Zuni, and the market for Zuni agricultural produce dissipated as the Army gained access to non-Indian suppliers. Nonetheless, the occupation and redevelopment of the farming villages at Nutria, Pescado, and Ojo Caliente continued unabated.

The Zuni Indian Reservation was established by Executive Order in 1877. Initially the reservation was small, but a number of additions over the next century increased its size to 169,273 ha (418,104 acres); its configuration at that time is shown in Figure 3.4 (Ferguson and Hart 1985: 92–99). Two years after the Zuni Indian Reservation was established, the first of a long series of anthropologists arrived at Zuni. The initial group of scholars, sponsored by the Smithsonian Institution, included Frank Hamilton Cushing and Matilda Coxe Stevenson. These two anthropologists produced the first detailed descriptions of Zuni culture and society (Cushing 1882, 1896, 1901, 1920; Stevenson 1887, 1904). Their ethnological work in the late nineteenth century was significantly augmented by the detailed mapping and photographic documentation of prehistoric and historic Zuni settlements by other researchers employed by the Smithsonian Institution, among them Cosmos and Victor Mindeleff and John K. Hillers (Mindeleff 1891). A number of archaeological investigations (Cushing 1890; Fewkes 1891) and narrative descriptions of the settlements at Nutria (Curtis 1883: 41–59, 74) and Ojo Caliente (Culin 1903: 30) made after 1879 also provide important information.

The Mindeleffs' outstanding documentation of Zuni Pueblo, Nutria, Pescado, and Ojo Caliente during the period from 1881 to 1885 resulted in the first maps of these sites. The scale and detail of their cartography provide an important baseline for studying architectural change in the nineteenth- and twentieth-century Zuni settlements. These plans are discussed in detail in the following chapter, but it is significant to note here that the work of the Mindeleffs documents the architectural change that was occurring at Zuni Pueblo and the outlying farming villages. At Zuni Pueblo, doors and windows were being installed in ground floor rooms that previously lacked fenestration. Until the 1880s, access into the massive room blocks of the pueblo had been by ladders that led to roof entries. This system of access provided a measure of defense because the ladders could be removed during raids, making entry into the interior of the pueblo more difficult. The Mindeleffs also documented the first buildings at Zuni Pueblo that were constructed outside the core pueblo on the south bank of the Zuni River.

Dispersion of buildings in the settlement plans of the farming villages was also documented. At Nutria and Pescado, houses were constructed beyond the tight clusters of buildings that comprised the earlier settlements, and at Ojo Caliente houses on the valley bottom had replaced earlier buildings defensively located on the flanks of the adjacent mesa. At the time the Mindeleffs undertook their fieldwork, the primary settlement at the farming village of Pescado was located at Lower Pescado (Fig. 3.4), about 3 km (1.9 miles) downstream from Pescado Springs (where Upper Pescado village was later established). A few isolated houses were situated upstream at Pescado Springs (Lange and others 1975: 298–299). The farming village at Nutria was in a cluster of buildings at a location referred to as Upper Nutria.

The occupation of Zuni Pueblo and the outlying farming villages formed the core of the nineteenth-century Zuni settlement system (Ferguson 1995). Surrounding each of these villages was a zone of intensively cultivated fields or gardens. On the banks of the river at Zuni Pueblo there were "waffle" gardens containing herbs and chiles grown in small earthen enclosures that could be watered by hand. At the farming villages there were fields irrigated by ditches from small reservoirs or springs. Surrounding these intensively cultivated plots was a much more extensive area of dispersed fields situated where surface runoff facilitated floodwater irrigation. Sheep and cattle grazed in a large open range surrounding the farming districts. After harvest in the fall, livestock was brought into the farming villages, where sheep herders could be more easily provisioned from Zuni Pueblo. The core area of settlement was surrounded by a much larger sustaining area used for hunting animals and gathering plants and for the ritual visitation to shrines and religious localities scattered throughout the region occupied by the prehistoric ancestors of the Zuni.

In the nineteenth century, Zuni Pueblo was the ceremonial center of the Zuni Tribe. As such, it was the mother village in a settlement system that entailed seasonal occupation of the outlying farming districts. During the winter, except for sheep herders and a few social outcasts who stayed at the farming villages, the entire Zuni population resided at Zuni Pueblo, where a series of important ceremonies was conducted. In the spring, summer, and early fall, most of the Zuni people

Table 3.1. Population of Zuni Pueblo and Farming Villages in 1880

Location		Population
Zuni Pueblo		1,613
Farming villages		1,493
Nutria	473	
Pescado	580	
Ojo Caliente	440	

left the Pueblo for the farming districts, where they stayed from planting through harvest of the crops. In a census conducted by Cushing in 1880 (Holmes 1983), 92 percent of the Zuni population was affiliated with the three major farming villages (Table 3.1). The rest of the population presumably farmed land near enough to Zuni Pueblo that they did not need to take up seasonal residence in an outlying farming district.

The peach orchard village at Heshoda Łuwal'a was still in use at the end of the nineteenth century, but it was only occupied during the short period when the ripening peaches needed protection from predators and processing for storage (Fewkes 1891: 111; Bender 1984: 119–121). In addition to Heshoda Łuwal'a, there was another prominent peach orchard settlement on the sandy east flank of Dowa Yalanne (Cushing 1920: 142). There were no aggregated room blocks at Dowa Yalanne, however, only dispersed field houses located adjacent to numerous, small orchards (Ferguson 1985: 106–109). The other prominent aggregated refuge period villages, Wimaya:wa, Kolliwa, and A'mossi'a, had apparently dropped out of the settlement system by this time and had been replaced by a number of more dispersed field houses, small farmsteads, and sheep camps (Mindeleff 1891: 82–88; Fewkes 1891: 112).

Population estimates for Zuni in the nineteenth century vary between 1,294 and 2,000 people (Fig. 3.2). Some of this variance is probably due to inaccurate reporting, but abrupt drops in population followed by a gradual recovery were common during the nineteenth century as epidemics of smallpox and other diseases ravaged the pueblo (Hart 1991a). After the turn of the century, the Zuni population began to slowly and steadily increase. By the 1920s, the population had grown to more than 2,000, and by the 1930s to more than 3,000. After 1950, the Zuni population underwent remarkable expansion, increasing to 4,000 by 1960, 5,000 by 1971, and 8,929 by 1988. The Zuni population has finally recovered from the decline that occurred during the Spanish period. The increasing population in the twentieth century played an important role in shaping the development of the Zuni settlement system.

At Zuni Pueblo, the steadily increasing population and the creation of more open space in the pueblo interior were major factors in the development of suburbs (Ferguson and Mills 1987). With less need for defense, more Zuni people began to live in ground floor rooms rather than on the higher terraces. The upper terraces of the pueblo were gradually dismantled. During this process, many people converted portions of room blocks into open space for use as streets to facilitate the access of wagons, and later automobiles, into the pueblo interior. The increase in open space resulted in a decrease in the area available to build new houses in the core pueblo. Consequently new houses were constructed in suburbs. By 1915, there were sizable suburbs located to the north of Zuni Pueblo and on the south bank of the Zuni River (Kroeber 1917: 198–204, Map 7). Eventually the majority of the population began to live in the suburbs, and the pueblo core became known at Zuni as the "Old Pueblo" or "Middle Village." The pueblo core remains the ceremonial heart of the tribe. All the dance plazas and kivas and most of the other ceremonial chambers are still located there. These sacred areas, and many additional areas of open space within the Pueblo that contain shrines, have been enlarged as the village was reconstructed in the twentieth century, but they have rarely been encroached on by remodeling (Ferguson and others 1990: 115).

In 1902 the first Bureau of Indian Affairs (BIA) subagency was established at Zuni Pueblo, with headquarters constructed at Blackrock east of Zuni Pueblo. Once established, the BIA worked hard to implement the standing federal policy to allot communally held reservation land to individual men, ignoring the fact that farmland at Zuni was owned by women. The keystone of this policy at Zuni entailed the construction of a large dam and reservoir at Blackrock, which were completed in 1909. This dam and reservoir were intended to provide irrigation water for a large agricultural development north of Zuni Pueblo. The general idea was to resettle farmers from the outlying farming villages on individually owned farmsteads, following a model for non-Indian farmers in the larger American society. The history of Blackrock Dam is long and tragic and is recounted in full elsewhere (Hart 1980: 214–435; Ferguson 1989). What is important to note here is that Blackrock Dam suffered a series of failures and lost 73 percent of its storage capacity within 20 years because of rapid siltation.

When the Zuni Irrigation Unit fed by Blackrock Dam was initially established, as many as half of the farmers at Nutria, Pescado, and Ojo Caliente were induced to take up newly irrigable farmland at Zuni Pueblo. After the abject failure of Blackrock Dam, many of these farmers could not return to their farming villages because they had given up their rights to farm there. Since there was not enough irrigation water to support intensive agriculture at Zuni Pueblo, these disfranchised farmers had to seek alternative forms of livelihood like raising livestock, arts and crafts production, or wage labor. In the meantime, with the loss of half of the labor pool at the outlying farming districts, the remaining farmers substituted mechanized technology for the communal work groups that were no longer viable. The Zuni found the mechanization of agriculture, encouraged by the BIA, preferable to rebuilding the labor force by allowing disfranchised farmers to regain land tenure. As the total area of Zuni land use became increasingly smaller due to land acquisition by the United States, land assignments on the reservation became more valuable. With the endorsement of the BIA, many Zuni began to assert individual rights over communal property. As a result, the social organization and patterns of land tenure at the farming villages were irrevocably changed.

In 1912 a small group of Zuni established a new farming village at Tekapo, about 10 km (6 miles) southwest of Zuni Pueblo (Fig. 3.4). The BIA constructed a small reservoir at Tekapo to capture the overflow water released from the irrigation canal from Blackrock Dam. Although the Zuni had long practiced dispersed floodwater farming in the area, there had been no prior aggregated settlement at Tekapo. The subsequent history of Tekapo is closely tied to that of Blackrock Dam, because ditch irrigated agriculture in the farming district was dependent on an ever decreasing volume of available water as Blackrock Reservoir filled with silt.

Sometime prior to 1912, the Zuni at Nutria constructed a second cluster of buildings slightly downstream from the original settlement. The original settlement at Nutria became known as Upper Nutria and the new settlement as Lower Nutria (Fig. 3.4). Lower Nutria was not in existence at the time of the Mindeleffs' fieldwork in 1885 (Mindeleff 1891). The first maps it appears on were produced in 1912 during the cadastral surveys of the General Land Office (Ferguson 1980: 69). From an archaeological perspective, Upper and Lower Nutria appear as two discrete villages, but from the Zuni perspective they are simply two settlement nodes in the same farming district.

At the same time that the BIA was constructing large reservoirs and attempting to allot the Zuni Indian Reservation, the landscape was rapidly degrading from stream bed erosion (Hart 1988). This erosion was caused by clear cutting of timber in the adjacent Zuni Mountains with subsequent overgrazing. With the removal of the vegetative cover, the erosive force of runoff was significantly increased. Overgrazing on the Zuni Indian Reservation exacerbated the problems with erosion. Between 1846 and 1912, the Zuni had lost 89 percent of their aboriginal land use area from land seizures by the United States (Ferguson 1989: 96). As a result, the Zuni were forced to restrict the geographic extent of the range where they grazed their livestock. Even with a substantial voluntary reduction in the number of livestock in the first three decades of the twentieth century, the carrying capacity of the reservation range was greatly exceeded.

As the amount of grazing land on the Zuni Indian Reservation was constrained, the Zuni began to develop permanent ranch facilities to lay claim to range land and support their livestock industry (Ferguson 1980: 137–148). These ranches took the form of small masonry buildings, often associated with wells and other improvements. A typical stockman developed several of these sheep camps in his grazing area that were used sequentially during an annual round. Today there are hundreds of these small sheep camps located throughout the Zuni Indian Reservation. After the exterior boundaries of the Zuni Indian Reservation were fenced for the first time in 1934, the open range of the Zuni Reservation was divided into individually assigned range units that could be more effectively managed by the BIA to force additional stock reduction (Ferguson and Hart 1985: 102–103).

Stream beds were eroded into deeply incised arroyos during the early twentieth century, and traditional methods of floodwater farming became difficult or impossible (Ferguson 1989). The soils that eroded from stream beds rapidly filled the reservoir at Blackrock, and the ditch-irrigated farming sponsored by the BIA lost its viability. The increasing population, in conjunction with the decreasing size and degradation of the land base, made the early twentieth century a difficult period for most Zuni people. Farming became more arduous, and the open grazing system was replaced by land assignments that made it impossible for new people to enter the livestock industry unless someone else dropped out of it. New BIA grazing policies conflicted with the use of dispersed floodwater farm sites, and many of these farms were abandoned. The seasonal use of most of the peach orchard villages ceased about this time, a situation apparently related to these changes in land use.

Acute erosion in the Pescado district led to the relinquishment of occupation at Lower Pescado about 1921 (Ferguson 1980: 101–102). New houses after 1921 were constructed on the south side of the river, which had access to State Highway 53. The focus of habitation shifted from Lower Pescado village to an area immediately around the springs now known as Upper Pescado (Fig. 3.4).

In the 1930s, the BIA constructed large dams and reservoirs at Nutria and Pescado to act as silt traps in an attempt to prolong the life of Blackrock Dam (Ferguson 1989: 107–114). These dams had a secondary purpose as sources of irrigation water in the farming districts. A large dam and reservoir was also built at Ojo Caliente at the same time. With the construction of these dams, all the farming districts were subjected to the same pattern of boom and bust as that experienced at the Zuni Irrigation Unit serviced by Blackrock Dam. Initially in the 1930s there was an increase in irrigation water, which was accompanied by new construction at the farming villages as Zuni farmers there intensified their agriculture. These dams soon lost their capacity because of rapid siltation, however, causing a gradual decline in the seasonal use of the farming villages.

CONTEMPORARY PERIOD

Zuni Pueblo today remains the primary settlement on the Zuni Indian Reservation. With the dramatic increase in population in the twentieth century, it is remarkable that the Zuni remain in a single large town rather than reoccupy multiple villages. There is a slight but increasing trend for people to move to the farming village of Pescado, where electricity, running water, and paved roads provide the modern amenities desired by most Zuni. By and large, however, the occupation of the farming villages is now restricted to day-use, a pattern facilitated by the availability of pickup trucks and the improvement of the road network on the reservation. A few elderly people and sheepherders still reside at the farming villages on a seasonal basis, but virtually the entire tribe now resides in Zuni Pueblo and the adjacent settlement of Blackrock throughout the year.

Even though the Old Pueblo has undergone a drastic change in its architectural style and arrangement of buildings, it remains the ceremonial center of the Zuni Tribe. The plazas in the Old Pueblo are still used for the performance of kachina dances and other rituals intended for viewing by the general public. The roofs ringing the plazas continue to be used as public space for the galleries viewing the ceremonies. The six kivas in the Old Pueblo retain many of the most traditional elements of Zuni architecture such as ladders and roof entries. Although only a small fraction of the Zuni population still lives in the Old Pueblo, nearly all Zuni regularly use the core architecture in the conduct of their ceremonial and ritual life.

In the Old Pueblo and throughout the suburbs of Zuni, buildings undergo constant changes stemming from repeated rehabilitation in the context of a long-standing Zuni tradition of innovation in architecture (Ferguson and others 1990: 105–108). Much of the continual change in the architecture of Zuni Pueblo is attributable to the annual Shalako ceremony held near the winter solstice. Each year six or seven houses are either constructed or rehabilitated specifically to host the ritual dances that are a part of this ceremony. Through the years, a substantial number of houses have been built or modified both in the core pueblo and in the outlying suburbs for the Shalako ceremony.

In building new houses or rehabilitating old structures, the Zuni make cost-effective and pragmatic decisions in upgrading the construction materials and building styles of vernacular architecture. Their primary goal is to provide modern, weatherproof housing, and the appearance of the façade is a secondary concern. Zuni Pueblo thus looks very different today than it did a century ago. The heavily plastered, tabular sandstone masonry style was replaced first by a bold, ashlar style and more recently by cinder block. Small, glass pane windows have been replaced by larger aluminum framed picture windows. The aesthetics of architectural surfaces and fenestration aside, in many respects Zuni vernacular architecture continues to function as it always has in housing the extended lineages that comprise traditional households.

Vernacular architecture at Zuni Pueblo, however, is increasingly being replaced with commercial housing sponsored by the federal government. Since the 1960s, more than 700 houses have been constructed under the auspices of the Department of Housing and Urban Development (HUD). HUD houses now constitute approximately 30 percent of the housing units of Zuni Pueblo. Some Zuni view HUD housing as a "Trojan Horse" (Ferguson and others 1990: 116–117). The incorporation of HUD housing into Zuni Pueblo seemed attractive at first because it solved a serious housing shortage. Through the years, however, the small spaces, the physical layout, the dispersion in siting, and the high cost of maintenance of HUD housing have worked to disintegrate Zuni social relations. Much of the new HUD housing is concentrated in subdivisions that are on the outskirts of Zuni Pueblo.

Vernacular housing has greatly expanded to the north and east of the Old Pueblo on lands formerly part of the Zuni Irrigation Unit. Today this housing is merging with recent HUD subdivisions located at Blackrock. The formerly separate settlements of Zuni Pueblo and Blackrock have coalesced into a single community with constant daily traffic between the two as people commute from home to work, some people residing in Blackrock and working in Zuni Pueblo, and vice versa. With the construction of commercial buildings, jewelry stores, offices housing the tribal government, four schools, and other institutional buildings, Zuni Pueblo has grown into a large town encompassing an area of more than 260 ha (642 acres).

ZUNI SOCIAL ORGANIZATION

The basic structure of Zuni society during the late nineteenth century was described in detail by Cushing (1882, 1920) and Stevenson (1904). Additional information and analyses of change were added through the early twentieth-century ethnographic research of Kroeber (1917), Curtis (1926), Bunzel (1932), and Parsons (1933, 1939). The various descriptions of Zuni social structure were codified and compared to other Western Pueblos by Eggan (1950), using a classic structural-functionalist paradigm. Most recently, Ladd (1979a, 1979b) has updated information about social structure from a Zuni perspective, pointing out that the complexities of Zuni social organization have defied conventional description by anthropologists for more than a century.

As described ethnographically, Zuni society is composed of four interlocking subsystems, each operating independently: clans, kiva groups, medicine societies, and priesthoods (Ladd 1979a: 482). The fundamental units of Zuni society are the extended matrilineal lineages that comprise households. Women traditionally owned the houses, as well as the farmland that was worked by husbands who took up residence at their wives' houses. Although postmarital neolocality has become a common residence pattern in the last half of the twentieth century, maternal lineages remain vitally important social groups that gather together during all the important ceremonial occasions. The segmentary lineages of Zuni society are organized into totemically named exogamous clans in a Crow system. Each clan conducts its own esoteric rituals, many of which occur in the houses of their matriarchs. Some clans also have hereditary roles of leadership in several of the most important religious organizations at Zuni Pueblo.

All members of a clan refer to themselves in the Zuni language as brothers and sisters in recognition of their close relationship. In the nineteenth century there were 16 active clans, but several of them have become extinct in the twentieth century. At Zuni Pueblo, Kroeber (1917: 103–122) found no evidence that clans were localized in architectural arrangements. Clans are not grouped together in spatial clusters and are distributed randomly through the village.

Although maternal clans provide the primary social identification, paternal clans also play an important role in social relations. To a certain degree, Zuni is thus really a bilaterally organized society. Patrilineal inheritance and organization of work groups among paternal relatives are particularly important with respect to livestock ownership and herding activities. In this regard, it may be speculated that the use of the outlying farming villages, tied as they were to livestock activities, were organized as much along paternal lines as maternal lines, especially in the eighteenth and nineteenth centuries before permanent sheep camp facilities became fixed features in the settlement system.

There are six kiva groups at Zuni Pueblo associated with the performance of masked kachina dances in the four plazas of the Old Pueblo (Bunzel 1932: 478–479, 518–519; Ladd 1979a: 484–485). The six kivas are divisions of a unified kachina society with a set of officers that directs their communal activities. In addition, each individual kiva also has its own set of internal leaders. Because every adult male should belong to a kiva, this organization assumes the role of a tribal cult. Each of the kivas is associated with a particular color and direction with ritual connotations in Zuni cosmology. The kivas are primarily men's religious organizations, although historically a few women past the age of reproduction were initiated into these groups. Membership in a kiva is originally designated by parents at a child's birth, but this membership is not binding and men can change their kiva membership for social or personal reasons later in life. Initiation into a kiva generally occurs at puberty and ritually marks the transition into adulthood. During kiva initiation, young men are made privy to esoteric secrets about the origin of the Zuni people and their responsibilities as Zuni adults. In a fashion similar to clans, kiva members refer to themselves as younger and older brothers. Each kiva maintains a separate ceremonial chamber within Zuni Pueblo, where it holds esoteric rituals and conducts organizational meetings. In the past, kiva chambers also served as male clubhouses. Kachina dances were occasionally conducted at the nineteenth- and twentieth-century farming villages, but no kiva groups were ever established with membership coterminous with the farming villages. No kiva buildings were ever constructed at the farming villages.

Membership in the 12 medicine or curing societies at Zuni is open to both men and women, but these societies are more restrictive than the kiva societies in that not every adult belongs to a medicine group (Stevenson 1904: 407–577; Ladd 1979a: 485). Membership in a medicine society is either by choice after benefiting from a cure or by "capture" when a person trespasses during one of their esoteric rites. Each of the medicine societies specializes in curing a particular malady or set of related maladies. The medicine societies hold, use, and transmit a voluminous amount of esoteric knowledge about medicinal herbs, general medicine, and specific cures for a wide range of maladies. Medicine men and women often ply their skills in the homes of their patients. Most of the group rituals of the medicine societies, however, are conducted in the houses of their leaders. These houses generally contain large rooms that are temporarily cleared of domestic activities during use by the medicine societies. In addition, the medicine societies ritually participate in a variety of religious ceremonies and rites in a complex association with kivas and priesthoods.

There are 16 Rain Priesthoods at Zuni whose membership, open to both men and women, is limited by clan affiliation (Eggan 1950: 203–210; Ladd 1979a: 485). Within the Rain Priesthoods are six principal priests associated with the six directions. The Rain Priesthoods have esoteric functions, and each of the principal priests goes into a spiritual retreat annually in conjunction with the activities of the kachina society. Historically there was a Sun Priest, but the duties of this office have not been filled in recent years, and the most critical ritual responsibilities of this office have been assumed by the Rain Priest of the North. Some anthropologists (for example, Bunzel 1932: 521–525) have classified a set of kachina priests independently from the kachina society, including the mudheads (Koyemshi) and a "Council of Gods" representing the most important kachinas in the Zuni pantheon.

Another powerful priesthood at Zuni are the Priests of the Bow or War Chiefs (Parsons 1924; Eggan 1950: 205–207). The membership of this society is restricted to men who have taken scalps in war. The Bow Priesthood originally served as the executive arm of the Rain

Priesthoods and was entrusted with great coercive power to deal with social deviance within the pueblo. Today the responsibilities of the Bow Priesthood are largely ceremonial, but it still plays a key role in coordinating many aspects of ritual activities. The Rain Priests and the Bow Priests form a Council of Priests who command community respect and obedience because of their revered position in Zuni society, but who do not amass or control wealth. The responsibilities of the highest priesthoods inhibit secular financial pursuits, and the financial outlay associated with sponsoring and participating in numerous rituals tends to keep their accumulation of worldly goods modest. All the priesthoods maintain or use special chambers for their esoteric activities within the core pueblo.

Eggan (1950: 210) observed that "The social organization of Zuni is perhaps the most complex to be found in the western Pueblos; the social integration here achieved is both strong and successful." He also noted that Zuni social organization favors the integration of the community as a whole over that of individual lineages and clans. With the tendency of humans to put the interests of one's family and kin before that of other members of society, the integrative functions of Zuni social organization as described ethnographically merit explicit recognition.

As Kroeber (1917: 183) explained:

> Four or five different planes of systematization cross cut each other and thus preserve for the whole society an integrity that would speedily be lost if the planes merged, and thereby inclined to encourage segregation and fission. The clans, the fraternities, the priesthoods, and kivas, in a measure the gaming parties, are all dividing agencies. If they coincided, the rifts in the social structure would be deep; by countering each other they cause segmentations which produce an almost marvelous complexity, but can never break the national entity apart.

Eggan (1950: 217–219) points out that Kroeber provides a brilliant synchronic summary of Zuni social integration, but that there is also a diachronic dimension carried out through the lineage principle. It is the lineage principle that provides a mechanism for the inheritance of ceremonial offices and the transmission and preservation of ritual paraphernalia. It is also through the female components of lineages that land is traditionally owned and held in trust to be worked by men who marry into the household.

The ultimate control of Zuni society remains vested in a hierarchy of priesthoods who are responsible for community welfare. There has been a secular governor and tribal council since the Spanish period (Ferguson and others 1988: 114–115). At first the officials of this secular government were appointed by religious leaders, but since 1934 these officials have been democratically elected. Nonetheless, the social roles of the traditional Zuni religious leaders remain important in Zuni society (Pandey 1977).

Although the Zuni settlement system has undergone a number of remarkable changes, Zuni social structure has been more stable. There has been some attrition in certain elements of Zuni society, like the number of clans and priesthoods, but the basic social organization has been maintained to a much greater degree than the more fluid settlement system.

The foregoing discussion only outlines the basic structure of the complex Zuni social system. The Zuni religion is a powerful spiritual force as well as a significant social activity, and individual Zuni men and women fulfill many ceremonial responsibilities throughout their lives. It is ultimately their religion and their language that bind the Zuni together culturally as a distinct people. While acknowledging and respecting the cultural power of the Zuni religion, this research seeks to understand the ways that Zuni people are bound together *spatially* and *socially* rather than *culturally*. It is through the analysis of architecture that this interest is best pursued.

CHAPTER FOUR

Historic Zuni Settlements

Fourteen historic Zuni settlements where the preservation of architecture enabled a productive application of the analytical techniques of space syntax form the basis of this study. The architecture of many historic sites is so obscured by the formation processes of the archaeological record that observations from surface remains do not yield site plans with enough resolution for analysis. Excavation would be necessary at such sites to obtain architectural details comparable to those for the sites selected. These fourteen settlements span an interval ranging from the Contact period through the Contemporary period (Table 4.1). They are distributed in all the major river drainages on the Zuni Indian Reservation (Fig. 4.1). Precise locations are not published in an effort to preserve site security.

For brevity, each site description presents information in a structured format. Site numbers are listed in terms of the three major systems that have been used for archaeological records management on the Zuni Indian Reservation: (1) sites numbered by Leslie Spier (1917) in his pioneering archaeological survey conducted in 1916, (2) the Zuni Archaeology Program (ZAP) site file numbering system, and (3) the Laboratory of Anthropology (LA) numbering system managed by the Museum of New Mexico. The synonymy of names is not exhaustive and includes only those names used in the anthropological literature cited herein. A synonymy that includes the variants for site names recorded in Spanish documents is provided in Hodge

Table 4.1. Grouping of Historic Zuni Settlements for Analysis

	17th-century villages	
(1)		Hawikku
(2)		Kechiba:wa
(3)		Kyaki:ma
(4)	Pueblo revolt of 1680 settlement on Dowa Yalanne	
	18th-century and early 19th-century farming villages	
(5, 6)		Kyaki:ma refuge sites
(7)		Shundekya
(8)		Wimaya:wa
(9)		Heshoda Łuwal'a
(10)	Zuni Pueblo:	Core in 1881
	1885 farming villages	
(11)		Lower Pescado
(12)		Ojo Caliente
(13)		Upper Nutria
	Zuni Pueblo:	Core in 1915
	Zuni Pueblo:	Suburbs in 1915
	1979 farming villages	
		Ojo Caliente
		Upper Nutria
(14)		Lower Nutria
	Zuni Pueblo:	Core in 1972
	Zuni Pueblo:	Vernacular suburbs in 1978
	Zuni Pueblo:	HUD suburbs in 1978

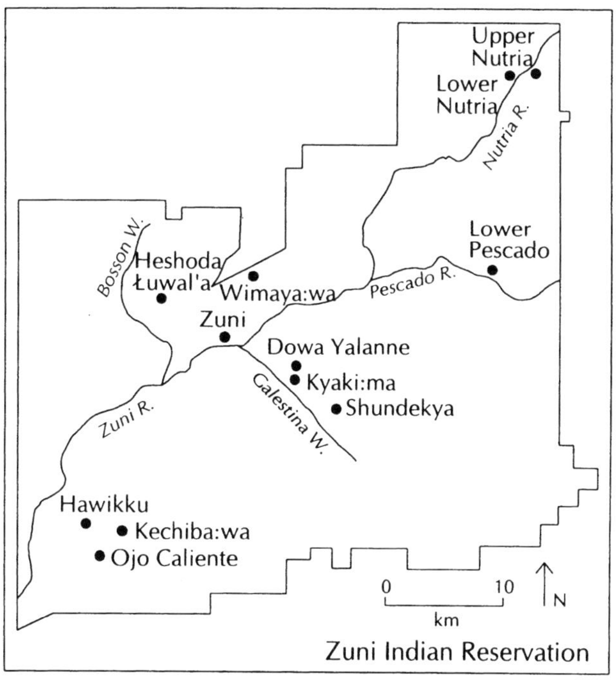

Figure 4.1. General location of historic Zuni settlements selected for analysis.

(1937: 128–134). The spelling of site names used as primary referents is the preferred orthography developed for the Zuni Archaeology Program by Zuni language consultants.

One entry in each site description cites the source of plans used as the cartographic basis for the analyses of space syntax. Additional maps and site plans consulted during research are cited where relevant. Site dimensions were calculated by drawing a rectangle around the convex space map of each site and measuring the maximal length and width of this geometric form, with the value rounded to the nearest meter. This measure includes 10 m of open space beyond the extent of architecture on each of the four sides of the site. The measure of site dimensions provides a standard for comparing the overall size of sites, but it does not measure the area enclosed by architecture or the total area of the site; these two attributes are analyzed in Chapter 5.

Population estimates for the settlements are given when they are available from either archaeological measures or documentary sources. Estimating population density is a notoriously difficult archaeological procedure (Cook 1972; Hassan 1981) and many alternative techniques have been applied using different variables, including the number of rooms, amount of floor space, and area of roofed architecture (Naroll 1962; LeBlanc 1971; Sumner 1979; Dohm 1990). Population estimates are provided primarily to facilitate comparisons among settlements and not to make definitive conclusions regarding Zuni demography, which is not a variable in the following analyses of space syntax.

A discussion of relevant aspects of settlement architecture not summarized in the previous sections concludes each description. The settlements are presented in the approximate chronological order in which habitation at them ceased. The Contact period villages occupied only until the Pueblo Revolt of 1680 appear first, and Zuni Pueblo is discussed last.

HAWIKKU

Site Numbers. Spier 25; ZAP:NM:13:A:2; LA 37.

Synonymy. Háwik'uh (Cushing 1896: 326); Hawikuh (Mindeleff 1891: 80); Hay-way-cu, Hay-we-cu (Fewkes 1891: 101, Map,); Hauicu (Bandelier 1890b: 171, 1892b: 338); Hawwikku (Kroeber 1916: 34; Spier 1917: 224); Ha'-wi-k'uh (Cushing 1920: 76).

Sources of Maps. Mindeleff (1891, Plate 46); Smith and others (1966, Fig. 1); Kintigh (1985: 60). Information from all three maps was used to produce the site plan (Fig. 4.2).

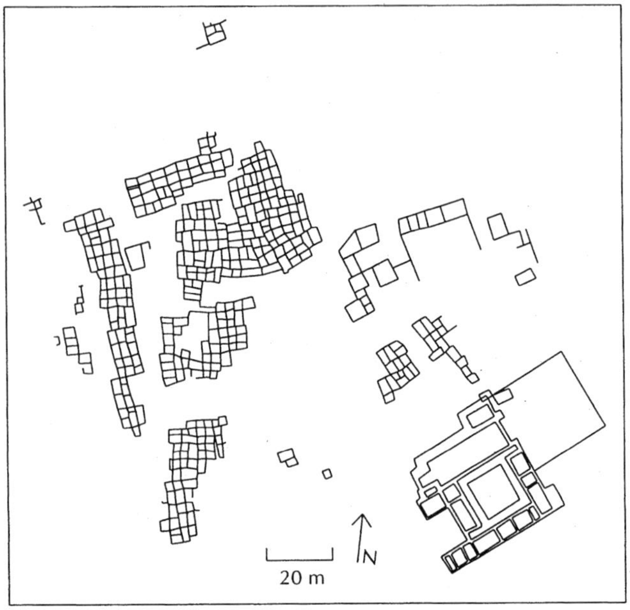

Figure 4.2. Ground story rooms at Hawikku (after Mindeleff 1891, Plate 46; Smith and others 1966, Fig. 1; Kintigh 1985: 60). The Catholic mission is outlined, *lower right*.

Elevation. 1,899 m.

Landform. Hawikku is located on the southern end of a low ridge in the Zuni River valley near the confluence of Plumasano Wash and the Zuni River. The principal room blocks of the settlement are on the ridge top and slopes, with additional room blocks on the valley floor at the base of the ridge.

Architectural Arrangement. The site is comprised of 20 pueblo room blocks in an irregular arrangement that encloses several plazas or streets (Fig. 4.2). On the ridge top the open space enclosed by the room blocks is constricted, whereas on the valley floor the open space is more expansive. A Catholic mission is located on the valley floor at the southeastern edge of the site.

Dimensions. 185 m by 193 m.

Room Estimate. The estimated number of rooms in the indigenous room blocks at Hawikku varies between 800 and 1,060. Smith and the Woodburys (1966: 11–12) estimated there were 470 ground story rooms at Hawikku. Assuming that all these rooms had a second story and one-fourth of the rooms had a third story, they derived the higher number.

Kintigh (1985: 60–61) analyzed the correspondence between the area of rubble as mapped by Mindeleff (1891, Plate 46) and the area of rooms exposed by excavation (Smith and others 1966, Fig. 1). Although the actual size of excavated rooms varied between 8.4

and 9.2 square meters, with an average size of 8.6 square meters, Kintigh found a correspondence of 7.9 square meters of rubble on Mindeleff's map for each excavated room. He applied this correspondence to the total area of architectural rubble as mapped by Mindeleff and calculated there were 457 ground story rooms. Assuming one-half of these rooms had a second story and one-fourth had a third story, Kintigh estimated 800 rooms. The Catholic mission built at Hawikku in 1629 comprised a large church with an adjoining friary containing about 30 rooms surrounding a garth, with a patio to the south of the complex.

Population Estimate. Population estimates for Hawikku vary and are derived from estimates of the number of occupied rooms at the settlement. Smith and his colleagues (1966: 13) thought that no more than 500 rooms were occupied at any one time, about 47 percent of their estimated number of rooms, and they assumed that the normal household unit contained three rooms with an average of four persons, or 0.75 room per person. These assumptions yield a momentary population estimate of about 660 people.

Kintigh (1985: 75) assumed that 65 percent of the rooms were occupied contemporaneously and that there were two persons per room, or 0.50 room per person. Using these assumptions and his estimated number of rooms, Kintigh calculated Hawikku had a momentary population of 1,040 persons.

The assumptions made by Smith and the Woodburys and by Kintigh regarding the number of people per room fit within the range for this variable as documented in 25 historic pueblos investigated by Dohm (1990: 212). Dohm recorded a range from 0.219 room to 1.344 rooms per person, with a mean of 0.60 room per person.

Temporal Placement. Hodge reported that roof beams in a kiva had dendrochronological dates ranging from A.D. 1381 to 1480 (Hodge 1939: 202), but subsequent reanalysis of these samples could not confirm the published dates (Bannister and others 1970: 12). Smith and the Woodburys (1966: 11) thought the occupation of Hawikku began some time before A.D. 1300 and continued until the Pueblo Revolt of 1680. Kintigh's (1985: 63) seriation of ceramics from Hawikku, however, suggested the settlement actually began about 1400. There is no doubt that Hawikku was occupied in 1540, as it was the first Zuni village encountered by Coronado during the Spanish Entrada. Occupation of Hawikku as a full-time residence ceased in 1680, but deep deposits of sheep dung in the patio adjacent to the friary provide archaeological evidence that the Zuni continued to use parts of the site as a sheep camp for an undetermined number of years (Smith and others 1966: 119).

Discussion. Archaeological excavations were undertaken at Hawikku from 1917 to 1923 under the direction of Frederick Webb Hodge as part of the Hendricks-Hodge Expedition sponsored by the Museum of the American Indian. These excavations yielded an accurate plan that encompassed most, but not all, of the site. The 20 room blocks of indigenous architecture at Hawikku enumerated for this analysis are illustrated in Figure 4.3. The Catholic mission was designated as room block Unit 19 (Fig. 4.2). Hodge concentrated his investigation on the room blocks at the crest of the ridge, the Catholic mission, and the room blocks adjacent to the mission (Units 1, 2, 3, 4, 5, 6, 7, and 16 in Figure 4.3). He did not investigate several room blocks on the valley floor north of the mission (Units 10, 11, 12, 13) and they do not appear on the published site plan (Smith and others 1966, Fig. 1). These room blocks were added to the plan using information provided in Mindeleff (1891, Plate 46). Kintigh mapped room block Units 10 through 13 using dashed lines to indicate that the plan of these buildings was more ambiguous than the rest of the site. However, the outlines of these room blocks as mapped by Mindeleff were sufficient to include them here.

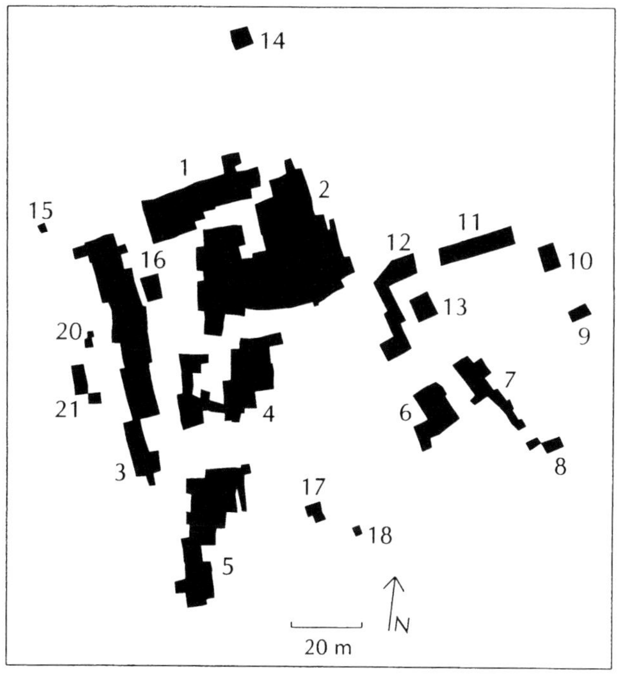

Figure 4.3. Room blocks of indigenous architecture at Hawikku as enumerated for analysis. Unit 19, the Catholic mission, was positioned over Unit 8 (*see* Fig. 4.2).

As analyzed in the report on Hodge's excavation prepared by Watson Smith, Richard B. Woodbury, and Natalie S. F. Woodbury (1966), the architecture of the site was divided into six primary "groups" or room blocks. These groups were designated A though F and they correspond respectively to room block Units 1 through 7 on Figure 4.3. Group F is actually two spatially discrete room blocks and is analyzed accordingly. Seven small room blocks to the north, west, and southeast of the major architectural groups labeled by Smith and his colleagues are assigned discrete numbers for this analysis (Units 8, 14, 15, 17, 18, 20, 21).

The architectural growth of Hawikku occurred through gradual accretion of rooms during a long period of time (Smith and others 1966: 14). The initial room blocks were buried under as much as 4.5 m of cultural debris (Hodge 1918: 370), with more recent room blocks constructed on top of this deposit. The archaeological excavation of the site did not fully expose the lower strata, so the original plan of the settlement is unknown. Hodge identified two distinct styles of masonry used in the construction of Hawikku, which he termed "ancient" and "recent." Many rooms that were built using the ancient architectural style were remodeled and occupied during the Spanish period (Smith and others 1966: 12–13). The Catholic mission was constructed on top of Unit 8, indicating that at least some of the room blocks on the valley floor were constructed and occupied prior to 1629. Nonetheless, Smith and the Woodburys (1966: 95) concluded that several valley floor room blocks must have been occupied during the Spanish period, perhaps for just a brief time.

Only a single structure definitely identified as a kiva was excavated at Hawikku (Smith and others 1966: 42–44; Hodge 1939). This subterranean building, designated Unit 16 in Figure 4.3, was located in a plaza. The kiva, built in a "recent" style of architecture, was apparently constructed relatively late in the sequence of occupation of Hawikku. The religious activities conducted in the kiva were probably suppressed and the building intentionally filled by the Spaniards soon after the establishment of the Catholic mission. Hodge (1939: 211) observed that during the historic period Zuni kivas underwent a transformation from being subterranean structures to becoming a part of the house block that was hard to distinguish from common dwellings. It may be that there were additional kivas at Hawikku that were not recognized during excavation or were not excavated at all. Smith and the Woodburys (1966: 43) suggested there may have been a kiva under the Catholic mission.

The indigenous architecture at Hawikku was stone masonry. During construction of the Catholic mission, the Spaniards introduced the technique of building with uniformly sized adobe bricks manufactured in forms. The Catholic mission, with its imposing edifice and massive walls 2.5 m thick, stood in marked contrast to the room blocks of Hawikku. The indigenous architecture, although massive in its own right, was formed from many small architectural components constructed and reconstructed throughout a long interval. The Catholic mission was monumental in comparison, comprising a single architectural complex built in one construction episode and then repaired after it was destroyed by the Zuni in 1630.

KECHIBA:WA

Site Numbers. Spier 13; ZAP:NM:13:A:3.

Synonymy. K'yá-na-we (Cushing 1890: 156); Chan-a-hue (Bandelier 1890a: 133); Chyanahue (Bandelier 1890b: 171; Chyanaue (Bandelier 1890a: 133); Chek-e-pã-wha (Fewkes 1891: 101); Ketchipauan (Mindeleff 1891: 81); Chyan-a-hue, Ketchip-a-uan (Bandelier 1892b: 338); Kechipawan, K'iánawa (Hodge 1937: 131); Kettcippawa (Spier 1917: 222); Ketchipaun (Bushnell 1955: 657).

Sources of Maps. Mindeleff (1891, Plate 49); Kintigh (1985: 68).

Elevation. 1,966 m.

Landform. Kechiba:wa is situated on a low rise on top of a mesa flanking the northern edge of Plumasano Wash.

Architectural Arrangement. The site consists of an irregularly shaped complex of several room blocks arranged around four plazas (Fig. 4.4). One large room block consists of a central row of rooms with three large wings attached to it. These rooms are connected into one large building, and this complex was enumerated as a single room block for analytical purposes. Two smaller room blocks attached to each other at a vertex are connected to the large room block by a single wall. A small visita, labeled as Unit 4 in Figure 4.4, is located in the largest plaza. This visita was used by priests from the Catholic mission at Hawikku. A stone corral was situated in the northwest plaza when Mindeleff (1891: 81) mapped the site, but this structure does not appear on his map. The corral is still visible today.

Dimensions. 152 m by 128 m.

Room Estimate. Kintigh (1985: 69) provided an approximate room estimate using the figure of 7.9 square meters of rubble for each room derived from his anal-

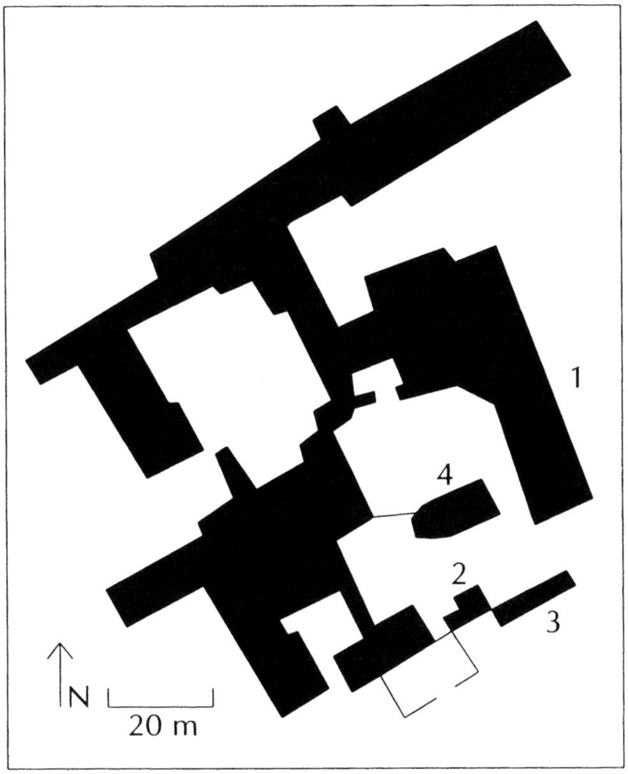

Figure 4.4. Room blocks at Kechiba:wa as enumerated for analysis (after Mindeleff 1891, Plate 49; Kintigh 1985: 68).

ysis of Mindeleff's map of Hawikku. As applied to Kechiba:wa, this formula yielded an estimate of 471 ground story rooms. Assuming that half the rooms had a second story and one-fourth had a third story, Kintigh estimated the total number of rooms at 824.

Population Estimate. Kintigh (1985: 75) used the same assumptions he applied at Hawikku to estimate a momentary population at Kechiba:wa of 1,071 persons.

Temporal Placement. Based on ceramic cross-dating, the primary occupation of Kechiba:wa was from about A.D. 1425 to the Pueblo Revolt of 1680 (Kintigh 1985: 69). The presence of a corral in one of the plazas indicates limited use of the site as a sheep camp after habitation ceased.

Discussion. Archaeological investigations were conducted at Kechiba:wa from 1919 to 1923 under the auspices of the Hendricks-Hodge Expedition. The work was directed by Samuel K. Lothrop of Cambridge University Museum of Archaeology and Ethnology (Bushnell 1955: 657); 90 rooms and 1 kiva were exposed (Kintigh 1985: 68), but an adequate map of the excavated site has yet to be drafted or published.

Mindeleff's map from 1885 thus remains the most informative plan. He illustrates some room spaces, but much of the site is depicted only by the extent of rubble. Figure 4.4, therefore, only shows the outlines of the room blocks.

The placement of the visita in a plaza with a wall connecting the building to the main room block effectively split this plaza into two open spaces. The visita was constructed of stone masonry and was used at some time between 1629 and 1680 (Mindeleff (1891: 82).

There is a reservoir 34 m in diameter approximately 92 m from the southeast corner of the settlement. This shallow reservoir, about 1.2 m deep, was formed by a low wall placed across a drainage where it discharges at the edge of the mesa.

Translated into English, Kechiba:wa means "gypsum place" (Eggan and Pandey 1979: 481). The settlement is near a source of gypsum that the Zuni use for whitewash.

KYAKI:MA

Site Numbers. Spier 45; ZAP:NM:12:K3:10.

Synonymy. Kyakima (Bandelier 1890a: 133); Kiakima (Bandelier 1890b: 172, 1892b: 337); K'iakima (Mindeleff 1891: 85); Ki-a-kime (Fewkes 1891: 108); Kyakkima (Spier 1917: 230); K'iákima (Hodge 1937: 133).

Sources of Maps. Mindeleff (1891, Plate 52); Ferguson and others (1977: 25).

Elevation. 1,969 m.

Landform. Kyaki:ma is on a small hill that forms part of the lowest bench on the southern edge of Dowa Yalanne. The site is located on the east side of a spectacular re-entrant that drains the entire top of Dowa Yalanne. A major spring is located west of Kyaki:ma, and in the nineteenth century a small stream issued from this spring (Mindeleff 1891: 85). Kyaki:ma overlooks the alluvial valley bottom of Galestina Wash.

Architectural Arrangement. Kyaki:ma comprises four irregularly shaped room blocks arranged around two plazas (Fig. 4.5). One massive room block, labeled Unit 1, wraps around and incorporates a small plaza that opens to the south. Units 2 and 3 are north of Unit 1 and define a second, much larger plaza or street. Units 2 and 3 are connected to one another by a short wall. Unit 4 is a freestanding room block at the east edge of the north plaza or street.

Dimensions. 101 m by 165 m.

Room Estimate. Kintigh (1985: 65) applied the assumptions he developed in the analysis of Hawikku to derive an estimate of 250 ground story rooms for Kyaki:ma. He thought there was no adequate surface evidence to calculate the number of stories, so he consid-

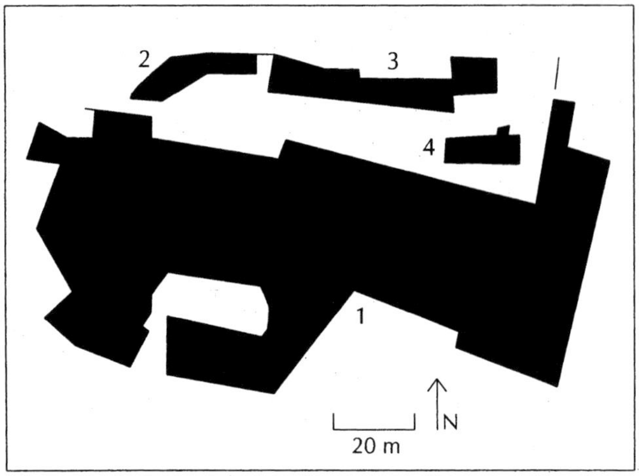

Figure 4.5. Outline of room blocks at Kyaki:ma as enumerated for analysis (after Ferguson and others 1977: 25).

ered Kyaki:ma to have only one story. Kintigh estimated that the site encompassed 1,972 square meters of rubble. The site plan Kintigh used for this estimate, however, was based on Mindeleff's map, which does not adequately represent the full extent of rubble at Kyaki:ma. As Spier (1917: 231) observed in 1916, Kyaki:ma covers a "fairly large area, larger in fact than shown on Mindeleff's plan."

Close examination of Kyaki:ma during mapping of the site by the Zuni Archaeology Program in 1977 revealed the presence of a series of definite wall alignments on the hill slope at the east edge of the site and small segments of wall alignments throughout the area of Unit 1 as mapped in Figure 4.5. These wall alignments suggest that Unit 1 was a continuous room block (Ferguson and others 1977: 24–37). Using these wall alignments and the extent of concentrated wall rubble, a much larger area was mapped for the room block of Unit 1 than that depicted by Kintigh (1985: 64). Disregarding Unit 4, the area of construction rubble at Kyaki:ma approximates 6,590 square meters. Using Kintigh's figure of 7.9 square meters of rubble per room, an estimate of 834 ground floor rooms is derived. Parts of Kyaki:ma may have had two stories, but the relatively low height of the rubble and the steep slopes on which the settlement was placed suggest that most of the village was only one story. The estimate of 834 is thus probably close to the actual number of rooms at the site.

Population Estimate. Kintigh (1985: 75–76) estimated the population of Kyaki:ma at 325, assuming that 65 percent of 250 rooms were occupied at any one time and that each of the occupied rooms had two inhabitants. Using these same assumptions with an estimate of 834 rooms yields an estimated population of 1,084 persons. The higher population estimate for Kyaki:ma is close to the estimated populations for the contemporaneous villages of Hawikku and Kechiba:wa.

Temporal Placement. Based on ceramic cross dating, Kintigh (1985: 65) thought Kyaki:ma was occupied from about A.D. 1400 to the mid-seventeenth century. Unit 4 appears to represent a limited occupation of the settlement in the seventeenth or eighteenth centuries.

Discussion. Most of Kyaki:ma has been reduced to rubble, making it difficult to record the internal structure of the architectural units. Nonetheless, the south plaza with its opening to the south and the north plaza or street are clearly defined by architectural rubble, and the basic outline of the pueblo can be established with enough resolution for space syntax analysis.

A series of upright slabs occurs at the northeast corner (Fig. 4.6). Mindeleff (1891: 85) thought these slabs were grave stones. Fewkes (1891: 109) observed that these stones resembled the Druid alignments in Brittany, but suggested that they may have functioned to prevent soil erosion. Reexamination of the feature in 1977 indicated the upright slabs were probably part of a wall constructed as a formal entry to the north plaza or street (Ferguson and others 1977: 36–37).

There is an area of construction rubble and trash located south of Kyaki:ma that does not appear on Mindeleff's map or on Figure 4.5. Although there were no clear wall alignments visible in 1977, one section of apparent wall fall suggested that there were one or more buildings in this area (Ferguson and others 1977:35). This location may be the site of the visita documented in historical records. The lack of resolution of this feature precluded its inclusion in the analysis of space syntax.

Most of Kyaki:ma was reduced to rubble long ago, but Unit 4 in the north plaza or street had standing walls in the nineteenth century (Mindeleff 1891: 85). One of these walls was still standing when the site was recorded in 1977 (Ferguson and others 1977: 30–31). Mindeleff observed that one of the rooms in Unit 4 contained the remnants of a chimney, and he suggested that other parts of the room block were enclosures used as corrals. He thought that this room block was more recent than the other architectural units of Kyaki:ma and that it was associated with the occupation of two small room block and corral complexes located on a bench north of the site. These complexes are described below, following Dowa Yalanne, as the Kyaki:ma Refuge Sites. Mindeleff's assessment of the date of occupa-

Figure 4.6. Upright slabs at Kyaki:ma in 1984, with T. J. Ferguson facing east. (Photograph by John Appel.)

tion of Unit 4 appears to be correct. Because Unit 4 probably postdates the major occupation of Kyaki:ma, it was excluded from the analyses of space syntax. An active Zuni shrine located at Kyaki:ma represents post-occupational use.

DOWA YALANNE

Site Number. Spier 47.

Synonymy. To-yo-a-la-na (Bandelier 1890a: 134); Tâaiyalana (Mindeleff 1891: 89); Tä-ya-ol-o-ne, Tay-a-ol-o-ne (Fewkes 1891: 110, Map); Tâaiyálane, Tâai-yá'hltona Hlúelawa (Cushing 1896: 429); Toyoalana, Old Zuni (Bandelier 1892b: 334); Heshoda Ayahltona (Hodge 1907: 544); Towwayallanna (Kroeber 1916: 28; Spier 1917: 231); Peñol de Caiquima (Hackett 1942a: 181); Mesa de Galisteo (Hodge 1937: 102); Tówayálane (Hodge 1954).

Sources of Maps. Mindeleff (1891, Plate 60); Victor and Cosmos Mindeleff (Item 2621); new fieldwork in 1989.

Elevation. Varies from 2,170 m to 2,192 m.

Landform. The site is located on the top of Dowa Yalanne at the south end of the mesa. The room blocks flank the two largest drainages on the mesa where they flow over the edge of a prominent re-entrant into the small wash that runs by Kyaki:ma.

Architectural Arrangement. Sixty-two architectural units were recorded within the area covered by the site plan in Figure 4.7. These units include room blocks, enclosures, walls, dams, and rubble areas. They are situated in several clusters on low rolling hills around

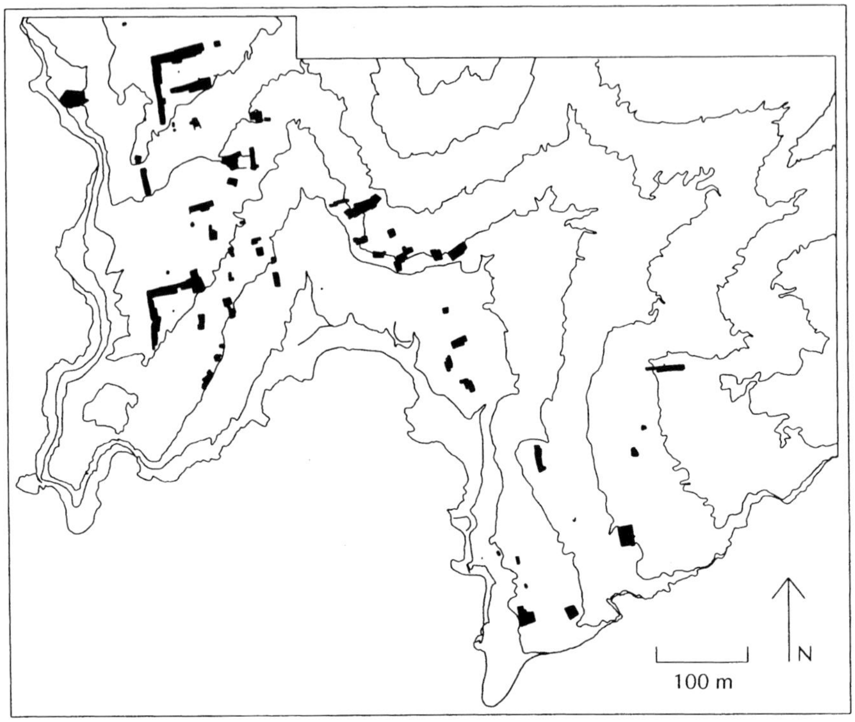

Figure 4.7. Architectural units mapped on Dowa Yalanne. The contour interval is 3 m.

the edge of the re-entrant. For purposes of analysis, the architectural units were divided into two classes: 14 units inferred to have been occupied prior to 1680 (Fig. 4.8), and 48 units inferred to have been occupied during the Pueblo Revolt from 1680 to 1692 (Fig. 4.9).

Dimensions. 738 m by 699 m.

Room Estimate. Thirty rooms were recorded in room blocks thought to have been occupied prior to the Pueblo Revolt. A total of 433 ground floor rooms was recorded in room blocks probably occupied during the Pueblo Revolt of 1680 to 1692. The height of the rubble at the two largest room blocks in the 1680 occupation indicates that many rooms in these units were at least two stories. Unit 1 contained 69 ground floor rooms, of which 54 were multistoried. Unit 27 contained 75 ground floor rooms, of which 73 were multistoried. Based on the multistoried architecture, 560 rooms were occupied on Dowa Yalanne during the Pueblo Revolt.

Population Estimate. Historical records document that the Zuni population numbered 2,500 during the Pueblo Revolt (Hart 1991a: 54). Documented population estimates before and after the Pueblo Revolt are lower. In 1664 the population was estimated at 1,200 and in 1706 at 1,500 persons. It is likely that either the documented population estimate for the Pueblo Revolt is too high or estimates preceding and following the Revolt are too low. Probably all the rooms on top of Dowa Yalanne were occupied during the relatively brief time span of the Pueblo Revolt. If two people occupied each room, as was assumed in estimating the populations of Hawikku, Kechiba:wa, and Kyaki:ma, then a population estimate of 1,120 is derived from archaeological data. This estimate seems low; it may be that Dowa Yalanne had a higher population density per room than the earlier villages. If the documented population estimate of 2,500 is accurate, there would have been about 4.5 persons per room.

Temporal Placement. Documentary evidence indicates Dowa Yalanne was briefly occupied in 1540, 1632, 1680, and 1703 (Hodge 1907: 544). The principal occupation was from 1680 to 1692.

Discussion. A map of the Pueblo Revolt village on Dowa Yalanne that complies with National Map Accuracy Standards was produced for this study. Photogrammetric base maps showing two-foot contour intervals and architectural features were prepared by Thomas R. Mann and Associates of Albuquerque using aerial photography exposed on June 2 and 8, 1988. Survey control was established by archaeologists from the University of New Mexico using a laser transit to tie into the State Plane Coordinate System, West Zone. The base maps were taken into the field and additional architectural details visible on the surface were plotted on the maps using a compass and tape measure to con-

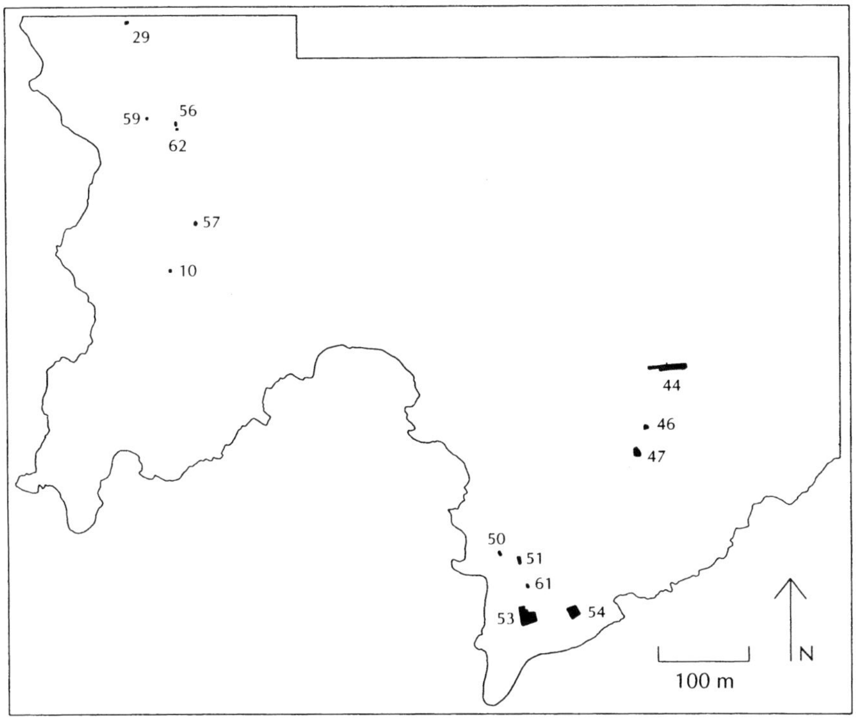

Figure 4.8. Distribution of architectural units mapped on Dowa Yalanne that date prior to A.D. 1680.

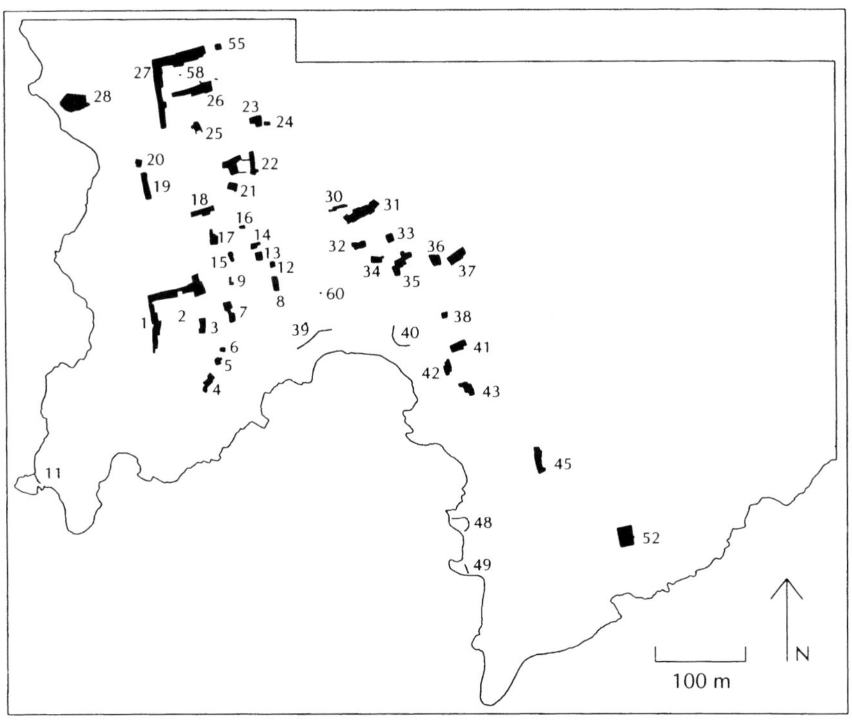

Figure 4.9. Distribution of architectural units mapped on Dowa Yalanne that date to the Pueblo Revolt of 1680.

nect with established points. Thirteen final maps were plotted on mylar at a scale of 1:360 and digitized using a digitizing tablet and computer aided drafting (CAD) software.

Earlier maps and descriptions of the settlement on Dowa Yalanne have been published by Cushing (1890: 156–157), Fewkes (1891: 110–111), Mindeleff (1891: 89–91, Plate 60), Bandelier (1892b: 334), Kroeber

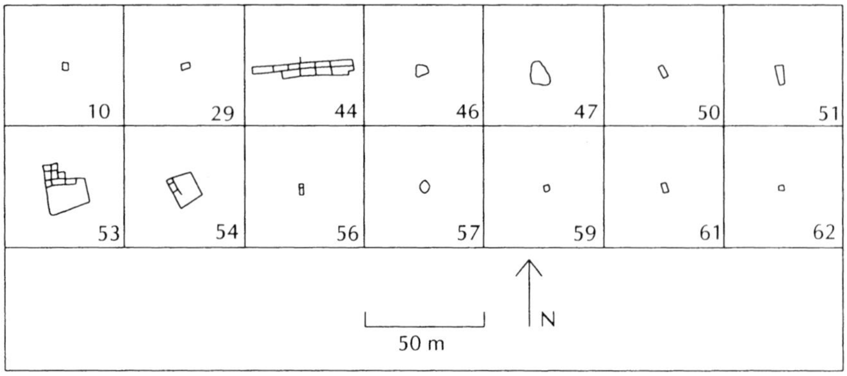

Figure 4.10. Plans of architectural units mapped on Dowa Yalanne that date prior to A.D. 1680.

(1916: 29), Spier (1917: 231), and Lange and Riley (1970: 47–50). None of these archaeologists, however, identified multiple components at the site. During my fieldwork it became clear that a number of room blocks had been "stone-robbed" or stripped of their building elements with only the wall foundations remaining (Units 29, 44, 50, 51, 53, 54, and 61). Other units had been reduced to low rubble piles and appeared to be the remains of temporary camp sites (Units 46, 47, and 57). These stone-robbed and small rubble units are notably different from the majority of room blocks on Dowa Yalanne, which are characterized by standing walls and substantial mounds of architectural debris.

The earlier archaeologists mapped 38 buildings on Dowa Yalanne. During mapping in 1989, 50 room blocks were recorded. Comparison of the historic maps with the plan prepared in 1989 indicates that the earlier scientists essentially mapped the major room blocks attributed to the Pueblo Revolt occupation. The room blocks associated with the occupations prior to 1680 do not appear on their maps. It is logical to think that the brief, historically documented use of Dowa Yalanne in 1540 and 1632 probably produced an archaeological record much different from that of the Pueblo Revolt occupation some 50 years later. The stone-robbed room blocks and low rubble piles mapped here for the first time are what would be expected to remain from the earlier occupations, and they are thus inferred to predate the Pueblo Revolt.

The collection of chronometric samples and other information needed to confirm the temporal placement of architectural units was not undertaken for this research, and the classification of the site into early and late components remains a working hypothesis. For this analysis, however, the classification of Dowa Yalanne into two components results in a conservative definition of the Pueblo Revolt occupation that is congruent with the characterization of the site by earlier archaeologists.

Fourteen architectural units are inferred to have been occupied prior to 1680 using criteria of stone-robbing, small size, meager amounts of rubble, and overall reduction of the features (Fig. 4.10). They include 11 room blocks ranging in size from 1 to 10 rooms (Table 4.2). Two of these room blocks incorporated unroofed open space in the form of courtyards or plazas. These units are primarily located at the margins of the Pueblo Revolt occupation. It is probable that additional early room blocks or features underlie many of the later architectural units and are therefore not visible today. Several architectural features on top of Dowa Yalanne outside of the mapped area have archaeological attributes similar to those units classified as part of the early component. These units may also be part of the 1540 or 1632 occupations.

Forty-eight architectural units are inferred to have been occupied during the Pueblo Revolt of 1680 using criteria of standing walls, preservation of architectural structure, and substantial mounds of architectural rubble. These units include room blocks, enclosures, wall segments, and dams. The plans of the 39 room blocks

Table 4.2. Number of Ground Story Rooms and Unroofed Spaces in Pre-1680 Room Blocks on Dowa Yalanne

Unit	Number of Rooms	Number of Spaces
10	1	
29	1	
44	10	
50	1	
51	1	
53	8	1
54	3	1
56	2	
59	1	
61	1	
62	1	

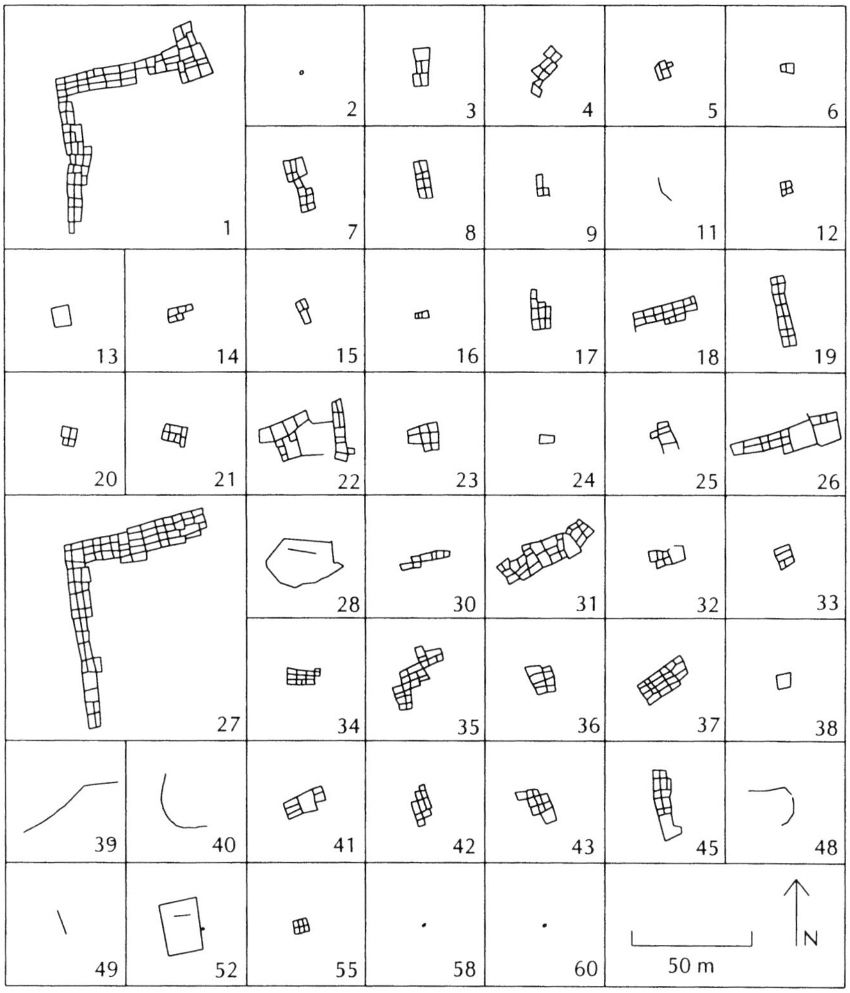

Figure 4.11. Plans of architectural units mapped on Dowa Yalanne that date to the Pueblo Revolt of 1680.

occupied during the Pueblo Revolt are illustrated in Figure 4.11, and the number of ground story rooms in them is given in Table 4.3.

The Pueblo Revolt room blocks range in size from 1 to 75 ground story rooms. The two largest room blocks, Units 1 and 27, have wings of rooms positioned at right angles to one another forming an ell that encloses an open space or plaza. Units 1 and 27 were undoubtedly multistoried and incorporated at least 123 rooms and 148 rooms, respectively. An unattributed photograph from the late nineteenth century in the archives of the Southwest Museum clearly shows a two-story wall at either Unit 1 or Unit 27 (Fig. 4.12). This wall has collapsed since the photograph was taken. Portions of these room blocks may have contained a third story, so the estimated number of rooms is conservative.

Mindeleff (1891: 90) thought four of the largest clusters may have attained a height of two or three stories. During fieldwork in 1989, only one additional room block (Unit 20) was observed to have a high rubble mound that may represent the remains of a multistoried building. Because the number of stories at Unit 20 was less certain than at Units 1 and 27, it was considered to have had only one story. Unit 20 is only four rooms, and a conservative room estimate for this unit does not substantially affect the total room count for the site as a whole.

Most of the Pueblo Revolt room blocks were relatively small compared to Units 1 and 27; 27 units have 9 rooms or less, and another 10 room blocks have between 11 and 27 rooms. The average size of the smaller Pueblo Revolt room blocks is 7.6 rooms, and 11 of the small room blocks incorporate one or more unroofed open areas within them. These unroofed areas appear to be courtyards or small plazas adjacent to the roofed rooms.

Four Pueblo Revolt architectural units were enclosures of various kinds. Two enclosures (Units 2 and 58)

Figure 4.12. Two-story construction in a room block on top of Dowa Yalanne. (Unattributed photograph from the late nineteenth century; courtesy of the Southwest Museum, Los Angeles; Negative No. 33,705.)

were less than a meter in diameter and appeared in the open area defined by the wings of the large room blocks. These features appear to be plaza shrines.

Table 4.3. Number of Ground Story Rooms and Unroofed Spaces in Pueblo Revolt Room Blocks on Dowa Yalanne

Unit	Number of Rooms	Number of Spaces	Unit	Number of Rooms	Number of Spaces
1	69		24	1	
3	4	1	25	3	1
4	8		26	12	3
5	4		27	75	2
6	2		30	7	
7	12		31	27	1
8	8		32	5	1
9	3		33	4	
12	4		34	12	
13	1		35	21	
14	5		36	8	
15	3		37	19	
16	3		38	1	
17	9		41	5	1
18	16	1	42	9	
19	14		43	9	1
20	4		45	11	1
21	7		55	6	
22	13	6	60	1	
23	8				

The other two enclosures were larger. Unit 28 is an irregularly shaped polygon defined by low walls near the west edge of Dowa Yalanne. Constructed with large stones, this feature encompasses an area of 437 square meters and has a short wall or linear alignment of rocks within it. There is a light scatter of sherds and lithics within the enclosure. In some respects Unit 28 looks like a corral, but there was no animal dung associated with it. The fourth enclosure, Unit 52, is a rectangular structure encompassing 319 square meters. Mindeleff mapped this unit with four interior rooms but no evidence of interior walls was seen in 1989. The feature looks like an unroofed space defined by walls. There was a shrinelike feature attached to the outside of the east wall of Unit 52.

Three Pueblo Revolt units were short walls situated on small outcrops of slickrock near the mesa edge. Unit 11 was an angled wall 11.7 m long. Unit 48 was a curving wall 34.9 m long, with a gate or opening in the middle of it. Unit 49 was a straight wall 10.6 m long. The function of these features is not known. They look like corrals, but their west sides are open to the sheer cliff face of Dowa Yalanne, making their use as corrals improbable. Whatever their purpose, they clearly demark areas adjacent to the mesa edge.

Units 39 and 40 were two dams built to impound reservoirs where the largest drainages flow off the mesa top. Unit 39 is 46.2 m long, with a slightly curving wall that has an angular wing on its east side. Unit 40 is 36.7 m long, with a pronounced curve to the wall. Both units are constructed of large building elements. Mindeleff noted a third reservoir along the mesa rim to the southeast beyond the limits of his plan. Two architectural features consisting of short wall segments are located in this vicinity (Units 48 and 49), but neither of them appears to be a dam or reservoir. Another reservoir was recorded in 1989 on the west side of Dowa Yalanne beyond the northern edge of the map in Figure 4.7. The Zuni reported to Mindeleff (1891: 91) that after snow storms their ancestors rolled up huge snowballs on the mesa to furnish water to these reservoirs. Cushing (1896: 330) noted that the reservoirs were filled by rain and snow.

Diego de Vargas (1914: 304–305) described three kivas (estufas) in the plaza of the pueblo he visited on the summit of Dowa Yalanne in 1692. The building Vargas described had to have been either Unit 1 or 27, because they are the two multistoried room blocks enclosing plazas. No indication of any kivas or subterranean features was discerned in these open areas during fieldwork, however. The only building tentatively identified as a kiva was Unit 13, which appeared to be partly subterranean.

Mindeleff (1891: 90) described buildings on Dowa Yalanne as roughly built, with dry-laid masonry walls displaying hasty and careless construction. Close examination of many walls during fieldwork in 1989, however, revealed that many of the room blocks have walls constructed with mud mortar, some of them in a masonry style using heavily dressed elements with chinking between courses of masonry. Most of the mortar used in construction has apparently eroded from the standing walls, giving them the appearance described by Mindeleff. No evidence of roof beams or other structural wood was observed during fieldwork. The standing walls in many of the room blocks are relatively high compared with other sites on the Zuni Indian Reservation, perhaps because the Zuni do not graze livestock on top of the mesa. Many observers have noted that the ruins on Dowa Yalanne are almost all associated with a heavy growth of cholla cacti (Mindeleff 1891: 90; Fewkes 1891: 110–111). Stands of cholla this thick do not commonly occur in the Zuni area and are a distinctive feature of the ruins on Dowa Yalanne.

There is a large, diffuse artifact scatter extending over the entire surface of the Pueblo Revolt village, and virtually all the room blocks have discrete middens adjacent to them. These middens contain a profuse amount of animal bone, ash, charcoal, lithics, and ceramics, including small traces of Cibola White Ware and gray corrugated utility ware and more numerous amounts of black ware, Kechipauan Polychrome, Matsaki Brown-on-buff, Matsaki Polychrome, Hawikuh Glaze-on-red, Hawikuh Polychrome, Ashiwi Polychrome, plain buff ware, red-on-buff ware, and plain red ware.

The distribution of the room blocks on Dowa Yalanne has fascinated many archaeologists. In this regard, Cushing (Item 155: 10–12, 1890: 156–157) applied a structuralist paradigm to the interpretation of Zuni architecture, arguing that the spatial layout of the settlement on Dowa Yalanne and other Zuni villages was organized around a central "Idea" entailing a sevenfold division of symbolic, social, and physical space. He thought this "Idea" was carried out in the extensive though temporary building of the Pueblo Revolt village on top of Dowa Yalanne. In various publications, Cushing refers to either six or seven clusters of buildings on Dowa Yalanne (Cushing 1896: 330, 1920: 131). In the final analysis, Cushing meant both six and seven clusters simultaneously. He thought that the structure of both Zuni society and architecture corresponded to the six directions (cardinal points with the addition of the zenith and nadir) and that a final division represented "the middle or mother and synthetic combination of them all" (Cushing 1896: 367). For Cushing, six spatial groups yielded a sevenfold division by the addition of the entire settlement to the six house clusters he perceived.

Cushing thought the key to the distribution or separation of the house clusters on Dowa Yalanne was the occurrence in each of an isolated, square, or nearly square, four-room chamber or kiva (Cushing 1890: 156–157). He marked the location of seven of these ceremonial structures and delineated six clusters of buildings on a map now in the archives of the Brooklyn Museum (Fig. 4.13; Bigelow, Map; Ferguson 1992: 89). Correlation of Cushing's map with the 1989 fieldwork indicates that these "kivas" are Units 9, 20, 24, 33, 34 38, and 55. These room blocks actually range in size from 1 to 12 rooms, and none of them could be identified as kivas using contemporary standards of archaeological classification. The one structure that was identified in 1989 as a possible kiva, Unit 13, does not appear on Cushing's map.

Cushing (1920: 131) and Bandelier (Lange and Riley 1970: 47–50) both believed that the clusters of buildings they perceived on Dowa Yalanne corresponded to the social organization of the six villages occupied at the time of the Spanish Entrada. In the words of Bandelier,

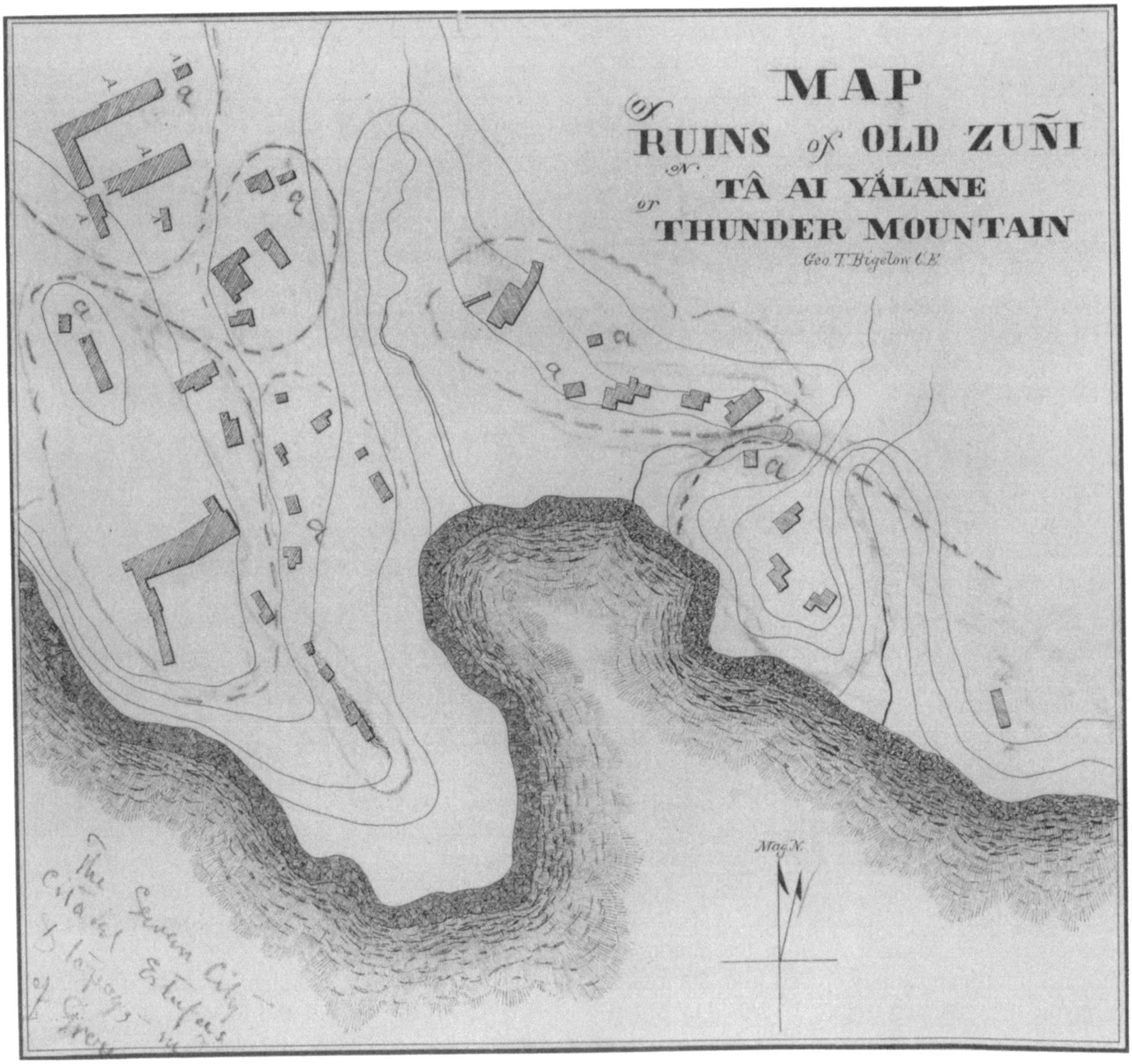

Figure 4.13. Map drawn by George Bigelow around 1888, with Frank Hamilton Cushing's notes showing the location of kivas ("a") and house clusters (dashed lines). Courtesy of the Brooklyn Museum Archives, Culin Archival Collection, Cushing Sketches (6.3.029): Zuni maps and plans, no date.

when the Zuni "fled onto the mesa, each pueblo of below built its own for itself, close by the others, but still a separate and distinct group" (Lange and Riley 1970: 47).

Archaeologists who subsequently investigated Dowa Yalanne disputed Cushing's and Bandelier's identification of six or seven house clusters. Fewkes (1891: 110–111) was not able to detect the seven house clusters described by Cushing, adding "nor does Mr. Bigelow's map show an arrangement as clearly as might be wished in support of such a theory." Mindeleff (1891: 89–90), who published a remarkably accurate plan of the settlement, also disputed the clustering of the house blocks, stating:

> An examination of the plan . . . will show that no such definite scheme of arrangement governed the builders. There are but three, or at most four groups that could be defined as distinct clusters, and even in the case of these the disposition is so irregular and their boundaries so ill defined, through the great number of small groups scattered about, that they can hardly be considered distinct.

Kroeber (1916: 28–30) and Spier (1917: 231) agreed with Mindeleff that they could not discern the house clusters claimed by Cushing. Spier felt strongly enough to characterize Cushing's idea as "absurd."

Kroeber (1916: 29) thought that the ruins on Dowa Yalanne were the largest in the Zuni area. He wrote: "It gives the casual impression of having sheltered a thousand people, but is so scattered that it cannot be surveyed in one sweep of the eye, and may have harbored twice as much." Kroeber also noted that although part of the mesa top was arable land, the area would have been too small, even if cultivated, to have supported more than a fraction of the population.

There are four major trails to the top of Dowa Yalanne, with approaches from the east, west, and south sides, plus additional routes that entail more strenuous climbing. Many of the trails incorporate hand and toe holds pecked into the steep sandstone slopes of the mesa. One trail leads directly down the slickrock of the re-entrant to the spring at Kyaki:ma (Mindeleff 1891: 89; Fewkes 1891: 110–111).

At many of the trail heads, there are low walls associated with adjacent rock piles. These features, still visible today, were interpreted by nineteenth-century Zuni Indians as defensive measures (Stevenson 1904: 287). The Indians could protect themselves behind the walls and use the stones as missiles to bombard unwanted visitors. The steep walls of the 300–m high mesa, along with the defensive walls and rock piles, transformed the Pueblo Revolt village on Dowa Yalanne into an almost impregnable fortress.

One Zuni name for the settlement on Dowa Yalanne, Heshoda Ayahltona, is translated by Hodge (1907: 544) as "ancient buildings above." Similarly, Cushing (1896: 429) translated another Zuni name, Tâaiyá'hltona Hlúelawa, as "Towns-all-above of-the-seed-all." The word Dowa means corn in the Zuni language, so the mesa is often referred to today as "Corn Mountain," a name conceptually related to Cushing's translation. Cushing also translated Tâaiyálane as "Mountain of Thunder" (Cushing 1896: 429), and this appellation was used by many non-Zuni in the late nineteenth and early twentieth centuries.

Active Zuni shrines located in and adjacent to the Pueblo Revolt village room blocks on Dowa Yalanne represent a postoccupational use of the mesa top and attest to the continuing significance of the site to the Zuni Indians (Whipple 1856, Plate 34; Hodge 1954).

KYAKI:MA REFUGE SITES

Site Numbers. ZAP:NM:12:K3:11; LA 48386.
ZAP:NM:12:K3:12; LA 48387.

Synonymy. These two sites do not have unique names distinct from the adjacent site of Kyaki:ma.

Sources of Maps. Mindeleff (1891, Plate 52); Ferguson and others (1977: 38, 42).

Elevation. 1,948 m.

Landform. The sites are 183 m apart on a narrow bench of Dowa Yalanne immediately above the site of Kyaki:ma. Both sites are bounded on the east by the vertical wall of the mesa and on the west by a steep escarpment. The sites form spatially distinct clusters situated on the highest points at both ends of the bench. The narrow bench they are on forms a natural walkway between them. Both sites have a commanding view of the surrounding valley.

Architectural Arrangement. Both sites consist of small, irregularly shaped complexes incorporating one-story rooms, unroofed enclosures, and corrals (Fig. 4.14). The most complex architectural feature is Unit 1 at ZAP:NM:12:K3:12, which consists of six rooms arranged in a configuration with two large enclosures. The other units at that site consist only of corral enclosures. At ZAP:NM:12:K3:11, two units have one room attached to corral enclosures, and the other units are simply enclosures.

Dimensions. 73 m by 69 m (ZAP:NM:12:K3:11).
74 m by 37 m (ZAP:NM:12:K3:12).

Room Estimate. NM:12:K3:11 has three rooms and five enclosures. K3:12 contains six rooms and four unroofed enclosures.

Population Estimate. The 1790 census of *Rancho de Galisteo* (Minge 1980: 51–56) enumerates 105 occupants. However, the two Kyaki:ma Refuge sites and other sites from this period documented in the drainage of Galestina Wash (Shundekya) do not appear large enough by themselves or in the aggregate to house this many people.

Temporal Placement. The presence of corrals at these sites is definite evidence that they were occupied in the historic period, but precise dates are not avail-

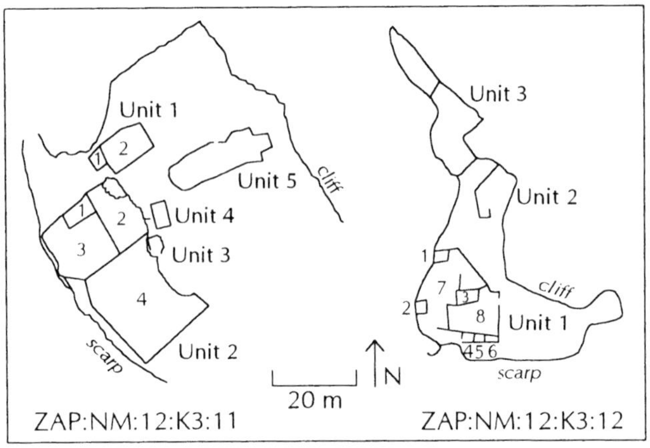

Figure 4.14. Plans of Kyaki:ma Refuge Sites (after Ferguson and others 1977: 38, 42).

able. The settlements are generally thought to have been used sometime between the occupation of Kyaki:ma and the mid-nineteenth century. The ceramic assemblages consist of a high frequency of black ware and low frequencies of Ashiwi Polychrome, Matsaki Polychrome, a matte black and red painted buff ware, and unidentified red wares (Ferguson and others 1977: 37–43). It is the presence of Ashiwi Polychrome, known to have been made from about 1700 to 1750 (Batkin 1987: 163), that provides the best archaeological evidence to date the refuge sites. Several petroglyphs on the cliff facing the east side of the settlements were executed in an incised style with subject matter relating to the historic period, for instance, a man on horseback, Shalakos, and kachina masks. The sites are considered herein to date to the eighteenth century.

Discussion. These two sites are grouped together not only because of their proximity but also because they may have functioned as a single settlement. The room block in the north plaza or street in the adjacent site of Kyaki:ma (Unit 4), as discussed above, may also have been occupied in conjunction with the two Kyaki:ma refuge sites, and, indeed, may have been the principal habitation occupied when the refuge settlements were in use. Nonetheless, as spatially distinct complexes, the two refuge sites on the bench above Kyaki:ma are similar to "fortified sheep camps" in other places on the Zuni Indian Reservation and for this reason are analyzed separately.

Like many other refuges, the Kyaki:ma sites were constructed using unshaped masonry elements dry laid into relatively crude walls, as compared with most Zuni habitations (Ferguson and others 1977: 37–43). The masonry contains no mortar or chinking. The sites are similar to the ruins on the summit of Dowa Yalanne in that they are covered with a thick stand of cholla cactus.

Two of the walled enclosures at both refuge sites were formed by wall segments abutting the adjacent cliff face or the large boulders or outcrops. The larger of these enclosures contained a yellowish-brown soil with a different color than the surrounding natural soils, and it was inferred to result from decomposing dung deposits. One of the large enclosures at the easternmost site is defined by a low wall with a gate or opening on the north side. This structure, Unit 5, encloses an irregularly shaped rectangular area with rounded corners at the west end and a small alcove at the east end. When Kroeber visited this feature in 1915, he was told by the Lieutenant Governor of Zuni that it was a "head man's dance house." There is no way to evaluate this interpretation, but Unit 5 does not appear to be a corral.

SHUNDEKYA

Site Number. Spier 44.

Synonymy. Shunntekkya (Kroeber 1916: 34; Spier 1917: 230) Shundek'yay'a (Ferguson and Hart 1985: 134).

Source of Map. New fieldwork in 1989.

Elevation. 2,012 m.

Landform. Shundekya is located on a bench of the mesa flanking the east side of Galestina Wash. A steep escarpment defines the north edge of the site; it commands a wide view of the northern portion of Galestina Canyon.

Architectural Arrangement. Two architectural units are situated on different levels of the bench (Fig. 4.15). Unit 1 consists of two rooms arranged in a configuration with two large enclosures interpreted to be corrals.

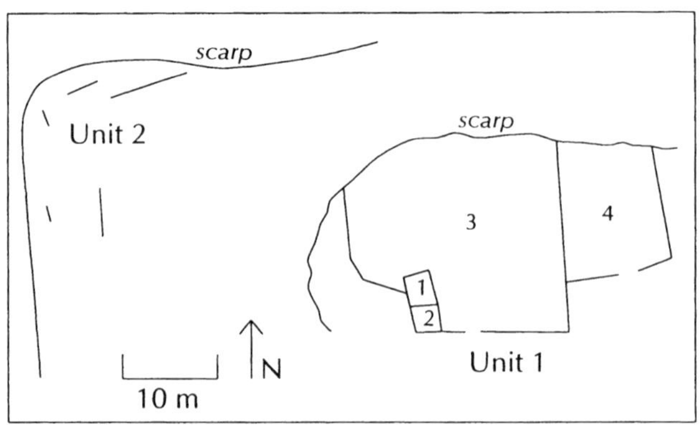

Figure 4.15. Plan of Shundekya.

Figure 4.16. Space 4 at Shundekya, looking southeast. (Photograph by T. J. Ferguson, 1989.)

Unit 2 consists of five isolated wall segments adjacent to several deep fissures or crevices in the bedrock on the bench below Unit 1. All architecture was one story.

Dimensions. 31 m by 47 m.

Room Estimate. Shundekya contains two rooms.

Population Estimate. These rooms were probably used by the minimal social unit involved in sheep herding: a man, his brothers, and their sons. The exact size of these social units is not known, but it is likely the settlement was never occupied by more than a few people at one time.

Temporal Placement. The corrals at the site indicate it was occupied during the historic period, but precise dates are not available. Kroeber's (1916: 16–20) analysis of the ceramics led him to classify Shundekya as a member of a late group of sites in "Period A." The other sites in Period A were all occupied in the late prehistoric and early historic eras, including the settlement on top of Dowa Yalanne and Wimaya:wa. The sparse artifact scatter associated with the site in 1989 contained Zuni Polychrome and black ware. Zuni Polychrome was made from about 1750 to the present (Batkin 1987: 163–165). The settlement was not used during the nineteenth century and for purposes of analysis it is considered to date primarily to the eighteenth century.

Discussion. The masonry walls of Shundekya are a single course wide and are constructed of irregularly shaped tabular sandstone elements (Fig. 4.16). The walls contain some notably large building stones. Most of the walls in Unit 1 have collapsed, but those portions still standing are about 70 cm high. Both of the corrals have openings in their south walls.

Shundekya can only be accessed by a steep trail up a small re-entrant along the edge of the mesa. A feature below the site looks like a masonry ramp constructed to facilitate driving sheep up to the bench. Unit 2 comprises a series of walls that perhaps protected the sheep where the trail is adjacent to deep crevices. Additionally, these walls may have impeded the progress of trespassers.

Kroeber (1916: 34) did not visit Shundekya in 1915, but he described it as a ruin from which he obtained some potsherds from a Zuni friend whose father had collected them six or eight years earlier while herding sheep. The walls of the site are visible from the valley floor (Spier 1917: 230). A prayerstick was observed in one of the walls in 1989, providing evidence that Shundekya retains ritual significance for contemporary Zuni.

WIMAYA:WA

Site Number. Spier 53.

Synonymy. Wimmayawa (Kroeber 1916: 30; Spier 1917: 233).

Sources of Maps. Spier 1917: 220; new fieldwork in 1989.

Elevation. 1,998 m.

Landform. Wimaya:wa is on the crest of a low hill in the drainage of Oak Wash north of Zuni Pueblo. It commands an unobstructed view of the entire valley.

Architectural Arrangement. This architectural complex comprises a single unit with 29 contiguous spaces incorporating one-story rooms, unroofed open areas, and corrals (Fig. 4.17). The overall plan has an irregular shape, and rooms are distributed in four parts of the site. In the southwest corner is a block of six rooms (Spaces 22–27) with four adjacent enclosures (Spaces 20, 21, 28 and 29). In the center of the site is a block of eight rooms (Spaces 11–14 and 16–19) surrounding an open enclosure (Space 15). A single room (Space 2) is at the northeast corner and two rooms (Spaces 5 and 6) are in the southeast corner. Five large enclosures (Space 3, 4, 8, 9, and 10) are located between the central room block and the rooms at the northeast and southeast corners. Enclosures are attached to the north wall of the room in the northeast corner (Space 1) and to the south wall of Rooms 5 and 6 (Space 7).

Dimensions. 111 m by 101 m.

Room Estimate. Wimaya:wa encompasses a total of 17 rooms.

Population Estimate. Wimaya:wa is not listed by this name in historical census records, so the size of the population that occupied the settlement cannot be estimated using documentary sources. Kroeber (1916: 30) thought Wimaya:wa could have housed two or three hundred people, but this is not a realistic estimate because the settlement is much too small for a population of this size. Considering the seasonal nature of occupation, it is doubtful whether an accurate population estimate can be derived using the assumptions applied to permanent pueblos. Population density may have been higher in this type of settlement than at a permanently occupied pueblo. Even assuming all rooms were occupied contemporaneously with a density of occupation twice that assumed for Hawikku (four persons per room rather than two), a momentary population estimate of 34 would result. The presence of four room clusters within the architectural complex suggest it was used by several small households or cooperative herding groups.

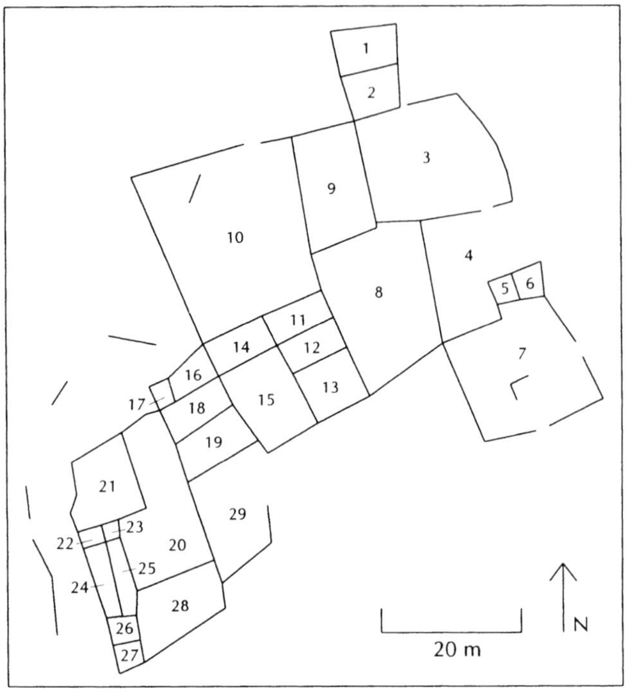

Figure 4.17. Plan of Wimaya:wa

Temporal Placement. Spier (1917: 265) classified this site as a "recent" or "post-Conquest" ruin in a group that also included Heshoda Łuwal'a.

Discussion. A comparison of Spier's (1917: 220) map and the plan prepared in 1989 show a close correspondence in many respects, especially to the larger enclosures. Both Kroeber (1916: 30-31) and Spier (1917: 233–234) thought that intermediate walls in the original structure of the settlement had been removed to enlarge the corrals to their present size. Kroeber suggested that rooms were enlarged into corrals, whereas Spier suggested small corrals were reconstructed into larger enclosures. The evidence for enlargement of the corrals has become obscured through time and is difficult to discern today. There are still many standing walls, the highest of which measures 1.7 m, but most of the walls are beginning to fall down and be reduced to rubble piles.

In 1989 more rooms were mapped in the central and southwest portions of Wimaya:wa than were shown by Spier. Six of the unroofed open areas (Spaces 1, 8, 9,

Figure 4.18. Space 10 at Wimaya:wa, looking north. (Photograph by T. J. Ferguson, 1979.)

20, 21, and 28) had no openings to the outside, which meant that if they were used as corrals the walls had to be dismantled and reconstructed. There is no evidence for such reconstruction, however, and it is more likely that these open areas were used as courtyards or plazas in conjunction with adjoining rooms. Space 29 has a low retaining wall that may have defined an exterior activity area. If only the enclosures with gates or openings are considered to be corrals (Spaces 3, 4, 7, and 10), then there are only four corrals at Wimaya:wa. The correlation between the number of room clusters and the number of corrals may be meaningful.

Walls are constructed of unshaped tabular sandstone masonry using mud mortar (Kroeber 1916: 30–31). Most of the mortar has eroded from the walls, giving them a rough appearance (Fig. 4.18). There are four short wall alignments at the west side of the site, as well as short wall segments in Spaces 7 and 10. The function of these wall segments is unclear.

As Kroeber noted, most artifacts are found in a scatter extending down the hill slope on the south side of the architectural complex. Spier (1917: 233–234) thought Wimaya:wa was "obviously" a refuge village occupied for only a short period. He decided the "ash heaps" were too shallow for stratigraphic excavations and only analyzed ceramics collected from the surface. The presence of a single corral in 1915, in good repair with a substantial dung deposit (Kroeber 1916: 30), suggests a portion of the site was still being used at that time by one herder to pen livestock.

HESHODA ŁUWAL'A

Site Number. Spier 42.

Synonymy. Hesh-o-ta-thlu-al-la (Fewkes 1891: 111), HeccotaLalla (Spier 1917: 230).

Sources of Maps. Spier (1917: 220); new fieldwork in 1989.

Elevation. The architectural units are positioned between the 2,030-m and 2,036-m contour intervals. The contour of the canyon rim depicted in Figure 4.19 is a composite of the 2,008-m to 2,011 m contour intervals.

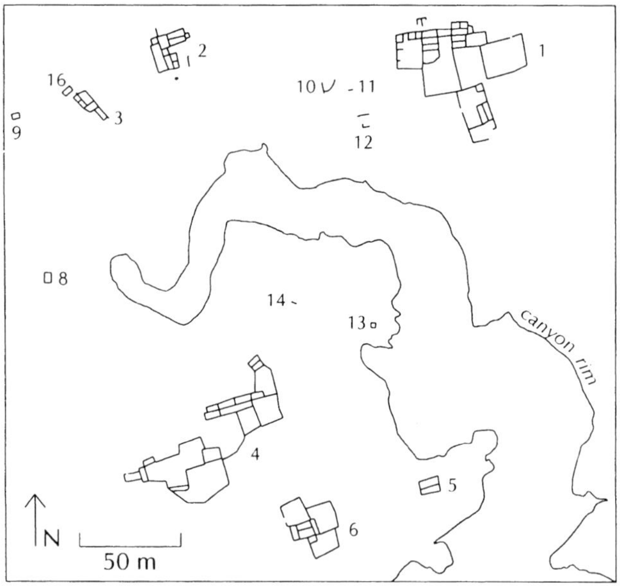

Figure 4.19. Plan of Heshoda Łuwal'a. The canyon rim is a composite of the 2,008-m to 2,011-m contour intervals.

Landform. Heshoda Łuwal'a is on the bench of Yala Lana (Big Mesa) northwest of Zuni Pueblo. The architectural units are located on several small knolls or rises on the bench surrounding the rim of a deep canyon. The canyon is an impediment to travel within the settlement; access between the northern and southern parts is possible only by detouring around it.

Architectural Arrangement. Heshoda Łuwal'a comprises 14 architectural units (Fig. 4.19). Five of these units consist of blocks of contiguous rooms in irregularly shaped configurations that contain corrals and open enclosures (Fig. 4.20). One unit is a two-room structure (Unit 5) and four units are one-room structures. Four units consist of isolated wall segments whose function is not entirely clear, although several of them appear to be retaining walls to prevent soil erosion.

Dimensions. 279 m by 255 m.

Room Estimate. There are 49 rooms incorporated in the architectural units of Heshoda Łuwal'a, along with 23 unroofed enclosures. All rooms appear to have been one story.

Population Estimate. Heshoda Łuwal'a is not listed by this name in historical census records. As discussed in Chapter 3, however, Heshoda Łuwal'a is probably either Rancho Colorado or Rancho del Cañon. In 1790, Rancho Colorado had a population of 96 and Rancho del Cañon had a population of 160 (Minge 1980: 51–56). Assuming all rooms were occupied contemporaneously, the number of persons per room at Heshoda Łuwal'a would have been 1.96 if the site was identified as Rancho Colorado and 3.27 persons if it was identified as Rancho del Cañon.

Temporal Placement. Spier (1917: 265) classified Heshoda Łuwal'a as a "recent" ruin in a group that also included Wimaya:wa. Black ware and early Zuni Polychrome sherds observed in the artifact scatter in 1989 confirm this temporal placement. Heshoda Łuwal'a was occupied by Lai-iu-ah-tsai-lu (alias Pedro Pino) for several years prior to 1821 (Cushing, Item 36). When Fewkes (1891: 102) visited Zuni in 1890, he met an "old woman of the tribe" who said she had been born in the buildings now in ruin, near the peach orchard north of town. For the purposes of analysis, the primary occupation of Heshoda Łuwal'a is considered to have been in the eighteenth and early nineteenth centuries.

Discussion. A map of Heshoda Łuwal'a was made that complies with National Map Accuracy Standards. A series of photogrammetric base maps showing two-foot contour intervals and architectural features was prepared by Thomas R. Mann and Associates of Albuquerque using aerial photography exposed on June 2 and 8, 1988. Survey control was established by archaeologists from the University of New Mexico using a laser transit to tie into the State Plane Coordinate System, West Zone.

The base maps were taken into the field and additional architectural details visible on the surface were plotted on the maps using a compass and tape measure to correlate with established points. Four final maps were plotted on mylar at a scale of 1:360 and were digitized using a digitizing tablet and computer aided drafting (CAD) software.

Comparison of Spier's (1917: 220) plan and the 1989 map show an excellent correspondence in the configuration of principal architectural units. As at Wimaya:wa, however, more internal walls were discerned in 1989 and more rooms were mapped within the complexes. Spier's map is somewhat schematic, with right angles shown at the corners of many walls that are actually curving to follow slight changes in topography. Whereas Spier mapped 4 of the architectural units in 1915, 14 were mapped in 1989.

The principal architectural units contain a mixture of rooms, unroofed open enclosures, and corrals. Many of the unroofed enclosures have no openings or gates in their walls and apparently functioned as courtyards or plazas rather than corrals. Unit 1 has sixteen rooms (Spaces 1-3, 5-7, 9, 11-16, 20, 22, 23), four enclosures with no gates (Spaces 4, 8, 10, and 17), and four

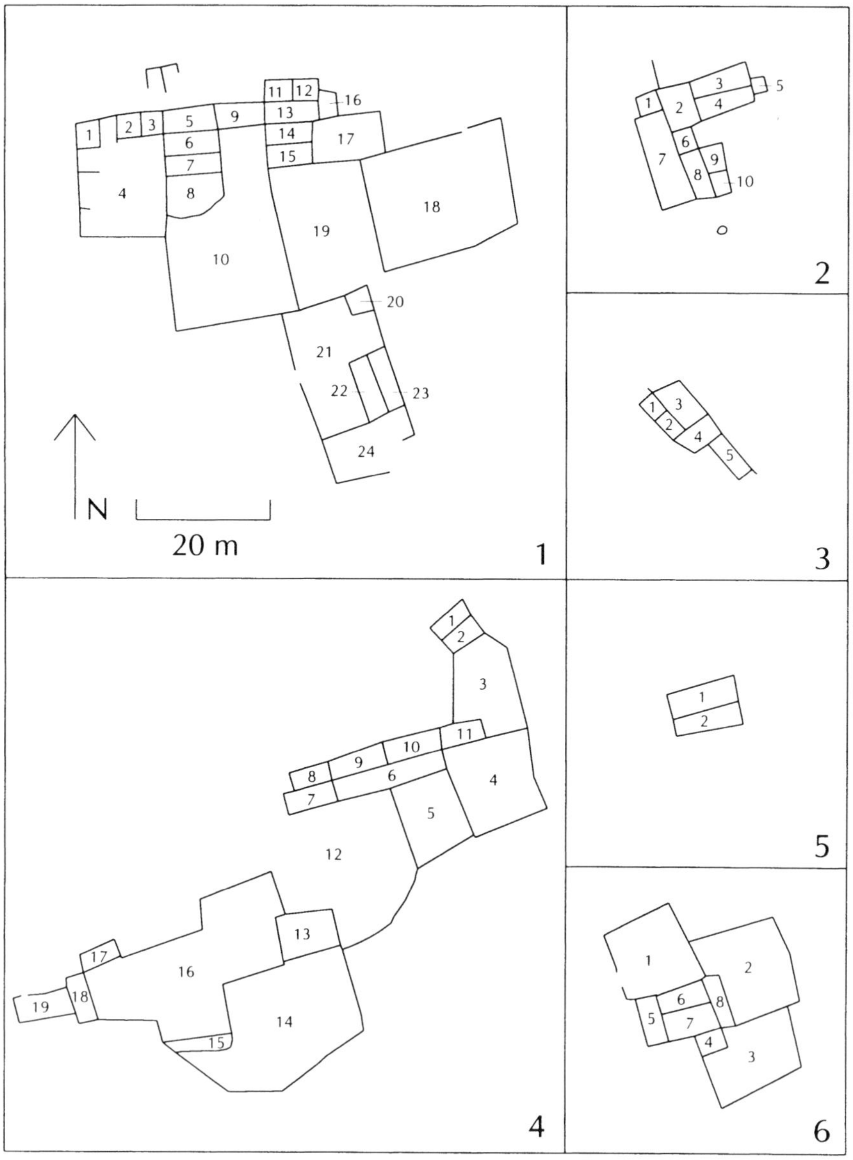

Figure 4.20. Plans of the principal architectural units at Heshoda Łuwal'a.

corrals (Spaces 18, 19, 21, 24). Unit 2 has eight rooms (Spaces 1, 3-6, 8-10) and two enclosures without gates (Spaces 2 and 7). Unit 3 has three rooms (Spaces 1, 2, 5) and two enclosures without gates (Spaces 3 and 4). Unit 4 has ten rooms (Spaces 1, 2, 6-11, 17, 18), seven enclosures without gates (Spaces 3-5, 13-16), one enclosure with a gate (Space 19), and one corral (Space 12). Unit 6 has five rooms (Spaces 4-8), two enclosures without gates (Spaces 2, 3), and one corral (Space 1).

A line drawing in Fewkes (1891: 111–112) illustrates substantial walls with at least one room standing full height, revealing how much the standing architecture has been reduced in the last century. Fewkes noted that the ruin was in a good state of preservation and that several houses retained their roofs. He observed that the architecture resembled that of the other inhabited Zuni pueblos. Masonry as it appeared in 1979 is shown in Figure 4.21. Spier (1917: 230) wrote that the "ash heaps" at Heshoda Łuwal'a were but a few inches thick.

Two small architectural units consisting of single room structures were recorded but were outside the area mapped in Figure 4.19. Toward the end of occupation, the aggregated room blocks were apparently vacated in favor of smaller, dispersed field houses located adjacent to individual orchards. The settlement pattern of dispersed field houses next to orchards is present at other sites occupied in the nineteenth and early twentieth centuries, and it may have occurred at Heshoda Łuwal'a

Figure 4.21. Masonry at Heshoda Łuwal'a. (Photograph by Barbara J. Mills, 1979.)

as well. Another example is a peach orchard on the east flank of Dowa Yalanne (Cushing 1920: 142–151; Ferguson 1985: 107–109). There was no way to confirm this settlement sequence at Heshoda Łuwal'a during fieldwork, and the notion remains a working hypothesis for future investigation.

Heshoda Łuwal'a was one of what Cushing described as the "seven Sónoli Hlúëlawe (the Towns of Sonora)," so called because the peach stones used to plant the orchards came from Sonora. Cushing (1896: 332) observed in the 1880s that there were numerous peach orchards among the cliffs and terraces of "Grand Mountain" and Twin Mountains north of Zuni, with large, neatly arranged gardens and many small cornfields.

Cushing proposed that "massive kivas" were built in the peach orchard villages where the Zuni could "escape from the irksome and oft-repeated spyings upon and interdictions of their sacred observances and mythic drama-dances" that the Spanish authorities were wont to make. No evidence of these kivas was found during mapping of the site in 1989; excavation might shed light on this issue.

In 1916, Spier (1917: 230) recorded a peach orchard and large cottonwoods at Heshoda Łuwal'a. There are no peach orchards today, and, in fact, only a few stumps from peach trees even remain. The best archaeological evidence that there were once peaches at the settlement comes from the peach stones that are in the middens.

When Spier described the sites, there was a permanent spring under the cliff that flowed in a small stream across the ledge into one of the canyons. He observed that: "The situation could hardly be bettered from the standpoint of defense and with its adequate water supply and fields near by might have sheltered a large population" (Spier 1917: 230).

A steep trail up the escarpment of the bench is used for access to Heshoda Łuwal'a. There are several walls or retained areas along this trail, which is beyond the area shown in Figure 4.19.

LOWER PESCADO

Site Numbers. ZAP:NM:12:I3:109; LA 34961

Synonymy. Hesh-o-ta-tzina (Fewkes 1891: 103); He-sho-ta-tsi'-na-kwe, Ojo del Pescado (Cushing 1920: 126, 363); Hé'shâkta-tsína (Curtis 1926: 93).

Source of Map. Mindeleff (1891, Plate 69).

Elevation. 2,042 m.

Landform. The site is on the alluvial floodplain on the north bank of the Rio Pescado.

Architectural Arrangement. Six room blocks form an irregularly shaped ellipse enclosing a large open space that contains a seventh room block, five corrals, and several wall segments (Fig. 4.22). The east end of the settlement has a diagonal alignment and the west end has a semicircular form.

Dimensions. 142 m by 201 m.

Room Estimate. Mindeleff's plan shows roofed areas instead of rooms. Because some roofs probably covered more than one room, a precise room count cannot be derived from his plan. As mapped by Mindeleff in 1885, Lower Pescado village had 65 one-story roofed spaces, 9 two-story roofed spaces, and 23 unroofed room spaces. These figures yield a minimum of 106 room spaces in the settlement, but the actual number of rooms was probably slightly higher. In 1885, 78 percent of the estimated number of rooms were being occupied or maintained.

Population Estimate. Cushing's 1880 census of Zuni enumerated 580 people associated with the farming village of Pescado (Holmes 1983). It is not known how many of these people actually resided at the farming village during the growing season, but it is likely that most of them did so at least part of the year. Some people had an association with more than one farming village and probably maintained buildings at each of the settlements they used (Fewkes 1891: 102). A few Zuni (for example, priests) may have been associated with a farming village but resided primarily in Zuni Pueblo in order to fulfill their religious and social responsibilities. If all 580 people affiliated with Pescado occupied the 83 roofed buildings, there would have been 6.99 persons per room. Probably the number of rooms is underestimated and the number of people in residence at one time is overestimated, and the actual number of persons per room in a momentary occupation of the settlement was less.

Temporal Placement. Eight tree-ring dates from standing buildings at Lower Pescado range from 1807 to 1931 (Rothschild and Dublin 1995, Appendix C). Four of these dates are from the 1890s and two dates are from the twentieth century. None of the tree-ring samples from Lower Pescado produced cutting dates.

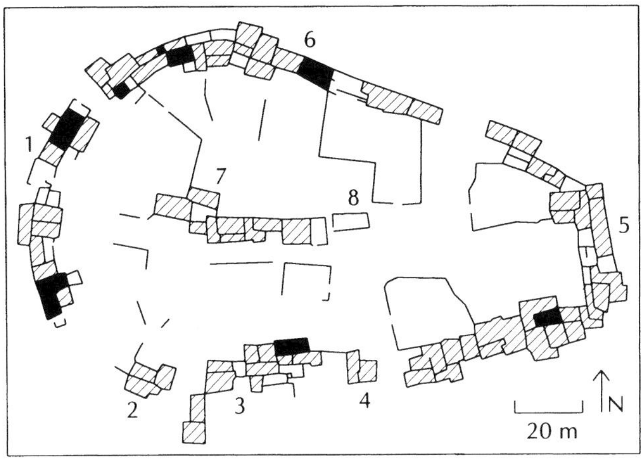

Figure 4.22. Lower Pescado in 1885, with occupied one-story buildings shown with hatching and second-story rooms shown with solid black.

Lower Pescado was occupied as a village until about 1921 (Ferguson 1985: 101). By this time the streambed of the Rio Pescado had been deeply eroded and access to the settlement across the river became impossible during parts of the year when there was high water flow in the narrow, incised channel. After 1921, most new houses in the Pescado district were constructed in a dispersed settlement along the highway on the south side of the Pescado valley and in a more concentrated settlement upstream adjacent to the springs in an area that came to be called Upper Pescado. Today only three standing buildings exist at Lower Pescado and these are used for storage (Rothschild 1991: 27; Rothschild and Dublin 1995: 19–21). The settlement mapped by Mindeleff has been reduced to low rubble mounds.

Discussion. Victor and Cosmos Mindeleff (Item 2621) mapped Lower Pescado on October 13 and 14, 1885. Their plan of the settlement was published without a scale, and it was their field notes that were used to calculate the scale of the published plan and to check architectural details during digitization of the map. The Mindeleffs' field map was produced on three sheets of graph paper using a scale of one inch to twenty feet (1:240). To calculate the scale of the published plan, several walls were measured in different portions of the field plan and compared to the published map. The measured scale of the published plan varied between 1:571 to 1:607 in different portions of the map, and it seemed reasonable to set an average scale of 1:600 for the digitized map.

Figure 4.23. Lower Pescado village in 1912. (Photograph by D. E. Winchester, Number 191, U.S. Geological Survey Library, Denver, Colorado.)

The historic farming village at Lower Pescado (Fig. 4.23) was built on top of a fourteenth-century pueblo, and it is thought that the historic configuration of the village closely conformed to the prehistoric settlement plan (Kintigh 1985: 55; Dublin and Rothschild 1994: 91–93). A stratigraphic profile of archaeological deposits exposed in the north bank of the Rio Pescado revealed a level of sterile sands separating the prehistoric and historic levels of the site. This stratigraphy was interpreted as indicating a hiatus between the prehistoric and historic occupations (Ferguson 1985: 193–196).

Mindeleff (1891: 95–96) observed wall fragments of carefully executed masonry that he thought formed part of the external wall of the prehistoric pueblo. He noted that this outer wall probably stood at full height surrounding the pueblo at one time. By 1885 the Zuni had constructed new buildings or refurbished prehistoric rooms to yield the plan in Figure 4.22. The nineteenth-century pueblo was constructed entirely of stone masonry. Several external stone steps provided access to the upper stories. A number of dome-shaped bread ovens were located outside the walls. Mindeleff (1891: 96) found no evidence of any kivas at Lower Pescado.

Mindeleff (1891: 94–95) wrote that "abandoned and roofless" houses were prevalent at Lower Pescado in 1885. His plan shows 23 such spaces, constituting 22 percent of the total number of spaces in the complex.

The Zuni name for the settlement, rendered variously as Hesh-o-ta-tzina, He-sho-ta-tsi'-na-kwe, or Hé'shâkta-tsína, is taken from a large boulder covered with petroglyphs that is in the vicinity of the spring at what is now known as Upper Pescado. Cushing (1920: 126) translated the Zuni name as "People of the Pictured Town." Curtis (1926: 93) translated it more literally as "ruin picture."

OJO CALIENTE

Site Numbers. ZAP:NM:13:A:33; LA 68910.

Synonymy. Ojo Cahente (Fewkes 1891, Map); Aguas Calientes (Bandelier 1890a: 133); Aguas calientes de Zuñi (Bandelier 1892a: 29); K'iap'-kwai-na-kwe, Los Ojos Calientes (Cushing 1920: 127, 363); Ky'áp-qaina (Curtis 1926: 93); Kyapkwainakwin (Hodge 1966: 280); K'ya'na'a, K'yapkwayina'a (Ferguson and Hart 1985: 125).

Sources of Maps. Mindeleff (1891, Plate 73); Borchers (1979a).

Elevation. 1,908 m.

Landform. Ojo Caliente is situated at the mouth of Plumasano Wash where it flows into the Zuni River valley. The village is at the southwestern base of a large mesa forming the north side of the valley draining Plumasano Wash, located on elevation contours that are 6 m to 12 m above the adjacent floodplain. There are three major springs in the vicinity of the village.

Architectural Arrangement. Ojo Caliente consists of multiple room blocks dispersed in a linear arrangement following the base of the mesa adjacent to the settlement. In 1885 there were 31 houses or room blocks in the village, configured in two clusters (Fig. 4.24). The plan of the village in 1979 (Fig. 4.25; see also Fig. 4.26) is similar to the 1885 plan, but with only 30 room blocks or architectural units. The eight smallest architectural units (6, 8, 9, 10, 12, 16, 18, and 20) represent outhouses, sheds, and small storage structures rather than houses. An *acequia* defines the southern edge of the settlement and a road runs through the center of the village. Corrals, pens, bread ovens, and roads are not depicted in Figure 4.25 to provide a plan with information comparable to that presented by Mindeleff.

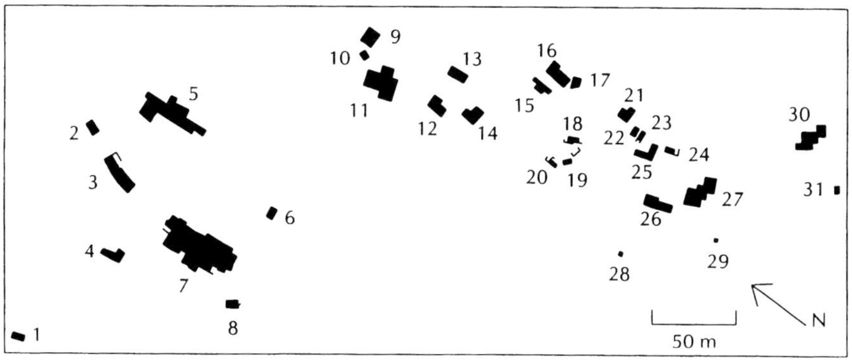

Figure 4.24. Plan of Ojo Caliente in 1885 (after Mindeleff 1891, Plate 73).

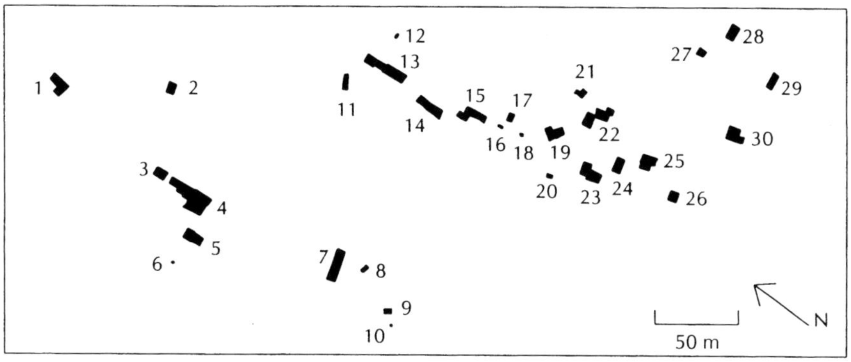

Figure 4.25. Plan of Ojo Caliente in 1979 (after Borchers 1979a).

Figure 4.26. Ojo Caliente in 1978. (Photograph by Perry Borchers, courtesy of the Zuni Heritage and Historic Preservation Office.)

Table 4.4. Stem and Leaf Display of Tree-ring Dates from Ojo Caliente

Decade	Year (underlined numbers represent cutting dates)
195	3
194	122
193	3
192	01223456666667899
191	000112222233334445555555666666667777799
190	01111112222223355577
189	00000000111111222222 44 555555 6666666 7777777777 8888888888888 999
188	0001222333 44 555566777 8888888999999999
187	0124455566666 7777888888 99999
186	022333566777 88 999
185	015555688
184	056899
183	4678
182	88
181	13
180	3456
179	44
178	
177	2256
176	4678
175	37
174	7
173	
172	6

Dimensions. 205 m by 531 m (1885); 197 m by 459 m (1979).

Room Estimate. Mindeleff's plan of Ojo Caliente in 1885 shows roofed areas rather than rooms, making a precise room count difficult. His plan depicts a minimum of 94 one-story rooms, of which 67 were roofed and apparently in use. The plan of Ojo Caliente in 1979 depicts 49 roofed spaces in 22 houses or room blocks, all one story.

Population Estimate. Cushing's 1880 census enumerated 440 people affiliated with the village of Ojo Caliente (Holmes 1983). Assuming there were 67 occupied rooms in 1885, this estimate yields a total of 6.57 persons per room. For the same reasons discussed for the population estimate of Lower Pescado, however, probably the ratio of persons per room was slightly less. The population of Ojo Caliente in 1979 is difficult to determine, because the primary use of the settlement was characterized by diurnal commuting from Zuni Pueblo, and only a few older people resided in the village during the summer.

Temporal Placement. The most reliable information for dating the occupation of Ojo Caliente comes from tree-ring dates derived from 261 roof beams and lintels collected in 1979 from 36 rooms in 16 buildings (Ferguson and Mills 1988). In the stem and leaf display in Table 4.4, the numbers in the bar charts are actual values rather than symbols. The stem represents decades and the leaves represent years within that decade; underlined leaves are cutting dates.

The tree-ring dates from Ojo Caliente range from 1726 to 1953. A cluster of dates in the 1700s represents reused wood from earlier structures in the vicinity of Ojo Caliente that was incorporated into the construction of later buildings. A second cluster of tree-ring dates from the 1820s to the 1890s, with a mode in the 1890s, records the development of Ojo Caliente as one of the three principal farming villages in the nineteenth century and documents a substantial amount of construction activity at the village around the time it was recorded by the Mindeleffs. A third cluster of tree-ring dates from 1900 to the 1920s, with a mode in the 1910s, represents a major episode of reconstruction at Ojo Caliente in the early twentieth century. The dates from the 1930s to the 1950s generally reflect the repair of structures.

Discussion. Mindeleff's plan of Ojo Caliente was published without a scale. The field notes of Victor and Cosmos Mindeleff (Item 2621) contain two sheets showing the room blocks at a scale of 1:240 and a series of

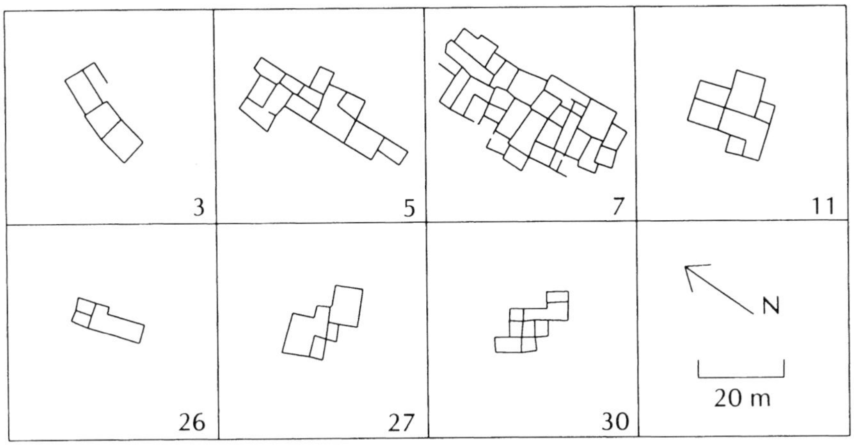

Figure 4.27. Plans of the principal architectural units at Ojo Caliente in 1885.

sheets depicting the entire village at a scale of 1:960. The average scale of the published plan was 1:746 and this value was used to set the scale of the digitized plan. The Mindeleffs recorded Ojo Caliente from September 23 to 25, 1885.

Borchers (1979a) plan of Ojo Caliente in 1979 is a photogrammetric map prepared at Ohio State University using aerial photography exposed on April 19, 1979, by Koogle and Pouls Engineering of Albuquerque. This map was drawn at a scale of 1:720. It was produced for an architectural and ethnohistorical study of the farming villages conducted by the Zuni Archaeology Program.

The earliest buildings at Ojo Caliente were constructed on the elevated rocky slopes of the mesa in a defensive position. These buildings were in an advanced state of decay in 1885 and today have been reduced to low foundations and rubble mounds. Mindeleff thought there had been a gradual relocation of houses to lower, more open sites as defense from Apache incursions became less of a problem. He observed that "The distribution of houses over sites of varying degrees of inaccessibility, suggests a succession of approaches to the occupation of the open and unprotected valley" (Mindeleff 1891: 96).

The plans of the seven largest room blocks at Ojo Caliente in 1885 are illustrated in Figure 4.27. The number of roofed and unroofed spaces in these buildings is listed in Table 4.5. The other architectural units shown on the 1885 plan contained from one to three roofed or unroofed spaces. Only two room blocks (Units 5 and 7) in 1885 contained more than ten roofed and unroofed spaces.

In 1885 Mindeleff (1891: 96) described the stone masonry of the village as "carelessly constructed," with less adobe plastering than at Zuni Pueblo. Virtually every building in the village was reconstructed or extensively remodeled in the early twentieth century. Many of the twentieth-century houses were built in a labor intensive, ashlar masonry style with heavily dressed and closely fitted elements. Others were constructed of adobe, including one house built after Hodge's excavation of Hawikku that reportedly used adobe bricks from the seventeenth-century Catholic mission at that site (Mills and others 1982: 44).

Table 4.5. Number of Roofed and Unroofed Spaces in the Principal Architectural Units at Ojo Caliente in 1885

Unit	Number of Roofed Spaces	Number of Unroofed Spaces
3	2	1
5	9	2
7	20	8
11	4	2
26	2	1
27	3	1
30	2	6

Mindeleff (1891: 96) observed that a large portion of the settlement was "untenanted" and described the inhabited village as including only "the large cluster toward the eastern extremity of the group, and the adjoining houses situated on the low, level ground. . . . " If roofed spaces are interpreted as maintained rooms in active use, then 71 percent of all spaces were being occupied in 1885.

In 1979 there were nine fewer houses at Ojo Caliente than there were in 1885, and these houses contained fewer rooms. The largest buildings in 1979 (Units 4 and 15) contained only five roofed spaces. Most of the buildings standing that year had between one and three rooms. The architectural units in 1979 were dispersed over an area approximately the same size as the area of

Figure 4.28. Unit 8 at Ojo Caliente in 1979. (Photograph by Barbara J. Mills.)

the village in 1885, resulting in more open space within the boundaries of the settlement.

At the time of Mindeleff's survey, several families were planning to occupy Ojo Caliente throughout the year, resorting to the parent village only during important ceremonials and festivals. In 1891 Fewkes reported that a few families stayed at Ojo Caliente during the winter (Fewkes (1891: 97–98). Full-time habitation at Ojo Caliente was never undertaken by more than a few individuals, however, and throughout the occupation of the settlement most people continued to reside in Zuni Pueblo during the late fall and winter.

In 1979 the basic observational unit during field recording was termed the "locus." The loci at Ojo Caliente and the other farming villages documented in 1979 often incorporated multiple buildings and were defined using ethnographic information to determine feature sets associated with individual households or family groups (Mills and others 1982). Because comparable information was not available for most of the other sites in this study, a more archaeological approach was taken in enumerating buildings such that each freestanding structure was considered as a separate architectural unit (Fig. 4.28). For comparability, information about roofed and unroofed structures for both 1885 and 1979 were derived solely from map analysis. Mills and her colleagues (1982) made more detailed observations about roofed and unroofed structures in 1979 than were made in 1885, resulting in slight differences in the values for this variable between their study and this research.

Three loci comprising wheat threshing areas paved with flat stones are at the edges of Ojo Caliente. Two are on the east side of the village on flat portions of the ridge forming the mesa escarpment and the third is at the northwest edge of the settlement. These threshing areas were not included in the analysis.

Cushing (1920: 127) said K'iap'-kwai-na-kwe, the Zuni name for Ojo Caliente, meant "People of the Town Whence the Hot Water Flows." Curtis (1926: 93) provided a more literal translation as "Hot-water come-out." This name derives from one of the major springs located in the vicinity of the village.

UPPER NUTRIA

Site Numbers. ZAP:NM:12:S2:60; LA 48682.

Synonymy. To-y-a, Toya (Bandelier 1892b: 340); Tâ'-ia-kwe, Las Nutrias, Tâi'ya (Cushing 1920: 126, 363); Táya-qin (Curtis 1926: 93).

Sources of Maps. Mindeleff (1891, Plate 67); Borchers (1979b).

Elevation. 2,079 m.

Landform. Upper Nutria is at the end of a gently sloping ridge forming part of the northwestern base of Mexican Hill, a small butte in the Rio Nutria valley. It is about 150 m east of Rio Nutria and 500 m southwest of the Hogbacks, a sharp anticlinal limestone ridge. The village is about 6 m above the floodplain of the Rio Nutria.

Architectural Arrangement. In 1885 Upper Nutria comprised two clusters of buildings (Fig. 4.29). Four large room blocks in a cluster at the west end of the village were arranged in a curving arc open to the southwest. Two additional room blocks in this cluster were positioned west of the arc, enclosing an open space within the cluster. A second cluster of four small buildings was located east of the large cluster. In 1979 Upper Nutria comprised 20 dispersed room blocks whose configuration bore little resemblance to that in 1885 (Fig. 4.30).

Dimensions. 106 m by 194 m (1885); 127 m by 256 m (1979).

Room Estimate. Mindeleff's plan in 1885 depicts 35 occupied one-story roofed areas, 7 occupied two-story roofed areas, and 25 unoccupied room spaces. The calculated minimum number of rooms at Upper Nutria in 1885 was 74, of which 49 (66 percent) were occupied. As Mindeleff (1891: 96) observed, there were many "abandoned and ruined rooms." In 1979 there were 45 discernible room spaces at Upper Nutria, most of which were in an advanced stage of disintegration. Only 14 (31 percent) of the total rooms mapped in 1979 were being maintained.

Population Estimate. Cushing's 1880 census enumerated 473 people affiliated with the village of Upper Nutria (Holmes 1983). Assuming there were 49 occupied rooms in 1885, this estimate yields a total of 9.65 persons per room. For the reasons discussed in the population estimate of Lower Pescado, the ratio of persons per room was undoubtedly less. The population using Upper Nutria in 1979 is difficult to determine because the primary use of the settlement was characterized by diurnal commuting from Zuni Pueblo and only one sheep herder actually resided in the village.

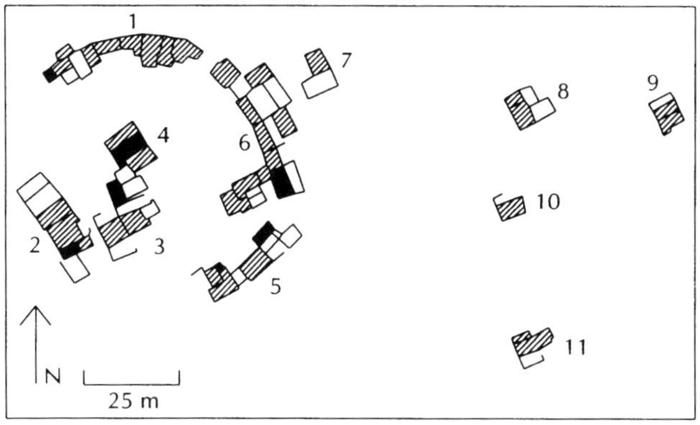

Figure 4.29. Plan of Upper Nutria in 1885; occupied one-story buildings are shown with hatching and second-story rooms with solid black (after Mindeleff 1891, Plate 67).

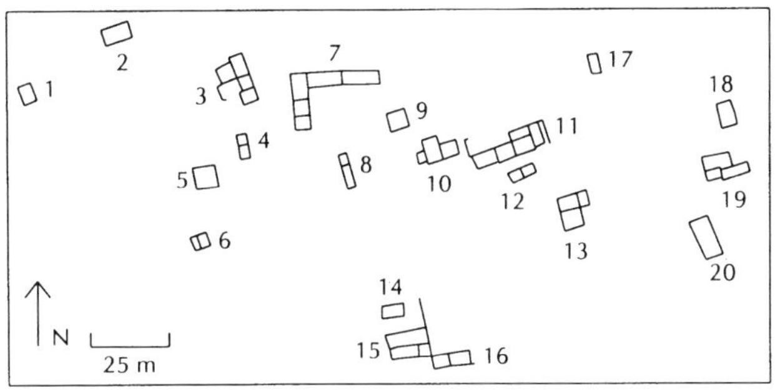

Figure 4.30. Plan of houses at Upper Nutria in 1979 (after Borchers 1979b).

Temporal Placement. The occupation of Upper Nutria is dated by tree-ring samples from 170 roof beams and lintels (Table 4.6) that were collected in 1979 from 22 rooms in 12 buildings (Ferguson and Mills 1988). The tree-ring dates from Upper Nutria range from 1771 to 1953. The early dates represent wood reused from earlier structures in the vicinity of the village. There are four modes in the dates from the nineteenth and twentieth centuries. Two modes represent the development of the settlement as a principal farming village in the mid-nineteenth century, and the other two represent substantial periods of reconstruction in the 1890s and the 1920s to 1930s. The lack of tree-ring dates after 1953 indicates the time when the Zuni stopped investing labor and materials in the maintenance of buildings at Upper Nutria.

Discussion. Mindeleff's plan of Upper Nutria was published without a scale. The field notes of Victor and Cosmos Mindeleff (Item 2621) contain one sheet depict-

Table 4.6. Stem and Leaf Display of Tree-ring Dates from Upper Nutria

Decade	Year (underlined numbers represent cutting dates)
195	0011222333
194	13336779
193	122244 5555555 6777 88
192	0022 3446 777 88 99
191	02347799
190	58
189	00011122233333 4444 5555666666 77977 88888 999
188	01344455555 89999
187	0347
186	002 56788
185	000357999
184	4
183	13488
182	28
181	366667
180	47
179	36
178	044
177	112

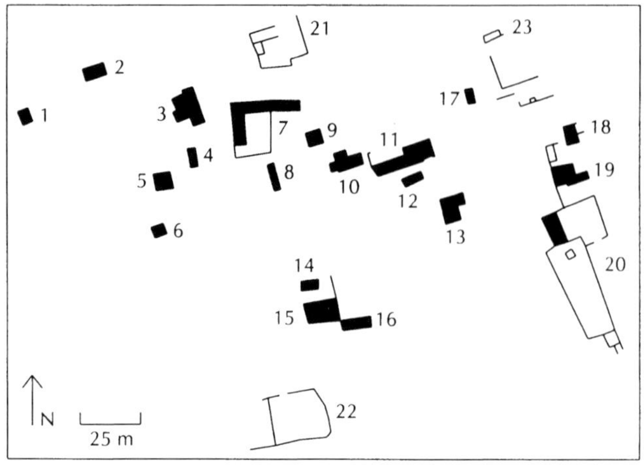

Figure 4.31. Plan of houses, corrals, and fences at Upper Nutria in 1979 (after Borchers 1979b).

ing the site at a scale of 1:240. The average scale of the published plan was determined to be 1:480; this value was used to set the scale of the digitized plan.

Borchers's (1979b) photogrammetric map of Upper Nutria in 1979 was drawn at a scale of 1:360, using aerial photography exposed on April 19, 1979 by Koogle and Pouls Engineering of Albuquerque. Additional information about room spaces and maintained buildings at Upper Nutria was derived from field notes made by the Zuni Archaeology Program in 1979.

Like Lower Pescado, Upper Nutria is built on top of a large prehistoric pueblo occupied in the late thirteenth and early fourteenth centuries (Kintigh 1985: 45). The available archaeological information indicates that there was a hiatus between the prehistoric and historic occupations of the settlement. Mindeleff (1891: 94) described the plan of Upper Nutria in 1885 as approximating the form of the underlying prehistoric pueblo, and in one figure depicts what he characterized as "ancient masonry" along the curving wall of the room block at the north edge of the site. The rubble remains of the nineteenth- and early twentieth-century structures that have collapsed or been dismantled at Upper Nutria have obscured the remains of the prehistoric pueblo. Today it is primarily the prehistoric ceramics in the artifact assemblage that attest to the presence of an earlier component.

To provide comparability with Mindeleff's plan, Figure 4.30 depicts only buildings at Upper Nutria, but there are a number of corrals and fences within the settlement as well (Fig. 4.31). Other features at the site include bread ovens, wood piles, and a circular area of stone pavement used for threshing wheat (Rothschild 1991: 29–30); they were not included in the analysis and are not depicted on the figures. The dimensions of the settlement, including the corrals, are 197 m by 270 m. The spatial syntax of Upper Nutria in 1979 is analyzed in Chapter 5 using both the plan showing only buildings and the plan showing buildings and corrals.

Tree-ring dates reveal several episodes of major reconstruction or rehabilitation of the village. The masonry styles changed though time, although the composition of the basic building elements (sandstone blocks) remained the same. New masonry styles, use of milled lumber, larger fenestration, and glass windows changed the appearance of the architecture (Figs. 4.32, 4.33). A more fundamental difference was effected in the plan in the twentieth century as the relatively large and tightly clustered room blocks were replaced with smaller houses dispersed over a larger area.

Cushing (1920: 126, 363) translates Tâi'ya, the Zuni name for Upper Nutria, as "People of the Planting Town" or "Place of Planting." Curtis (1926: 93) simply translates it as "planting place."

Figure 4.32. Upper Nutria village about 1901. (Photograph by N. H. Darton, Number No. 873, U.S. Geological Survey Library, Denver, Colorado.)

Figure 4.33. Building in Upper Nutria in 1979, showing adjacent activity and storage area. (Photograph by Barbara J. Mills.)

LOWER NUTRIA

Site Numbers. Pending.

Source of Map. Borchers (1979c).

Elevation. 2,067 m.

Landform. Lower Nutria is 2.4 km (about 1.5 miles) southwest of Upper Nutria. It is on a gentle slope at the base of a mesa on the west side of the Rio Nutria valley. This topographic position elevates the village above the adjacent floodplain. Blind Canyon Draw flows into Rio Nutria immediately to the east of Lower Nutria.

Architectural Arrangement. Lower Nutria in 1979 comprised 18 scattered buildings interspersed with 6 major corrals and fences, and additional corrals and animal pens were outside the area illustrated in Figure 4.34. The houses were arranged in two clusters. The south cluster coincided with a contour that followed an approximate east-west axis. The north cluster was upslope on the high point of the land.

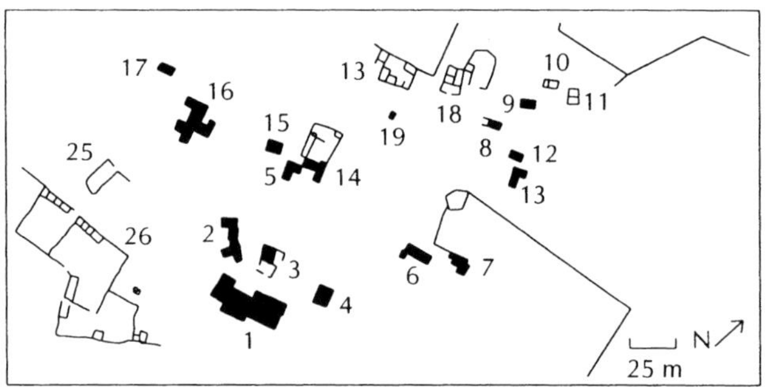

Figure 4.34. Lower Nutria village in 1979; buildings are shown with solid black.

Dimensions: 202 m by 411 m.

Room Estimate. Of the 60 rooms in the 17 buildings that are interpreted as habitations, 28 were occupied or maintained in 1979. Additional rooms in the form of small sheds and storage structures were appended to corrals, but they were not quantified in this room count.

Population Estimate. A reliable population estimate for Lower Nutria is not available. Assuming a similar range in the number of persons per room as that determined for the other farming villages and only 60 percent occupancy of the rooms at any one time, a maximum population of Lower Nutria is estimated between 237 to 347 persons. The actual number of inhabitants at any particular time was probably less.

Temporal Placement. Lower Nutria first appears on maps in 1912. The fact that it was not recorded by the Mindeleffs indicates the village was founded between

Table 4.7. Stem and Leaf Display of Tree-ring Dates from Lower Nutria

Decade	Year
193	0001
192	33479988
191	002444455
190	8
189	558
188	456
186	15
184	6

1885 and 1912. The 31 tree-ring dates from 4 buildings at Lower Nutria support the idea that the village was established after 1880 (Rothschild and Dublin 1995, Appendix C) and suggest that there was substantial construction in the 1910s and 1920s (Table 4.7). The subsequent occupation of Lower Nutria mirrors that of Upper Nutria. Today the village is used primarily on a diurnal basis.

Discussion. Borchers's (1979c) photogrammetric map of Lower Nutria was drawn at a scale of 1:480 using aerial photography exposed on April 17, 1979. An acequia runs through the southern portion of the village. Bread ovens and other small architectural features at the settlement were not analyzed and are not depicted in Figure 4.34. All the houses at Lower Nutria were one story. Some of the architectural units housed more than one family (Rothschild 1991: 27). In 1989 a single house was being used at Lower Nutria on a regular basis (Rothschild and others 1993: 136).

ZUNI PUEBLO

Site Numbers. ZAP:NM:K3:1; LA 9093.

Synonymy. Halona, Hal-onan (Bandelier 1890a: 335, 337); Hal-o-na-wan (Fewkes 1891: 100); Hallonawa (Kroeber 1917: 202; Spier 1917: 227); Shiwwanakwe, I'tiwawa (Kroeber 1917: 202); Halona:wa North (Kintigh 1985: 69).

Sources of Maps. Mindeleff (1891, Plate 76); Kroeber (1917, Maps 6 and 7); Stubbs (1950: 93); Borchers (1972); Dederich (1978a).

Elevation. 1,920 m.

Landform. The core architecture of Zuni Pueblo (Fig. 4.35) is situated on the crest and slopes of a small knoll on the north bank of the Zuni River. During the last century, the pueblo has grown to encompass an area larger than 500 ha (1,235 acres) on the alluvial valley floor on both sides of the Zuni River.

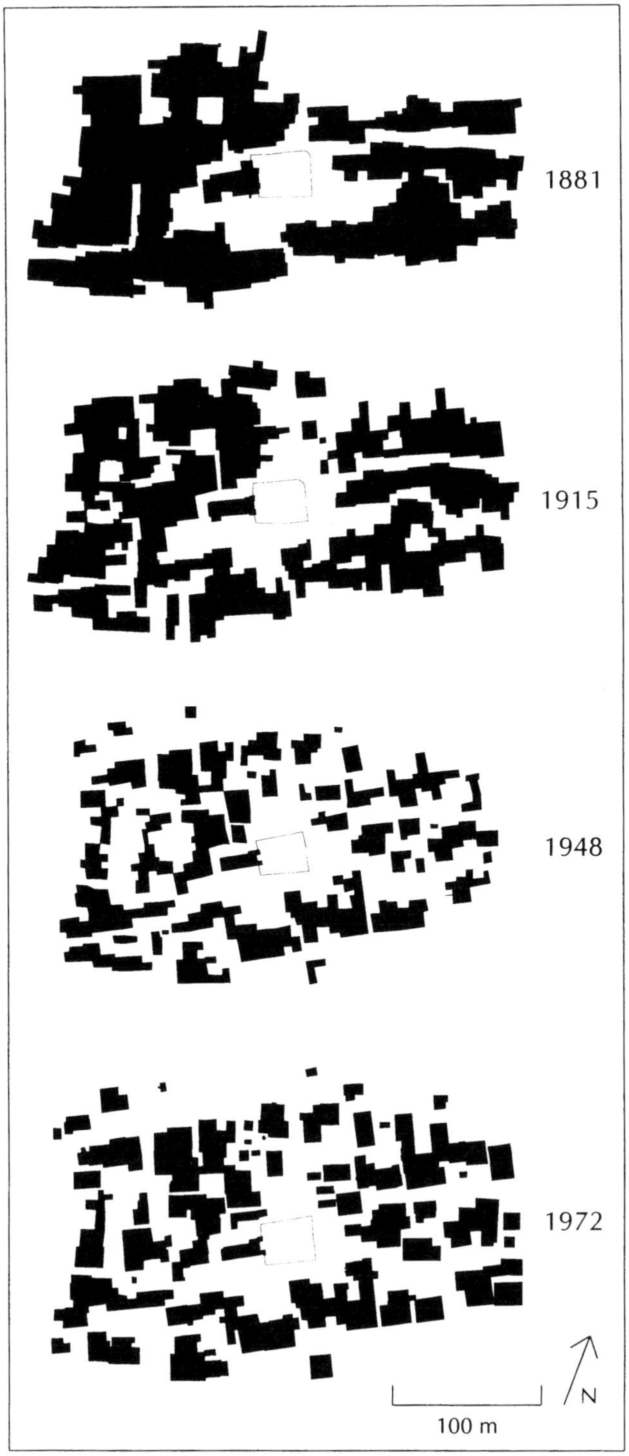

Figure 4.35. Block diagrams of the core architecture in Zuni Pueblo between 1881 and 1972.

Architectural Arrangement. In 1881 the core architecture of Zuni Pueblo consisted of four, large, irregularly shaped room blocks arranged around four plazas and a number of narrow streets. Access into the pueblo was restricted and there was little open space within the pueblo interior. Large corrals ringed the pueblo on all sides. In the twentieth century, the massive room blocks in the pueblo core were reconstructed into smaller buildings with more open space between them. At the same time, new houses were built in a suburban pattern outside the pueblo core (Figs. 4.36, 4.37).

The size of the room blocks and houses in Zuni Pueblo and its suburbs gradually decreased as single-family dwellings became more common than multi-family units. Through time, the arrangement of buildings in the suburbs has been increasingly oriented toward streets and roads.

Dimensions. The core architecture was 202 m by 357 m in 1881; 201 m by 378 m in 1915; 231 m by 346 m in 1948; and 230 m by 337 m in 1972. The full extent of the settlement as analyzed here was 883 m by 1,073 m in 1915 and 2,058 m by 2,463 m in 1978.

Room Estimate. There are no reliable estimates for the number of rooms at Zuni Pueblo for any specific time. The plans of Zuni Pueblo depict roofed areas rather than rooms, and a single roof often covered multiple rooms. The fact that the late nineteenth- and early twentieth-century room blocks in the pueblo core were multistoried introduces additional difficulty in estimating the number of rooms. Because houses were built terraced up the sides of the knoll, many rooms were concealed deep within the massive buildings and the floors of adjacent houses were often at different levels. This arrangement resulted in a situation where a two-story house often sat next to a three-story house, with both appearing to be part of the same terrace (Mindeleff 1891: 97).

Mindeleff's plan of the core architecture in 1881 (Fig. 4.38) indicates approximately 406 roofed spaces, 5 of which were in apparent disrepair because roof beams are depicted in whole or in part as opposed to a completely plastered roof surface. Three room spaces were unroofed. The count is approximate because Mindeleff shows a number of walls that do not extend fully across a roofed space; whether these were counted as one or two spaces depends on the interpretation of other attributes, such as the configuration of the space, the extent of the wall, and roof features. Mindeleff's plan uses four or five shades of gray to illustrate the various terraces supporting the roofed areas. The darkest shade of gray evidently depicts the lowest terrace and the lightest shade of gray the highest terrace. This shading cannot be used by itself, however, to determine the number of stories that the roof covered. The terraces

Figure 4.36. Suburbs of Zuni Pueblo in 1915.

Mindeleff illustrates were roofs at the same approximate elevation, and these roofs did not always cover buildings with the same number of stories. The roofs surrounding the interior of the small plaza in the most massive room block, for instance, are depicted in the second gray level but historic photographs clearly show these rooms to be only one-story (Mindeleff 1891, Plate 82). The gradation of gray within a particular terrace also varies across the plan, which makes consistent interpretation problematical.

The number of stories for most of the roofed areas depicted in Mindeleff's plan could be determined through an intensive analysis of contemporaneous photographs, but this information was not needed for the analysis of space syntax. Assuming that 50 percent of the 401 roofed spaces covered two stories and 25 percent covered three stories, a minimal estimate of 701 rooms is derived. Because many roofed spaces covered more than one room, this is a low estimate, and there were undoubtedly many more rooms than this in Zuni Pueblo in 1881.

Kroeber's plan of Zuni in 1915 has 469 roofed areas in the core architecture of Zuni Pueblo (Fig. 4.39). Many rooms on the upper terraces of Zuni Pueblo had been dismantled by 1915, and ground-story houses had become more prevalent. Although there is more open space within the plan, several of the room blocks were expanded by the construction of new rooms at their perimeters, resulting in an increase in the number of roofed spaces. Several room blocks had encroached on the area formerly used for corrals. Assuming that 30 percent of the roofed areas covered two stories and that 10 percent covered three stories, a minimal room estimate of 657 rooms is derived. Because many of the roofed areas covered more than one room, this is a low estimate.

The estimated number of roofed areas or rooms in the core of Zuni Pueblo in 1915 must be considered in relation to the number of houses occupied in the newly constructed suburbs. Kroeber (1917: 109–123) documented a total of 220 families at Zuni in 1915, of which 139 lived in the core pueblo and 81 lived in the suburbs. There were only 52 vacant houses in the core pueblo, and Kroeber interpreted the difference between the number of these vacant houses and the number of houses in the suburbs as representing an increase of 30 families. Kroeber's figures indicate that 37 percent of the core architecture was not being occupied in 1915.

The plan of the core architecture of Zuni Pueblo in 1948 depicts 254 roofed spaces (Fig. 4.40). Stubbs (1950: 93) documented that only two of these roofed spaces were two stories; the rest were one story. The estimated minimum of 256 rooms in the core architecture in 1948 is low, because many of the roofed spaces

Figure 4.37. Suburbs of Zuni Pueblo in 1978.

depicted in Figure 4.40 covered more than one room. The plan of the core architecture of Zuni Pueblo in 1972 depicts 217 roofed areas, all of which were one story (Fig. 4.41). Most of these roofed areas covered more than one room, so there were more than 217 rooms in the core architecture in 1972.

Population Estimate. Virtually all the Zuni maintained a residence at Zuni Pueblo, so the population estimates graphed in Figure 3.2 represent the population of the village. In 1880, the year before the core architecture was mapped by the Mindeleffs, the population of Zuni was enumerated by Cushing as 1,493 (Holmes 1983). In 1915 Kroeber (1917: 123) counted a population of 1,664 persons. In 1947, the year before Stubbs mapped the core architecture, the population of Zuni Pueblo was 2,552; in 1972 the population had doubled to 5,155 persons (Hart 1991a: 60).

Temporal Placement. The analysis of ceramics from Zuni Pueblo indicates a settlement was established on the north bank of the Zuni River sometime before A.D. 1300, but that its major occupation began about 1450 (Kintigh 1985: 70; Ferguson and Mills 1987: 243–244).

Figure 4.38. Plan of the core architecture in Zuni Pueblo in 1881, showing room blocks and corrals (after Mindeleff 1891, Plate 76).

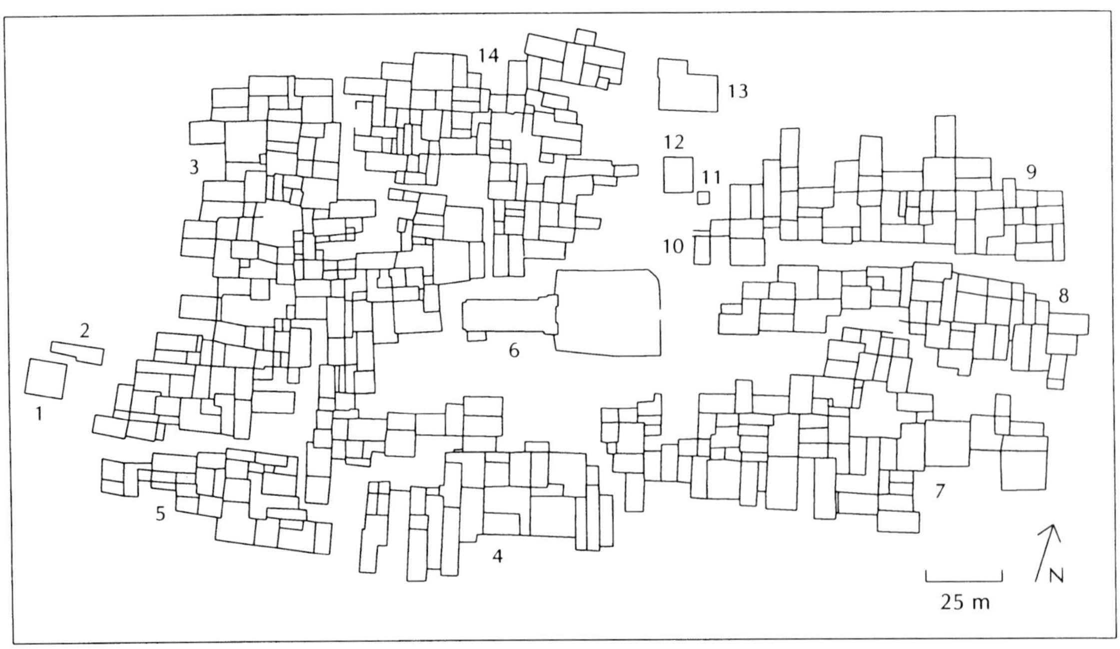

Figure 4.39. Plan of the core architecture in Zuni Pueblo in 1915 (after Kroeber 1917, Map 7).

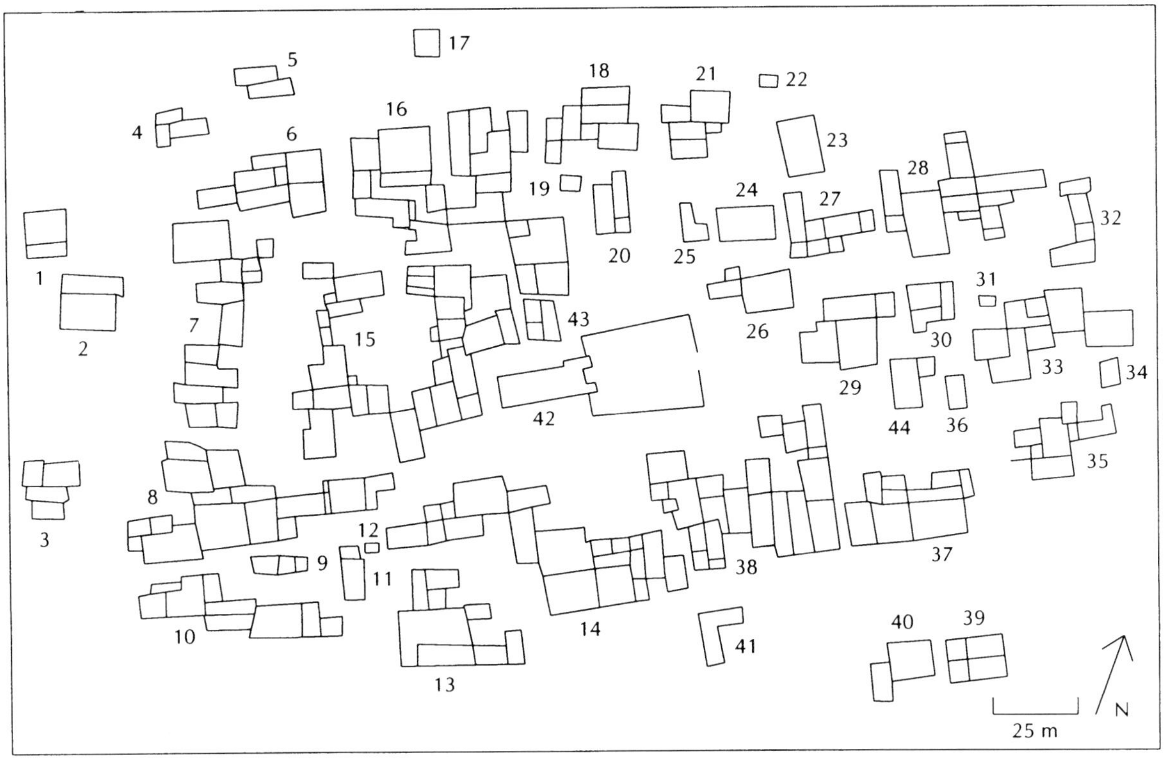

Figure 4.40. Plan of the core architecture in Zuni Pueblo in 1948 (after Stubbs 1950: 93).

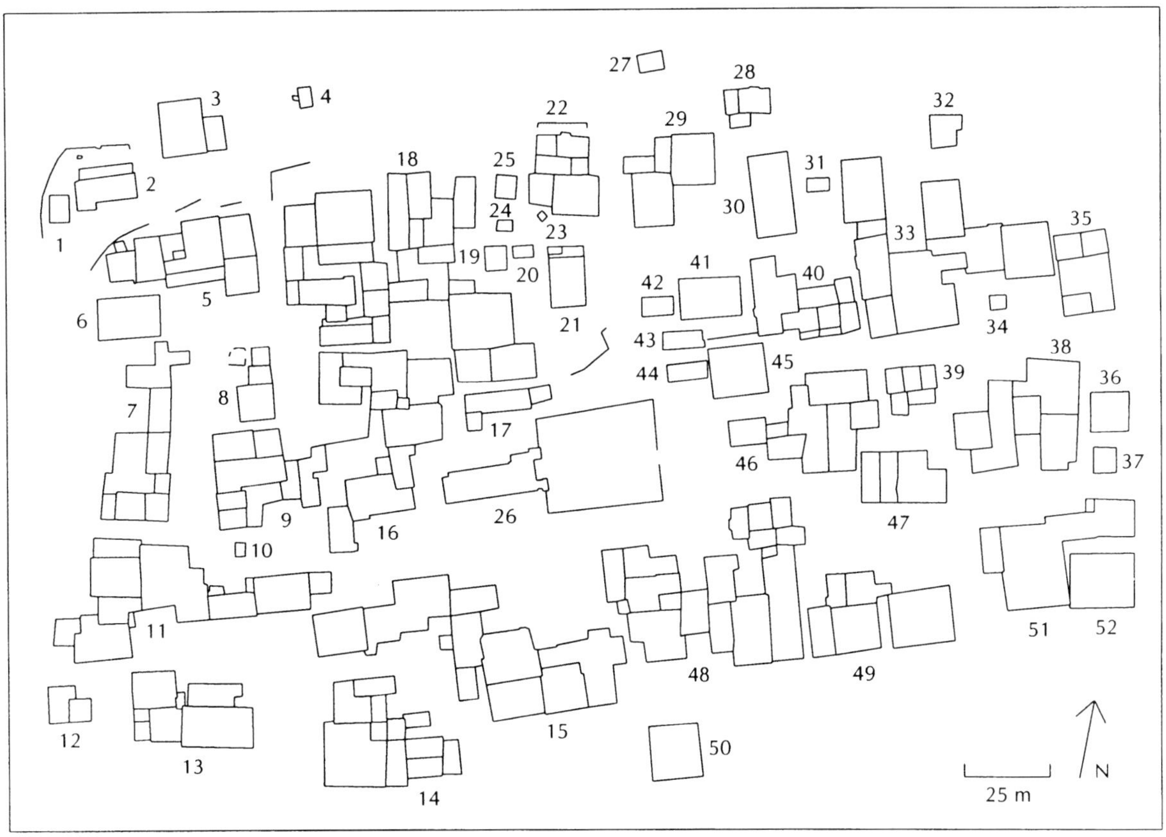

Figure 4.41. Plan of the core architecture in Zuni Pueblo in 1972 (after Borchers 1972).

There is another large, plaza-oriented pueblo on the south bank of the Zuni River that was occupied about A.D. 1275 to 1325. The recent growth of Zuni Pueblo has encompassed the site of this earlier pueblo, called Halona:wa South (Kintigh 1985: 45–48). The pueblo on the north bank of the river was occupied during the Spanish Entrada of 1540, at which time it was known as Halona:wa, and it remained inhabited until the Pueblo Revolt of 1680. In 1693, following the Pueblo Revolt, Halona:wa was the only contact period village reoccupied by the Zuni. The village became known as Zuni Pueblo and has been continuously occupied since then.

Discussion. The Mindeleff plan of Zuni Pueblo in 1881 was produced using a compass and tape and was primarily intended to record information that could be used to produce a scale model of the pueblo for the Smithsonian Institution (Mindeleff 1891: 44–45). Mindeleff's plan was published without a scale or north arrow. Kroeber (1917: 190–194) computed the scale of Mindeleff's map at 1:516 and produced a plan of the core architecture in 1915 at this scale with a north arrow that can be used to orient Mindeleff's plan. Kroeber's plan was surveyed with a transit; the exterior walls of the buildings were measured with a chain, and the interior walls were plotted using a stadia rod to measure distances. Kroeber noted that his plan ignored the deviations from straight lines that characterized many Zuni walls.

Stubb's plan of the core architecture of Zuni Pueblo in 1948 was produced using an aerial photograph with the scale established by measuring structures at the settlement (Stubbs 1950: xii). The 1948 plan is published at a scale of 1:3250. Borchers's (1972) plan of the core of Zuni Pueblo in 1972 is a photogrammetric map plotted at the scale of 1:480 using aerial photography exposed by the New Mexico State Highway Department in September, 1972. The plan of the suburbs of Zuni Pueblo in 1978 was drawn by Devon Dederich (1978a, 1978b: 5) for the National Park Service using a series of 1:6000 scale aerial photographs of Zuni Pueblo to produce a planimetric map of all houses, corrals, and gardens at an approximate scale of 1:3000.

The architectural history of Zuni is reviewed in detail by Mindeleff (1891:97-99), Kroeber (1917: 198–205), Bunting (1976: 31-51), and Ferguson and Mills (1987) and is not recapitulated here. The discussion instead focuses on the settlement patterns relevant to the analysis of spatial syntax.

The Zuni name for the village, Halona:wa, means "ant place." It is derived from *Halo*, the Zuni word for red-ant (Ferguson and Mills 1987: 247). It is interesting that many non-Indians who visited Zuni Pueblo in the nineteenth century compared the core architecture to an immense beehive or anthill (Whipple 1856: 68; Stevenson 1881: 9).

Several scholars have commented on the defensive character of nineteenth-century Zuni architecture. In the traditional Zuni history recounting the movement to Zuni Pueblo following the Pueblo Revolt of 1680, Stevenson (1881: 26) states:

> A grand council of all of the Pueblos of the vicinity was held, and it was decided, after long and grave deliberation, to adopt a style of architecture which seemed to promise the end they had in view -- their desire being to hold the position they occupied. They determined to build their houses one upon another, so that the topmost tier would give them a good lookout, while the consolidation of buildings would afford strong fortification in case of attack.

Stevenson (1881: 26) added that however defective or inaccurate this tradition may be in some particulars, the necessity for adequate defense of the community from the attacks of their enemies undoubtedly gave rise to the manner in which the Zuni constructed their houses.

Mindeleff (1891: 97) thought the "defensive efficiency" of Zuni Pueblo came from its well-planned and well-constructed buildings arranged in a remarkably compact configuration that grew through accretion. In achieving this arrangement, Mindeleff noted that the stone masonry dwellings in the oldest part of the pueblo, centered around the two small plazas in the northwest quadrant, were subject to spatial constraint from the landform beneath them. The spatial constraints on lateral growth in this location led to the vertical expansion of the village, and five distinct terraces were constructed in this part of the pueblo. Mindeleff (1891: 97) observed:

> The summit of the knoll upon which the older portion of Zuni has been built is so uneven, and the houses themselves vary so much in dimensions, that the greatest disparity prevails in the height of the terraces. A three-terrace portion of a cluster may have but two terraces immediately alongside, and throughout the more closely built portions of the village the exposed height of terraces varies from 1 foot to 8 or 10 feet.

Mindeleff (1891: 99) thought the kivas and other ceremonial rooms used in meetings of various religious orders and esoteric societies were "crowded into the innermost recesses" of the most ancient portion of Zuni Pueblo during the Spanish period, presumably to protect their activities from the purview of Spanish authorities.

When Zuni Pueblo was expanded after the Pueblo Revolt to incorporate the population of the entire tribe, new room blocks were added south and east of the original pueblo, running down the hill slope to the flat land at its base (Mindeleff 1891: 97–98). These room blocks were initially built almost entirely of adobe brick manufactured in standardized forms, a construction technique introduced by the Spaniards when the Catholic mission was built in the seventeenth century (Ferguson and Mills 1987: 247). The Catholic mission was originally located at the edge of the pueblo on a trash mound (Spier 1917: 228; Caywood 1972), but it came to occupy a spatially central position when the largest plaza of the village was formed by the arrangement of the south and east room blocks.

Although the terraces of Zuni are often described as being oriented along cardinal north-south and east-west axes (Bunting 1976: 45; Ferguson and Mills 1987: 248), in actuality the settlement has a vertical axis that is 18 degrees west of north. The horizontal axis of the village thus extends along a northeasterly-southwesterly direction rather than true east-west. The orientation of the axes is primarily a symbolic rather than a true cardinal directionalism. Nonetheless, the rooftop terraces of Zuni Pueblo in the nineteenth century were built to take advantage of the optimal southern and eastern exposures for passive solar heating.

The orientation of the rooftop terraces along consistent axes resulted in a fundamental uniformity in the plan of the pueblo, but the varying configuration of individual roofs introduced many distinct spaces. Dohm's (1992) analysis of the architecture and portable artifacts documented in nineteenth-century maps and photographs conclusively demonstrated that changes in the elevation of rooftop terraces, partial enclosure by walls of various heights, and the visibility of extramural areas from room interiors all worked to mark privacy in Zuni Pueblo.

The eastern room blocks were lower than the buildings at the crest of the hill and were not as densely clustered. During the dramatic reconstruction of Zuni Pueblo in the late nineteenth and early twentieth centuries, the east room blocks were razed and new stone houses were built to replace them. The adobe construction in this area facilitated redevelopment, as the walls were easily knocked down and the adobe construction elements were pulverized and smeared into horizontal clay deposits using horse-drawn scrapers. In the original room blocks of stone masonry located around the two small plazas, rooms were converted to open space by cutting roofs and collapsing them into the interior of room columns and then filling the area with trash or clean sand (Ferguson and Mills 1987: 253).

Kroeber (1917: 195) wrote about the Zuni custom of rehabilitating old structures or building new houses for the annual Shalako ceremony and the important impact it had on the rate and character of architectural change:

> People apparently vie with each other to make their houses as imposing as possible on this occasion, and the result is that every year the front or main living rooms of eight different houses are with few exceptions pulled down to be rebuilt on an enlarged scale. The degree to which this custom leads to alterations has possibly been intensified in recent years. Under present conditions, the feeling is of sufficient strength to bring about that the exterior walls of nearly every house in Zuni are altered in the course of thirty or forty years.

During the last century, Shalako has resulted in the construction or rehabilitation of 600 to 800 houses at Zuni Pueblo (Ferguson and Mills 1987: 256).

Although the Zuni first became incorporated into a "world system" during the Spanish period (Hall 1989: 50–74), it was not until the construction of the transcontinental railroad in 1881 through Gallup, New Mexico, 40 miles north of Zuni that the Zuni gained access to an abundant source of new construction materials for use in vernacular architecture (for example, milled lumber and glass windows). After 1881, several different masonry and fenestration styles became successively popular and the appearance of the pueblo greatly changed. Plastered tabular sandstone buildings with small selenite windows were replaced with unplastered ashlar sandstone buildings with larger, six-pane glass windows, and these were followed by the currently popular cinder block buildings with aluminum sliding windows.

Even though the structure and appearance of Zuni Pueblo has changed dramatically in the last century, there are a number of enduring architectural features of cultural importance. Scholars interested in how architecture represents culture have noted that the spatial organization of Zuni Pueblo reflects the affirmation of the Puebloan world view through ritual and ceremony (Saile 1982; Huang 1985), and, in fact, the reconstruction of Zuni Pueblo has centered around the preservation of the open space used for the performances of kachina dances and other rituals. Much of the continuity in the spatial arrangement of the room blocks results from the inviolability of the sacred areas; they have been enlarged but rarely encroached upon. The sacred dance plazas are the most stable spaces in the village, and the reorganization of space in the pueblo has been oriented toward their integrity as open spaces. Similarly, the roofs surrounding the plazas are still used as public space for viewing dances (Ferguson and Mills 1987: 262).

Open space in the core architecture of Zuni Pueblo has greatly increased, but the basic outlines of the older room blocks can still be discerned. At the same time, the size of individual buildings has decreased. As documented in Table 4.8, the average size of room blocks as measured by the number of contiguous roofed spaces decreased from 101.50 spaces in 1881 to 4.17 spaces in 1972. Regarding these calculations, it should be noted that Mindeleff (1891, facing page 97) divided the core architecture into eight units, which yields an average of 50.75 roofed spaces per room block. Using the criterion applied in this study wherein all contiguous roofs constitute a single building, there are only four distinct room blocks. Regardless of how the 1881 plan is partitioned, there is a clear trend at Zuni Pueblo toward a larger number of smaller buildings with more open space surrounding them in the core architecture.

Kroeber's (1917: 103–123) investigation of Zuni kin and clan in relation to the spatial organization of the architecture of Zuni Pueblo revealed that related families often resided in adjacent houses, but there was no localization of clans in the village. Clans were dispersed throughout the settlement and their social solidarity did not derive from their spatial location.

Kroeber (1917: 198, Maps 5 and 6) elucidated an interesting movement to the suburbs (Fig. 4.42) based on a directionalism congruent with a family's original placement in the pueblo. Kroeber noted that when families moved their residences to the suburbs they generally settled in that part of the village that corresponded to the section of town they originally occupied. All the new houses in the suburbs faced inward with their doors toward the village core. The inward-facing orientation of the settlement was thus retained even as it was greatly expanded.

Kroeber (1917: 121) thought the movement to the suburbs resulted as much from the development of neolocal households as from a lessening of the need for defense in the pueblo core. In the new residential patterns that were developing in the early twentieth century, husbands often built new houses for their wives and families. Whereas sisters generally occupied adjoining houses in the pueblo core, in the suburbs adjoining houses were sometimes occupied by a set of brothers. Multistoried family architectural units were common at Zuni in 1915, and the 81 families living in the suburbs occupied 52 buildings (Kroeber 1917: 117–123). Another 16 buildings in the suburbs were used for stores, missions, schools, and government offices.

Table 4.8. Average Number of Roofed Spaces per Building in the Core Architecture at Zuni Pueblo

Date	Number of Room Blocks	Number of Roofs	Mean
1881	4	406	101.50
1915	14	469	33.50
1948	44	254	5.77
1972	52	217	4.17

Prior to the 1930s, the locations of roads and paths seemed to have little bearing on the positioning of new houses (Dederich 1978b: 15, 18, 24). Once houses were built, roads and paths to them subsequently appeared on later aerial photographs. By the 1930s, a rectangular grid of roads and irrigation canals had been superimposed on the earlier radial pattern of roads and trails that emanated from the core architecture (Dederich 1978b: 14–16). After the 1930s, there was a tendency to place houses along roads and utility corridors. With the exception of a few HUD subdivisions, there has not been any zoning by housing type or time period. There is a mix of old and new buildings, and vernacular and commercial housing, throughout the settlement. Even though there is a well-established road network, aerial photographs in 1978 show numerous foot trails, bike paths, and two-track roads that cross-cut and make interconnections throughout the rectangular grid of paved roads (Dederich 1978b: 23–24).

The houses built recently at Zuni are oriented more to streets and roads than are the earlier buildings. Because the road grid runs approximately parallel to the major axes of the core architecture, many new houses on the east and west edges of the village face north or south rather than toward the pueblo core. The suburbs of Zuni Pueblo have today merged with the community of Blackrock 6.4 km (4 miles) east of the pueblo core. In 1978 this conurbation was not as pronounced as it is today, but the delineation of the suburbs as mapped in Figure 4.37 is still somewhat arbitrary. There were additional houses in Zuni Pueblo east of the area depicted in Figure 4.37. The course of the Zuni River clearly divides the settlement into northern and southern halves.

Figure 4.42. Zuni Pueblo about 1912, showing suburbs on the south bank of the Zuni River. (Photograph by Jesse Nusbaum, Negative No. 61721, Museum of New Mexico.)

The 1,354 structures outlined in Figure 4.37 encompass a wide range of Zuni architecture, including houses, outbuildings, sheds, corrals, animal pens, and gardens. Eight neighborhoods bounded by streets and roads were selected to analyze the spatial syntax of the suburbs in 1978. The smallest structures interpreted as animal pens and other minor architectural features were deleted from the analysis. Six of the sampled suburban areas primarily contain vernacular architecture with only minor in-fill of HUD housing, and these samples are consequently referred to as vernacular suburbs. The remaining two areas are recent HUD subdivisions.

Sample 1 (Fig. 4.43) encompasses 64 structures northwest of the core architecture of Zuni Pueblo. The 78 structures in Sample 2 are situated immediately northeast of the core architecture. Sample 3 includes 71 structures located directly east of the core architecture on the north side of Zuni River.

Sample 4 comprises 97 structures on the south bank of the Zuni River in an area that includes the Halona Plaza store, the Christian Reformed Mission, and the Halona:wa South archaeological site, as well as many vernacular buildings. The 71 structures in Sample 5 are in an area immediately northwest of the HUD subdivision in the southwest corner of the settlement. Sample 6 includes 29 structures situated along the south bank of the Zuni River at the west edge of the village. Sample 7 is a HUD subdivision in the southwest corner of the settlement that contains 66 houses constructed in the late 1960s. The HUD subdivision in Sample 8 at the southeast corner of the settlement contains 37 houses built in the late 1970s.

In conclusion, the architectural history of Zuni Pueblo reveals that architectural change has largely occurred in a piecemeal fashion, with each family building, repairing, demolishing, and often rebuilding its own indi-

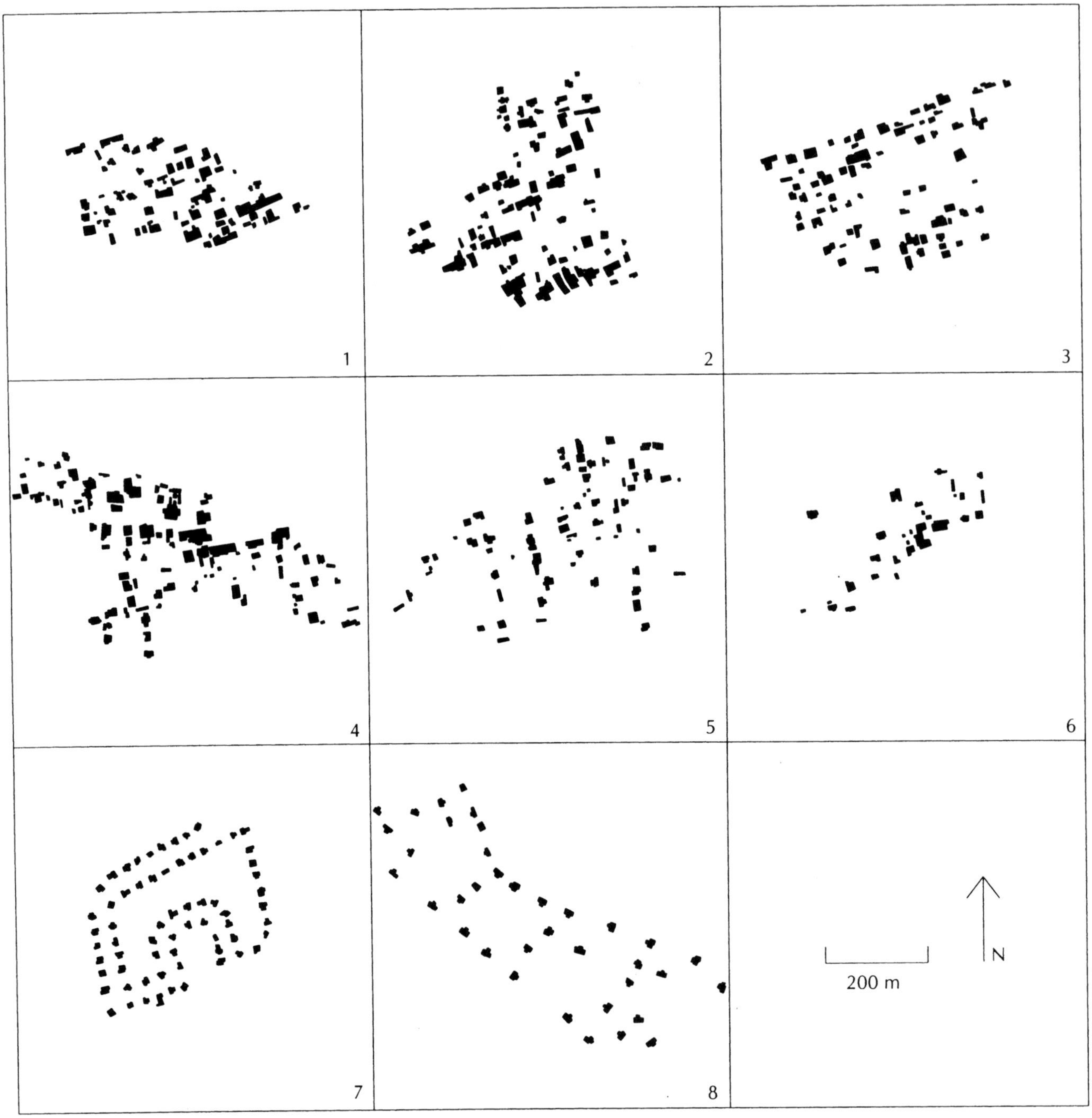

Figure 4.43. Zuni suburbs in 1978 selected for the analysis of space syntax.

vidual dwelling. The vernacular architecture of Zuni Pueblo incorporates a marvelous individuality while a uniform aesthetic provides continuity. There is a coherent global structure to the settlement plan that derives from many different individual actions rather than from any central planning. The increase in the amount of commercial housing has indelibly altered the arrangement of buildings and open spaces within the village, but a substantial amount of vernacular architecture is still being constructed at Zuni Pueblo.

CHAPTER FIVE

Organization of Open Space in Historic Zuni Settlements

The primary focus of analyzing variation in the organization of open space at historic Zuni settlements is to identify structural change through time and to generate new information about Zuni architecture and society. Secondarily, the syntactic measures of open space developed by Hillier and Hanson (1984) are evaluated to determine which measures have methodological utility in the study of Puebloan architecture. The analysis is organized to address four basic questions:

What variation exists in the open space structure of Zuni settlements?

Does the open space structure of Zuni settlements change through time?

How does the open space structure of Zuni Pueblo differ from the contemporaneous seasonally occupied farming villages?

What does the variation in the open space structure of settlements mean in terms of the social logic of space and structuration theory?

VARIATION IN OPEN SPACE STRUCTURE

The syntactic measures defined in Chapter 2 may be used to analyze the axial and convex dimensions of open space in terms of the spatial relations of distributedness and asymmetry. By reducing site plans to graphs, different spatial relations can be quantified and used to compare the structural layouts of different settlements. The techniques developed by Hillier and Hanson (1984: 82–142) are based on graph theory that describes the structure of open space in terms of (1) the deformation of the grid that is formed by the open space around buildings, and (2) the local and global relations of asymmetry and control in the axial spaces that constitute the routes of access within a settlement.

The number and variety of identifiable architectural features differ between occupied settlements and archaeological sites. Rothschild's (1991) ethnoarchaeological research at the Zuni farming villages demonstrates the role that small architectural features play in the incorporation of the outdoors as living space. These small architectural features include semifixed facilities like outhouses and bread ovens and portable features like wood piles and chairs. The formation processes of the archaeological record tend to obscure these small architectural features as abandoned buildings and other structures are reduced to rubble mounds. For the sake of analytical comparability between archaeological sites and occupied settlements, these small architectural features are generally ignored at occupied villages. The following analysis of open space only incorporates the major architectural units that are best preserved in the archaeological record such as room blocks, enclosures, and walls. The analysis thus concentrates on the global structure of open space within a settlement rather than on the localized use of space by individual households.

Size of Settlements and Amount of Open Space

The quantity of different types of space within historic Zuni settlements is summarized in Table 5.1. The space occupied by room blocks, unroofed enclosures, and open space was measured and the percentage of convex space at each site was calculated. Some sites contain unroofed enclosures that were difficult to classify in terms of the convex space system. These enclosures are defined by low walls or fences with openings that give them direct permeability to the convex space system. Most, but not all, of these enclosures appear to be corrals or other types of animal pens. When the corrals and animal pens were in use they would have constituted a barrier to movement. When not in use, however, there was relatively open access through the corral spaces. I decided to analyze corrals and pens with openings as part of the convex space system because axial lines could penetrate these spaces. Access to the interior spaces of room blocks and to other types of unroofed enclosures would require one or more steps beyond that

Table 5.1. Area of Buildings, Enclosures, and Open Space in Square Meters

Settlement	Room blocks	Unroofed enclosure not open to convex space	Unroofed enclosure open to convex space	Open space	Total area	% of convex space
Hawikku, no church	3,414			13,064	16,478	79
Hawikku, with church	4,503			15,564	20,067	78
Kechiba:wa, no church	4,256			8,695	12,951	67
Kechiba:wa, with church	4,366			8,579	12,945	66
Kyaki:ma	6,590			7,094	13,684	52
Dowa Yalanne	6,983		271	190,570	197,824	96
Kyaki:ma Refuge Site 11	274	352	419	2,492	3,537	82
Kyaki:ma Refuge Site 12	53		533	1,058	1,644	97
Shundekya	17		537	534	1,088	98
Wimaya:wa	517	1,018	1,079	4,208	6,822	77
Heshoda Łuwal'a	945	2,247	1,336	42,993	47,521	93
Lower Pescado 1885	3,648			15,744	19,392	81
Ojo Caliente 1885	2,719			40,943	43,662	94
Upper Nutria 1885	1,633			12,600	14,233	89
Ojo Caliente 1979	1,448			35,883	37,331	96
Upper Nutria 1979, no corrals	1,307			17,370	18,677	93
Upper Nutria 1979, with corrals	1,307	819	1,048	32,091	35,265	94
Lower Nutria 1979, no corrals	1,603			21,949	23,552	93
Lower Nutria 1979, with corrals	1,603	1,934	2,073	52,653	58,263	94
Zuni Core 1881, no corrals	27,201			21,398	48,599	44
Zuni Core 1881, with corrals	27,201		16,944	53,729	97,874	72
Zuni Core 1915 (B)	26,037	1,077		27,297	54,411	50
Zuni 1915, North Suburbs	7,167			201,721	208,888	97
Zuni 1915, East Suburbs	1,326			42,175	43,501	97
Zuni 1915, South Suburbs	3,758			46,238	49,996	92
Zuni Core 1972	21,402			39,634	61,036	65
Zuni 1978, Suburb 1	12,545			63,202	75,747	83
Zuni 1978, Suburb 2	18,869			97,250	116,119	84
Zuni 1978, Suburb 3	13,322			104,984	118,306	89
Zuni 1978, Suburb 4	19,369			107,794	127,163	85
Zuni 1978, Suburb 5	9,913			114,652	124,565	92
Zuni 1978, Suburb 6	4,520			45,476	49,996	91
Zuni 1978, Suburb 7	8,942			86,545	95,487	91
Zuni 1978, Suburb 8	6,691			128,852	135,852	95

entailed in accessing corrals and pens, that is, up ladders or through doors that had to be opened. Axial lines cannot penetrate these completely enclosed architectural features.

Unroofed enclosures, then, were divided into those spaces with no direct connection (permeability) to the convex space system and those spaces with a direct connection. Unroofed space not connected to the convex space system includes small open spaces within room blocks (for example, in the core of Zuni Pueblo in 1915) and unroofed enclosures with no gates. Identifiable plazas within settlements were analyzed as part of the convex space system (as open space). Spaces classified as unroofed space connected to convex space were added to the area of open space to calculate the percentage of convex space as a proportion of the total area of the settlement.

There is substantial variation in the size of historic Zuni settlements, ranging from Shundekya with an area of 1,088 square meters to Dowa Yalanne with an area of 197,824 square meters (Fig. 5.1). The suburbs of Zuni Pueblo sampled for analysis are even larger, with areas ranging up to 208,888 square meters. Most of the sites are large: 13 are 50,000 square meters or more, and another 10 are between 20,000 and 50,000 square meters. Only 11 sites have areas smaller than 20,000 square meters. The information on site size reveals that, with the exception of the early farming villages, the size

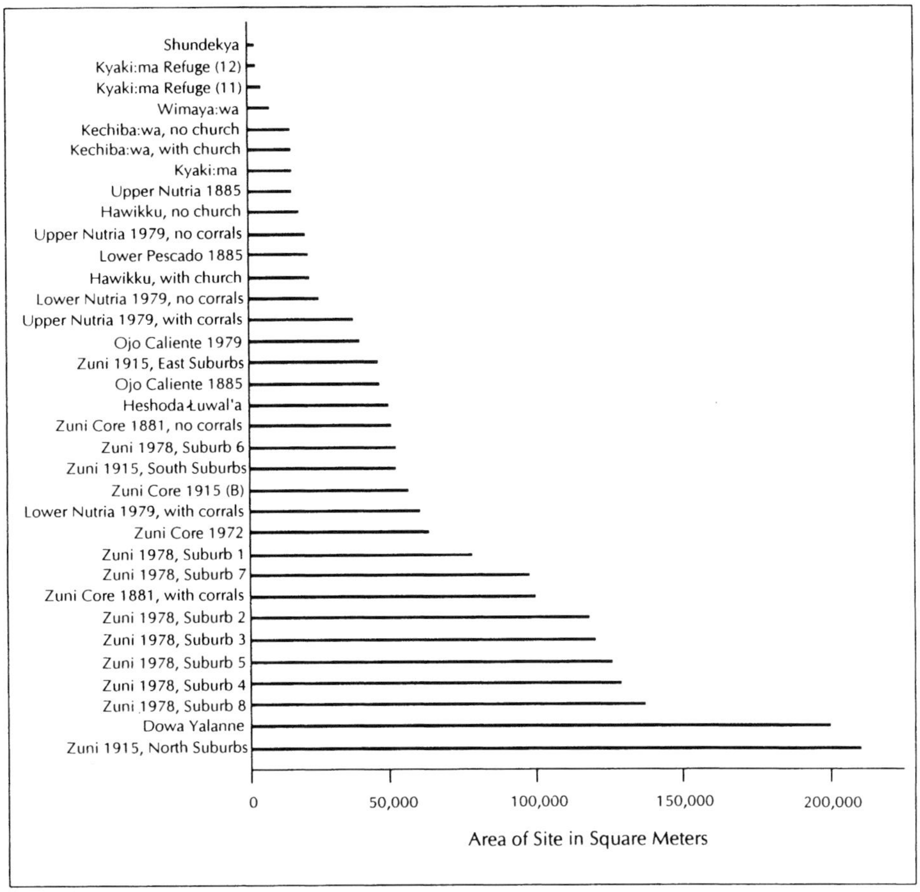

Figure 5.1. Settlement size in rank order.

of historic Zuni settlements has greatly increased through time. It is noteworthy, however, that the later historic settlements contain less area enclosed in room blocks and more open space than do the earlier sites.

The percentage of open space within settlements is illustrated as a bar chart in Figure 5.2, with the settlements presented in rank order from the least to the most open space. This figure graphically illustrates that most Zuni settlements contain a substantial amount of open space between and around buildings and other architectural units: 17 contain more than 90 percent open space, and 7 contain between 80 to 90 percent open space. Only 6 sites contain less than 80 percent open space: the early seventeenth-century sites of Hawikku, Kechiba:wa, and Kyaki:ma; the early farming village of Wimaya:wa; and the core architecture of Zuni Pueblo in 1881 and 1915. Only the core of Zuni Pueblo in 1881 contains less than 50 percent open space.

Syntactic Measures Describing the Open Space Structure as a Grid

A suite of statistics describing the character and deformation of open space in terms of a grid is generated using three variables: the number of "islands," the number of axial spaces, and the number of convex spaces (Table 5.2). Islands are spatially discrete architectural units completely surrounded by open space. The number of architectural units and the number of islands at a settlement are not always the same. Hawikku, Kechiba:wa, Kyaki:ma, Dowa Yalanne, Upper Nutria, Lower Nutria, and Zuni Pueblo have architectural units that are joined by a connecting wall or at the corners of room blocks. The joined architectural units at these sites form a single island, because access between them is blocked and the constituent room blocks are not completely surrounded by open space. At Wimaya:wa, a single architectural unit is interrupted by gates in enclosure walls such that three islands are formed.

Several settlements are analyzed in different configurations: Hawikku and Kechiba:wa are analyzed with and without the Catholic churches; and Upper Nutria, Lower Nutria, and Zuni Pueblo in 1881 are analyzed with and without corrals. The core of Zuni Pueblo in 1915 has several axial spaces that are not connected to the open space system (they are completely contained within room blocks), and it was analyzed with and without these spaces. Zuni 1915 (A) is the village with these spaces and Zuni 1915 (B) without them.

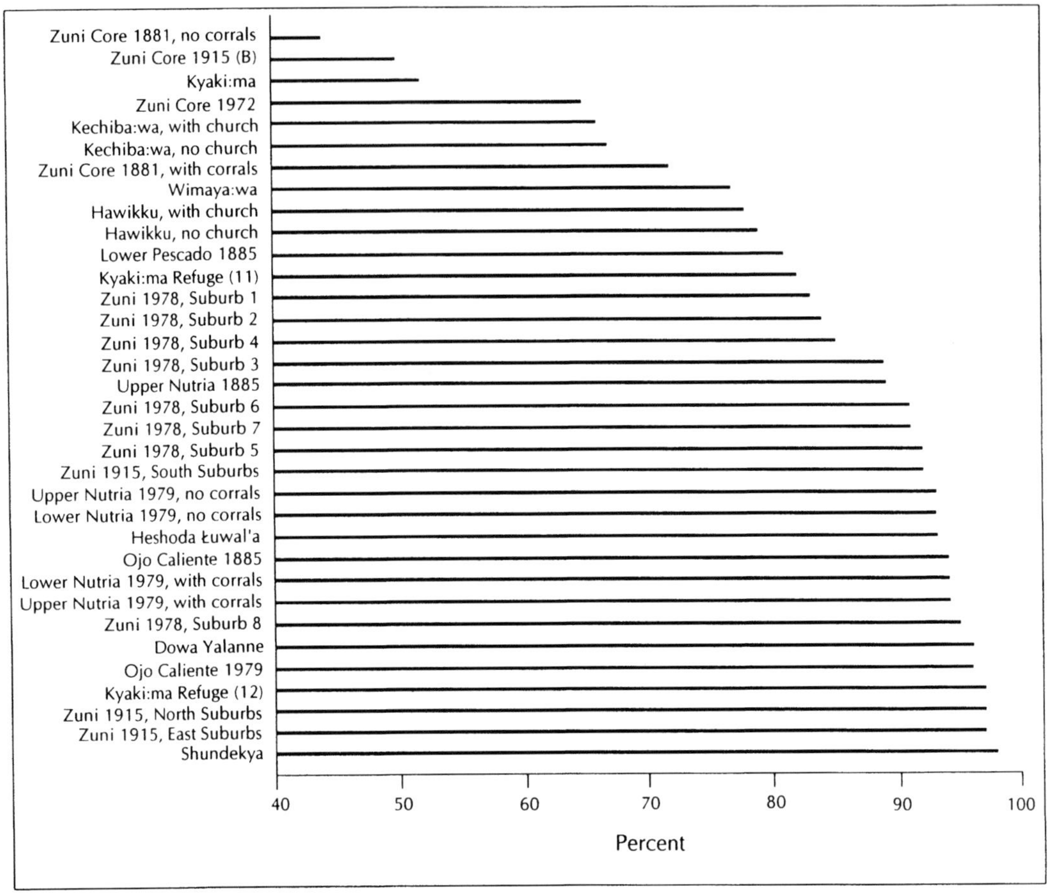

Figure 5.2. Settlements ranked in order of the percentage of open space within them.

Four syntactic measures characterize the graphs derived from the axial lines drawn through the open space of settlements (Table 5.2). The axial space graphs of all the Zuni settlements except the suburbs of Zuni Pueblo are depicted below in Figures 5.26 to 5.33.

The measure of *axial articulation* quantifies the degree to which open space is broken up into axial lines by architectural units. Higher values for axial articulation indicate a greater breakup of axial space. The values of the measure of axial articulation for Zuni settlements are illustrated in rank order from low to high in a bar chart (Fig. 5.3). Most Zuni settlements have a low value for axial articulation. The villages with the highest values (> 10) for axial articulation include the core architecture of Zuni Pueblo in 1881 and Wimaya:wa. Other settlements with relatively high values (> 4) include the core of Zuni Pueblo in 1915, two of the three villages occupied in the early seventeenth century, several early farming villages, and one farming village occupied in 1885.

The measure of *axial integration of convex spaces* compares the number of axial lines to convex spaces in the same way that the measure of axial articulation compares the number of axial lines to the number of architectural units. Figure 5.4 illustrates the values for axial integration of convex spaces in a bar chart with settlements presented in rank order from low to high values. Low values for this measure indicate a higher degree of axial integration of convex spaces and high values a lower degree. Several settlements with high values for axial articulation also have high values for axial integration of convex spaces: the early seventeenth-century village of Kyaki:ma and the early farming villages of Shundekya and Wimaya:wa. However, several other villages with low values for axial articulation have high values for axial integration of convex spaces: Kyaki:ma Refuge Sites 11 and 12. Conversely, several sites with high values for axial articulation have lower values for axial integration of convex spaces, most notably the core architecture of Zuni Pueblo in 1881 and 1915.

Grid axiality is a measure that compares axial spaces to an orthogonal grid. High values for grid axiality indicate stronger approximation to a grid, whereas low values indicate greater deformation of the axial space system. The values for grid axiality are illustrated as a

Table 5.2. Syntactic Measures Relating to the Axial Space Grid

Settlement	n Units	n Islands	n Axial spaces	n Convex spaces	Axial articulation	Axial integration of convex spaces	Grid axiality	Axial ringiness
Hawikku, no church	20	18	46	142	2.3000	0.3239	0.2279	0.2069
Hawikku, with church	21	18	50	159	2.3810	0.3145	0.2097	0.1895
Kechiba:wa, no church	3	1	15	41	5.0000	0.3659	0.2667	0.0400
Kechiba:wa, with church	4	1	17	45	4.2500	0.3778	0.2353	0.0345
Kyaki:ma	3	2	13	27	4.3333	0.4815	0.3714	0.0952
Dowa Yalanne	48	45	35	170	0.7292	0.2059	0.4405	0.6923
Kyaki:ma Refuge Site 11	5	2	10	24	2.0000	0.4167	0.4828	0.1333
Kyaki:ma Refuge Site 12	3	3	12	22	4.0000	0.5455	0.4553	0.1579
Shundekya	1	1	6	11	6.0000	0.5455	0.6667	0.1429
Wimaya:wa	1	3	11	26	11.0000	0.4231	0.4967	0.1765
Heshoda Łuwal'a	10	10	20	73	2.0000	0.2740	0.4162	0.2857
Lower Pescado 1885	8	8	33	100	4.1250	0.3300	0.2320	0.1311
Ojo Caliente 1885	31	31	34	112	1.0968	0.3036	0.3863	0.4921
Upper Nutria 1885	11	10	21	77	1.9091	0.2727	0.3964	0.2703
Ojo Caliente 1979	30	30	21	90	0.7000	0.2333	0.6169	0.8108
Upper Nutria 1979, no corrals	20	20	19	54	0.9500	0.3519	0.5760	0.6061
Upper Nutria 1979, with corrals	24	21	24	64	1.0000	0.3750	0.4652	0.4884
Lower Nutria 1979, no corrals	19	18	16	68	0.8421	0.2353	0.6553	0.6667
Lower Nutria 1979, with corrals	23	23	36	96	1.5652	0.3750	0.3220	0.3433
Zuni Core 1881, no corrals	4	4	59	165	14.7500	0.3576	0.1017	0.0354
Zuni Core 1881, with corrals	19	19	68	230	3.5789	0.2957	0.1576	0.1450
Zuni Core 1915 (A)	14	13	68	235	4.8571	0.2894	0.1355	0.0992
Zuni Core 1915 (B)	14	13	73	215	5.2143	0.3395	0.1262	0.0922
Zuni 1915, North Suburbs	33	33	29	113	0.8788	0.2566	0.4651	0.6226
Zuni 1915, East Suburbs	9	9	8	33	0.8889	0.2424	1.0000	0.8182
Zuni 1915, South Suburbs	26	26	23	80	0.8846	0.2875	0.5303	0.6341
Zuni Core 1972	52	51	86	275	1.6538	0.3127	0.1893	0.3054
Zuni 1978, Suburb 1	64	64	42	172	0.6563	0.2442	0.4286	0.8101
Zuni 1978, Suburb 2	78	78	56	238	0.7179	0.2353	0.3511	0.7290
Zuni 1978, Suburb 3	71	71	50	193	0.7042	0.2591	0.3770	0.7474
Zuni 1978, Suburb 4	97	97	75	299	0.7732	0.2508	0.2893	0.6690
Zuni 1978, Suburb 5	71	71	56	187	0.7887	0.2995	0.3366	0.6636
Zuni 1978, Suburb 6	28	28	19	88	0.6786	0.2159	0.6623	0.8485
Zuni 1978, Suburb 7	37	37	23	123	0.6216	0.1870	0.6159	0.9024
Zuni 1978, Suburb 8	66	66	46	217	0.6970	0.2120	0.3967	0.7586

bar chart in Figure 5.5, with the settlements presented in rank order from lowest to highest values. Eight villages have high values (> 0.5) of grid axiality, including Shundekya, Upper and Lower Nutria in 1979 without corrals, and several of the suburbs of Zuni Pueblo in 1915 and 1978. The most deformed axial space systems are in the core architecture of Zuni Pueblo in 1881, 1915, and 1972.

The distributedness of axial space in a settlement is characterized using the measure of *axial ringiness*. This statistic measures distributedness in terms of the number of rings or circuits in a spatial arrangement as a proportion of the maximum number of planar rings possible given the number of spaces in the settlement. Axial ringiness quantifies the degree to which a global spatial structure encompasses circuitous as opposed to nonintersecting routes between spaces. The values for axial ringiness are shown as a bar chart in Figure 5.6, with the settlements presented in rank order from low to high values. Places with a high degree of distributedness of axial space (> 0.6) include Dowa Yalanne, Upper Nutria in 1885, and most of the suburbs of Zuni Pueblo. Those with low values of axial ringiness (< 0.2) include the early seventeenth-century villages of Kechiba:wa, Kyaki:ma, and Hawikku, several farming villages, and the core of Zuni Pueblo in 1881 and 1915.

Three syntactic measures characterize convex space within settlements in a manner similar to that of axial

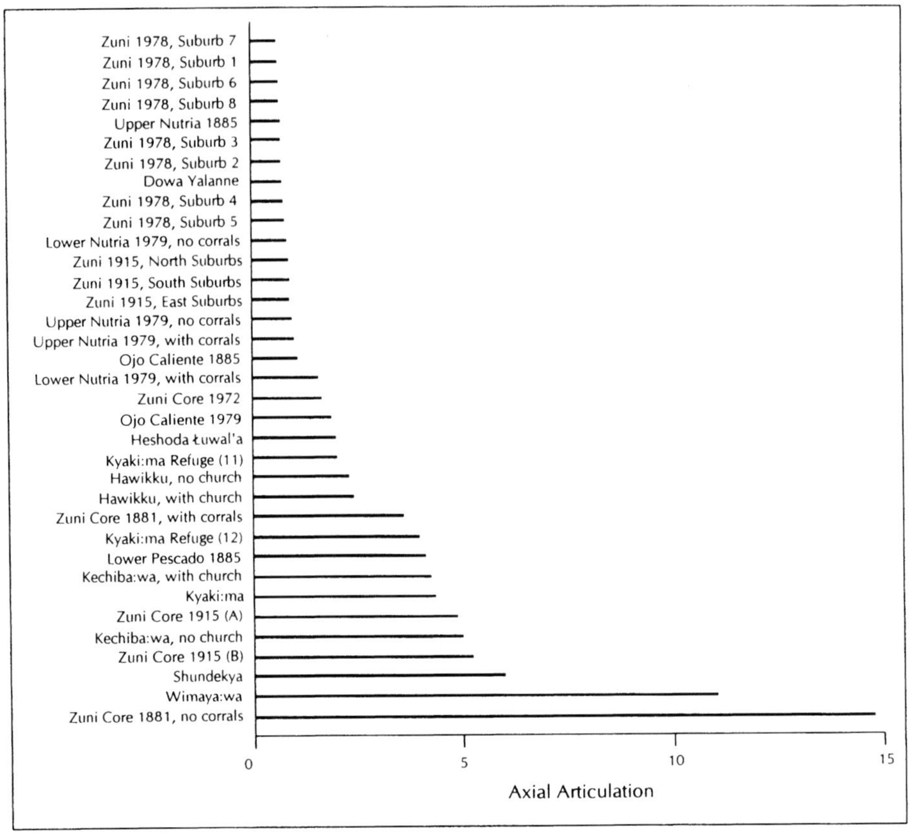

Figure 5.3. Axial articulation values in rank order.

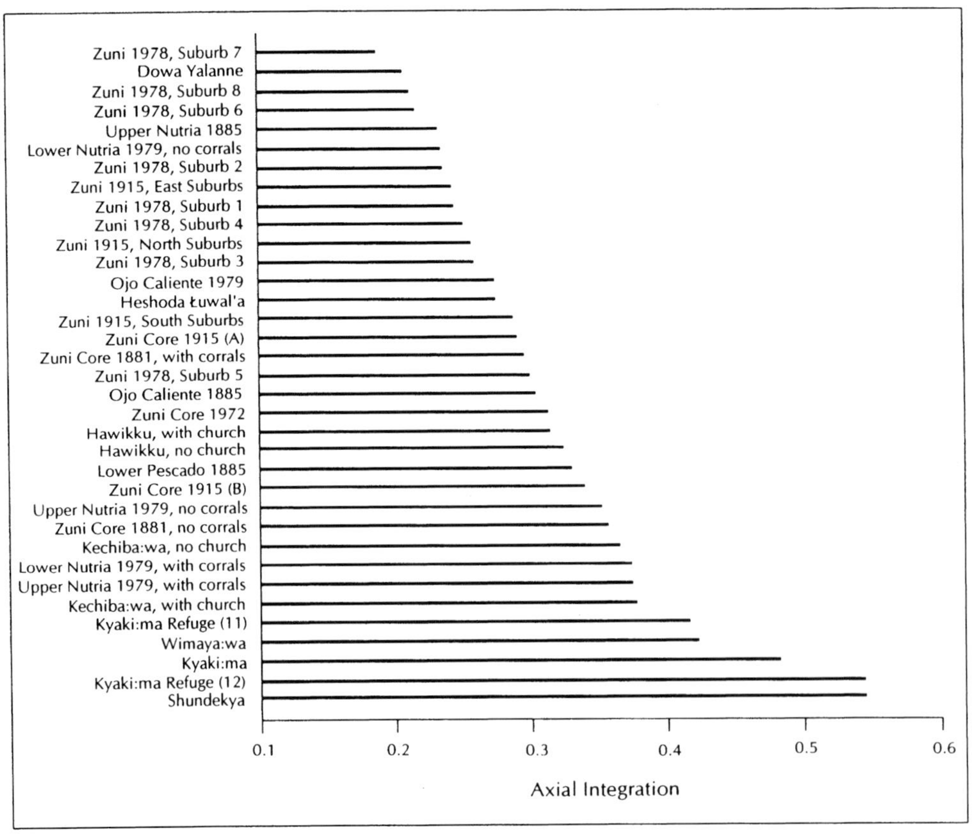

Figure 5.4. Axial integration of convex space values in rank order.

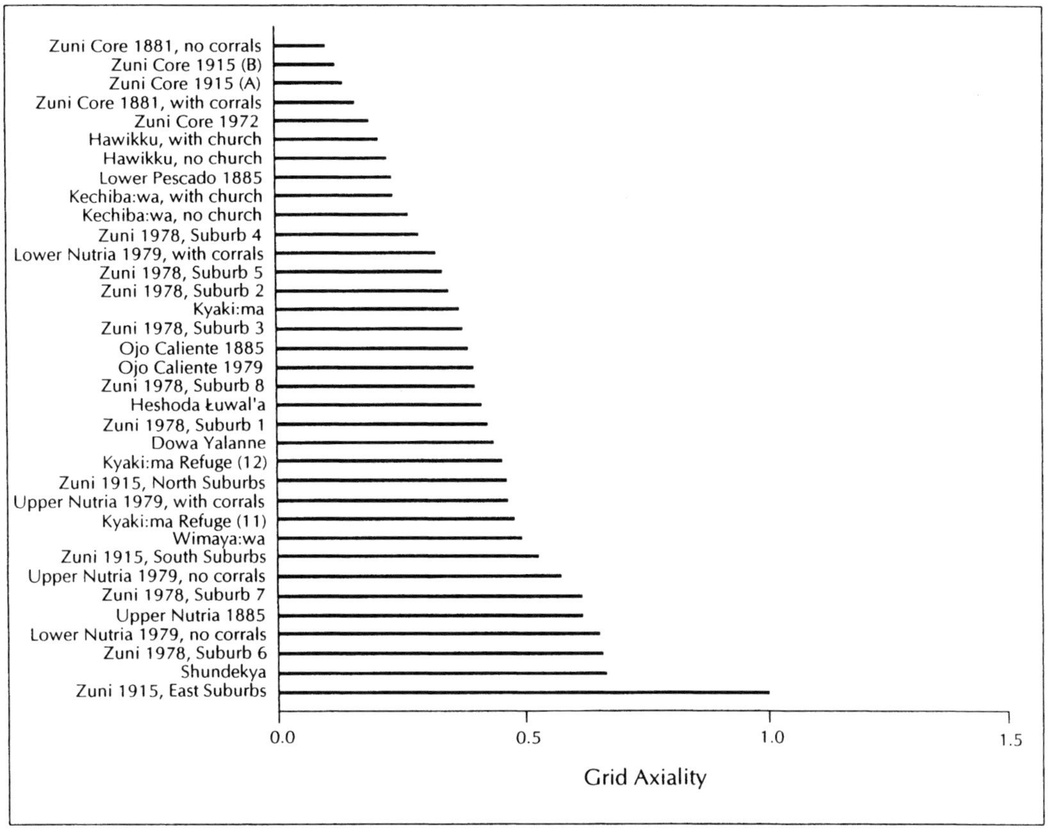

Figure 5.5. Grid axiality values in rank order.

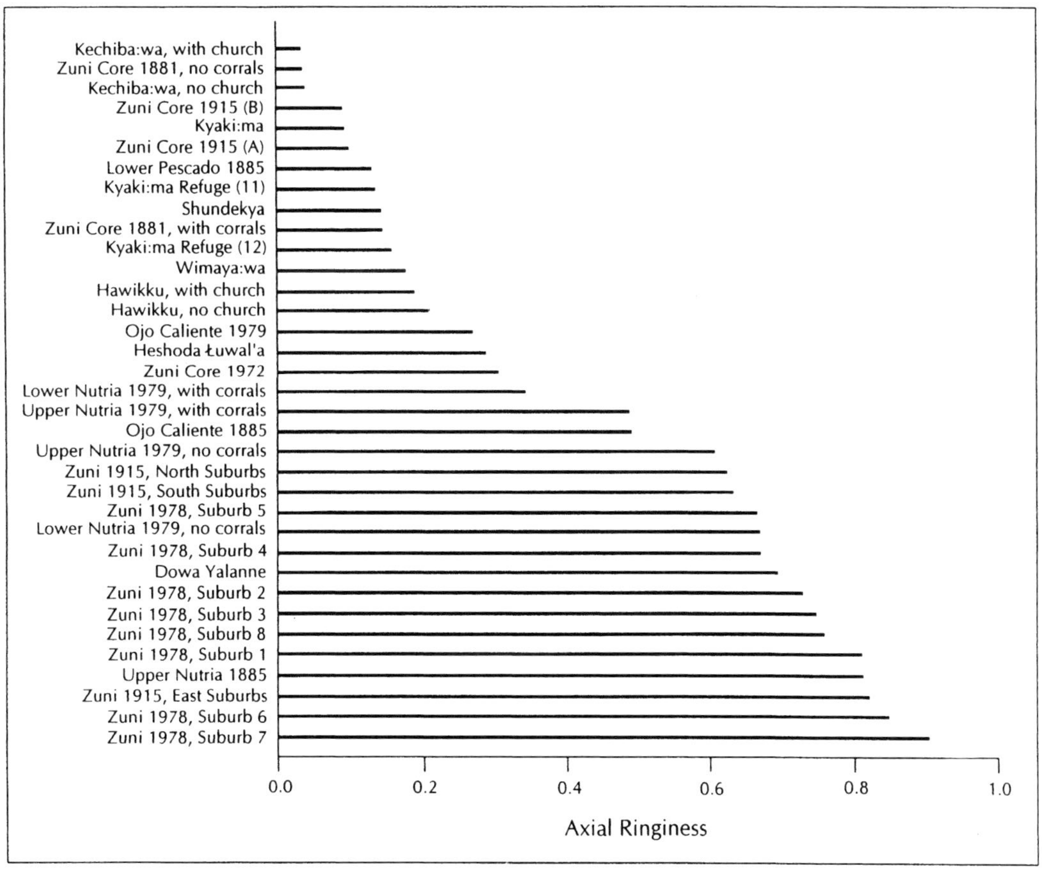

Figure 5.6. Axial ringiness values in rank order.

Table 5.3. Values of Syntactic Measures Relating to the Convex Space Grid

Settlement	Convex articu- lation	Grid con- vexity	Convex ringi- ness
Hawikku, no church	7.10	0.1936	0.0645
Hawikku, with church	7.57	0.1729	0.0575
Kechiba:wa, no church	13.67	0.0976	0.0130
Kechiba:wa, with church	11.25	0.0889	0.0118
Kyaki:ma	9.00	0.2159	0.0408
Dowa Yalanne	3.54	0.3495	0.1343
Kyaki:ma Refuge Site 11	4.80	0.2429	0.0465
Kyaki:ma Refuge Site 12	7.33	0.3393	0.0769
Shundekya	11.00	0.3636	0.0588
Wimaya:wa	26.00	0.2871	0.0638
Heshoda Łuwal'a	7.30	0.2373	0.0709
Lower Pescado 1885	12.50	0.1466	0.0410
Ojo Caliente 1885	3.61	0.3851	0.1416
Upper Nutria 1885	7.00	0.2250	0.0671
Ojo Caliente 1979	3.00	0.4662	0.1714
Upper Nutria 1979, no corrals	2.70	0.5545	0.1942
Upper Nutria 1979, with corrals	2.67	0.4870	0.1707
Lower Nutria 1979, no corrals	3.58	0.4042	0.1374
Lower Nutria 1979, with corrals	4.17	0.3499	0.1230
Zuni Core 1881, no corrals	41.25	0.0545	0.0123
Zuni Core 1881, with corrals	12.11	0.1249	0.0418
Zuni Core 1915 (A)	16.79	0.0903	0.0280
Zuni Core 1915 (B)	15.36	0.0987	0.0306
Zuni 1915, North Suburbs	3.42	0.4026	0.1493
Zuni 1915, East Suburbs	3.67	0.4848	0.1475
Zuni 1915, South Suburbs	3.08	0.4650	0.1677
Zuni Core 1972	5.29	0.2410	0.0936
Zuni 1978, Suburb 1	2.69	0.4709	0.1888
Zuni 1978, Suburb 2	3.05	0.4061	0.1656
Zuni 1978, Suburb 3	2.72	0.4604	0.1864
Zuni 1978, Suburb 4	3.08	0.3936	0.1636
Zuni 1978, Suburb 5	2.63	0.4751	0.1924
Zuni 1978, Suburb 6	3.14	0.4498	0.1637
Zuni 1978, Suburb 7	3.32	0.4078	0.1535
Zuni 1978, Suburb 8	3.29	0.3836	0.1538

space (Table 5.3). *Convex articulation* quantifies the degree to which open space is broken up into convex space by architectural units. Higher values for convex articulation indicate a greater breakup of convex space. The values for convex articulation are illustrated as a bar chart in Figure 5.7 with settlements depicted in rank order from low to high.

Like axial articulation, most Zuni settlements have a low value for convex articulation, indicating little breakup of convex space. Most of the villages with high values of axial articulation also have high values of convex articulation (> 10): the early seventeenth-century village of Kechiba:wa, the early farming villages of Shundekya and Wimaya:wa, the 1885 farming village of Lower Pescado, and the core of Zuni Pueblo in 1881 and 1915.

A second measure of convexity is *grid convexity* (Fig. 5.8). This statistic measures the degree of convex deformation of a grid by comparing the convex map to an orthogonal grid. Grid convexity quantifies the actual number of convex spaces in relation to the minimum that could exist for a regular grid with the same number of room blocks. Low values of grid convexity indicate more deformed grids.

The set of settlements with the lowest values of grid convexity (< 0.2) is similar to that with the lowest values of grid axiality: the early seventeenth-century villages of Kechiba:wa and Hawikku, the 1885 farming village of Lower Pescado, and the core architecture of Zuni Pueblo in 1881 and 1915. The settlements with the highest values of grid convexity, however, differ from those with high values of grid axiality. Villages with the least deformed convex grids include Upper Nutria and most of the suburbs of Zuni Pueblo.

The third measure of convexity, *convex ringiness*, is derived from spatial properties inherent in y-graphs. This statistic measures the actual number of rings or circuits in a spatial arrangement as a proportion of the maximum number of planar rings possible with the amount of convex spaces in the settlement. The rings or circuits actually formed by convex spaces are depicted in y-graphs that are derived by placing dots in the center of each convex space and connecting all adjacent spaces with straight lines (Figs. 5.26–5.33). The values of convex ringiness are presented in rank order as a bar chart in Figure 5.9. The set of settlements with high and low values of convex ringiness are almost identical to those with high and low values of axial ringiness and those with the least distributed convex space system include the early seventeenth-century villages, the 1885 farming village of Lower Pescado, and the core of Zuni Pueblo in 1881 and 1915. The settlements containing convex spaces that form the most rings include most of the Zuni suburbs in 1915 and 1978 and Upper Nutria in 1885 and 1979.

The ordering of Zuni settlements by values of the syntactic measures describing open space as a grid suggests that several of the measures are correlated. For instance, there is a similarity in the ranking of settlements by values of axial articulation and convex articulation and by values of axial ringiness and convex ringiness. To statistically investigate the correlation of the syntactic measures, bivariate plots of all settlements were generated using all pairs of measures (Figs. 5.10,

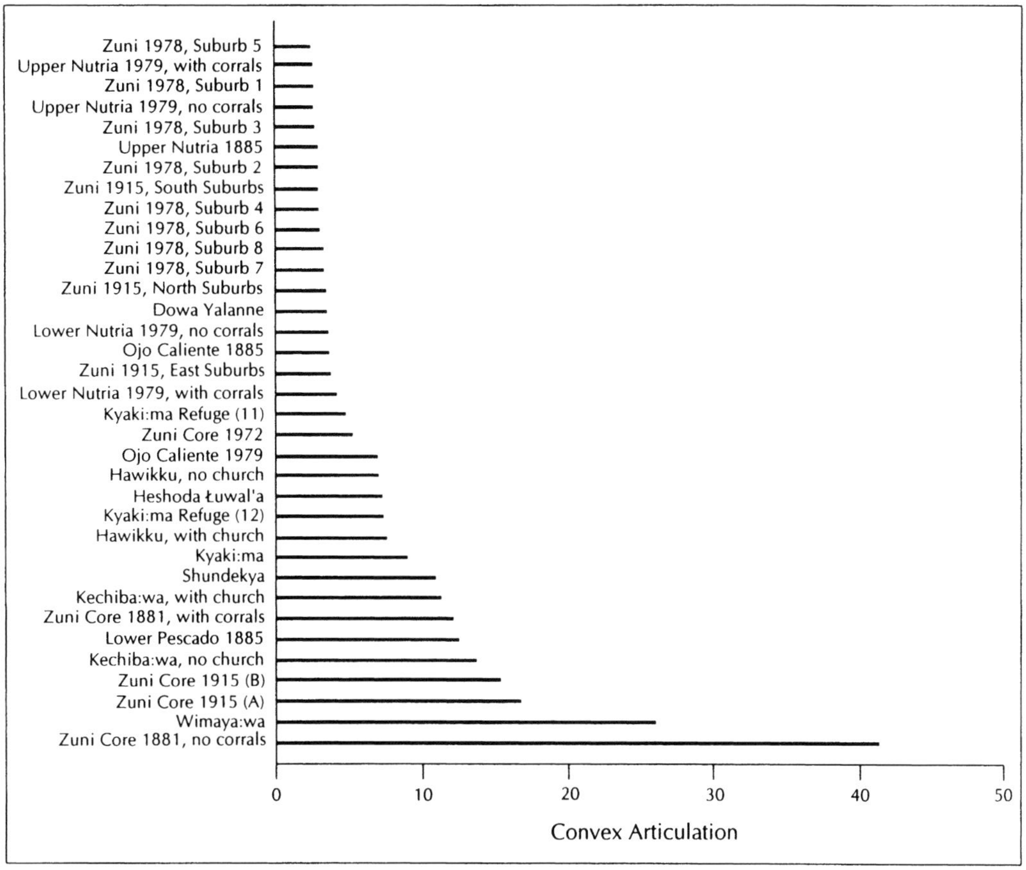

Figure 5.7. Convex articulation values in rank order.

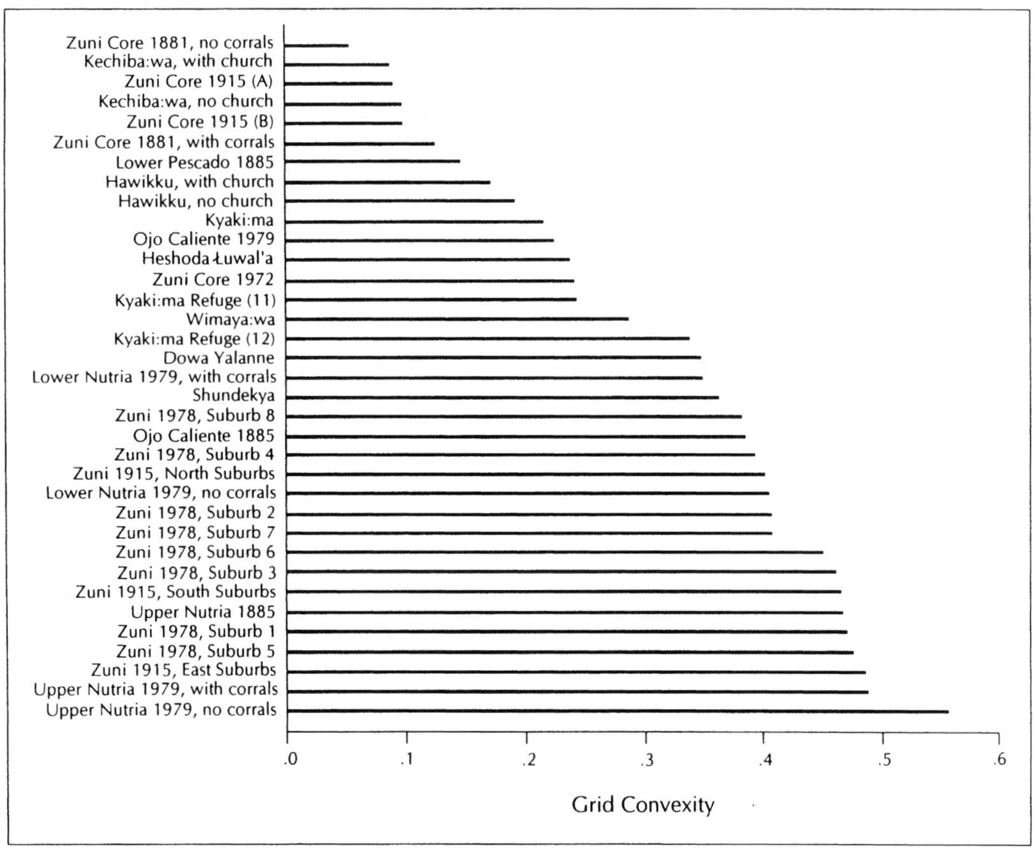

Figure 5.8. Grid convexity values in rank order.

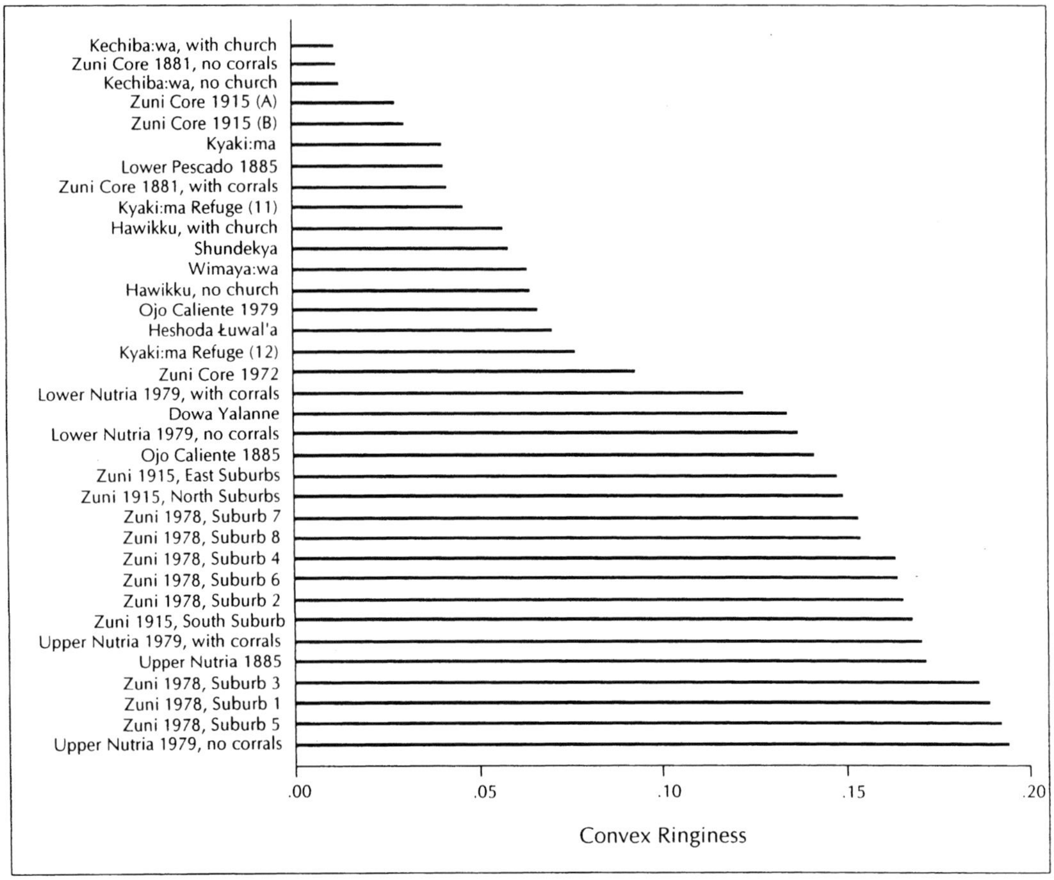

Figure 5.9. Convex ringiness values in rank order.

5.11) and a Pearson correlation matrix was calculated (Tables 5.4, 5.5). The 11 Zuni suburbs were analyzed as a group separately from the other Zuni settlements because they contain tracts of commercial housing and are more oriented toward a road network than are earlier Zuni settlements. To simplify the analysis of Zuni settlements other than the suburbs, the configurations of villages containing churches and corrals were not included, yielding a sample of 22 settlements.

In the bivariate plots of Zuni settlements excluding the suburbs, the large site of Dowa Yalanne constitutes an outlier with respect to the variable of settlement area, constraining the spread of the other values. A series of bivariate plots and a correlation matrix were calculated excluding Dowa Yalanne, but the results obtained without the outlier were not statistically different from the analysis including it and are not presented here. The bivariate plots and Pearson correlation matrix (Fig. 5.10, Table 5.4) show three significant ($R > 0.9$) correlations. Convex articulation is correlated with axial articulation, and convex ringiness is correlated with axial ringiness and grid convexity. The correlation matrix is presented for heuristic purposes; the unadjusted alpha with respect to experiment-wise error values calls for a cautious interpretation of the matrix.

The correlations of convex articulation with axial articulation and convex ringiness with axial ringiness suggest that axial spaces and convex spaces have similar trends in the intersection of routes in the open space structure. The correlation of convex ringiness with axial articulation and grid convexity suggests that the distributedness of convex space is positively related to both the breakup of axial space and the deformation of the convex space grid.

The bivariate plots and heuristic Pearson correlation matrix for the suburbs of Zuni Pueblo in 1915 and 1978 show a different pattern than the other Zuni settlements (Fig. 5.11, Table 5.5). In the Zuni suburbs, there is only a single significant correlation ($R = -0.973$) between the variables of convex ringiness and convex articulation. This is an inverse relationship such that as convex ringiness increases, convex articulation decreases. The lack of correlation between the axial ringiness and convex ringiness variables indicates these two dimensions of the open space structure operate differently in the Zuni suburbs than they do at other Zuni settlements. The fact that different variables are correlated in the Zuni suburbs than in the other Zuni settlements is another indication that the structure of open space in suburbs differs from that of other settlements.

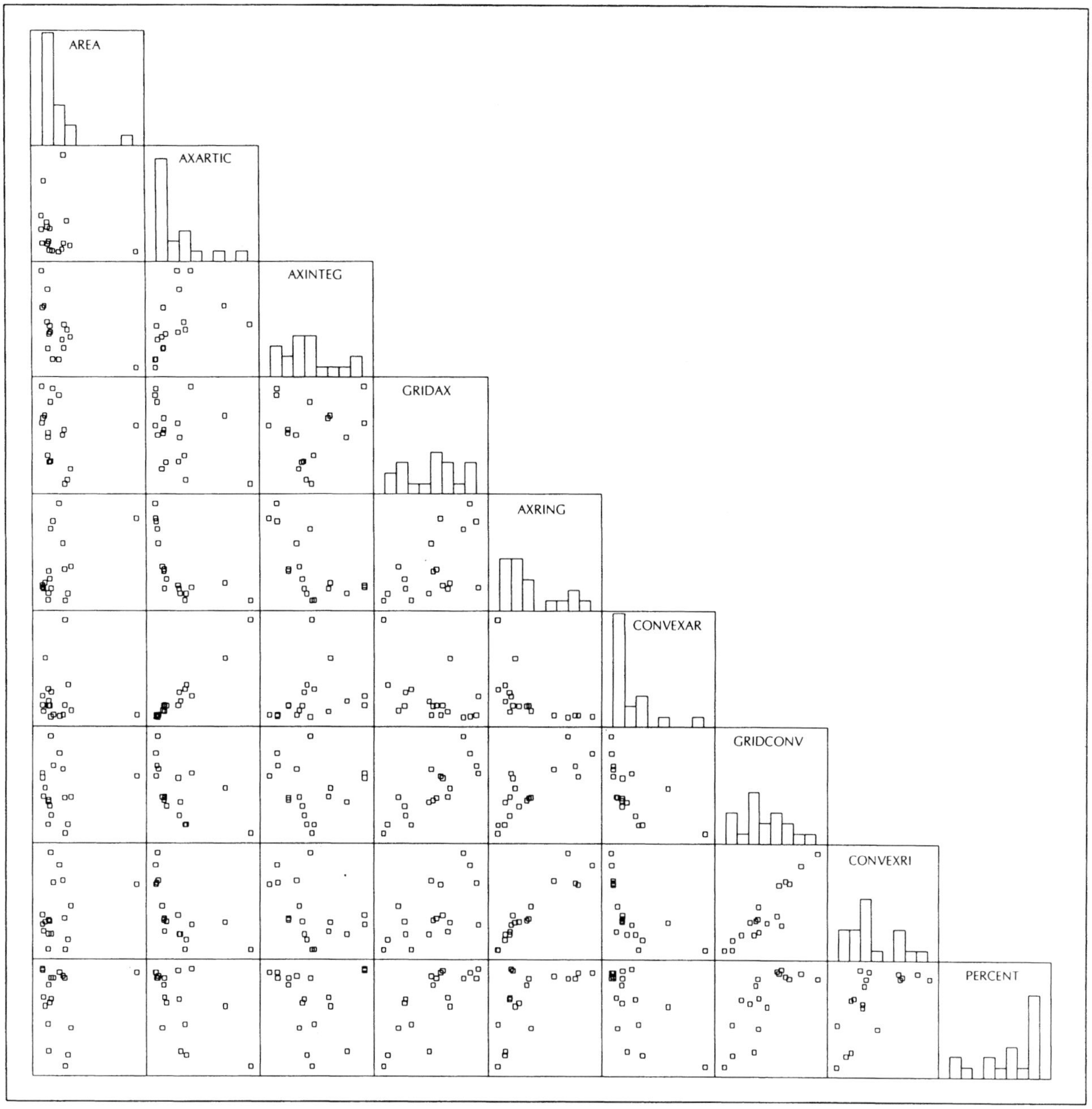

Figure 5.10. Histograms and bivariate plots of syntactic measures, settlement area, and percent of convex space for Zuni settlements, excluding the suburbs of Zuni Pueblo.

Table 5.4 Pearson Correlation Matrix of Syntactic Variables at Zuni Settlements, Excluding Zuni Suburbs

	Area	AxArt	AxInteg	GridAx	AxRing	ConArt	GrCon	ConRing	% Conv
Area	1.000								
AxArt	-0.193	1.000							
AxInteg	-0.565	0.424	1.000						
GridAx	-0.152	-0.364	0.087	1.000					
AxRing	0.445	-0.616	-0.643	0.568	1.000				
ConArt	-0.104	0.977	0.245	-0.472	-0.568	1.000			
GrConv	0.048	-0.530	-0.095	0.835	0.796	-0.600	1.000		
ConRing	0.275	-0.617	-0.441	0.604	0.938	-0.607	0.914	1.000	
% Conv	0.048	-0.592	-0.151	0.762	0.609	-0.642	0.757	0.648	1.000

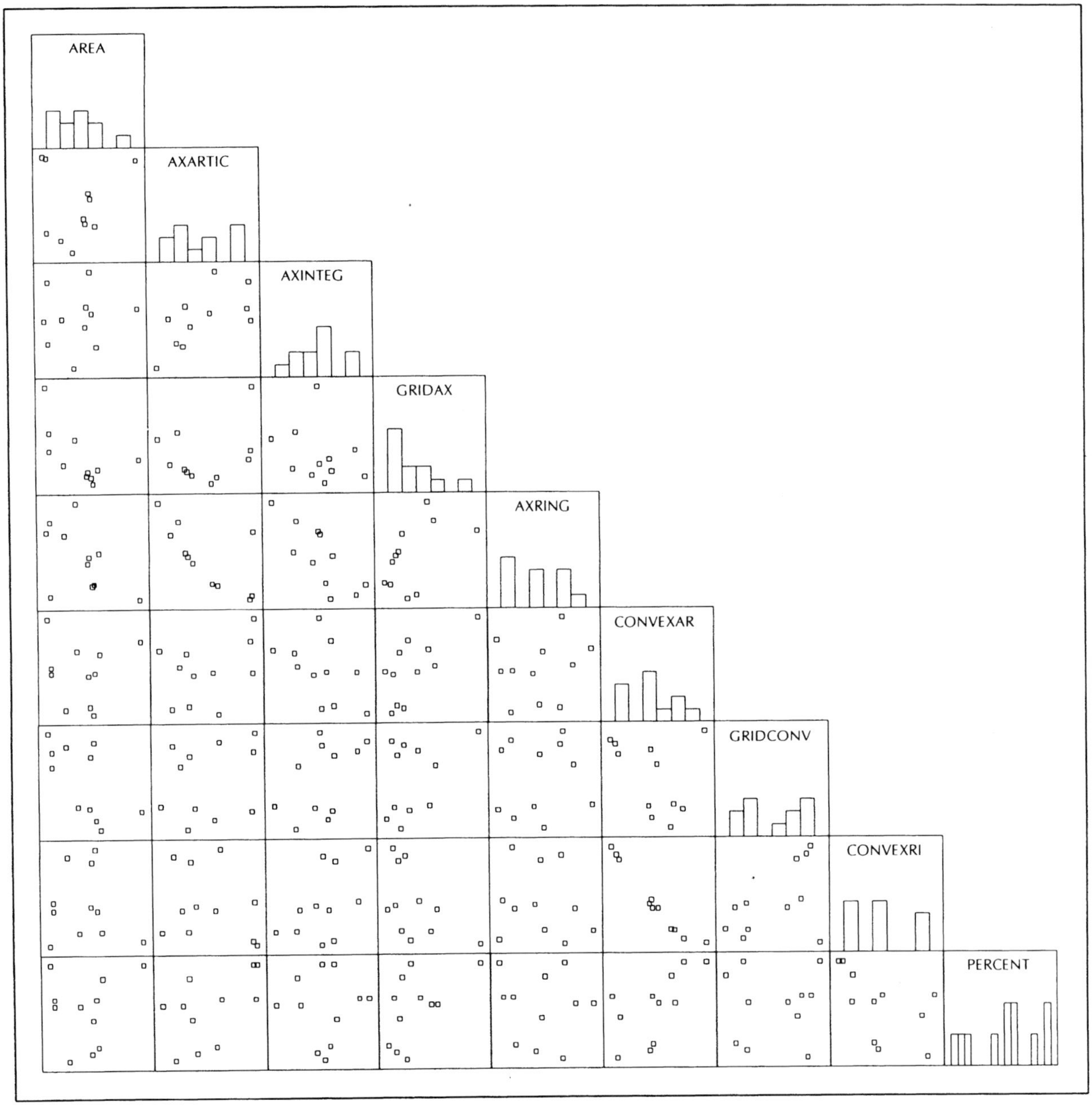

Figure 5.11. Histograms and bivariate plots of syntactic measures, settlement area, and percent of convex space for the suburbs of Zuni Pueblo.

Table 5.5. Pearson Correlation Matrix of Syntactic Variables at the Zuni Suburbs

	Area	AxArt	AxInteg	GridAx	AxRing	ConArt	GrCon	ConRing	% Conv
Area	1.000								
AxArt	0.086	1.000							
AxInteg	0.092	0.646	1.000						
GridAx	-0.588	0.276	-0.284	1.000					
AxRing	-0.517	-0.671	-0.789	0.520	1.000				
ConArt	-0.011	0.369	-0.468	0.679	0.197	1.000			
GrConv	-0.622	0.246	0.506	0.422	0.103	-0.322	1.000		
ConRing	-0.097	-0.272	0.542	-0.521	-0.156	-0.973	0.515	1.000	
% Conv	0.140	0.533	0.018	0.534	-0.085	0.636	0.048	-0.553	1.000

Table 5.6. Summary Data for Real Relative Asymmetry (RRA) Values

Settlement	n	Min	Max	Mean	s.d.
Hawikku, no church	46	0.5800	1.7200	1.0155	0.258
Hawikku, with church	50	0.5500	1.7700	0.9828	0.279
Kechiba:wa, no church	15	0.7200	2.2100	1.2620	0.397
Kechiba:wa, with church	17	0.7900	2.3600	1.3512	0.435
Kyaki:ma	13	0.7100	1.4300	1.0215	0.242
Dowa Yalanne	35	0.2200	1.3700	0.5157	0.217
Kyaki:ma Refuge Site 11	10	0.7300	2.3600	1.4890	0.519
Kyaki:ma Refuge Site 12	12	0.8300	2.9300	1.6483	0.571
Shundekya	6	0.2900	2.0000	1.1433	0.570
Wimaya:wa	11	0.5300	1.8100	1.1373	0.370
Heshoda Łuwal'a	20	0.7800	1.7900	1.2505	0.331
Lower Pescado 1885	33	0.6100	1.3100	0.8903	0.166
Ojo Caliente 1885	34	0.3600	1.1700	0.6659	0.215
Upper Nutria 1885	21	0.2300	0.7700	0.5286	0.157
Ojo Caliente 1979	21	0.4500	1.8200	0.9248	0.317
Upper Nutria 1979, no corrals	19	0.1900	0.6700	0.3963	0.143
Upper Nutria 1979, with corrals	24	0.1100	0.5900	0.3113	0.105
Lower Nutria 1979, no corrals	16	0.4900	1.3700	0.7681	0.262
Lower Nutria 1979, with corrals	36	0.7100	1.9000	1.1008	0.275
Zuni Core 1881, no corrals	59	0.9800	2.4300	1.4461	0.334
Zuni Core 1915 (A)	78	0.0000	1.7000	0.9558	0.426
Zuni Core 1915 (B)	68	0.7000	1.8000	1.1582	0.243
Zuni 1915, North Suburbs	29	0.2200	1.0900	0.5576	0.204
Zuni 1915, East Suburbs	8	0.4400	1.3100	0.8000	0.319
Zuni 1915, South Suburbs	23	0.3100	1.5500	0.7561	0.298
Zuni Core 1972	86	0.6200	1.4600	0.8719	0.162
Zuni 1978, Suburb 1	42	0.4500	1.1900	0.7762	0.192
Zuni 1978, Suburb 2	56	0.3500	1.1900	0.7011	0.172
Zuni 1978, Suburb 3	50	0.2900	0.9500	0.5926	0.148
Zuni 1978, Suburb 4	75	0.4700	1.5800	0.9143	0.229
Zuni 1978, Suburb 5	56	0.4900	2.3500	0.9459	0.354
Zuni 1978, Suburb 6	19	0.4000	1.4700	0.9089	0.291
Zuni 1978, Suburb 7	47	0.2300	0.8500	0.5230	0.127
Zuni 1978, Suburb 8	23	0.3900	1.5100	0.7574	0.288

Syntactic Measures Describing Asymmetry and Control of Axial Spaces

Three syntactic measures describe the spatial properties of axial space in a settlement in terms of asymmetry and control. *Relative asymmetry* (RA) measures the integration or segregation of an individual axial line by quantifying the number of spaces that axial line is away from the outside of the settlement in terms of how many intervening spaces must be traversed to arrive there.

Relative asymmetry generalizes the relation of depth by comparing how deep the system is from a particular point with how deep or shallow it could theoretically be, with the least depth being when all spaces are directly connected to the outside of the settlement, and the most depth when all spaces are arranged in a unilinear sequence away from exterior space. Low values of relative asymmetry indicate a space from which the system is shallow, that is, a space that tends to integrate the system, and high values indicate a space that tends to be segregated from the system. The mean value of relative asymmetry provides a general measure of integration for the system as a whole.

Values of relative asymmetry are useful in analyzing the variation in the distribution of values within a particular settlement and in comparing settlements with the same number of axial spaces. A transformation of relative asymmetry is required to compare settlements of different sizes, however, as described in Chapter 2.

Transformed values are named *real relative asymmetry* (RRA). The mean values for RRA are the primary measures of integration used in this chapter, because the Zuni settlements being analyzed differ in size. Summary information about RRA values for Zuni settlements is presented in Table 5.6, and the shape of the distribution of all the RRA values is illustrated as a histogram in Figure 5.12.

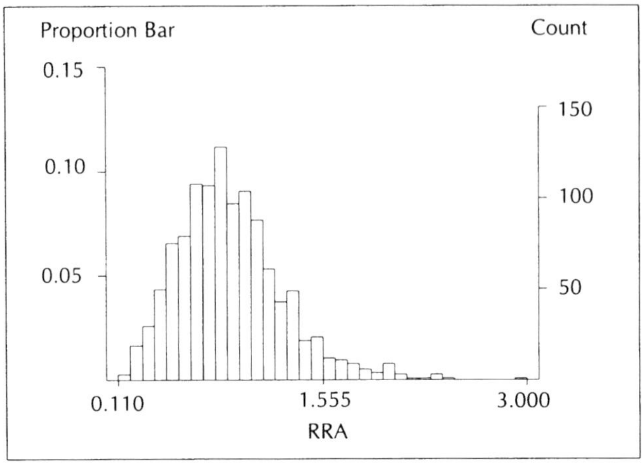

Figure 5.12. Histogram of RRA values for all Zuni settlements.

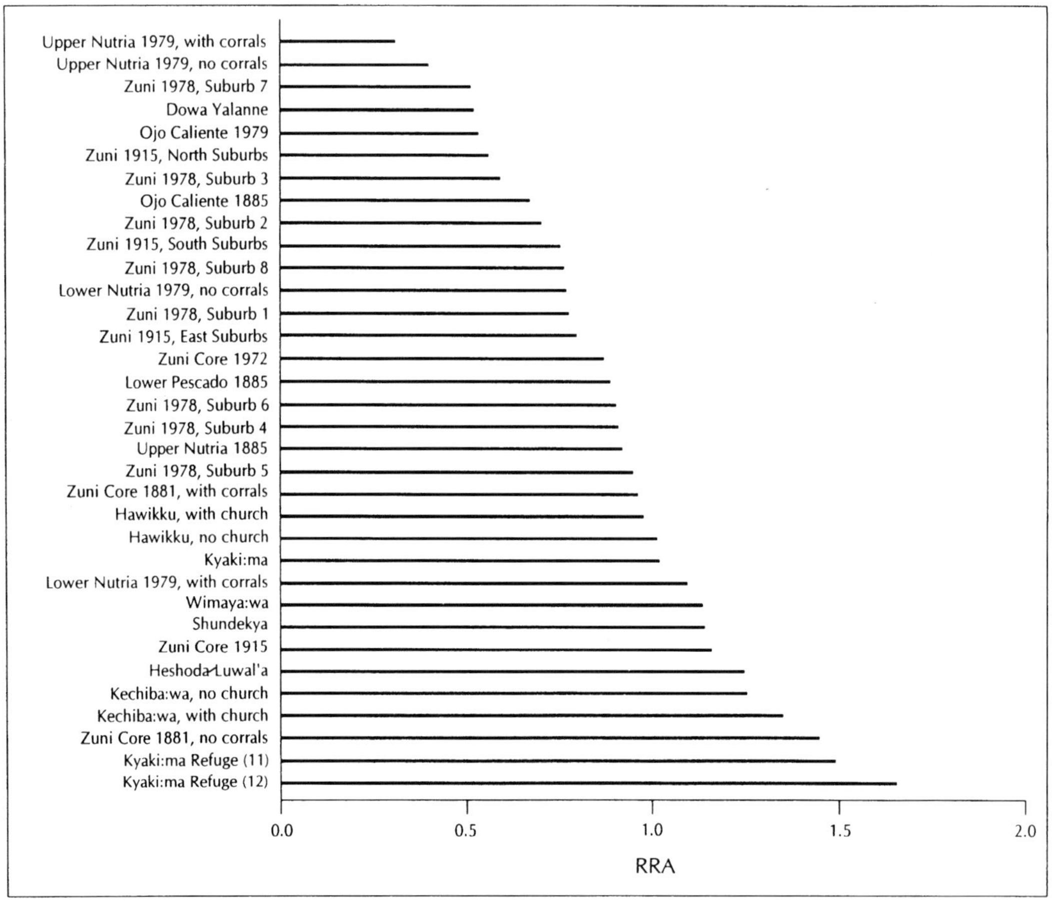

Figure 5.13. Mean RRA values for Zuni settlement in rank order.

The mean RRA values for Zuni settlements are illustrated as a bar chart in Figure 5.13 in rank order from low to high. Some obvious trends are apparent in this chart. Dowa Yalanne, the 1979 farming villages, and the Zuni suburbs all have low values of RRA, indicating high integration of axial space. The early seventeenth-century villages, the early farming villages, and the core of Zuni Pueblo in 1881 and 1915 all have high values of RRA, indicating their axial space system is more segregated.

A final syntactic measure is that of *control*. Control is a *local* measure; it only takes into account the spatial relations between an axial line and its immediate neighbors. In contrast, the RA and RRA measures of integration are *global* measures; they incorporate the relations of a space to every other space in the system. Control only quantifies the spatial relation between one space and the other axial spaces it directly bisects. Each space is given a value of 1/n where n is the number of other spaces it bisects. This value is then assigned to each of the axial spaces it bisects. The values each space receives from its neighbors are summed to yield the control value of that space. Higher values indicate stronger control. High values for control are generated when a space provides a route of access to many other spaces or when it provides the only route of access to another space. The highest control values are generally derived from spaces that control other spaces in both of these ways.

A histogram of control values obtained from all the Zuni settlements illustrated in Figure 5.14 shows the values are skewed and do not form a normal distribution. Considering the manner in which the statistic is calculated, it is not surprising that most axial spaces have low values of control and only a few spaces have high values.

Summary information about the measure is presented in Table 5.7. The median rather than the mean control value is tabulated because the mean value for each of the settlements is 1. Although the median shows variation in the distribution of values at different settlements, the control statistic is a local rather than a global measure and its values are of use primarily in intrasite rather than intersite comparisons. The range of values and standard deviations of the control data in Table 5.7 indicate that there is substantial variation in the distribution of control values at different settlements.

Information on the length of axial spaces at Zuni settlements was examined to investigate whether this dimension has an effect on the values yielded by the RRA and control measures (Table 5.7) The absolute length of axial space ranges from a minimum of 3 m at Hawikku to a maximum of 760 m in the north suburbs of Zuni Pueblo in 1915, and the mean length ranges from a low of 20 m at Kyaki:ma Refuge Site 12 to 261 m in the north suburbs of Zuni Pueblo in 1915. A histogram of the length of axial spaces (Fig. 5.15) shows that this variable is highly skewed and not normally distributed. Most axial lines are relatively short and the number of axial lines greatly decreases as their length increases.

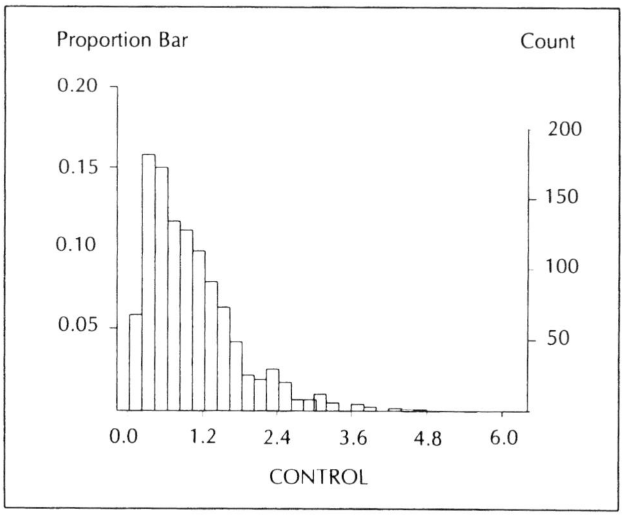

Figure 5.14. Histogram of control values for all settlements.

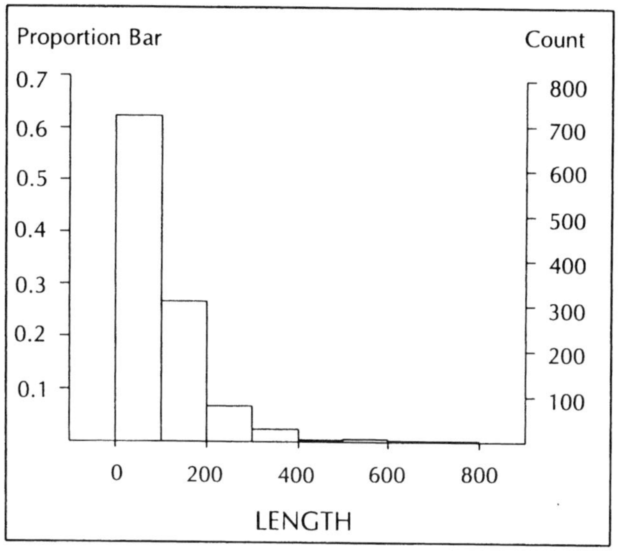

Figure 5.15. Histogram of length of axial lines for all settlements.

Bivariate plots were generated to determine if the length of axial lines has an effect on RRA and control values (Figure 5.16). These scatter plots show a cloud-like rather than a linear distribution of values, indicating that the RRA and control measures are not correlated with the length of axial lines. Figure 5.16 depicts the values for all settlements except the suburbs of Zuni Pueblo. Bivariate plots of the Zuni suburbs with similar scatters are not presented here. A Pearson correlation matrix yields insignificant correlations for all pairs of the three variables. RRA and length have an R value of -0.475, length and control have an R value of 0.399, and RRA and control have an R value of -0.263.

Table 5.7. Summary Data for Control Values of Axial Spaces and for Length of Axial Space in Meters

Settlement	n	Control Values of Axial Spaces Min	Max	Median	s.d.	Length of Axial Space in Meters Min	Max	Mean	s.d.
Hawikku, no church	46	0.1111	4.2512	0.7500	0.950	3	146	42	34
Hawikku, with church	50	0.1000	4.4917	0.7250	0.884	3	146	43	35
Kechiba:wa, no church	15	0.2000	3.1667	0.8333	0.722	18	120	54	28
Kechiba:wa, with church	17	0.2000	3.1667	0.8333	0.724	18	120	49	28
Kyaki:ma	13	0.2500	2.0000	0.8333	0.596	13	131	62	35
Dowa Yalanne	35	0.1576	2.6222	0.8551	0.648	35	656	242	157
Kyaki:ma Refuge Site 11	10	0.5000	1.5000	0.9167	0.380	18	61	36	15
Kyaki:ma Refuge Site 12	12	0.5000	2.0000	1.0000	0.477	9	36	20	10
Shundekya	6	0.2500	2.5000	0.7500	0.806	15	35	27	7
Wimaya:wa	11	0.2500	2.5000	0.6667	0.763	26	95	48	23
Heshoda Łuwal'a	20	0.2000	2.8333	0.7583	0.765	22	717	141	148
Lower Pescado 1885	33	0.1250	3.1833	0.7833	0.745	12	134	56	34
Ojo Caliente 1885	34	0.0833	5.5095	0.7068	1.604	7	296	103	79
Upper Nutria 1885	21	0.1429	2.4507	0.9134	0.650	12	146	73	38
Ojo Caliente 1979	21	0.4500	1.6167	0.9929	0.305	31	263	123	58
Upper Nutria 1979, no corrals	19	0.4004	2.1036	0.8933	0.435	37	225	103	53
Upper Nutria 1979, with corrals	24	0.2679	2.2202	1.0195	0.520	20	271	136	63
Lower Nutria 1979, no corrals	16	0.2000	2.4500	0.8417	0.609	15	217	99	66
Lower Nutria 1979, with corrals	36	0.1000	4.2143	0.7816	0.978	14	357	107	79
Zuni Core 1881, no corrals	59	0.2000	2.5000	0.8167	0.685	5	164	49	37
Zuni Core 1915 (A)	78	0.0000	3.8690	0.7750	0.777	9	151	48	34
Zuni Core 1915 (B)	68	0.1000	3.8690	0.8333	0.769	10	151	52	33
Zuni 1915, North Suburbs	29	0.1111	3.6714	0.4825	1.126	20	760	261	195
Zuni 1915, East Suburbs	8	0.2500	2.2500	0.5000	0.845	43	323	191	83
Zuni 1915, South Suburbs	23	0.1250	3.7576	0.6826	0.906	12	357	148	87
Zuni Core 1972	86	0.1000	3.8012	0.7917	0.763	9	212	62	38
Zuni 1978, Suburb 1	42	0.1250	2.5206	0.9324	0.952	24	237	116	61
Zuni 1978, Suburb 2	56	0.0769	4.7198	0.6181	0.773	27	426	121	86
Zuni 1978, Suburb 3	50	0.0667	3.2274	0.8000	0.787	19	426	151	107
Zuni 1978, Suburb 4	75	0.1111	3.6012	0.7262	0.925	12	319	112	63
Zuni 1978, Suburb 5	56	0.0833	4.9857	0.7584	0.425	19	329	131	78
Zuni 1978, Suburb 6	19	0.3333	2.1167	0.9762	0.685	25	310	135	69
Zuni 1978, Suburb 7	47	0.2361	2.8790	0.7139	0.702	36	371	150	75
Zuni 1978, Suburb 8	23	0.2361	2.2917	0.8373	0.605	24	665	245	206

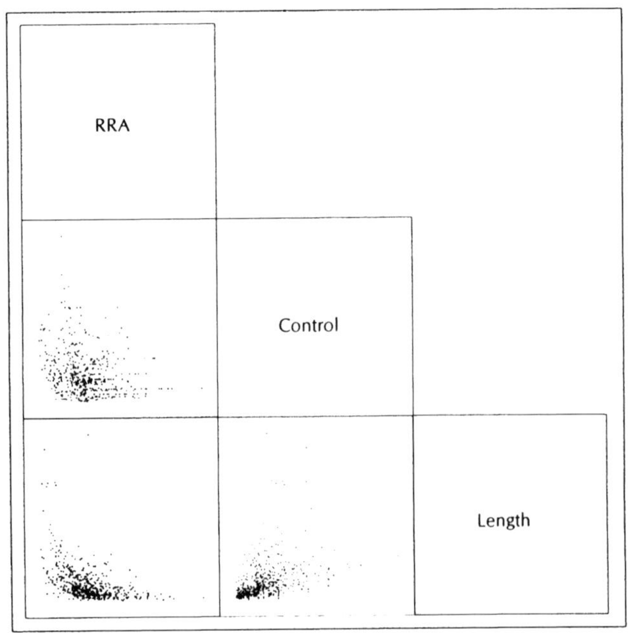

Figure 5.16. Bivariate plots of RRA, control, and length values of axial spaces.

Open Space Structure Analyses

The analytical techniques of space syntax yield substantial variation in the syntactic measures of the grid structure of open space and in the measures of asymmetry and control. This variation is used to investigate intrasite differences, diachronic change through time, and functional differences between Zuni Pueblo and the contemporaneous farming villages. The results of these analyses are then evaluated in terms of the social logic of space and structuration theory.

INTRASITE ANALYSIS OF ASYMMETRY AND CONTROL

The syntactic measures of asymmetry and control are used to address one methodological issue and two substantive questions regarding spatial variation within settlements. The methodological issue concerns the usefulness of visual pattern recognition procedures using the analytical techniques recommended by Hillier and Hanson (1984: 82–140). The substantive questions are whether the inclusion of Catholic churches at two early seventeenth-century villages and the inclusion of corrals at two 1979 farming villages have a significant effect on the mean RRA values for integration of the open space structure at these settlements. If there is no significant difference between the settlements with configurations including or excluding the churches and corrals, investigation of diachronic change in the open space structure of settlements can be simplified by including only one configuration in subsequent analyses.

Application of Visual Pattern Recognition Techniques

Hillier and Hanson (1984: 122–123) recommend that the syntactic relations characterizing the open space structure of settlements be interpreted using a combination of visual and quantitative analyses. Once integration and control values are derived quantitatively, maps showing the core distribution of these values (the top 5, 10, or 25 percent of the most integrating or controlling spaces) can be produced for use in visual pattern recognition. Various permutations of integration and control maps can be generated for different purposes according to the interests of the analyst. The analytical goal is to determine how space is invested and structured in relation to global and local organization and how these syntactic relations structure the interaction of inhabitants and outsiders. Hillier and Hanson suggest this procedure will yield a general description of how the structure of the open space generates and controls social interaction.

Several applications of the visual pattern recognition procedures are presented here as examples of the technique and to illustrate graphically the spaces differentiated by the measures of integration and control. RA rather than RRA values are used for the measure of integration, because only one settlement is analyzed at a time.

The first example depicts a graph of the 25 percent most integrating axial spaces (lowest RA) at Hawikku superimposed on the plan of the room blocks and church (Fig. 5.17). All the indigenous room blocks at Hawikku were well integrated into the open space structure in that the routes of access between them could be traversed with relatively few intervening steps. The Catholic church, however, was not well integrated into the settlement. It was situated both at the edge of the village and at the edge of the network of the most integrated axial spaces. Only one entrance to the church faced onto a well-integrated axial space: a small entryway at the southwest corner of the friary at the rear of the church complex. The formal entrance into the church itself, through the *campo santo* or graveyard and the front door of the nave, was not well integrated into the axial space system. The spatial arrangement of Hawikku suggests that Catholicism as represented by its church was not well integrated into Zuni society prior to the Pueblo Revolt of 1680. This interpretation is congruent with the fact that the Zuni burned the Catholic

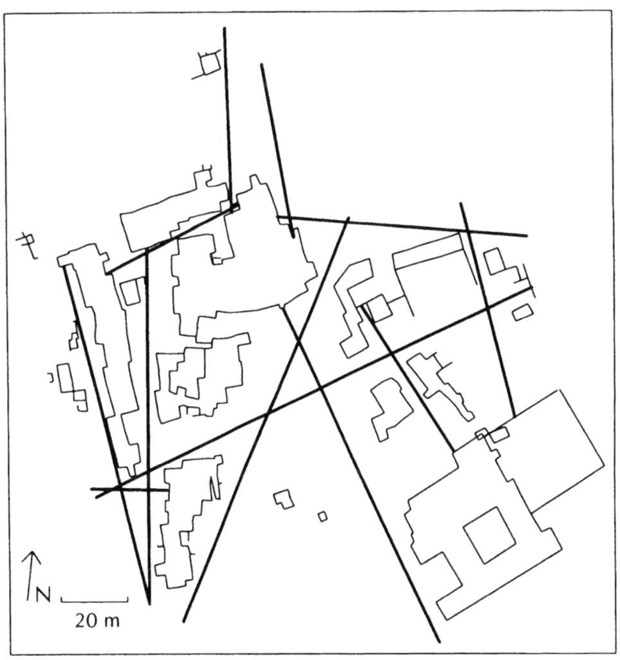

Figure 5.17. Distribution of the most integrating (low RA) axial spaces at Hawikku.

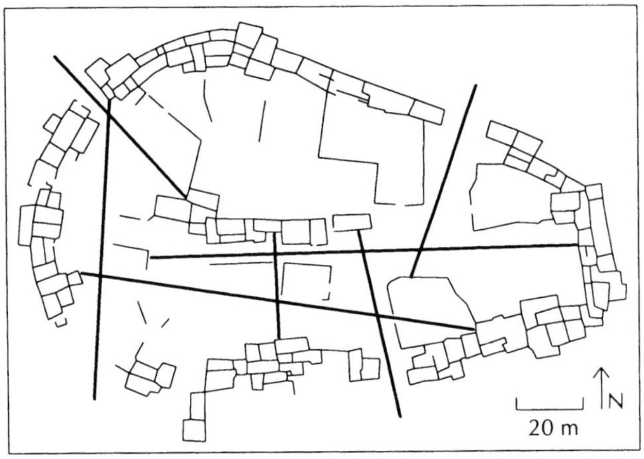

Figure 5.18. Distribution of the most integrating (low RA) axial spaces in Lower Pescado in 1885.

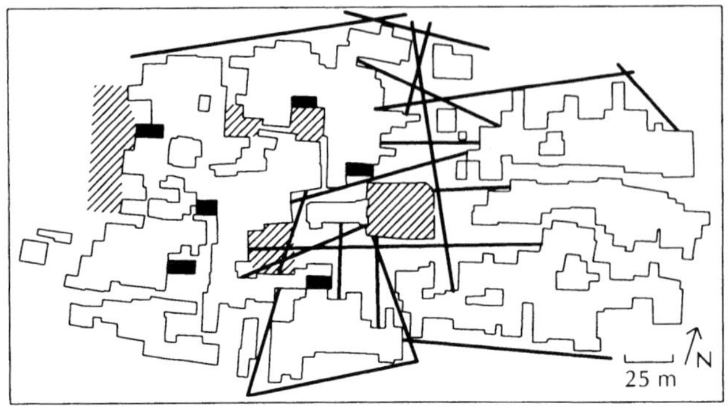

Figure 5.19. Distribution of the most integrating (low RA) axial spaces at Zuni Pueblo in 1915. Kivas are denoted with solid black, sacred plazas and the campo santo with hatching (Kroeber 1917, Map 1; Tedlock 1979: 503).

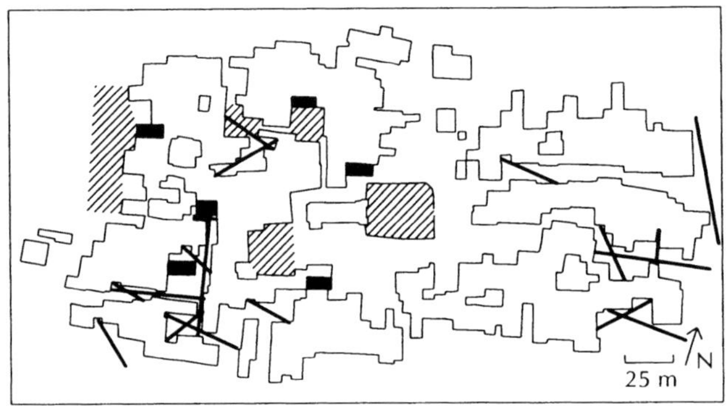

Figure 5.20. Distribution of the most segregating (high RA) axial spaces at Zuni Pueblo in 1915. Kivas are denoted with solid black, sacred plazas and the campo santo with hatching (Kroeber 1917, Map 1; Tedlock 1979: 503).

missions in 1630 and 1680 in an attempt to rid their society of this foreign institution.

The graphic display of the 20 percent most integrating axial spaces in the 1885 farming village of Lower Pescado (Fig. 5.18) shows that four of the seven most integrating spaces were positioned to regulate access to the interior of the settlement. The other three highly integrated axial spaces structured internal movement within the village. Figure 5.18 illustrates how the axial structure of open space at Pescado in 1885 was oriented toward the interface between the interior and the exterior of the settlement. Although the overall plan of Pescado suggests the settlement was focused on its interior, four out of seven of the most integrating spaces connected the interior with the exterior. The points of access into the village were relatively constricted, however, and therefore easily regulated. The overall structure of open space at Pescado appears to have been oriented toward moving livestock into and out of the settlement in a controlled fashion that otherwise facilitated protective enclosure of the settlement.

Displays of the most integrating and segregating axial spaces in the core of Zuni Pueblo in 1915 are useful in evaluating how graph analytical techniques relate to important spaces as defined culturally (Figs. 5.19, 5.20). One of the plazas was an open area on the western flank of the pueblo rather than a completely enclosed architectural space.

Although historically associated with the Catholic church, the campo santo in front of the church has become culturally important to the Zuni people. There is now a second cemetery on the outskirts of Zuni Pueblo, but the campo santo is still used as the burial site for important Zuni religious and community leaders. The importance of the cemetery in Zuni culture is symbolized by the fact that although the Zuni Tribe has leased the church to the contemporary Catholic mission at Zuni Pueblo, it has not leased the cemetery, which remains under tribal control.

The 25 percent most integrating (low RA) axial spaces are depicted in Figure 5.19. Unlike Hawikku, where the church was on the periphery of the axial integration network, the Catholic church at Zuni Pueblo is completely surrounded by well-integrated axial lines. The original church at Zuni Pueblo, as at Hawikku, was built outside of the village as it existed in the early seventeenth century. Following the Pueblo Revolt, Zuni Pueblo was expanded and room blocks were constructed east of the church, enclosing it in a central position in the plan of the village. In terms of spatial structure, the Catholic church was integrated into the settlement of Zuni Pueblo.

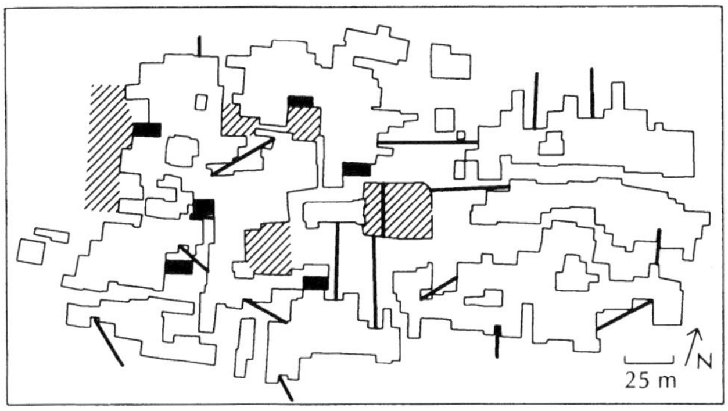

Figure 5.21. Distribution of axial spaces with low control values at Zuni Pueblo in 1915. Kivas are denoted with solid black, sacred plazas and the campo santo with hatching.

Figure 5.22. Distribution of axial spaces with high control values at Zuni Pueblo in 1915. Kivas are denoted with solid black, sacred plazas and the campo santo with hatching.

Zuni Pueblo in 1915, unlike Lower Pescado in 1885, had a network of highly integrated spaces that included both exterior and interior axial lines. There was more integration of exterior space at Zuni Pueblo in 1915 than at Pescado thirty years earlier. Although there were more points of access into Zuni Pueblo than into Pescado, the most integrated axial lines funneled access to the pueblo interior at only two points leading to the church at the center of the village. Only two of the six kiva buildings and one of the four Zuni plazas were located adjacent to or were bisected by highly integrated axial spaces. In terms of the structure of open space, the majority of the sacred areas at Zuni Pueblo were not situated in the most accessible places. These ritual areas were not positioned with respect to the open space interface with visitors to the village, but toward the localized routes of access of the village inhabitants.

The 25 percent most segregated spaces (high RA) at Zuni Pueblo in 1915 are illustrated in Figure 5.20. These spaces were segregated in the sense that access to them required the most travel along other intervening spaces. As might be expected, most of the axial spaces mapped in Figure 5.20 were associated with small cul-de-sacs or situated at the edges of the pueblo. The most segregated axial spaces were adjacent to two kiva buildings and intersected one plaza.

Figures 5.21 and 5.22 depict the axial spaces with the lowest and highest control values. Low control values indicate spaces that do not intersect many other spaces. High control values indicate spaces that intersect many other spaces or that provide the only intersection or route of access with another space. The highest control values are assigned to axial spaces that combine both of these local properties. The map of the 25 percent axial spaces with the lowest control values shows these spaces were distributed in a fragmented fashion throughout the settlement. Low control values were found in the axial spaces associated with the campo santo and in areas adjacent to two kivas. Axial spaces with high control were distributed in all parts of the village, with many more interconnections than the axial spaces with low control.

The distribution of the 10 percent largest convex spaces superimposed on the high control axial spaces (Fig. 5.23) shows that a large amount of open space was invested in the areas of the village that were characterized by high local control of the axial space system. Most of the high control axial spaces were associated with large convex spaces and vice versa. The distribution of the large open spaces associated with high control axial lines extended well beyond the integration core focused on a north-south axis at the center of the village. This pattern is another indication of how the open space structure of Zuni Pueblo in 1915 was oriented toward the inhabitants of the village rather than toward visitors.

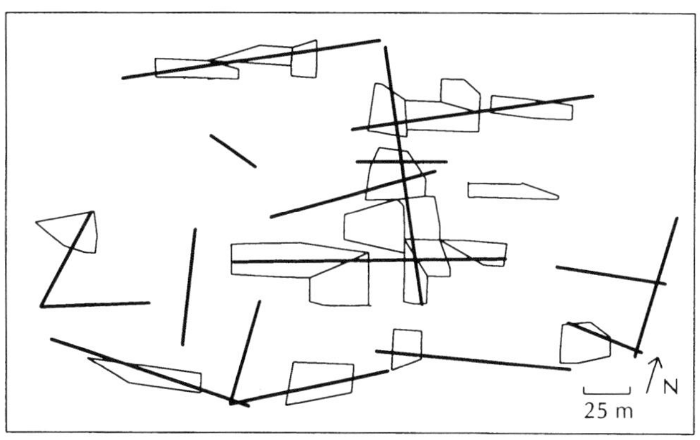

Figure 5.23. The 10 percent largest convex spaces superimposed on high control axial lines at Zuni Pueblo in 1915.

Comparison of Figures 5.19 through 5.22 reveals that integration and control values are independent of one another and form a number of different combinations. For instance, four highly integrated axial lines have low control values, and seven highly integrated lines have high control values. Similarly, five axial lines with low integration (high RA) have low control values, and four axial spaces with low integration have high control values. The various permutations of integration and control values for axial lines at Zuni Pueblo in 1915 have no readily apparent social or behavioral correlates.

Although there are some interesting features in the axial maps of Hawikku, Lower Pescado, and Zuni Pueblo in 1915, the visual interpretation of integration and control patterns applied to the full set of Zuni settlements yielded less interesting results. By and large, the pattern recognition study of intrasite variation using RA and control variables was not especially productive. Many of the settlements are so small or have so few axial spaces that mapping a percentage of the most integrating or controlling spaces did not produce displays that were easily interpreted. The limitations of an analysis that only includes open space at ground level also obviate a robust assessment of real access within the multistoried pueblos of the early seventeenth century and Zuni Pueblo in 1881 and in 1915, because many routes of travel within the villages were over rooftop terraces and not through streets or plazas.

The application of visual pattern recognition procedures in this study failed to adequately capture the cultural aspects of space at Zuni Pueblo as known ethnographically. In a purely formal analysis of open space, neither the measures of integration nor control consistently intersected key culturally defined spaces within Zuni Pueblo. The ritual areas of Zuni Pueblo in general are associated with axial spaces that are in the middle range of integration and control values rather than at the highest or lowest ends of the distribution of these syntactic variables. The spaces that are the most differentiated using the graph analytical techniques are not easily recognizable in cultural terms.

A less formal research design that assigns value according to a hierarchical ordering of cultural space might be more productive in terms of the analysis of culturally defined space, but such a research design presupposes the very information that an archaeological investigation seeks to determine. In the absence of preexisting information, the graph analytic techniques proposed by Hillier and Hanson (1984) produce a type of information about access within a settlement that appears to be more fundamental to social interaction than to the ideational aspects of cultural symbolism.

A critical review of Hillier and Hanson's use of various displays of integration and control values of axial space reveals that they use these maps as much for discursive explication of settlement organization as for explicit and controlled comparisons between settlements. For the purposes of this study, the use of such displays to investigate intrasite variation in the syntactic characteristics of individual axial spaces proved to be less informative than the use of an average RRA value as a summary description of the pattern of access for the settlement as a whole. Because control is a local rather than a global measure, little use is made of this variable in comparing settlements. The following analyses thus concentrate on average RRA values as a global measure.

The Spatial Effect of Catholic Churches on RRA at Early Seventeenth-Century Villages

The two early seventeenth-century villages of Hawikku and Kechiba:wa were analyzed in configurations with and without the Catholic churches to determine what effect the imposition of a Spanish institutional facility had on the open space structure of these villages. A notched box plot is an analytical technique that may be used to determine if there are statistically significant differences in the median RRA values between the configurations with and without churches.

Box plots provide a simple graphical summary of a set of data (Wilkinson 1990: 166). A horizontal axis provides a scale of the values of the RRA variable. The median of the data set is marked by a vertical line in the center of the box, and the edges of the box are formed at the lower and upper hinges (that is, quartiles) of the distribution. Statistically, the center of the box thus splits the data set in half and the hinges at the ends of the box split the remaining halves in half again. The box illustrates the interquartile range, which is called the Hspread (the difference between the values at the limits of the middle 50 percent of the data). The lines extending beyond the box are called whiskers and they depict the range of values that fall within 1.5 Hspreads of the hinges. Values beyond the end of the whiskers are plotted with asterisks to denote outliers and with open circles to denote far outlying values (the values beyond three Hspreads from the hinges). Notching of the box plot establishes confidence intervals on the median of several grouped data sets. The boxes are notched at the median and return to full width at the lower and upper confidence intervals. The confidence

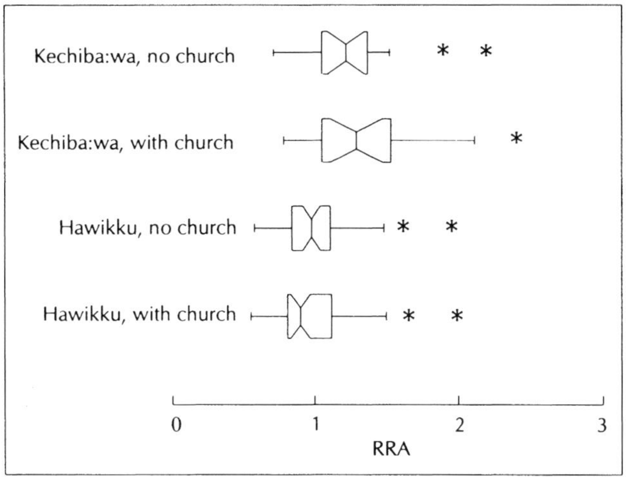

Figure 5.24. Notched box plots of RRA values of early seventeenth-century settlements analyzed with and without churches.

intervals occasionally extend beyond the hinges, providing an unaesthetic but accurate depiction of the statistical property. If the confidence intervals around two medians do not overlap, there is a 95 percent level of confidence that the two population medians are different. Notched box plots, therefore, offer a relatively straightforward and useful means to judge differences between groups.

Notched box plots of the RRA values for Kechiba:wa and Hawikku with and without churches are illustrated in Figure 5.24. The box plots show that the two villages are different from each other, but the inclusion or exclusion of the churches does not make a significant difference in the median RRA values for either Kechiba:wa or Hawikku considered separately.

The intrasite analysis of Hawikku showed the Catholic church was not well integrated into the axial space system, so it is not surprising that the church has little spatial impact on the statistical distribution of RRA values. Because there is no statistical difference in the early seventeenth-century villages analyzed with or without churches, the diachronic analysis of settlements in the next section uses only information derived from the analysis of the settlements excluding the churches.

The Spatial Effect of Corrals on RRA at Two Farming Villages Occupied in 1979

The inclusion or exclusion of corrals in the analysis of axial space at Upper Nutria and Lower Nutria in 1979 were analyzed using the same logic and techniques as those discussed in the preceding analysis of early seventeenth-century villages with and without churches. Notched box plots of the RRA values of two 1979 farming villages are illustrated in Figure 5.25.

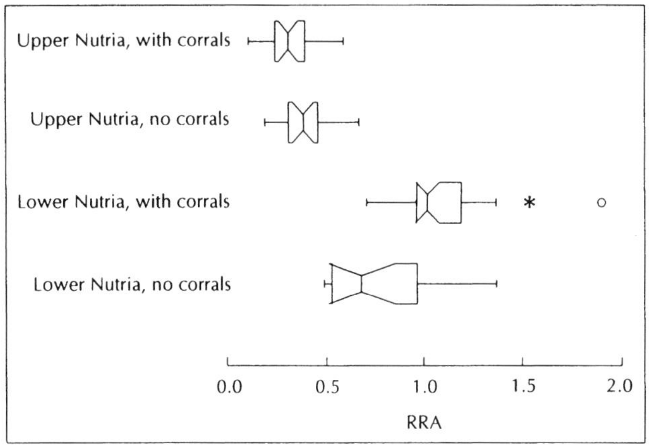

Figure 5.25. Notched box plots of RRA values of 1979 farming villages analyzed with and without corrals.

In this analysis the RRA values for Upper Nutria, analyzed with and without corrals, have confidence intervals that overlap, indicating there is no statistically significant difference between the two groups. At Lower Nutria, however, the confidence intervals do not overlap, indicating that the configurations of the village without corrals is statistically different from the configuration with corrals. The inclusion of corrals in the analysis of Lower Nutria significantly heightens the median RRA value, indicating a much less integrated axial space system in the structure of open space. Without the corrals, Lower Nutria exhibits more integration in the axial organization of open space. Figure 5.25 also indicates that Upper Nutria and Lower Nutria are different from each other, regardless of whether corrals are included or excluded from the analysis.

In the analyses below, Upper Nutria and Lower Nutria are analyzed using configurations excluding corrals to provide information more comparable to Ojo Caliente and the 1885 farming villages. This simplifies the analysis, but it should be kept in mind that the exclusion of corrals at Lower Nutria yields more segregated RRA values.

SYNCHRONIC VARIATION AND DIACHRONIC CHANGE IN OPEN SPACE STRUCTURE

Change in the open space structure of Zuni settlements is analyzed in terms of (1) the open space grid, and (2) the integration of axial space. Because one focus of the analysis is diachronic change, the primary criterion used to group settlements is chronological association. Considering the major differences in size and function between Zuni Pueblo and the contemporaneous satellite farming villages, however, these settlements are analyzed in separate groups. A secondary criterion used to derive analytical groups, therefore, is site function: permanent versus seasonal occupation. A series of figures depicting the settlement plans, axial graphs, and y-graphs for all villages except the Zuni suburbs are presented to supplement the verbal description and comparison of spatial patterns.

Synchronic Variation and Diachronic Change in the Structure of the Open Space Grid

The syntactic measures that describe the grid structure of open space are recapitulated in Table 5.8. The values for syntactic grid measures obtained in the analysis of Zuni settlements are summarized in Table 5.9 by using a plus sign to denote values above the mean of all the villages and a minus sign to denote values below the mean. Several trends are evident in Table 5.9.

The early seventeenth-century villages of Hawikku, Kechiba:wa, and Kyaki:ma (Figure 5.26) are similar in some respects and different in others. The axial and convex spaces at all three settlements have a weak approximation to a grid, and all three have low distributedness, that is, there are relatively few intersecting routes considering the number of axial and convex spaces. Where the three villages differ is in the breakup of axial and convex space. Hawikku has less breakup of axial and convex space than Kechiba:wa or Kyaki:ma. The inclusion of the church at Kechiba:wa makes no difference in the summarized values of syntactic variables for that village. At Hawikku, however, the inclusion of the church decreases the axial integration of convex space and increases the breakup of convex space.

The Pueblo Revolt village on Dowa Yalanne (Fig. 5.27) exhibits spatial characteristics that are virtually the mirror reverse of the attributes of the early seventeenth-century villages. The structure of axial and convex space at the Dowa Yalanne settlement has a strong approximation to a grid and is also highly distributed with numerous intersecting routes. There is relatively low breakup of axial and convex space, and the convex space system has more axial integration.

The five early farming villages of Heshoda Łuwal'a, Wimaya:wa, Shundekya, Kyaki:ma Refuge Site 11, and Kyaki:ma Refuge Site 12 exhibit some variation with respect to the syntactic grid measures (Figs. 5.28, 5.29). Three of the settlements have axial space systems with a strong approximation to a grid. Only two of them, however, have convex space systems with a strong approximation to a grid: Shundekya and Wimaya:wa. Heshoda Łuwal'a and the Kyaki:ma refuge sites have convex space systems with only a weak approximation to a grid. The configuration of the curving axial graph and y-graph of Heshoda Łuwal'a is determined by the geological barrier of the canyon around which the settlement is arranged. All the early farming villages have axial and convex space that is not highly distributed, that is, there are relatively few intersecting routes in the y-graphs. The amount of breakup of axial and convex space varies among the early farming villages.

Table 5.8. Spatial Properties Quantified by Syntactic Measures

Measure	Spatial Property
Axial articulation	Higher values mean greater breakup of axial space
Axial integration of convex space	Higher values mean less integration of convex space
Grid axiality	Higher values mean stronger approximation to a grid
Axial ringiness	Higher values mean more intersecting routes
Convex articulation	Higher values mean greater breakup of convex space
Grid convexity	Higher values mean stronger approximation to a grid
Convex ringiness	Higher values mean more intersecting routes

Heshoda Łuwal'a and Kyaki:ma Refuge Site 11 have low breakup of axial space, and the other villages have high breakup. Heshoda Łuwal'a and the two Kyaki:ma refuge sites have low breakup of convex space, and Shundekya and Wimaya:wa exhibit a high convex space breakup. The early farming villages are similar to the early seventeenth-century villages in terms of their low distributedness of axial and convex space. The strong grid approximation of the axial space systems of the early farming villages, however, is similar to the Pueblo Revolt village rather than to the early seventeenth-century villages. With respect to the other syntactic variables, Heshoda Łuwal'a is similar to Dowa Yalanne, and the other settlements are similar to the early seventeenth-century villages.

There is more variation in the 1885 farming villages of Ojo Caliente, Upper Nutria, and Lower Pescado (Figs. 5.30, 5.31) than in any other group of settlements. Ojo Caliente and Upper Nutria have convex space systems that strongly approximate a grid, but the convex space structure at Pescado has a weak approximation to a grid. With respect to the axial space system, Pescado

Table 5.9. Summary of Syntactic Grid Measures of Zuni Settlements

	AxArt	AxInteg	GrAx	AxRing	ConArt	GrCon	ConRing
Settlement group	+ = above the mean value; − = below the mean value; ( ) = beyond 1 s.d.						
Early 17th-century Villages							
Hawikku, no church	−	+	(−)	−	−	−	−
Hawikku, with church	−	−	(−)	−	+	−	−
Kechiba:wa, no church	+	+	−	(−)	(+)	−	(−)
Kechiba:wa, with church	+	+	−	(−)	(+)	−	(−)
Kyaki:ma	+	+	−	(−)	(+)	−	(−)
Pueblo Revolt Village							
Dowa Yalanne	−	(−)	+	+	−	+	+
Early Farming Villages							
Kyaki:ma Refuge Site 11	−	(+)	−	(−)	−	−	(−)
Kyaki:ma Refuge Site 12	+	(+)	+	−	−	+	−
Shundekya	(+)	(+)	(+)	(−)	+	+	−
Wimaya:wa	(+)	(+)	+	−	(+)	−	−
Heshoda Łuwal'a	−	−	−	−	−	−	−
1885 Farming Villages							
Lower Pescado	+	+	(−)	(−)	+	(−)	(−)
Ojo Caliente	−	−	−	+	−	+	+
Upper Nutria	−	−	(+)	(+)	−	(+)	+
1979 Farming Villages							
Ojo Caliente	−	−	−	−	−	−	−
Upper Nutria, no corrals	−	+	+	+	−	(+)	(+)
Upper Nutria, with corrals	−	+	+	+	−	(+)	+
Lower Nutria, no corrals	−	−	(+)	+	−	+	+
Lower Nutria, with corrals	−	+	−	−	−	+	+
Zuni Core							
Zuni 1881	(+)	+	(−)	(−)	(+)	(−)	(−)
Zuni 1915	+	+	(−)	(−)	(+)	(−)	(−)
Zuni 1972	−	−	(−)	−	−	−	−
Zuni Suburbs							
1915, North	−	−	+	+	−	+	+
1915, East	−	−	+	(+)	−	(+)	+
1915, South	−	−	+	+	−	(+)	+
1978, Suburb 1	−	−	+	(+)	−	(+)	(+)
1978, Suburb 2	−	−	−	+	−	+	+
1978, Suburb 3	−	−	−	(+)	−	+	(+)
1978, Suburb 4	−	−	−	+	−	+	+
1978, Suburb 5	−	−	−	+	−	(+)	(+)
1978, Suburb 6	−	(−)	(+)	(+)	−	+	+
1978, Suburb 7	−	(−)	(+)	(+)	−	+	+
1978, Suburb 8	−	(−)	−	(+)	−	+	+

and Ojo Caliente have a weak approximation to a grid, but Upper Nutria has a strong approximation to a grid. Ojo Caliente and Upper Nutria have a more distributed axial and convex space structure than does Pescado, which has fewer than the average number of intersecting routes. Pescado has a high amount of breakup in axial and convex space, and the other two villages have a low breakup. Pescado also has less axial integration of convex space than either Upper Nutria or Ojo Caliente.

The spatial structure of the 1885 farming villages was undergoing transition at the time they were documented, and the variation in syntactic grid measures reflects this change. Lower Pescado, which has a spatial structure with the most similarity to the earlier farming villages, was apparently the least changed in 1885. Ojo Caliente, which is similar in many respects to the settlement on Dowa Yalanne, was the most transformed. The earlier houses at Ojo Caliente were located defensively on the higher slope of the mesa east of the pueblo. By

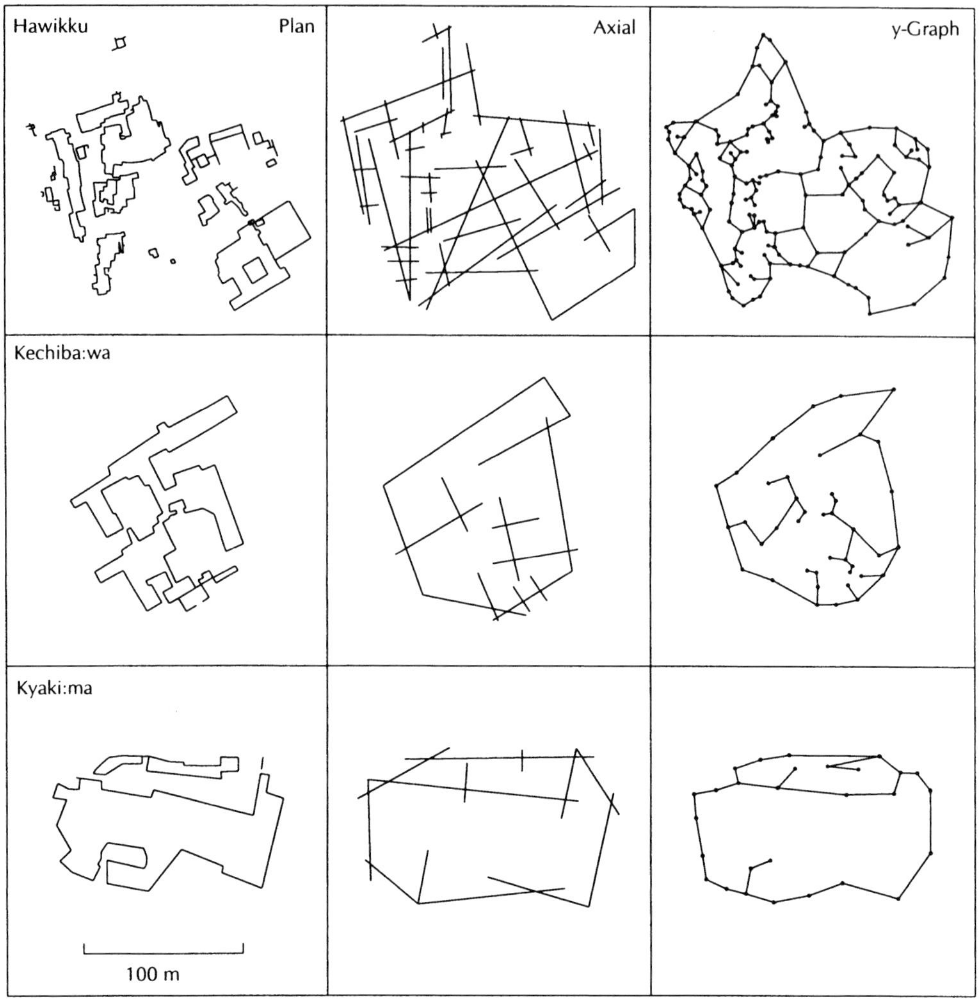

Figure 5.26. Plan views, axial graphs, and y-graphs of early seventeenth-century Zuni villages.

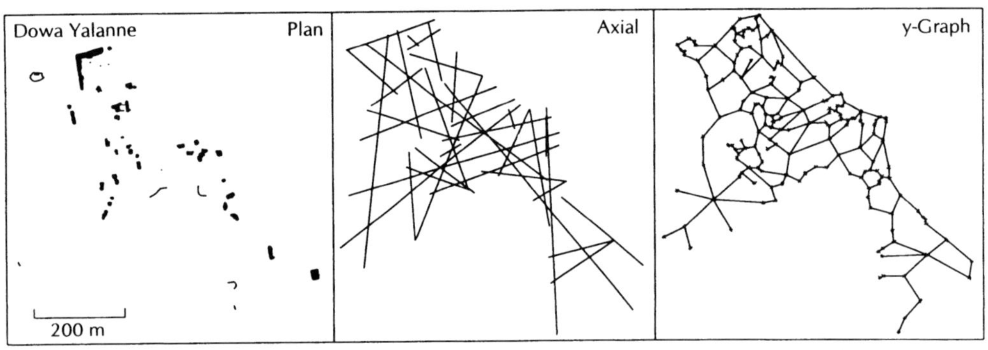

Figure 5.27. Plan view, axial graph, and y-graph of the settlement on Dowa Yalanne.

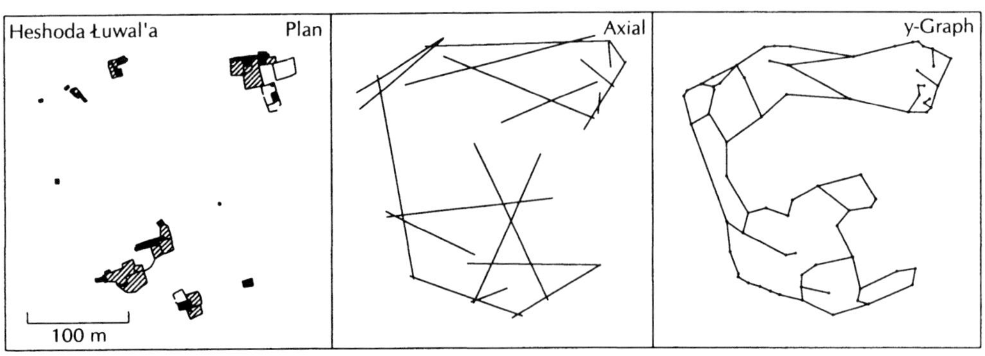

Figure 5.28. Plan view, axial graph, and y-graph of Heshoda Łuwal'a.

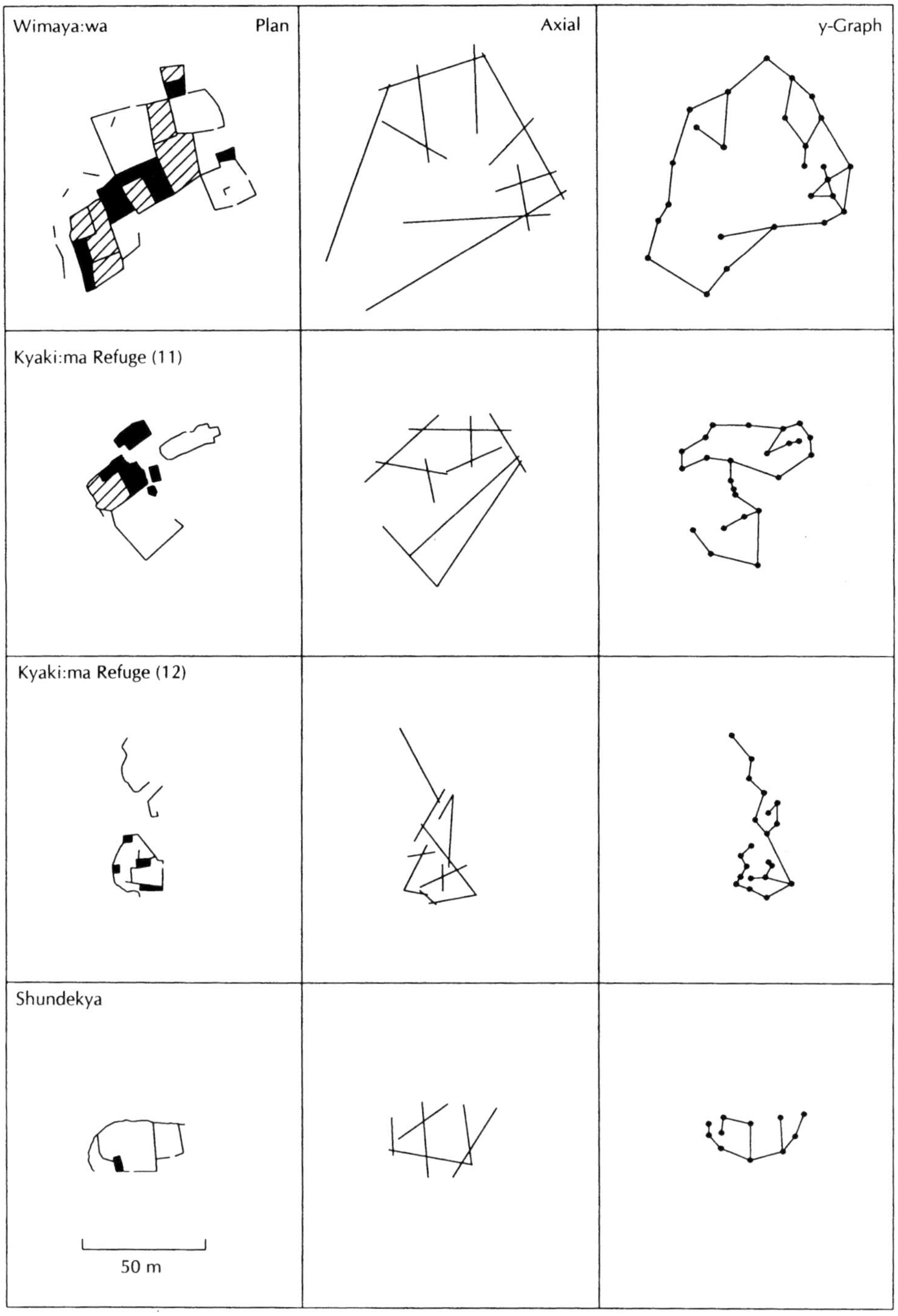

Figure 5.29. Plan views, axial graphs, and y-graphs of Wimaya:wa, Kyaki:ma Refuge Sites 11 and 12, and Shundekya.

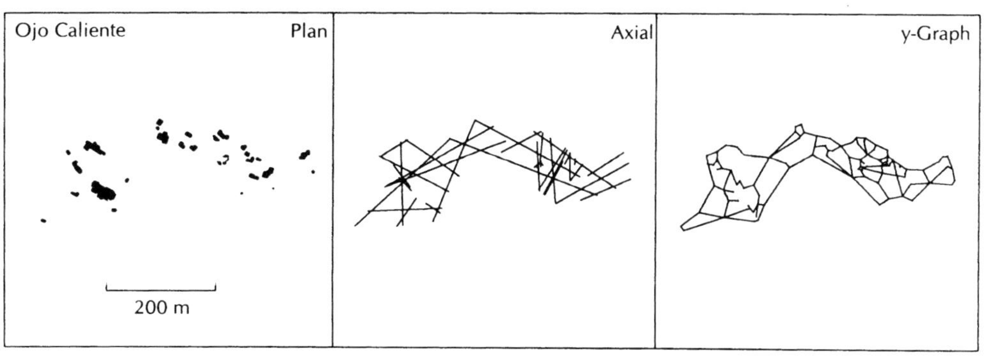

Figure 5.30. Plan view, axial graph, and y-graph of Ojo Caliente in 1885.

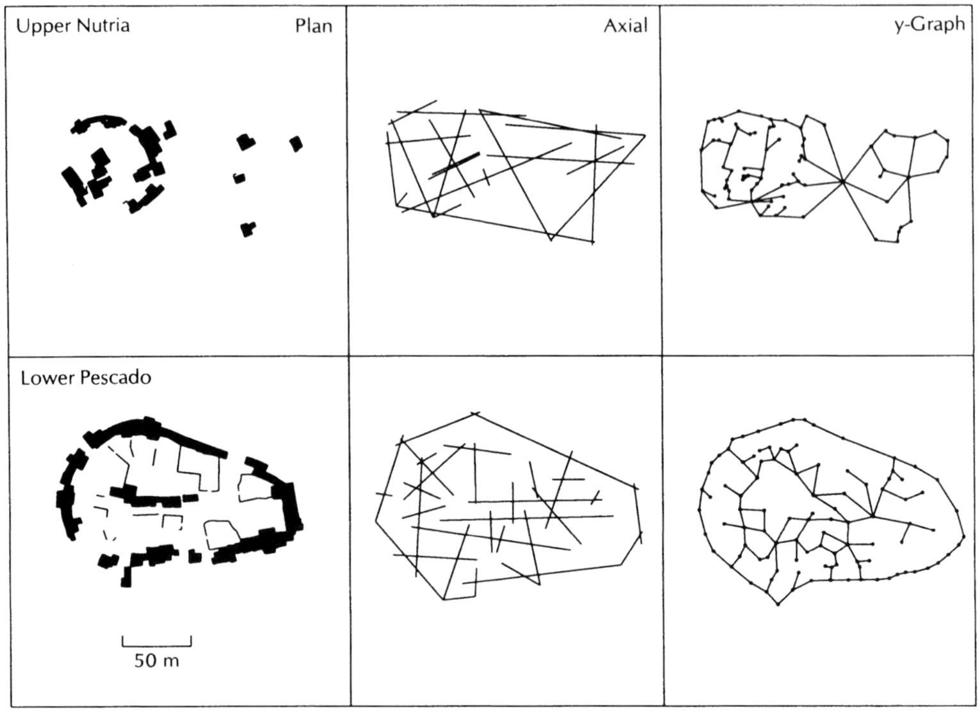

Figure 5.31. Plan views, axial graphs, and y-graphs of Upper Nutria and Lower Pescado in 1885.

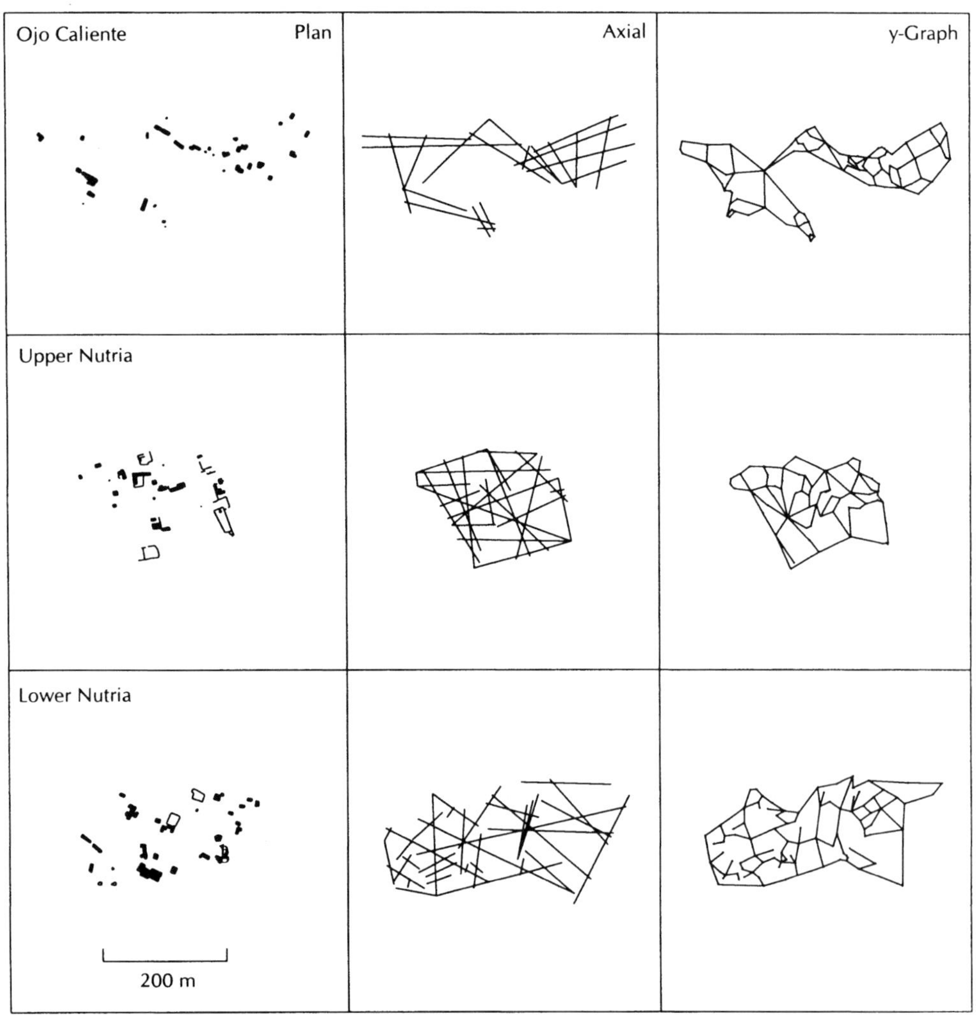

Figure 5.32. Plan views, axial graphs, and y-graphs of Ojo Caliente, Upper Nutria, and Lower Nutria in 1979. Upper Nutria and Lower Nutria are mapped with corrals.

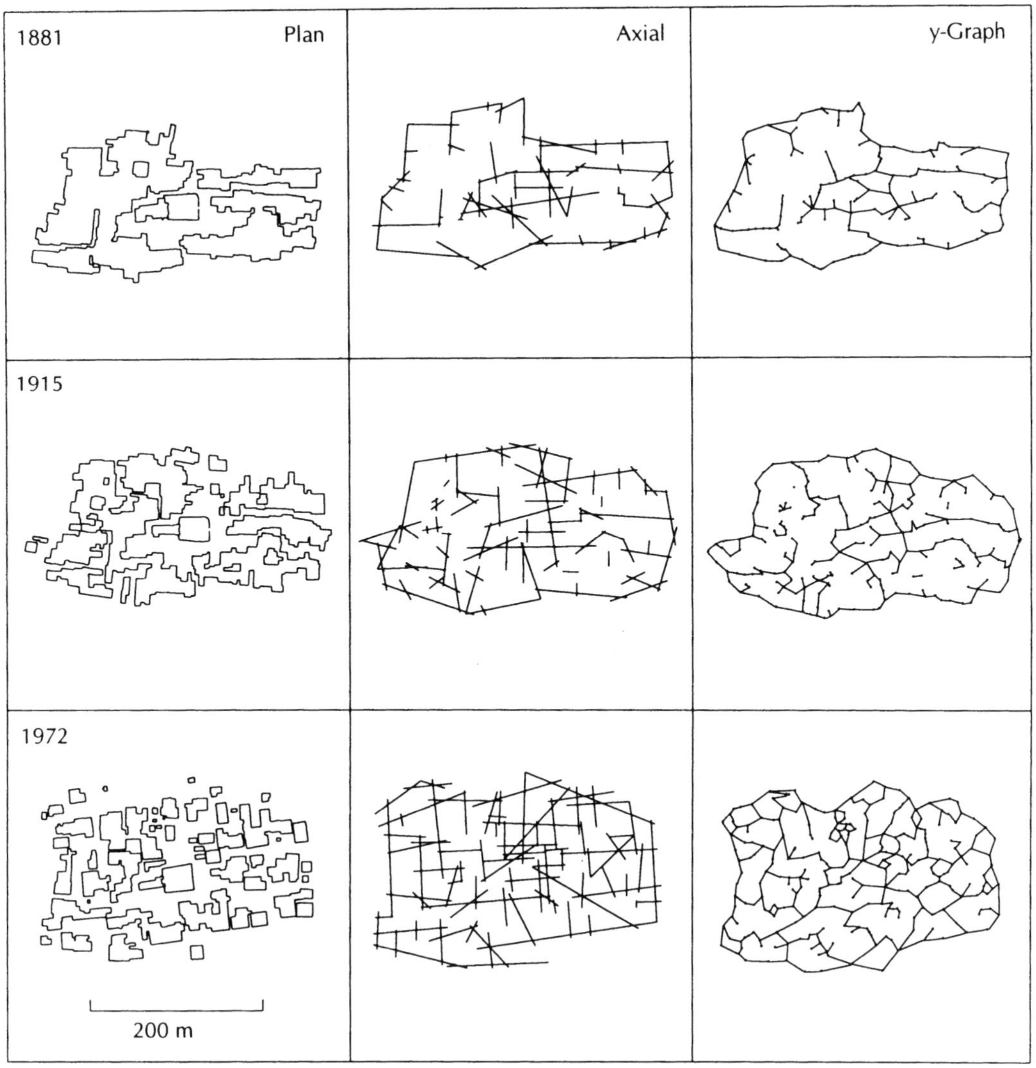

Figure 5.33. Plan views, axial graphs, and y-graphs of Zuni core architecture in 1881, 1915, and 1972.

1885, when defense was no longer a consideration, the settlement at the village had shifted to flatter, more open ground at the base of the mesa.

At Upper Nutria in 1885, the four dispersed houses at the east end of the settlement had been recently constructed, and the curving, more tightly clustered group of room blocks at the west end retained its earlier configuration. On a small scale, Upper Nutria combines the clustered room block orientation of Lower Pescado with the more open and dispersed arrangement of Ojo Caliente. It is not surprising, then, that Upper Nutria shares some spatial attributes with Pescado and others with Ojo Caliente. Upper Nutria is like Pescado in terms of axial ringiness, grid convexity, and convex ringiness, and like Ojo Caliente in terms of axial articulation and axial integration of convex spaces.

By 1979, all the occupied farming villages had been transformed with spatial structures similar to that of Ojo Caliente a century earlier (Fig. 5.30). With two exceptions, the axial and convex space systems have a strong approximation to a grid and many intersecting routes (high distributedness; Fig. 5.32). The exceptions are Ojo Caliente and Lower Nutria analyzed in a configuration that includes corrals. These settlements have a weak approximation to a grid and low distributedness. There is very little breakup of axial space and low convex articulation at all the 1979 farming villages. The axial integration of convex space is high at Upper Nutria with and without corrals and at Lower Nutria with corrals. At Ojo Caliente and Lower Nutria, excluding corrals, there is less of this type of integration. Spatially the 1979 farming villages share many of the properties exhibited at the settlement on Dowa Yalanne, especially the strong approximation of the open space to a grid and high distributedness.

The core architecture of Zuni Pueblo in 1881, 1915, and 1972 has some spatial attributes that are consistent and some that change through time (Fig. 5.33). The core architecture of Zuni Pueblo has consistently low distributedness, indicating relatively few intersecting routes, and the axial and convex space systems have a consistently weak approximation to a grid. The core of Zuni Pueblo in 1881 and 1915, however, has a greater breakup of axial and convex space, and less integration of convex space than the core in 1972.

The spatial structure of the core of Zuni Pueblo in 1881 and 1915 is similar to the early seventeenth-century villages of Kechiba:wa and Kyaki:ma in terms of the weak approximation to a grid, the low amount of distributedness, the greater breakup of axial and convex space, and less axial integration of convex space. The core of Zuni Pueblo in 1972 is similar to Upper Nutria in 1885, with low values for all syntactic grid variables.

The settlements with the least variability in the summarized spatial attributes are the suburbs of Zuni Pueblo. The suburbs in 1915 have consistently high values or consistently low values for the variables, as do the suburbs in 1978 with the exception of the variable of grid axiality. All the suburbs in 1915 and 1978 have high distributedness, indicating many intersecting routes. The convex space system of all the suburbs shows a strong approximation to a grid. Only two of the eight suburbs in 1978, however, have axial space systems with a strong approximation to a grid. One of the suburbs in 1978 with axial space that strongly approximates a grid is a HUD subdivision and the other is a Zuni vernacular suburb. All the suburbs in 1915 and 1978 have low breakup of axial and convex space and high axial integration of convex space. In general, the Zuni suburbs in 1915 and 1978 have spatial attributes that are more similar to the spatial attributes of Dowa Yalanne than to those of any other settlements.

Synchronic and Intragroup Variation in the Integration of Axial Space

The synchronic variation in the integration of axial space of settlements organized into chronological-functional groups is analyzed as a prelude to the diachronic and functional analysis of change in axial integration that follows. The investigation of synchronic variation includes an analysis of variance of RRA values to determine if there is significant intragroup variation, supplemented by notched box plots to visually isolate variation in RRA. A Kolmogorov-Smirnov one-sample test shows that RRA is not normally distributed (number of cases = 1,158; maximum difference = 0.592; 2-Tail probability = 0). Therefore, the nonparametric Kruskall-Wallis One-Way Analysis of Variance statistic is used to determine if there are significant differences between the RRA values within temporal-functional groups of settlements. In the Kruskall-Wallis analysis of variance the null hypothesis that the samples are equal is rejected when the probability is less than 0.05.

The three early seventeenth-century villages are analyzed in configurations excluding the churches at Hawikku and Kechiba:wa. The analysis of intrasite variation presented above indicated that the exclusion of the churches at these settlements makes no statistical difference in the distribution of RRA values. The analysis of variance in the RRA values of the early seventeenth-century villages indicates that there is no significant variance in this variable with the three of them taken as a group (Table 5.10). The notched box plots presented in Figure 5.34, however, show some variation between individual pairs of villages. Although the integration of axial space at Kyaki:ma is similar to both Kechiba:wa and Hawikku, Hawikku and Kechiba:wa are significantly different in this regard. Of the three, Kechiba:wa has the least integration of axial space. Kyaki:ma and Hawikku have almost the same median value for RRA, but Hawikku has a wider range of values and a narrower interquartile spread.

The analysis of variance of RRA of the five early farming villages indicates there is no statistically significant difference between the samples in the group. The notched box plots confirm this observation, as all the villages have overlapping confidence intervals (Fig. 5.35). Although the range of RRA values and the interquartile spread of the villages varies, all of them have a similar level of integration of axial spaces.

The results of the analysis of variance for the 1885 farming villages indicate there is a significant difference in RRA values among the settlements composing this group (Table 5.10). Examination of the notched box plots of RRA values for these villages reveals that Pescado has a significantly less integrated axial space structure than either Upper Nutria or Ojo Caliente (Fig. 5.36). The confidence intervals for Upper Nutria and Ojo Caliente overlap, indicating there is no significant difference in axial integration between them.

The 1979 farming villages were analyzed in configurations excluding corrals at Upper Nutria and Lower Nutria. As the analysis of variance indicates, the three 1979 farming villages have significant variation in their RRA values (Table 5.10). The notched box plots show that Upper Nutria has a significantly more integrated axial space structure than either Ojo Caliente or Lower Nutria, as well as a narrower spread of values (Fig. 5.37). The confidence intervals around the distribution of RRA values at Ojo Caliente and Lower Nutria overlap, indicating these two villages have similar median values. In interpreting these results, it is important to note the intrasite analysis of the effect of corrals on RRA values at Upper Nutria and Lower Nutria. Although the inclusion or exclusion of corrals made no difference in integration at Upper Nutria, at Lower Nutria the inclusion of corrals resulted in an axial space system that was significantly less integrated (higher RRA) than the configuration excluding the corrals. An analysis of Lower Nutria with corrals compared to Ojo Caliente shows confidence intervals that do not overlap, indicating the axial integration of Lower Nutria with corrals is significantly less than the other 1979 farming villages.

The analysis of variance of RRA values for the core architecture of Zuni Pueblo in 1881, 1915, and 1972 indicates there is a significant difference in the median values of the samples comprising this group (Table 5.11). The notched box plots show that the axial space in the core of Zuni Pueblo became increasingly more integrated through time (Fig. 5.38). None of the confidence intervals for the core of Zuni Pueblo overlap, indicating there is a significant difference in the integration of the core at all three points in time.

The three Zuni suburbs in 1915 present an anomalous statistical case. The analysis of variance indicates the three samples do not have equivalent medians (Table 5.11). However, the notched box plots show overlapping confidence intervals for all three samples, suggesting there is no difference between the samples (Fig. 5.39). The north suburbs exhibit more integration than the east and south suburbs, and seemingly that set of box plots fits into the 5 percent of cases outside the confidence intervals.

The analysis of variance of the suburbs in 1978 indicates the median values of integration of the samples are not equal (Table 5.11). The notched box plots depict a substantial amount of variation among different samples of suburbs (Fig. 5.40). The variation in median integration cross-cuts the distinction between vernacular and HUD subdivisions. Suburbs 1 through 6 are vernacular suburbs, and Suburbs 7 and 8 are HUD subdivisions. The suburbs with overlapping confidence intervals are tabulated in Table 5.12. All the suburbs have confidence intervals that overlap with at least one other suburb. One vernacular suburb (Suburb 2) overlaps only with a HUD subdivision (Suburb 8). Similarly, one HUD subdivision (Suburb 7) overlaps only with one vernacular suburb (Suburb 3). One HUD subdivision (Suburb 8) has a similar level of axial integration as five of the six vernacular suburbs. Although this variation in the integration of axial space in the suburbs is interesting, it is relevant to note that the median RRA value of all the suburbs is less than 1. All the suburbs of Zuni Pueblo in 1978 are relatively well integrated compared to other Zuni settlements.

Diachronic and Functional Variation in the Integration of Axial Space

Diachronic and functional variation in the integration of axial space is investigated by comparing the RRA values of eight groups of settlements. Zuni Pueblo and its suburbs in 1915 and 1978 are compared in a separate analysis.

An analysis of variance of the RRA of the Zuni settlements grouped by time and function indicates that there is significance difference between the various groups of settlements (Table 5.13). Notched box plots show where this variation occurs (Fig. 5.41). The median RRA value for the eight groups is 0.914. Groups with RRA values above the mean thus include the early seventeenth-century villages, the early farming villages, and the core architecture of Zuni Pueblo in 1881 and 1915. The settlements in these groups have significantly less integration of axial space than do the settlements in the other groups. Spatially, the most integrated settlements include Dowa Yalanne, the 1885 and 1979 farming villages, and the core of Zuni Pueblo in 1972.

Only two sets of grouped settlements in Figure 5.41 have overlapping 95 percent confidence intervals. The confidence intervals of early farming villages overlap with those of the core of Zuni Pueblo in 1881 and in 1915, and the confidence intervals of the 1885 and 1979 farming villages also overlap. These overlaps indicate these two sets of groups have similar levels of axial space integration. All the other groups have significantly different levels of spatial integration.

The earliest group, the villages occupied in the early seventeenth century, have a median RRA value that is close to but above the median. This value indicates the settlements in this group have relatively less spatial integration than Dowa Yalanne, the 1885 and 1979 farming villages, and the core of Zuni Pueblo in 1972, but more integration than the early farming villages and the core of Zuni Pueblo in 1881 and 1915.

The settlement on Dowa Yalanne has the lowest median RRA value of any group, indicating it has the most integrated axial space structure. The axial space of Dowa Yalanne is significantly more integrated than that of the earlier villages whose occupation was relinquished at the time of the Pueblo Revolt in 1680.

Table 5.10. Analysis of Variance of RRA Values

Settlement group	Count	Krusskall-Wallis Test Statistic	Probability
Early Seventeenth-century Villages			
Hawikku, no church	46	5.880	0.053
Kechiba:wa, no church	15		
Kyaki:ma	13		
Early Farming Villages			
Heshoda Łuwal'a	20	7.854	0.097
Kyaki:ma Refuge Site 11	10		
Kyaki:ma Refuge Site 12	12		
Shundekya	6		
Wimaya:wa	11		
1885 Farming Villages			
Upper Nutria	21	36.920	0.000
Lower Pescado	33		
Ojo Caliente	34		
1979 Farming Villages			
Upper Nutria	19	31.512	0.000
Ojo Caliente	21		
Lower Nutria	16		

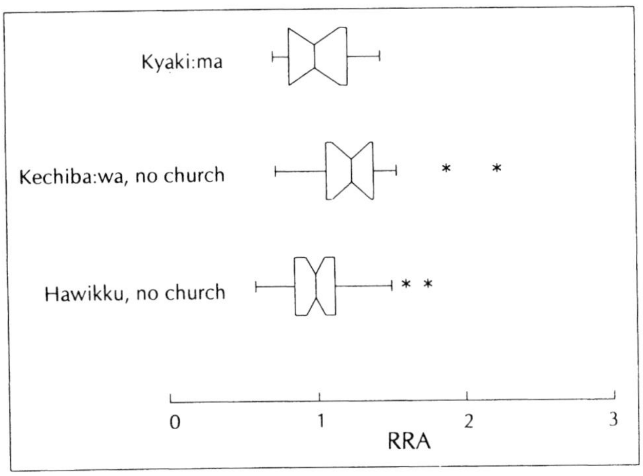

Figure 5.34. Notched box plots of RRA values of early seventeenth-century villages.

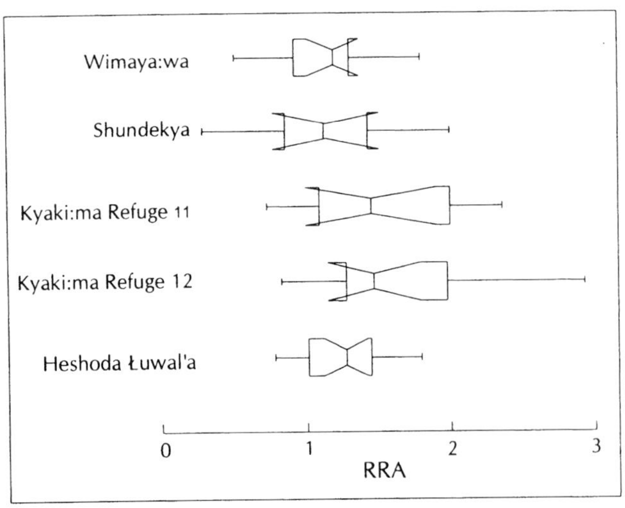

Figure 5.35. RRA values of early farming villages.

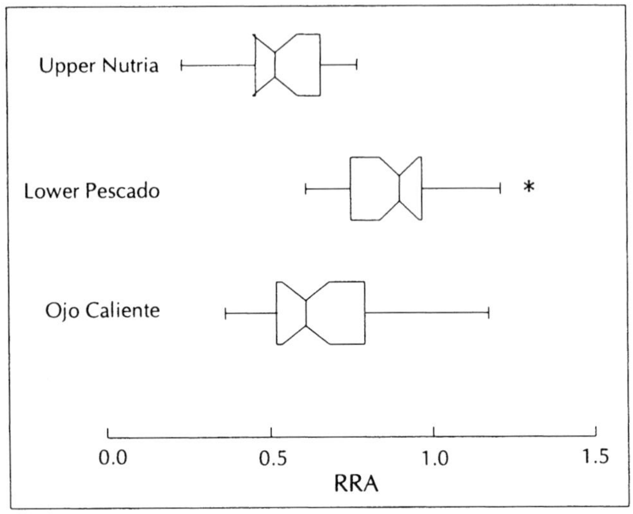

Figure 5.36. RRA values of 1885 farming villages.

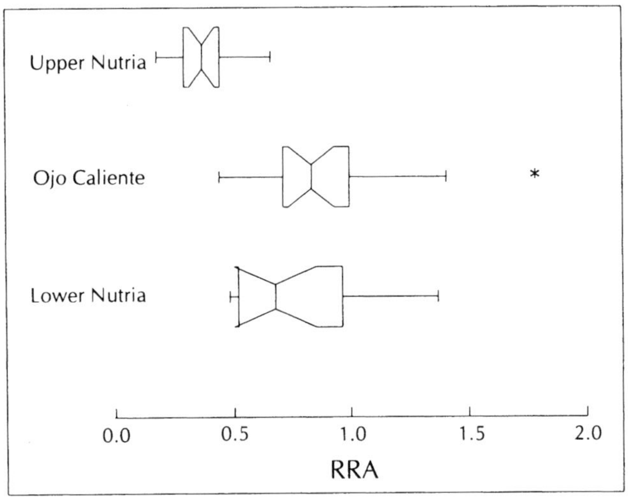

Figure 5.37. RRA values of 1979 farming villages.

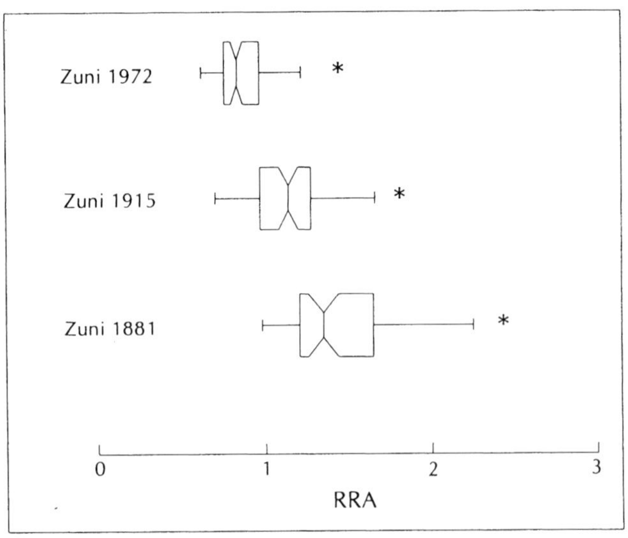

Figure 5.38. RRA values of core architecture in Zuni Pueblo in 1881, 1915, and 1972.

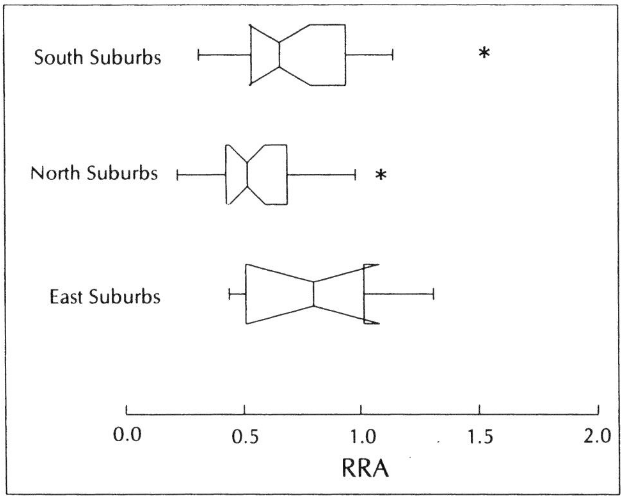

Figure 5.39. RRA values of Zuni suburbs in 1915.

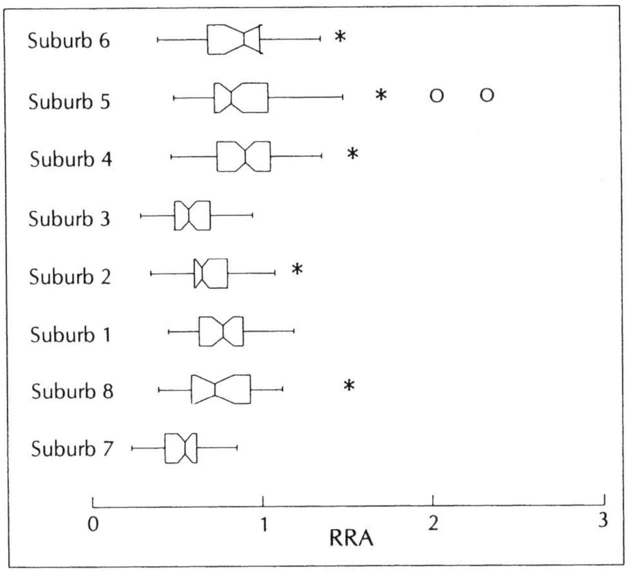

Figure 5.40. Notched box plots of Zuni suburbs in 1978.

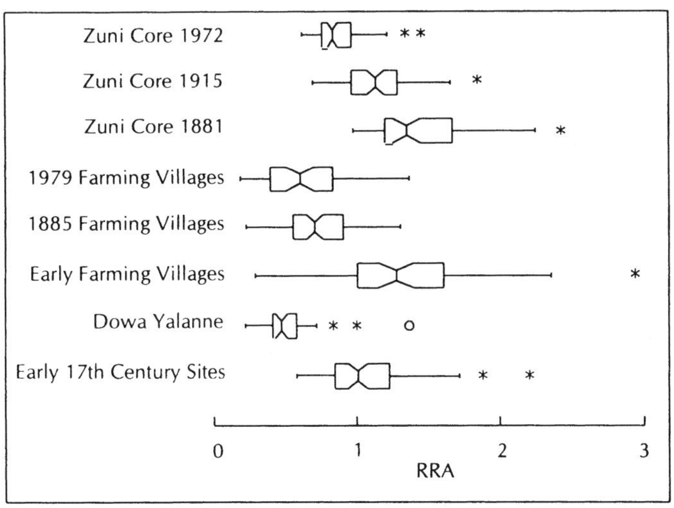

Figure 5.41. RRA values for Zuni settlements grouped by time and function.

Table 5.11. Analysis of Variance of RRA Values

Settlement group	Count	Krusskall-Wallis Test Statistic	Probability
Zuni Pueblo, 1881, 1915, 1972			
1972	86	116.377	0.000
1915	68		
1881	59		
Zuni Suburbs, 1915			
North Suburbs	29	8.264	0.016
East Suburbs	8		
South Suburbs	23		
Zuni Suburbs, 1978			
Suburb 1	42	133.459	0.000
Suburb 2	56		
Suburb 3	50		
Suburb 4	75		
Suburb 5	56		
Suburb 6	19		
Suburb 7	47		
Suburb 8	23		

Table 5.12. The 1978 Zuni Suburbs with Overlapping 95 Percent Confidence Intervals

Zuni	95% Confidence Intervals Overlap with:
Suburb 1	5, 6, 8
Suburb 2	3, 8
Suburb 3	2, 7, 8
Suburb 4	5, 6
Suburb 5	1, 4, 6, 8
Suburb 6	1, 4, 5, 8
Suburb 7	3
Suburb 8	1, 2, 3, 5, 6

Table 5.13. Analysis of Variance of RRA Values of Zuni Settlements

Settlement group	Count	Krusskall-Wallis Test Statistic	Probability
Grouped by Time and Function			
Early 17th-century Villages	74	278.238	0.000
Dowa Yalanne	35		
Early Farming Villages	59		
1885 Farming Villages	88		
1979 Farming Villages	56		
Zuni Core 1881	59		
Zuni Core 1915	68		
Zuni Core 1972	86		
Zuni Core and Suburbs			
Zuni Core 1972	86	168.446	0.000
Zuni Core 1915	68		
1915 Suburbs	60		
1978 HUD Suburbs	70		
1978 Vernacular Suburbs	298		

The early farming villages occupied in the eighteenth and early nineteenth centuries have a spatial structure much less integrated than that of Dowa Yalanne. This structure is also less integrated than that of the early seventeenth-century villages.

The spatial structure of the nineteenth- and twentieth-century farming villages is much more integrated than that of the early farming villages, but less integrated than that of Dowa Yalanne. The 1885 farming villages have a median RRA that is slightly higher than the 1979 farming villages, but the overlapping confidence intervals of the two groups indicate that they have essentially the same level of integration. The analysis of synchronic variation should be kept in mind when considering the three 1885 farming villages as a group. As previously discussed, the farming villages in 1885 were undergoing a transformation at the time they were documented. Lower Pescado was apparently the least changed and had the highest median RRA. Upper Nutria and Ojo Caliente had a more integrated spatial structure than Pescado at the time. Integration continued to increase at the farming villages, and the results of this trend are clearly evident in all of the farming villages occupied in 1979.

The axial space structure of the core of Zuni Pueblo becomes significantly more integrated through time, and the range and interquartile spread of RRA becomes increasingly compressed. The confidence intervals of the core of Zuni Pueblo in 1881 and 1915 do not overlap with each other, but they both overlap with those of the early farming villages. The core of Zuni Pueblo in 1881 and in 1915 are among the least integrated of all Zuni settlements. The core of Zuni Pueblo in 1881 and the core in 1972 are both significantly less integrated than the axial space structures of the contemporaneous farming villages. Thus, although the core of Zuni Pueblo becomes increasingly integrated through time, it remains the least integrated of any occupied Zuni settlement.

An analysis of variance of RRA of the core of Zuni Pueblo and its contemporaneous suburbs indicates there are significant differences between the median values in the group of samples (Table 5.13, p. 113). For purposes of analysis, the six 1978 vernacular suburbs were differentiated from the two 1978 HUD subdivisions. Notched box plots of the core and suburbs in 1915 and 1978 show that the only samples with overlapping confidence intervals are the 1915 suburbs and the 1978 HUD subdivisions (Figure 5.42). All the other samples have significantly different levels of integration. In 1915 the suburbs were considerably more integrated than the core of the pueblo. Although the axial integration of the pueblo core greatly increased by the 1970s, the contemporaneous suburbs still had significantly higher median RRA values. The decrease in integration between the 1915 suburbs and the 1978 vernacular suburbs shows that integration of axial space decreased as the relatively open suburbs in 1915 were gradually filled with many additional houses. Although there is still a significant difference between the core architecture and the suburbs, the overall trend is toward these settlement units becoming more similar in terms of integration.

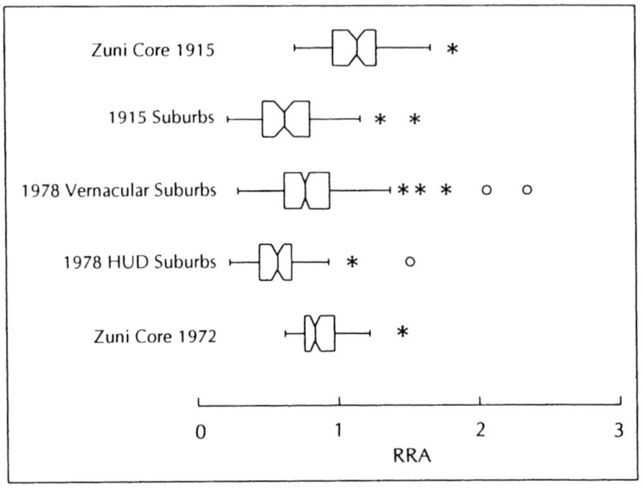

Figure 5.42. Notched box plots of RRA values of Zuni Pueblo core and suburbs.

These analyses have demonstrated that (1) there is variation in the open space structure of historic Zuni settlements, (2) this spatial structure has changed through time, and (3) the open space structure of Zuni Pueblo is different from that of the contemporaneous farming villages. The remaining question to be addressed is what this variation means in relation to the structure of Zuni society, and for that the variation in open space structure is interpreted using the precepts of the social logic of space.

SOCIOLOGICAL INTERPRETATION OF STRUCTURAL VARIATION IN OPEN SPACE AT ZUNI SETTLEMENTS

In the process of constructing new settlements and reconstructing existing villages to facilitate their socioeconomic activities, the Zuni have continually replicated their society. Zuni society is not static, however, and social change has occurred during the replicative process. At the same time that the Zuni have recreated many elements of their society in their previously existing form, they have also eliminated other elements and added some new features. Since the arrival of the Spaniards in the sixteenth century, the Zuni have increasingly participated in a world system involving successive political states that have imposed external social and architectural forms on the reproductive process (Hall 1989). A remarkable continuity in the overall structure of Zuni society has been accompanied by a modification of some social and architectural forms. Social structure derives from and takes form in social praxis or action, and the architectural facilities constructed as a part of that praxis provide a material trace that can be used as archaeological evidence to chart the development of Zuni society.

Theoretical Considerations Applied to Zuni Settlements

Interpretation of settlement structure using the social logic of space focuses on the interface that open space creates for social interaction among inhabitants and between inhabitants and outsiders. Both types of social interaction are important in understanding Zuni settlements. Social interaction among the Zuni binds them together in a well-integrated society, and this social interaction is constrained and enabled by the spatial structure of their villages. Two types of interaction between the Zuni and outsiders have also been historically important. First is the interaction with non-Indian political states, represented architecturally in this analysis by the occupation of Dowa Yalanne, the incorporation of Catholic churches into the settlement plans of some Zuni villages, and the recent development of government office buildings and HUD-sponsored subdivisions. Second are the occasionally hostile relations with Navajo and Apache bands that raided Zuni settlements prior to the late nineteenth century. These hostile social relations, and the concomitant need for defense in structuring social interaction with other Indian groups, have architectural correlates.

According to Hillier and Hanson (1984: 142), the principal axiom for the social logic of space is that spatial organization is a function of social solidarity and different forms of social solidarity are contingent on the structure of society as both a spatial and a transpatial system. In Durkheimian terms, mechanical solidarity requires a segregated and dispersed space, whereas organic solidarity requires an integrated and dense space. In interpreting the syntactic measures of spatial arrangements, Hillier and Hanson (1984: 96–97) postulate that asymmetry is related to social segregation and symmetry is related to social integration. Similarly, distributedness is related to the diffusion of social control and nondistributedness is related to the unitary and superordinate control of social interaction.

Hillier and Hanson (1984: 256–261) elaborate the notions of mechanical and organic solidarity as related to spatial structure by distinguishing between correspondence and noncorrespondence in spatial and social systems. In a correspondence system, spaces and socially labeled groups correspond to each other, a situation that occurs at the expense of relations with members of other spatial groups. In Zuni society, the primary spatial group corresponding to a social group is the household. In a noncorrespondence system, spaces and socially labeled groups do not correspond; the social groups are transpatial in that they are distributed among the various spatial groups. Transpatial social groups at Zuni include clans, kiva organizations, and other religious sodalities whose membership is not defined by spatial proximity. People belong to both spatial and transpatial groups simultaneously, and all societies exhibit a mix of correspondence and noncorrespondence subsystems in their spatial arrangements. At Zuni, as Kroeber (1915: 185) described in ethnographic terms, social integration at the community level derives from the transpatial groups that crosscut household lineages.

Because social encounters in correspondence systems result from physical proximity through membership in a spatial group, these encounters will reinforce each other at the expense of relations with members of other spatial and transpatial groups. The logic of the correspondence principle is territorial and the strength of the spatial system is a function of its ability to maintain correspondence, resulting in a spatial arrangement characterized by exclusivity, strong rules, strong boundaries, and an internally hierarchical organization. Open space within the arrangement structures deterministic rather than probabilistic encounters. The segregation and the strong control of space in correspondence systems are logical entailments of mechanical solidarity.

The logic of noncorrespondence systems entails the fact that spatial and transpatial groupings are separated. Members of spatial groups interact locally, whereas members of transpatial groups operate across space to relate individuals in different spatial groups to each other, leading to their interaction. The noncorrespondence system must maximize probabilistic encounters across space if it is to reproduce itself, because transpatial social groups depend on interaction among members of spatial groups to retain an identity as the system is reproduced. Noncorrespondence systems depend spatially on openness in the interaction of both inhabitants and noninhabitants and are facilitated by a relatively weak and diffused local organization that orients the system toward the global level. The integration of space and the diffusion of social control in noncorrespondence systems are logical entailments of organic solidarity.

Because all settlements house both spatial groups and transpatial groups, their spatial arrangements must have both local and global order (Hillier and Hanson 1984: 257–258). As settlements grow in size, the global order becomes increasingly important because there is more to hold together. Settlements can grow by either (1) adding cells to architectural units to make them larger (change in size of the spatial group), or (2) adding more cells without increasing the size of constituent architectural units, resulting in dispersion of the settlement on the landscape (change in the size of the transpatial group). The growth of the core architecture in Zuni Pueblo following the Pueblo Revolt of 1680 is an example of the former mode, and the development of the suburbs of Zuni Pueblo in the twentieth century is an example of the latter.

Spatial Properties of Zuni Settlements

The spatial properties of Zuni settlements organized into temporal-functional groups are summarized in Table 5.14. The table uses a plus sign to denote mean RRA values that are higher than the average value of all settlements (high asymmetry or segregation) and a minus sign to denote values below average (low asymmetry or integration). Plus and minus signs are also used to denote high or low distributedness based on the summary of both axial and convex ringiness presented in Table 5.9. High distributedness indicates there are many rings or intersecting routes within a settlement, and low distributedness indicates a treelike or branching structure. The differences in variables of asymmetry and distributedness are used with an evaluation of the correspondence or noncorrespondence of spatial and social systems to interpret the development of Zuni society in relation to the social logic of Zuni settlements.

It is noteworthy that the variation in the spatial structure of historic Zuni settlements is a matter of degree rather than kind. *All* the historic Zuni settlements analyzed have distributed open space systems, suggesting that a noncorrespondence system has long been a fundamental aspect of the social solidarity that spatially binds the Zuni people in communities. This

Table 5.14. Summary of Spatial Properties of Zuni Settlements

(+ = high values; − = low values)

Settlement group	Asymmetry	Distributedness
Early 17th-century Villages	+	−
Dowa Yalanne	−	+
Early Farming Villages	+	−
1885 Farming Villages	−	+
1979 Farming Villages	−	+
Zuni Core 1881	+	−
Zuni Core 1915	+	−
Zuni Core 1972	−	−
Zuni Suburbs 1915	−	+
Zuni Suburbs 1978	−	+

noncorrespondence system may not always have been in place. A number of Zuni sites that were occupied in the thirteenth and fourteenth centuries have nondistributed open space systems bounded by high walls that totally enclose the room blocks constituting the sites (Spier 1917: 246; Kintigh 1985: 21–56). The occupation of this nondistributed type of settlement, however, was relinquished prior to the beginning of the historic era in favor of villages with more open, distributed settlement plans like that exemplified by Hawikku.

Although all the historic Zuni settlements have distributed space systems, there is significant variation in the degree to which these villages include intersecting versus treelike routes. This variation is compounded by the inclusion of symmetric and asymmetric elements in the spatial syntax or rules that generate particular settlement forms. Some of the Zuni settlements like the 1979 farming villages and the Zuni suburbs incorporate the relatively simple generative rule characterized as the "clump syntax" in Chapter 2 (Table 2.1., Fig. 2.2). Other settlements like Hawikku and the core architecture of Zuni Pueblo incorporate a longer set of more complex generative rules that combine an asymmetric "central space syntax" with a symmetric syntax producing settlement plans containing both plazas and ring streets. The syntactic notion of control is linked to the generative rules that produce order in settlement plans. The longer the formula specifying the generative rules, the more control there must be in reproduction of architectural units.

Most, but not all, of the architectural units and open spaces that constitute Zuni settlements are interchangeable, that is, the syntactic relations generating the settlement obtain between any pair of symmetric features. A few architectural units at Zuni settlements are noninterchangeable, however, in that their syntactic relations are between a single feature and all other features in the settlement. Examples of noninterchangeable units at Zuni settlements include shrines, sacred areas, and Catholic churches. Noninterchangeable units require strong control of local spatial relations, which often leads to a lack of features in their immediate vicinity. The typical noninterchangeable building will thus be freestanding and surrounded by an open space barrier. The incorporation of a noninterchangeable unit into a settlement entails additional generative rules to specify its structural relation to the rest of the units and thus more control in syntactic relations.

Early Seventeenth-century Villages

The early seventeenth-century villages of Hawikku, Kechiba:wa, and Kyaki:ma are characterized by a spatial structure that exhibits relatively low integration (high asymmetry) and low distributedness. All three villages incorporate plazas that entail a relatively long set of generative rules governing their growth and that impose greater control over syntactic relations. These plazas, along with a set of shrines and sacred areas that probably existed but have not been identified archaeologically, are the main elements that constitute the global structure of the villages. The plazas at the early seventeenth-century villages are assumed to have functioned in a manner similar to the nineteenth- and twentieth-century plazas at Zuni Pueblo; they are open areas where the public gathered to observe ritual and social events. The plazas thus played a key role in structuring the dense, probabilistic encounters that a noncorrespondence system requires for social integration.

The kiva identified at Hawikku was also important in providing the global structure of the noncorrespondence system. The location of this architectural unit in an open area transected by a well-integrated axial line worked in conjunction with the plazas to encourage social encounters in the open space system. Men on their way to and from the kiva had a high probability of meeting other inhabitants of Hawikku, and any public ceremonies conducted at the kiva would attract the attention of a large segment of the community.

A complete interpretation of the encounter space of the early seventeenth-century villages is constrained by the fact that only ground level open space was analyzed. Much of the social interaction between inhabitants probably occurred on rooftop terraces, as was known to be the case at Zuni Pueblo in the nineteenth century. How these terraces structured either probabilistic or deterministic encounters was not investigated. The relatively segregated open space system, discounting the effect of the plazas, seems to suggest that mechanical rather than organic solidarity was the primary mode of social integration at the early seventeenth-century villages, but this observation may be a facile and erroneous inference. The segregated and dispersed spatial arrangement that Hillier and Hanson (1984: 142) postulate for mechanical solidarity does not fit well the early seventeenth-century villages, which are characterized by a *relatively* segregated and *dense* spatial arrangement. Although the open space of the settlements is segregated, the housing units themselves and their adjacent rooftop terraces are densely packed together in large room blocks.

In many respects, the open space system analyzed at the early seventeenth-century villages is more relevant to examining the interface that structures social interaction between the occupants of villages and visitors than that among the inhabitants themselves. The segregation in ground level open space at these villages is understandable as a means to control social interaction with visitors within the village. Access into most of the open areas at the early seventeenth-century villages was controlled at relatively few points of entry. Occupation of the rooftop terraces at these points conferred a military advantage to the inhabitants of the village during incidents where visitors tried to force their way into the settlement, as Coronado discovered during his battle at Hawikku in 1540. Hawikku is the most open of the three early seventeenth-century villages analyzed. At Kechiba:wa none of the open space within the settlement forms a ring, and at Kyaki:ma there is only one route through the pueblo forming a ring. The nondistributed open space at these settlements means that during raids the Zuni could remove the ladders that provided access onto roofs and thus prevent ingress by noninhabitants. The noninhabitants could then only circle the perimeter of the pueblo and not directly intervene in the domain of the inhabitants. Even at Hawikku, if raiding bands gained access to the open space within the perimeter of the settlement, they could only circle the perimeter of the individual, massive room blocks.

The introduction of churches at Hawikku and Kechiba:wa were effected differently at the two villages. At Hawikku, the church was situated at the edge of the community and completely surrounded by open space; it was not well integrated into the spatial structure of the settlement. At Kechiba:wa, the church was situated inside one of the plazas, with a wing wall connecting it to the edge of a room block. The fact that the church at

Kechiba:wa was only a visita, with no resident Spaniards as there were at the friary attached to the church at Hawikku, may have played a role in where the Zuni allowed the church to be constructed. The church at Kechiba:wa was surrounded by open space, but this open space was contained within one of the plazas, isolating the visita from the most integrated routes of travel through the village. Perhaps the Spaniards wanted to place the church in a plaza because it was a locus of the Zuni ceremonial activity that they were trying to supplant, and the Zuni wanted to place it there to isolate it from the rest of the village.

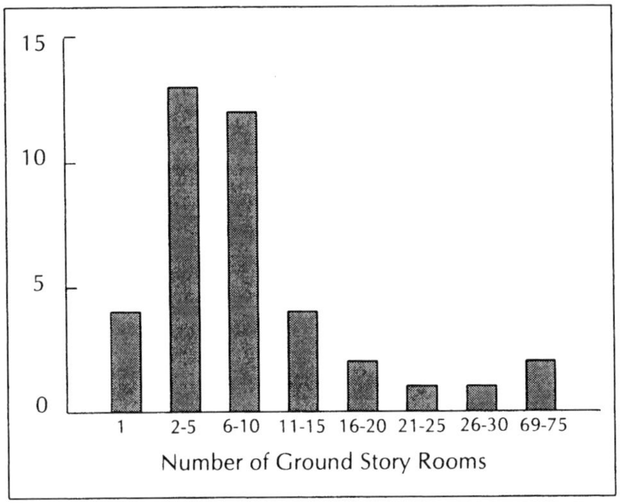

Figure 5.43. Size of architectural units in the settlement on Dowa Yalanne.

Pueblo Revolt Settlement on Dowa Yalanne

By the time of the Pueblo Revolt in 1680, the Zuni population had been substantially reduced by disease epidemics. Precise demographic figures are not available, but the population in 1680 was probably one-third or less the size of the population in 1540. This population decline required the restructuring of Zuni society in the late seventeenth century. The consolidation of Zuni settlement during the Pueblo Revolt created both the need and opportunity to restructure in a fashion that made a dramatic break with previous settlements. The relocation of the entire tribe to a single settlement on top of Dowa Yalanne thus affords an opportunity to investigate how Zuni social structure was reproduced at a critical juncture in Zuni history by analyzing the architectural arrangements constructed to house social units in the new community.

The spatial structure of the settlement on Dowa Yalanne is different from that of the early seventeenth-century villages: it is both highly integrated and highly distributed. The most prominent features of Dowa Yalanne are the individual room blocks rather than the village itself. There is a substantial amount of variation in the size and configuration of room blocks and not much global organization in the settlement. Although the two largest architectural units (Units 1 and 27) partially enclose plaza spaces with the ells of their room blocks, the entire village is not arranged with respect to these plaza areas. The few noninterchangeable features include what appear to be two small shrines (Units 58 and 60) in the center of the open space at Units 1 and 27 and perhaps one or more of the enigmatic enclosures (Units 28, 48, 49, and 52). These presumed noninterchangeable features are located at the periphery of the settlement and do not play a major role in its global organization.

Although the exact nature of the social groups that constituted the settlement on Dowa Yalanne is not known, the number of ground-story rooms in the individual room blocks provides some information about their size. There are a large number of small room blocks and relatively few large room blocks (Fig. 5.43): 74 percent of the room blocks contain 10 or fewer ground-story rooms, and another 21 percent contain between 11 and 30 rooms. There is a large jump from these relatively small room blocks to the two large room blocks that contain 69 and 75 ground-story rooms. When the multistoried architecture at the two large room blocks is considered, the difference in settlement size is even more pronounced; the two room blocks encompassed a total of 123 and 152 rooms. Together these two room blocks contain almost half the total number of rooms in the settlement.

About 25 percent of the room blocks on Dowa Yalanne incorporated unroofed enclosures in their room blocks, and many of these enclosures split the configuration of rooms into different sets. The small size of the room blocks in general and the small size of room sets in settlements containing unroofed enclosures suggest that most of the structures were built and occupied by small social groups. The theory of space syntax does not offer a means to identify the ethnographic character of these social groups, but they were probably single lineages and groups of closely related lineages or clan segments.

In contrast to the small room blocks, each of the two large room blocks on Dowa Yalanne appears to represent a much larger social grouping. Cushing (1920: 131) and Bandelier (Lange and Riley 1970: 47–50) thought that all six or seven of the contact period villages were spatially realized in clusters of room blocks on Dowa Yalanne. Such a clustering of room blocks is not readily apparent and it does not seem as if all the contact period villages are represented in the settlement pattern of Dowa Yalanne. However, some social organization larger than a small lineage or household group is needed to satisfactorily explain the two large room blocks. These two architectural units may have reproduced the social grouping of two of the earlier villages and thus be remnant communities that attempted to maintain social identity through spatial cohesion.

The diversity in the size of the room blocks provides evidence that there were different types of social groups being replicated. Slightly more that half of the rooms are distributed in the smaller room blocks that maintained open space around them, suggesting much of the community was organized around a correspondence between social and spatial groups. The two large room blocks had to have been organized with social groups characterized by a noncorrespondence or transpatial system that crosscut the local residence units that the room blocks incorporated. The apparent combination of both correspondence and noncorrespondence systems at Dowa Yalanne suggests there was a substantial amount of social experimentation going on in the settlement as the members of six or seven villages sought to reorganize themselves into a single community. Some of this experimentation appears oriented toward increasing the mechanical solidarity of the community at the expense of organic solidarity.

The dispersion of room blocks is an important component of the settlement structure. Each of the architectural units on Dowa Yalanne is a freestanding entity in the midst of a gridlike, well-integrated open space. This spatial structure would serve to maximize face-to-face encounters and social interaction as people moved around the settlement. The encounter space provided in this arrangement would be useful in fostering the social interaction needed to integrate the diverse social groups that apparently constituted the settlement.

The highly distributed and well-integrated open space of the settlement at Dowa Yalanne is apparently at odds with the defensive character of the settlement as a refuge during the Pueblo Revolt. It is clear that it was the location of the settlement on top of a sheer-sided, 300-m high mesa that provided defensibility, not the architectural arrangement of the room blocks. The settlement on Dowa Yalanne was virtually impregnable because of the difficulty in gaining access to the mesa top if the Zuni did not allow passage up one of the few, easily defended trails. Once on the mesa top, the routes of movement within the settlement were open and well distributed.

Early Farming Villages

The early farming villages occupied after the Pueblo Revolt have a spatial structure more like that of the early seventeenth-century villages than does Dowa Yalanne. The settlements of Wimaya:wa, Shundekya, Heshoda Łuwal'a, and the two Kyaki:ma refuge sites all have spatial structures that are neither highly integrated nor well distributed, even though their axial space systems have a strong approximation to a grid.

The location of these settlements on elevated landforms and their internal spatial arrangement worked together to inhibit movement into the villages from the outside, presumably for defensive purposes. The early farming villages were used to support livestock and agricultural activities on a seasonal basis. When occupied, the small size, the isolation, and the attractive resources (livestock) of these settlements put them at risk from raids from neighboring Navajo and Apache tribes. This risk was offset by locating the settlements so that they were relatively arduous to get to and by structuring the architecture to make access to them difficult. The asymmetric and nondistributed open space systems at the early farming villages were clearly oriented toward the needs of the inhabitants and not those of "visitors," or, more precisely in this case, raiding enemies.

The topography of the landforms underlying the settlements served to accentuate the attributes of spatial organization that hindered access by visitors. Intruders could be readily seen on their approach to the settlements. Heshoda Łuwal'a, in particular, was arranged around a canyon rim in a manner that would impede rapid movement through it. This obstacle would have provided time for the occupants of room blocks on one side of the canyon to prepare themselves if the room blocks on the other side were subjected to attack.

The smallest settlements at Shundekya and at the Kyaki:ma refuge sites were probably used by the minimal social units involved in the livestock industry. These architectural units consist of corral enclosures attached to a single room or small room block. The structure of Wimaya:wa appears to be an aggregation of several of these small units compounded into a single structure. The largest early farming village, Heshoda

Łuwal'a, consists of multiple architectural units that are similar to the single compound structure at Wimaya:wa. The major differences between the early farming villages are scale and the number of constituent units rather than a real difference in the organization of their internal structure.

Most of the architectural units at the early farming villages are quite small, precluding an interpretation of global versus local settlement structure. There is an apparent correspondence between the spatial and social units at the settlements in that all the architectural units have strong spatial boundaries and are spatially segregated from one another, even at the largest village of Heshoda Łuwal'a. The only evidence of transpatial social groups comes from the historical information provided by Pedro Pino, who told Cushing that the Zuni used Heshoda Łuwal'a as a refuge for conducting rituals that they wanted to keep private from the Catholic priest resident at Zuni Pueblo (Cushing, Item 36). In this situation, of course, the transpatial groups are as much associated with Zuni Pueblo as with Heshoda Łuwal'a.

The small size and the association of the early farming villages with livestock facilities suggest that their use may have been organized as much along patrilineal lines as matrilineal lines. The livestock industry today is primarily organized along patrilineal lines involving relatively small groups of men, and all available historic evidence suggests this has been the pattern for a long time. In contrast, farming has traditionally been organized along matrilineal lines, with farm land owned by women and passed within their matrilineal clans. Some of the early farming villages appear to be primarily oriented toward livestock (Shundekya and the Kyaki:ma refuge sites), and others appear to be oriented toward livestock and agriculture (Wimaya:wa and Heshoda Łuwal'a). The early farming villages, therefore, may demonstrate the initial architectural realization of a bilateral social organization that has become more prominent at Zuni Pueblo in the twentieth century.

Core Architecture of Zuni Pueblo in 1881, 1915, and 1972

The core of Zuni Pueblo provides architectural evidence about how the Zuni resolved the architectural and social experimentation they had engaged in at the Pueblo Revolt settlement on Dowa Yalanne. Following the Pueblo Revolt, the Zuni coalesced at Zuni Pueblo and greatly expanded the earlier village that had existed there. The solution to integration of the Zuni Tribe was consolidation into a single, densely packed community with a spatial structure characterized by relatively low integration and low distributedness. The spatial structure of the core of Zuni Pueblo, especially in 1881 and in 1915, is most similar to that of the early seventeenth-century villages.

The core of Zuni Pueblo is strongly oriented around a number of plazas, shrines, and sacred pathways that form noninterchangeable architectural features in the spatial structure of the settlement. These ritual spaces are integral to the global structure of the core settlement, and, in fact, have formed the nodes around which the pueblo has been transformed. As the pueblo was reconstructed in the late nineteenth and early twentieth centuries to incorporate more open space, these sacred areas have been enlarged but rarely encroached upon. The sacred spaces of Zuni Pueblo were not well delineated by the analytical techniques of space syntax, but these sacred spaces nonetheless play a critically important role in the integration of Zuni society.

Ethnographic knowledge about the location of Zuni sacred spaces clarifies the interpretation of many aspects of the open space structure. It is the plazas, shrines, and other sacred areas that provide a public space for ritual performances of the transpatial groups that crosscut the fundamental Zuni spatial group, the household. The success of Zuni Pueblo as a noncorrespondence social system hinges on the interaction of people from different households in the performance and observance of rituals, and these ceremonies require public space for their reenactment. The spatial consolidation of Zuni Pueblo following the Pueblo Revolt suggests reintegration of society based more on the principles of organic rather than mechanical solidarity.

In addition to Zuni sacred spaces, another key noninterchangeable architectural unit at Zuni Pueblo is the Catholic church. This building was originally situated at the edge of the pueblo, but it came to occupy a spatially central position when the village was expanded following the Pueblo Revolt. The Catholic church and adjacent campo santo is a classic noninterchangeable unit that is characterized by strong control of local spatial relations and a lack of other features in its immediate vicinity. The location of the Catholic church in the center of the high integration axial space network indicates how this building came to be integrated into the spatial structure of the village.

The integration of the Catholic church into the core settlement testifies to the successful imposition of new social and political forms at Zuni Pueblo derived from the forced interaction with the cultural representatives of the Spanish state, the Catholic priests. The contribution of this singular building to the global structure of Zuni Pueblo is typical of the impact that state-sponsored public architecture has on vernacular settlements. Although the church had a major impact on the spatial structure of Zuni Pueblo, it is significant that the full suite of Spanish settlement forms mandated for pueblos by Spanish law (Jojola 1993) was never implemented at Zuni. The spatial structure of Zuni Pueblo is evidence that the Zuni's participation in the Spanish state was only marginal.

The interface of the open space system at Zuni Pueblo, as described for the core in 1915, is structured more for the social interaction of the inhabitants than it is for social interaction with visitors. Visitors following the route of the highly integrated axial space network are directed toward the Catholic church and away from the dance plazas and other areas sacred to the Zuni people. The location of these sacred features is oriented toward their use by local residents.

Much of the social interaction between the inhabitants of Zuni Pueblo prior to the mid-twentieth century occurred on the densely packed rooftop terraces of the massive room blocks. The degree to which these terraces structured probabilistic or deterministic encounters was not analyzed, but examination of Mindeleff's 1881 plan suggests that these terraces have a relatively well integrated and highly distributed spatial structure that would support probabilistic social encounters.

The spatial structure of the rooftop terraces is contrasted by the asymmetrical and relatively poorly distributed ground level, open space structure at Zuni Pueblo, especially in 1881. As at the early seventeenth-century villages, the structure of this open space, combined with massive, multistoried room blocks, provided an important defensive component to the settlement plan. As the 1881 plan of Zuni Pueblo clearly illustrates, access to the pueblo interior was possible at only three points, all highly controlled. The fact that Zuni Pueblo was rarely attacked by hostile neighbors, and that when it was little damage was done, attests to the successful incorporation of defensive features into the spatial structure of the settlement.

Once the need for defense was no longer manifest at Zuni Pueblo, the Zuni people began to reconstruct their core settlement to create more open space and single story houses. This reconstruction was accomplished in a long process wherein individual families rebuilt single houses at a time. There was never a community-wide redevelopment, nor any centralized planning. Individual Zunis made decisions about what to build and where to build it based on their participation in the Zuni social system. The ritually important open spaces were preserved because the Zuni people used them; encroaching on these sacred open spaces was subject to severe social criticism. The fact that the global orientation of the pueblo toward the plazas and other ritually used open areas was preserved through many individual building episodes is a good illustration of how architectural structure derives from the reproduction of Zuni society through social interaction.

By 1972 the ground level open space system of Zuni Pueblo became virtually congruent with the social encounter space, that is, the reduction of the multistoried edifice into single story buildings resulted in the retention of only a few rooftop terraces. It is meaningful that those remaining rooftop terraces were all oriented around the plazas; the terraces served as galleries to observe ritual performances and provided an important spatial means to realize probabilistic social encounters. Today, however, most Zuni people have social encounters on the open ground surface rather than on rooftop terraces.

The increase in open space in the core architecture resulted in a significant change to more symmetry and more distributedness in the spatial structure of the pueblo. Nonetheless, the spatial structure of Zuni Pueblo remains the least symmetrical and least distributed of all occupied Zuni settlements.

The 1885 and 1979 Farming Villages Compared with Zuni Pueblo

The farming villages occupied in 1885 and 1979 form a counterpoint to Zuni Pueblo. These seasonally occupied satellite communities have a spatial and social structure that differs from that of the mother pueblo. In 1885 the farming villages of Lower Pescado, Upper Nutria, and Ojo Caliente had spatial structures characterized by more symmetry and more distributedness than the contemporaneous Zuni Pueblo.

The highly integrated and circuitous spatial structures of the nineteenth-century farming villages were used by social groups organized with a different emphasis than at Zuni Pueblo. The social organization of the farming villages was oriented toward subsistence level food production rather than toward the integration of Zuni society as a whole. As at Zuni Pueblo, the primary spatial group at the farming villages was the household. The only transpatial group of importance at the farming villages, however, was the clan. Clan members cooperated by forming communal labor parties instrumental in accomplishing the large tasks of hoeing and harvesting that were beyond the capabilities of individual households.

The farming villages were distinct from Zuni Pueblo in that Zuni ceremonialism was not fixed within their architectural structure. There were no formal plazas at the farming villages where ritual performances were regularly conducted, and, unlike Zuni Pueblo, there were no kivas or other specialized religious architecture dedicated to transpatial groups. There were occasional dances performed in the farming villages, and although these rituals were important in integrating the communities, they were not performed often enough to result in space dedicated solely for that purpose. The lack of emphasis on transpatial groups was apparent in the less global organization of the space system as compared to Zuni Pueblo.

In 1885, Lower Pescado and, to a lesser extent, Upper Nutria retained a spatial structure wherein the room blocks provided a strong boundary controlling the interior of the settlement. This settlement form requires a syntax with more rules than the "clump syntax" inherent in Ojo Caliente, which specifies only that a building be associated with an open space facing it. It is significant that as the farming villages were transformed by reconstruction in the twentieth century, their internal spaces were not maintained as discrete open areas in the same way that the plazas and sacred areas of Zuni Pueblo were preserved. The interior spaces of the farming villages had little spatial stability, in large part because these spaces had relatively limited roles in social interaction. The structure of corrals and fences inside Pescado, for instance, clearly indicate the interior of the pueblo was used primarily to protect livestock.

In 1885 Lower Pescado retained more defensive attributes than Upper Nutria or Ojo Caliente. The spatial structure of Pescado was the least integrated of the three farming villages, and its constricted entries enabled the greatest control over access into the village. Upper Nutria was in transition at the time, and four new houses had been built east of the original clustered room blocks, opening up the spatial structure as a result. By 1885 the original buildings at Ojo Caliente, located in a more defensible position on the slope of the adjacent mesa, had been abandoned in favor of more open and dispersed locations strung out along lower contours.

The trend toward a more open and dispersed settlement structure continued at the farming villages. In 1979 the farming villages had a well-integrated open space structure that was also well distributed with circuitous routes. The spatial properties of the open space structure at Upper Nutria and the new village of Lower Nutria converged with those of Ojo Caliente. Although Ojo Caliente still retained an elongated plan in comparison to the other farming villages, all the 1979 farming villages had relatively high amounts of asymmetry and distributedness compared to Zuni settlements from other periods. The open space structure at the 1979 farming villages had developed a stronger approximation to a grid than that of the 1885 villages.

Through time the architectural arrangement of the Zuni farming villages and Zuni Pueblo has changed in similar ways; there has been a trend toward more well-integrated and more distributed open space. Even so, the structure of Zuni Pueblo is still significantly less integrated than that of the farming villages. The relatively greater segregation of open space at Zuni Pueblo results in large measure from the global organization of the mother pueblo with respect to ritual spaces.

The Suburbs of Zuni Pueblo

Compared to the core of Zuni Pueblo, the suburbs in both 1915 and 1978 are predicated on a shorter set of generative rules that requires more reproductive events and less control to produce the settlement form. The primary generative rule is that of the "clump syntax," which only specifies that a building has an open space facing it. The suburbs of Zuni Pueblo are thus characterized by a spatial structure that has high integration and high distributedness.

The 1915 suburbs and the 1978 HUD subdivisions have a strong approximation to a grid. Interestingly, however, five out of six of the 1978 vernacular suburbs only have a weak approximation to a grid. This arrangement is the result of infilling of Zuni vernacular housing, which, until recently, was not positioned with regard to the road network. There is little breakup of axial or convex space at any of the suburbs. The HUD subdivisions have the clearest global structure, with the greatest regularity in the spacing of houses, but this structure is really the result of planning that is external to the pueblo and not founded in Zuni social interaction. The spatial structure of the HUD subdivisions is more integrated than that of the contemporaneous vernacular suburbs, but is similar to the level of integration of the Zuni suburbs in 1915.

Several buildings in the Zuni suburbs have either a temporary or permanent role in the transpatial organization that structures the use of public encounter space. Buildings with a temporary role include the six or seven

Shalako houses constructed every year to house a set of major ceremonies conducted prior to the Winter solstice. During the Shalako ceremony, much of the population of Zuni Pueblo visits one or more of the houses, and the neighborhood surrounding each house comprises a dense encounter space for social interaction. This effect is relatively brief for each house. It involves the kin and clan members who help construct the house during the course of a year, and it culminates at the evening performance when the Shalako figures bless each house with their dancing. Shalako houses also exist in the core pueblo and were once more numerous there than in the suburbs. With the great expansion of the Zuni population, more people now live in the suburbs than the core, however, and most of the new Shalako houses are consequently constructed in the suburbs.

There are also a few medicine societies or clan leaders who conduct ceremonies in houses in the suburbs, but this activity is not widespread there. The short term spatial effect of Shalako houses on social interaction and the relative sparsity of other ritual buildings contribute to a local rather that a global orientation in the spatial structure of the suburbs. There are several shrines spread throughout the suburbs, and although these result in small open areas that are not impeded by construction, they do not lead to a global structure tied to social interaction. Most of these shrines are used solely by members of esoteric religious groups who conduct private rather than public rituals at the shrines.

The Zuni Tribal Building housing the administrative headquarters of the tribe is located adjacent to the major east-west road in one of the northern suburbs of the town; it was not analyzed. Like other noninterchangeable units, the Zuni Tribal Building is surrounded by open space (used for vehicular access and parking) that provides a strong control over its boundary and sets it apart from the other buildings in the vicinity. Other than this exception, the tribal headquarters building has little apparent impact on the suburb where it is located.

Other institutional and therefore noninterchangeable buildings in the suburbs of Zuni Pueblo include several schools, Christian missions, and stores. These buildings serve a type of transpatial function by bringing together people from a wide range of different spatial groups, that is, different households. It is significant that not one of these institutional buildings appears to control the global structure of the suburb where it is situated in the same manner as do the plazas in the core of Zuni Pueblo.

Although HUD housing at Zuni Pueblo has been called a "Trojan Horse" and vilified for introducing unanticipated social change (Ferguson and others 1990: 116), the open space structure of HUD subdivisions is actually similar to that of the Zuni vernacular subdivisions. The major difference is one of density of occupation. The HUD subdivisions contain fewer houses per unit of space compared to the more closely packed Zuni vernacular subdivisions. Density, of course, is important in promoting probabilistic social encounters in the open space of Zuni Pueblo. Without further ethnographic study of actual human behavior, however, it is not known whether the denser vernacular suburbs also have a denser encounter rate in their open spaces. There is now substantial pedestrian and vehicular traffic in both HUD and Zuni vernacular suburbs.

Aside from the spatial correlates of social interaction, the assignment of housing in the HUD subdivisions bears little relation to the more traditional spatial arrangements where interrelated families, often a mother and her daughters, lived in proximity to one another. One interpretation of recent architectural change at Zuni Pueblo is that there is an increasing lack of articulation between the structure of architecture and Zuni social structure (Ferguson and others 1990: 117). As observed by Louis Hieb in 1993, however, another perspective is that the new architectural arrangements serve to articulate a reorganized Zuni society. The structure of Zuni society is currently undergoing a slow but fundamental change from a matrilineal to a bilateral organization, and neolocal residence patterns are becoming more common. These social changes are evident in the organization of the livestock industry, wage labor, and the ways that individual Zuni elect to accept HUD housing assignments.

From the perspective of space syntax, the reorganization of open space in the suburbs of Zuni Pueblo is primarily a function of the manner in which the Zuni reproduce society through their actions in selecting house locations and in building homes or allowing houses to be constructed for them. Individual selection of house location is the essential process connecting the open space structure of settlements to society, and the impact of this process is evident in all the historic Zuni settlements analyzed.

CHAPTER SIX

Internal Structure of Residential Space

The purpose of analyzing the recent architecture at Zuni Pueblo is to determine how the spatial structure of Zuni vernacular houses differs from that of HUD housing and to interpret this variation in terms of the social logic of space and structuration theory. The results add another dimension to our understanding of the relationship between historic Zuni architecture and social integration, and they provide insight to the drastic changes now being made to that long-held historic Zuni social organization. This study demonstrates procedures for the syntactic analysis of internal space that are applicable to well-documented settlements.

The syntactic analysis of building interiors is contingent on detailed plans that show doorways or other means of access between room spaces (for example, roof entries). Such plans are not available for any of the settlements analyzed in Chapter 5 except modern Zuni Pueblo. The two adequate sets of house plans document (1) Zuni vernacular housing and (2) HUD houses, whose construction was subsidized by the federal Department of Housing and Urban Development.

SOURCES OF INFORMATION

In this chapter, the term "house" is used as a generic expression for all residential units, including free-standing single-family dwellings and apartments. A house as an analytical unit is thus not isomorphic with a building as defined in previous chapters. It is common for large Zuni room blocks to be divided into a number of domiciles or apartments. Similarly, some HUD housing is in the form of apartment buildings.

Zuni Vernacular Housing

Information on Zuni vernacular housing came from material on file at the Zuni Archaeology Program. These records were compiled in 1967 and 1970 during a comprehensive "Housing Improvement Physical Survey" conducted by the Zuni Agency, Bureau of Indian Affairs. Each house recorded during this survey was documented with a measured plan view; a listing of the occupants by name, age, and relationship to the head of the household; photographs of the dwelling; and a description of the proposed improvements to the house. The function of most of the room spaces as used by the occupants was generally documented on the plan views.

Unfortunately, comprehensive information from only four of the seven zones documented in the survey have been archived at the Zuni Archaeology Program, along with a number of houses from a "Home Improvement Program Priority List," which crosscuts zones and includes a few houses from zones not otherwise represented. Detailed records are available from Zones 2 and 6 in the northern suburbs of Zuni Pueblo, Zone 5 in the eastern suburbs, and Zone 7 in the suburbs south of the Zuni River. Less comprehensive reports from the Priority List are also available from Zone 1 in the Old Pueblo (the core architecture of Zuni Pueblo) and Zone 4 in the suburbs south of the Zuni River.

Of the 308 houses described in the Housing Improvement Physical Survey files, only 155 were documented well enough to permit syntactic analysis. The remaining houses lacked measurements, did not depict doorways on the plan views, or suffered from other deficiencies that precluded inclusion in the analysis.

The improvements proposed for the houses documented in 1967 and 1970 included partitioning of large rooms into smaller rooms, installation of plumbing for kitchens and bathrooms, installation of electrical wiring, construction of hipped and pitched roofs to cover flat roofs, construction of plasterboard ceilings to shield roof beams, plastering of exterior and interior walls, construction of new floors, and installation of major appliances (stove, refrigerator, water heater). These improvements attest to the relatively recent acquisition by many Zuni families of amenities considered part of the normal standard of living in the United States.

Many of the Zuni houses documented in the survey are apartments contained within larger room blocks. The connection of these apartments to the larger room blocks was often, but not always, documented on plan views. In some cases this information could only be discerned by examining photographs. The documentation of many apartments without reference to the larger room blocks containing them is one indication of how the Zuni perceive these apartments as the domiciles of individual households. The apartments contained within large Zuni room blocks are occasionally interconnected by doors, especially when adjacent apartments are occupied by closely related families. In this case, the different households are socially demarcated by the presence of their own kitchens. No examples of such interconnected apartments, however, were documented in the survey.

HUD Housing

Information about HUD houses was derived from nine, "as built" architectural drawings obtained from the Zuni Housing Authority by Roger Anyon, the Director of the Zuni Archaeology Program. These architectural drawings were prepared by the commercial architectural firms who designed the housing units. Represented in this sample are plans for two-bedroom and three-bedroom apartments constructed in 1977; plans for three-, four-, and five-bedroom single-family dwellings constructed in 1980; and plans for two-, three-, four-, and five-bedroom single-family dwellings constructed in 1984.

Room function discerned from the HUD housing plans is the use envisioned by the architect, not necessarily how the Zuni have actually used those spaces. Casual visitation at a number of HUD houses shows that most rooms are generally used for their intended purposes: living rooms contain televisions for entertainment and are where guests sit while visiting, bedrooms are used for sleeping, and so forth. One notable modification is the presence of jewelry workshops in living rooms or bedrooms. Several Zunis have also built large living rooms attached to their HUD houses, much larger than the original living room in the HUD plan. Modifications of this type are not included in this analysis.

The Zuni who are selected as clients of the Zuni Housing Authority generally choose the house plan they want built and, occasionally, the type of siding or façade from the two or three alternatives offered. Other than these restricted choices, the Zuni have had no influence in the design process of HUD housing, which is driven by a concern for "prototype cost," that is, maximizing the number of houses that can be built with a finite amount of funding from HUD.

SIZE OF HOUSEHOLDS OCCUPYING VERNACULAR ARCHITECTURE

Household size was documented for 151 of the houses recorded during the Housing Improvement Physical Survey. There were 1,249 persons living in these houses, constituting about 26 percent of the 1970 population, which was 4,869 (Hart 1991a: 60). The number of people comprising households varied between a minimum of 2 and a maximum of 23, with a mean household size of 8.39 persons (Table 6.1). A histogram of household size depicts a distribution with a bell-shaped curve and one outlier (Fig. 6.1).

There is substantial variation in the actual populations of households, as well as in two of the proxy measures of population commonly used by archaeologists. For instance, the number of persons per room in households varies from a minimum of 0.18 to a maximum of

Table 6.1. Size of Zuni Households

Measure	Minimum	Maximum	Mean	s.d.
Population/household	2.00	23.00	8.39	4.07
Population/rooms	0.18	8.50	1.66	1.25
Area (sq. m) /population	2.29	132.00	18.63	15.39

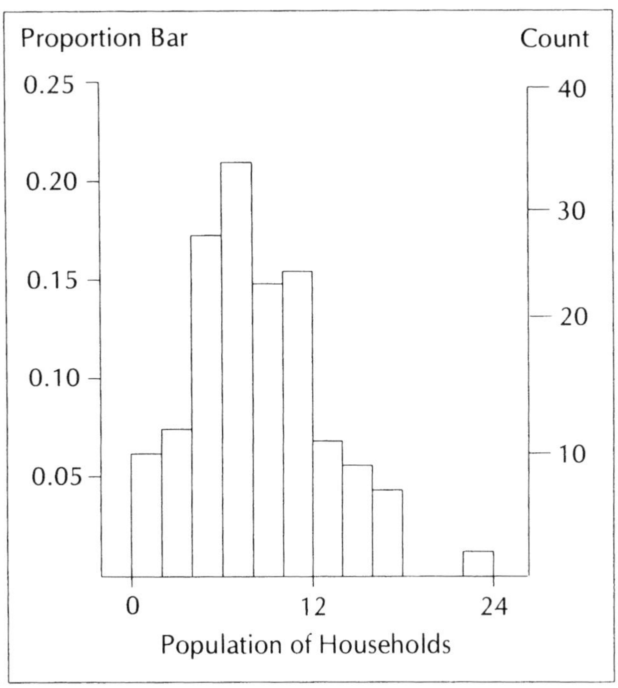

Figure 6.1. Histogram of the size of Zuni households in vernacular houses.

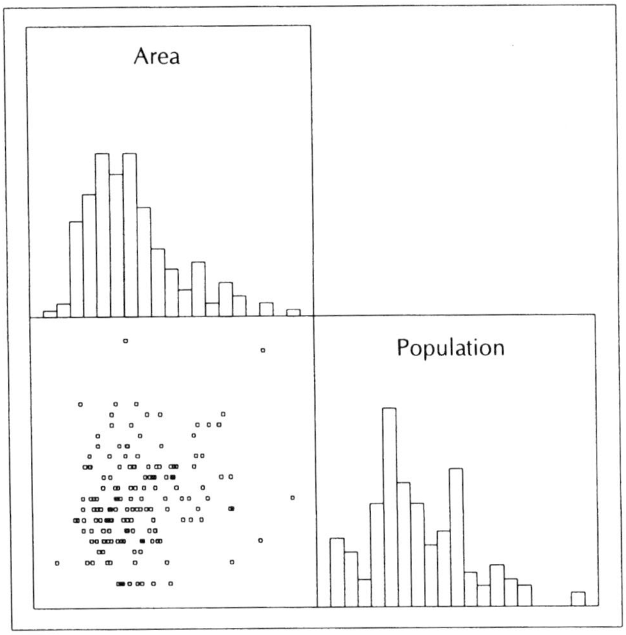

Figure 6.2. Bivariate plot of area of houses (in square meters) and household population.

of 8.5, with a mean of 1.66 (Table 6.1). Similarly, the number of square meters per person in households varies from a minimum of 2.29 to a maximum of 132.00, with a mean of 18.63 (Table 6.1). The lack of correlation (R = 0.226) between the area of households and household size is seen in the wide spread of values in a bivariate plot of these two variables (Fig. 6.2). The variation in the size of households is indicative of a concomitant variation in the social structure of Zuni households, ranging from dyads to large extended families. This variation seems to reflect both the developmental cycle of the domestic group (Goody 1971) and the occurrence of a number of different household types.

Although the "ownership" of Zuni houses is attributed to both men and women, it is men who are predominantly listed as "owners." This is a surprising change because Zuni houses were traditionally owned by Zuni women. To some degree the frequent attribution of male ownership reflects new patterns of bilateral and neolocal residence, but it probably also represents the application of non-Zuni classificatory criteria. The BIA Home Improvement Program survey forms required "ownership" to be attributed, and in most cases the Zuni surveyors apparently used the male "head of household" to complete this category. It may be that the term "ownership" is better interpreted as head of household.

EXAMPLES OF ZUNI VERNACULAR AND HUD HOUSING

The numbering system of the Housing Improvement Physical Survey was retained for the labeling of Zuni vernacular houses. In the following justified graphs of both vernacular and HUD houses, the carrier space is represented by a filled circle. The numbers of spaces on the graphs correspond to the numbered and labeled room spaces on the plan view. A tabulation of the room functions in vernacular and HUD houses that decodes the abbreviations used in the plan views is provided in Table 6.3 (p. 133). The standardized measures of real relative asymmetry (RRA) and relative ringiness (RR) are presented with each graph. The RRA statistic presented is the mean value of the RRA of all the individual spaces in the house.

Zuni Vernacular Houses

The spatial structure of Zuni vernacular houses ranges from simple to complex. The simplest structure entails a vernacular house comprised of a single room, exemplified by House 660A in Figure 6.3. The relative asymmetry of houses with less than four rooms cannot be standardized using the conversion table provided by Hillier and Hanson (1984: 112), so no RRA is presented for this house.

Other relatively simple vernacular houses have nondistributed permeability in their spatial structure, that is, the rooms occur on nonintersecting branches of treelike spatial structures. This type of house is exemplified by Houses 665 and 614 (Fig. 6.3). The mean RRA values characterizing these graphs are a global measure of the relative distance spaces are from each other and from the carrier. Because there are no rings or circuits in the spatial structure, the RR values are zero. House 665 is an unusual case in that Room 3, a workshop, is not directly accessible from the rest of the house. In order to access Room 3, one must travel through the exterior space surrounding the house, that is, the carrier space. House 614 exhibits a structure with branches that bifurcate into other branches as one moves deeper in the house.

Zuni vernacular houses with distributed spatial systems have a more complicated spatial structure than those with nondistributed spatial systems. A few vernacular houses have spatial systems that are completely distributed with every space occurring on a ring or circuit. House 785 depicted in Figure 6.4 is an example of this type of structure, with three rings emanating from

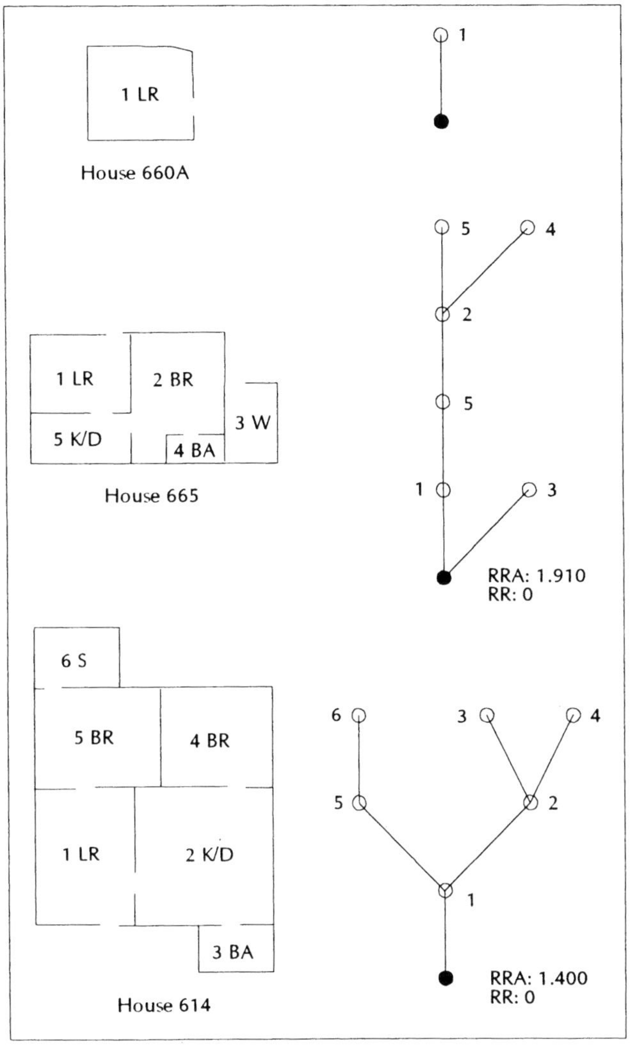

Figure 6.3. Plans and graphs of three Zuni vernacular houses with nondistributed permeability.

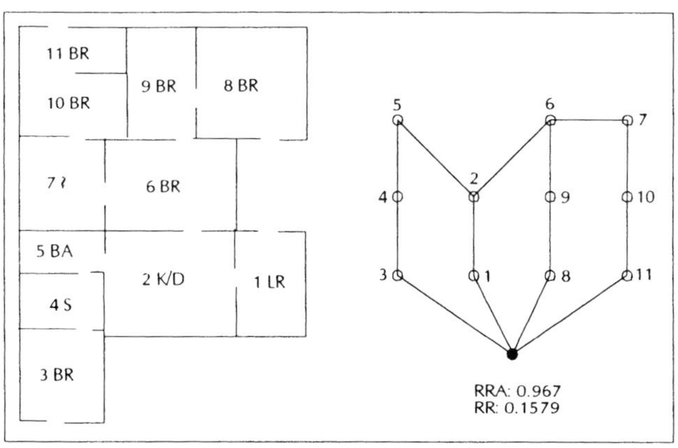

Figure 6.4. Plan and graph of Zuni vernacular House 785.

the carrier space that connect all the rooms in the house. This house exemplifies a common feature of many Zuni vernacular houses in that two of the six bedrooms (Rooms 9 and 10) can only be reached by moving through other bedrooms. This structural feature indicates the privacy of the occupants of Rooms 9 and 10 was not a primary concern when the house was designed. The integration of the spatial structure in House 785 is a physical indicator of close social relations between household members.

Many Zuni vernacular houses combine distributed and nondistributed elements in their spatial structure (Fig. 6.5). Two rings in House 630 emanate from the carrier space, and a third ring connecting the living room, kitchen-dining room, a bedroom, and a hallway is a completely interior circuit. The nondistributed branches in this house provide access to one bedroom (Room 9) located off the living room and to one room with an unknown function located off the kitchen-dining room. One of the five bedrooms (Room 7) in House 630 can only be reached by traversing other bedrooms.

The spatial structure of Zuni vernacular houses becomes more complicated when more rooms are added farther from the carrier space. For instance, House 511 (Fig. 6.6) has five graph levels encompassing three rings and nine nondistributed branches. The three rings

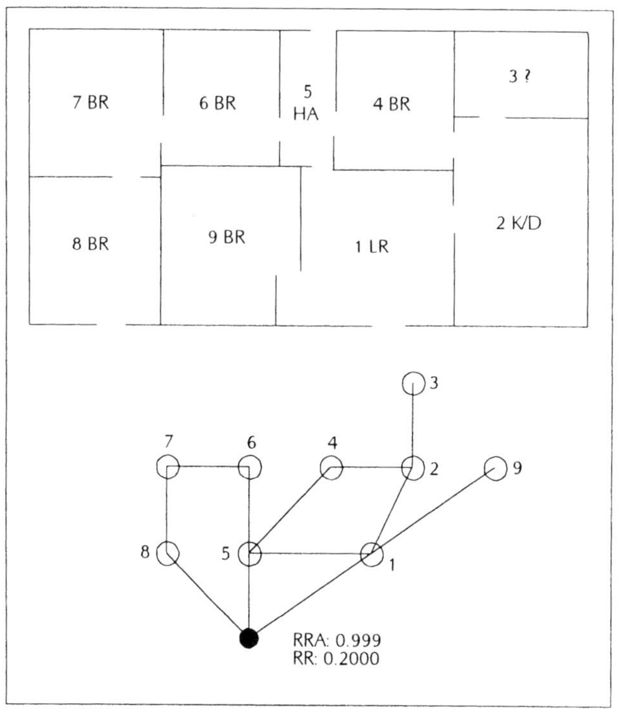

Figure 6.5. Plan and graph of Zuni vernacular House 630.

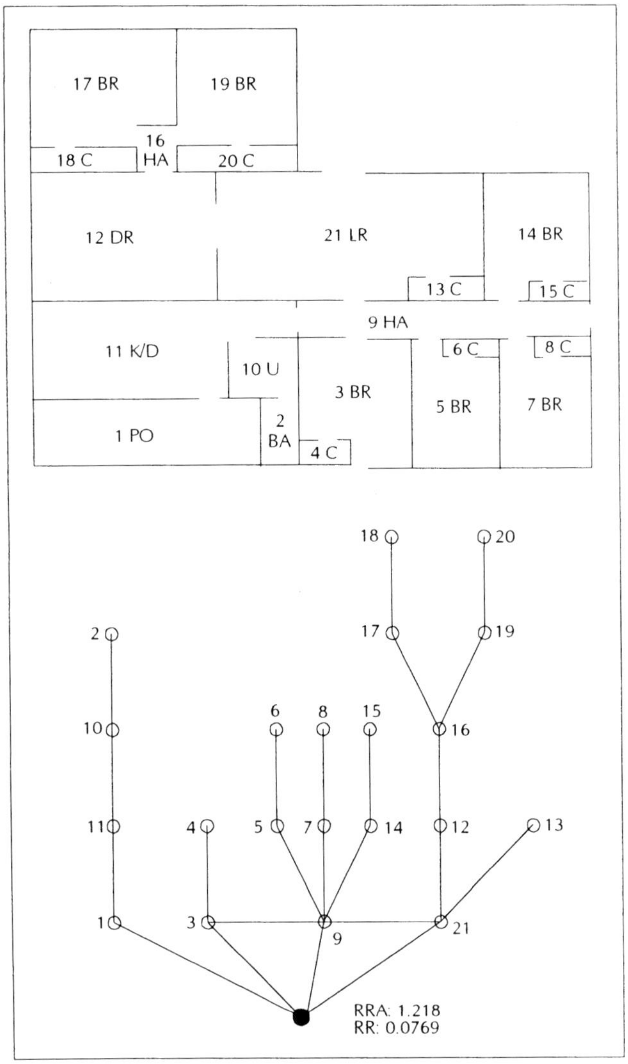

Figure 6.6. Plan and graph of Zuni vernacular House 511.

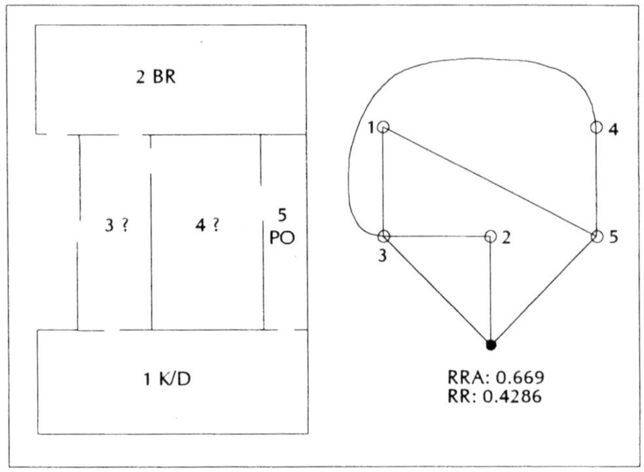

Figure 6.7. Plan and graph of Zuni vernacular House 670.

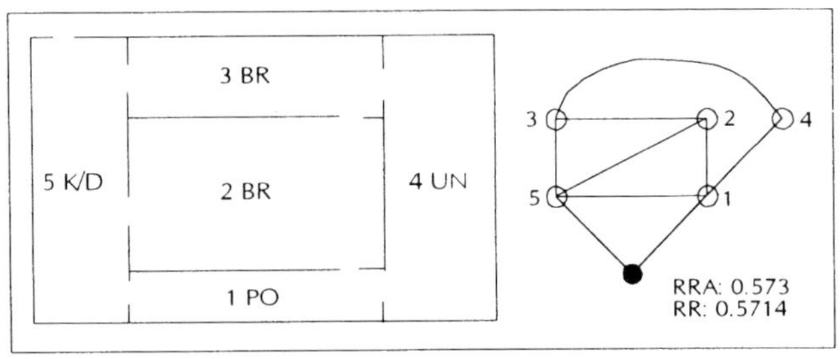

Figure 6.8. Plan and graph of Zuni vernacular House 274A.

emanate from the carrier space, connecting the exterior space with the living room, kitchen-dining room, and one bedroom via a central hallway and porch. The distributed elements exemplify how the most spatially integrated rooms in the house are those used by the entire household, the living room and kitchen-dining room. The nondistributed branches in House 511 include all the bedrooms accessed off the rings, as well as a utility room and bathroom.

Houses 670 and 274A (Figs. 6.7, 6.8) exemplify one of the most common layouts for Shalako houses in the 1970s, with a large central room, three long interconnected rooms flanking the central space, and a porch in the front of the house. The central room is where the principal public aspects of the Shalako ritual take place. It is in this room that a temporary altar is installed, the Shalako dances, and the religious leaders pray and sing during the ceremony. The most honored guests of the Shalako host are also seated in this room. The public views the Shalako ritual from the flanking rooms, the porch, or through the large picture windows that are installed in both the external and internal walls surrounding the central room. The ritual feasting that accompanies Shalako ceremonies occurs in one or more of the flanking rooms, with the food prepared in the kitchen.

The room functions labeled in Houses 670 and 274A indicate the residential use of Shalako houses following the Shalako ceremony, with no further reconstruction of the house. The large rooms of many Shalako houses, however, are partitioned for use as residential space (Fig. 6.9). The large central room in House 719 was divided into two smaller rooms, and the three flanking rooms were each divided into three rooms. The basic arrangement of a four-room Shalako house with a completely distributed spatial structure was modified to encompass thirteen rooms with a spatial structure entailing both distributed and nondistributed elements. Comparison of the mean RRA values for the three Shalako

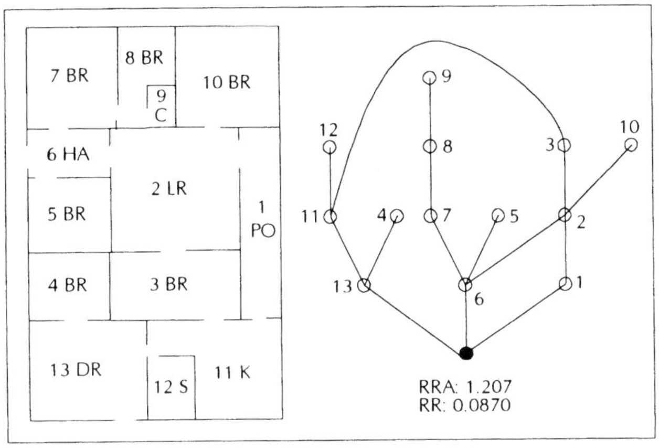

Figure 6.9. Plan and graph of Zuni vernacular House 719.

houses documents how the partitioning of the house for residential purposes decreased the overall integration of the spatial structure.

HUD Housing

Only one of the nine HUD house plans entails a nondistributed spatial structure. This is the prototype of the three-bedroom houses constructed in 1980 (Fig. 6.10). In this layout all the rooms in the house are arranged on branches that emanate from the living room. Two of the three bedrooms are on branches off a hallway connected to the living-dining room, and the third bedroom (the master bedroom) forms its own branch off the living-dining room. The living-dining room is L-shaped with both ells connected to the kitchen. These ells compose separate convex spaces and if the internal structure of the house were analyzed with convex spaces rather than rooms as the unit of analysis, the living-dining room and kitchen would form a ring. This three-bedroom house (Fig. 6.10) exhibits one important characteristic common to all HUD houses: the occurrence of small spaces located on branches off the bedrooms and other spaces. Some of these spaces were too small to label with functional codes in the figures illustrating HUD houses, but they are all closets. The presence of closets greatly increases the number of rooms (partitioned spaces) per house. The HUD three-bedroom house has four levels in its spatial structure; because there are no rings, the RR value is zero.

The plan and graph of the prototype of the four-bedroom HUD houses constructed in 1984 are depicted in Figure 6.11. This arrangement entails two rings and several nondistributed branches. One of the rings connects the carrier space with the living room, central hallway, utility room, and back porch. The other ring, completely internal to the house, connects the utility room, kitchen, dining room, and central hallway. All the bedrooms are accessible from branches located off

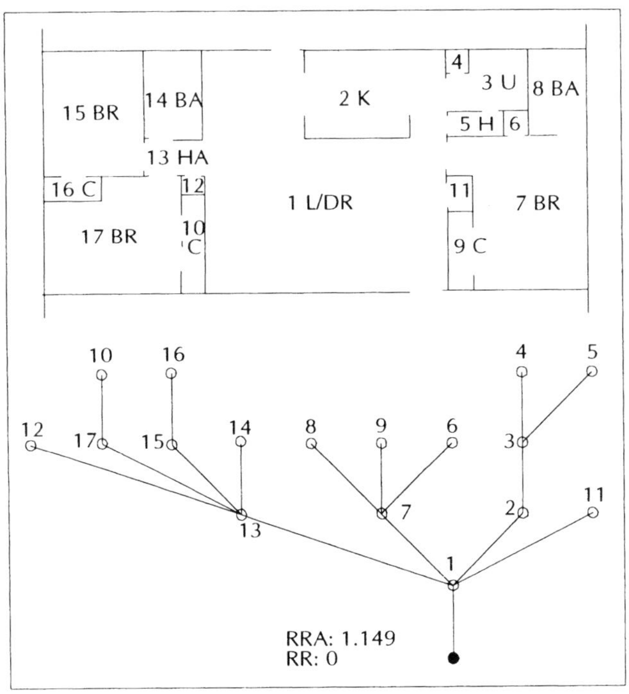

Figure 6.10. Plan and graph of a 1980 HUD three-bedroom house.

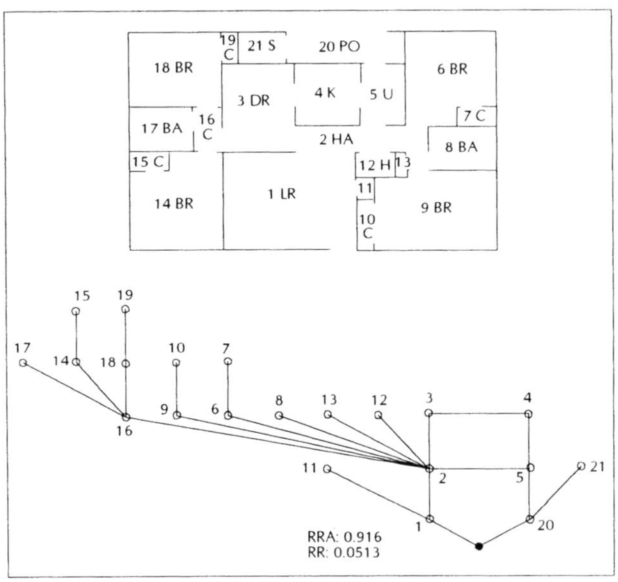

Figure 6.11. Plan and graph of a 1984 HUD four-bedroom house.

the central hallway. The only other branches are a closet accessible from the living room and a storage room accessible from the back porch. Although they are not illustrated, the two-bedroom, three-bedroom, and five-bedroom prototype designs for the 1984 houses all share the same essential structure as the four-bedroom house. All the houses have two rings, with most of the other rooms in nondistributed branches accessible from a central hallway. The major structural difference is in the number of branches and levels. The two-bedroom and three-bedroom houses only have four levels, whereas the four-bedroom and five-bedroom houses have five levels.

The prototype of a five-bedroom HUD house constructed in 1980 (Fig. 6.12) has a spatial structure similar to that of the 1984 HUD houses. There are three rings and six depth levels. The major ring connects the carrier space with the front porch, entry hallway, living-dining room, kitchen, and utility room. Two other rings are completely internal to the house. One of these connects the kitchen, the utility room and a room containing the mechanical heating appliances. A third ring connects the living-dining room, the kitchen, and the central hallway. All the bedrooms are located in nondistributed branches off hallways. Most bedrooms only have one branch that terminates in a single closet. The master bedroom, however, has three branches terminating in two closets and a bathroom.

In addition to single-family dwellings, HUD has sponsored the construction of several apartment buildings used for low income housing; all are located in the satellite community of Blackrock east of Zuni Pueblo (Fig. 6.13). These apartments are arranged in two-story buildings containing six units (Fig. 6.14). The two-bedroom units flank both ends of the apartment building, with two three-bedroom apartments between them.

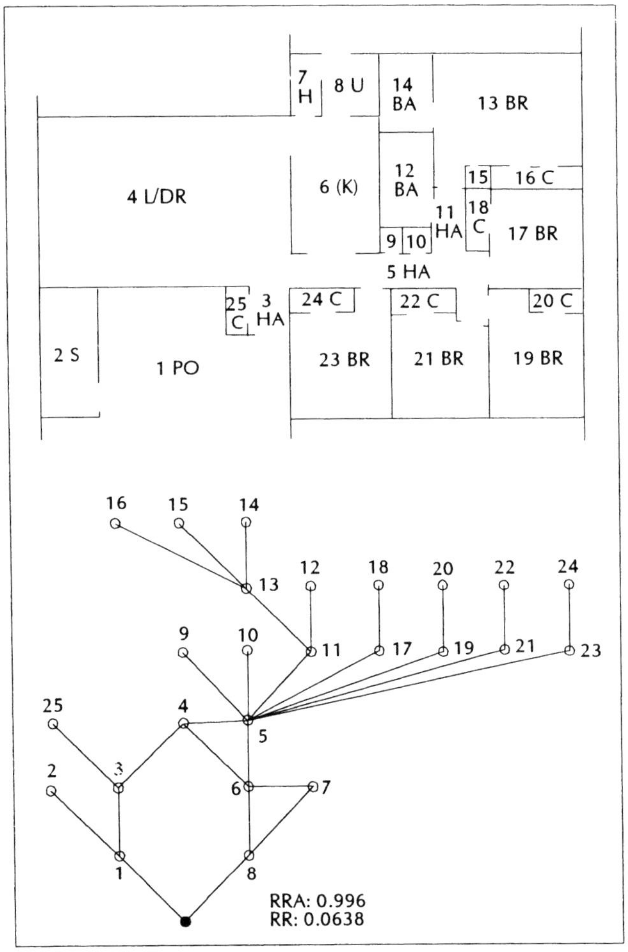

Figure 6.12. Plan and graph of a 1980 HUD five-bedroom house.

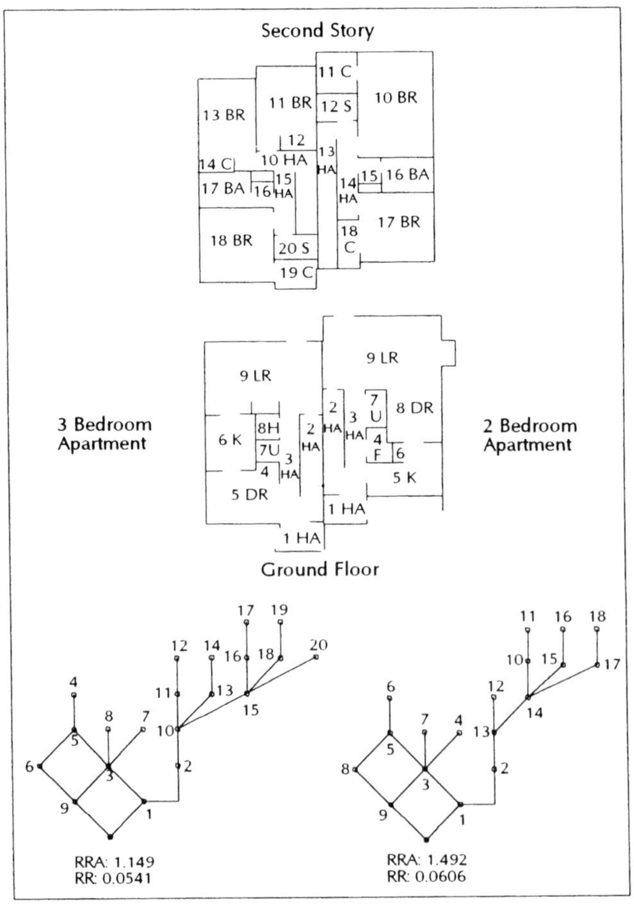

Figure 6.13. Plans and graphs of HUD two-bedroom and three-bedroom apartments in 1977.

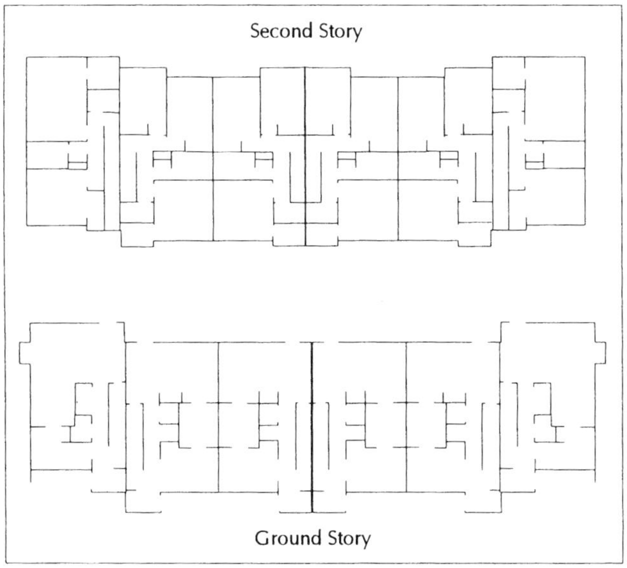

Figure 6.14. Plan of a 1977 HUD apartment building.

The two-bedroom and three-bedroom apartments have virtually the same spatial structure, entailing a combination of distributed and nondistributed components. Both apartments have two rings. One ring connects the carrier space with an entry hall, an internal hallway, and the living room. A second ring, completely internal to the units, connects the hallway with the kitchen, dining room, and living room. Branches from these rings provide access to closets, utility rooms, and rooms containing the mechanical heating equipment. All the apartments have two stories, and the second story is accessed up a stairway (Space 2 on both plans). The difference in the spatial structure of the apartments is in the organization of space on the second story to accommodate either two or three bedrooms. The three-bedroom units use two hallways to provide access to the bedrooms, whereas the two-bedroom unit has a single hallway.

COMPARISON OF ZUNI VERNACULAR AND HUD HOUSING

Zuni vernacular and HUD housing may be compared using the syntactic variables of real relative asymmetry, control, and relative ringiness, as well as the nonsyntactic variables of area and function. Before comparing the two types of housing, some consideration is given to the nature of the distribution of values for the variables and to the correlation of variables.

Nature of Distribution and Correlation of Variables

The variables of area, RRA, and control have values for each of the room spaces and carriers in the sample of Zuni vernacular and HUD houses. Relative ringiness only has a value for each house calculated from the base of the justified graph, that is, the carrier space. A Kolmogorov-Smirnov one sample test was used to see if the variables pertaining to all room spaces were normally distributed; the results showed that none of the variables was normally distributed (Table 6.2). For this reason, nonparametric statistics are used in the comparative analyses.

Bivariate plots of room area, control values, and mean RRA for Zuni vernacular and HUD houses were generated to investigate whether or not these variables are correlated (Fig. 6.15). The cloudlike spread of val-

Table 6.2. Kolmogorov-Smirnov One Sample Test of Area, RRA, and Control Using Standard Normal Distribution

Variable	N of cases	MAX DIF	Probability (2-Tail)
Room Area	1295	0.782	0.000
RRA	1295	0.569	0.000
Control	1295	0.540	0.000

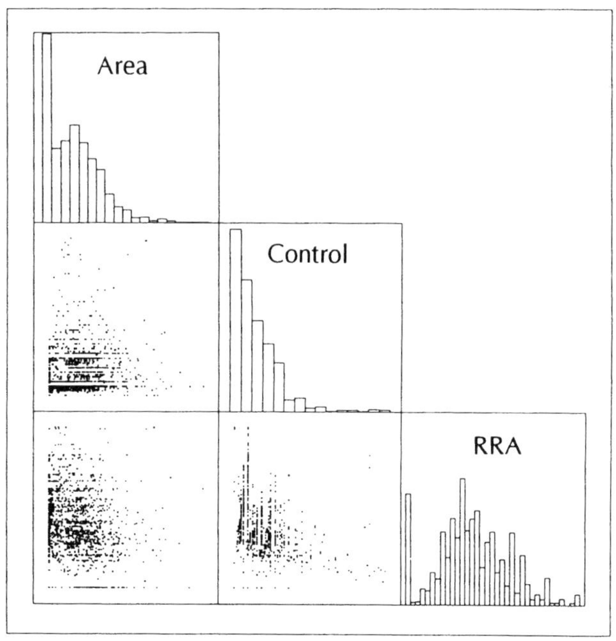

Figure 6.15. Bivariate plots of room area, control values, and mean RRA for vernacular and HUD houses.

ues in these plots suggests there is no correlation between the variables, an observation verified by a Pearsons correlation matrix that yields low correlation values for all three pairs of variables. Room area and control have an R of 0.105, room area and RRA have an R of -0.186, and control and RRA have an R of -0.319.

The histograms of these variables in Figure 6.15 show how the distributions are skewed. The spike on the left side of the RRA histogram represents houses with less than five rooms that have no standardized values and thus have an RRA of zero. Because this spike may affect the normality of the distribution, a Kolmogorov-Smirnov one sample test was calculated for RRA excluding cases with values of zero; the results indicated that excluding buildings with less than five rooms still yielded a distribution that was not normal.

Bivariate plots of mean RRA and relative ringiness for Zuni vernacular and HUD houses with distributed space systems are illustrated in Figures 6.16 and 6.17. Figure 6.16 plots seven houses with a mean RRA of 0, that is, houses with less than five rooms. No significant correlation is found for either vernacular houses (R = -0.495) or HUD houses (R = -0.152).

Number of Rooms, Room Function, and Room Size

The number of rooms per domicile in Zuni vernacular and HUD housing is depicted as a bar chart in Figure 6.18. With one exception, Zuni vernacular houses contain less than 15 rooms and HUD houses contain 15 rooms or more. The exception is a single Zuni vernacular house with 21 rooms. Although the number of rooms per Zuni vernacular house ranges from 1 to 21, the mean is only 6.25 rooms. In comparison, HUD houses have many more rooms, with a mean per HUD house of 19.68 rooms. One reason HUD houses have more rooms than Zuni vernacular houses is that the closets that occur with virtually every room are counted. Such storage areas are relatively uncommon in Zuni houses. Nonetheless, it is clear that there are a great many Zuni houses with relatively few rooms.

Room function, frequency, and size are summarized in Table 6.3. There are 24 categories of room function for Zuni vernacular houses, and only 12 for HUD houses. The greater number of categories of room function in vernacular houses is in large part a function of compounded room use. For instance, bedrooms are com-

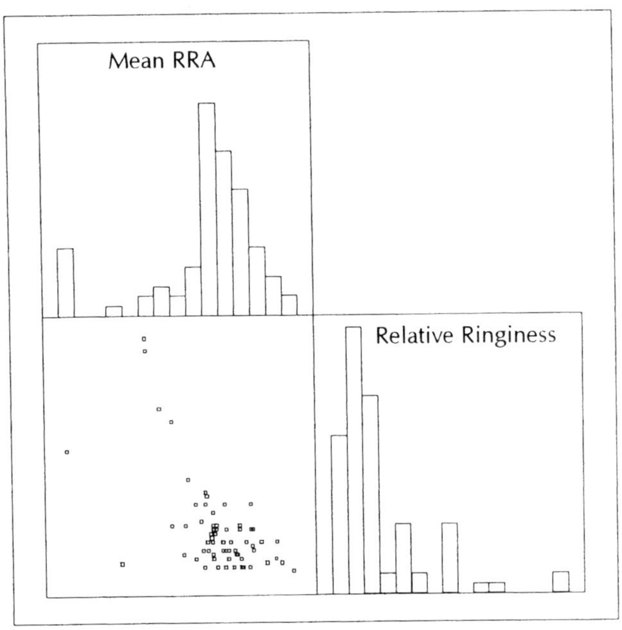

Figure 6.16. Bivariate plots of mean RRA and relative ringiness for Zuni vernacular houses with distributed space systems.

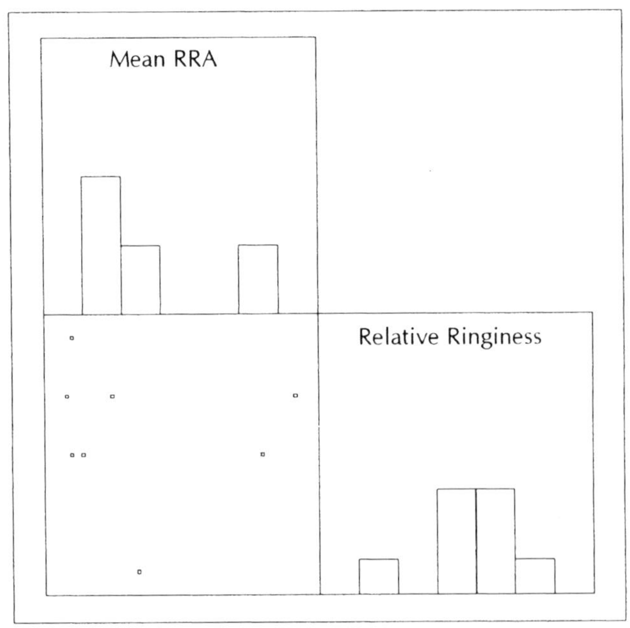

Figure 6.17. Bivariate plots of mean RRA and relative ringiness for HUD houses with distributed space systems.

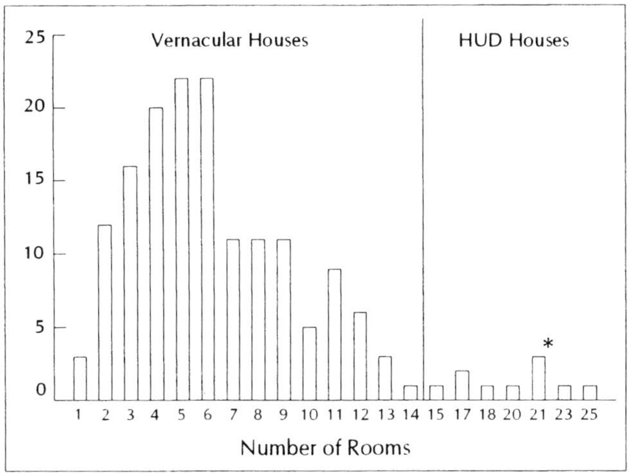

Figure 6.18. Bar chart of number of rooms in Zuni vernacular and HUD houses. One vernacular house (*) has 21 rooms.

pounded with many other room functions, including workshops, bathrooms, dining rooms, kitchens, and living rooms. One compounded room function that is normal for vernacular houses is the kitchen-dining room. The occurrence of 92 bathrooms in vernacular houses indicates that only about 60 percent of them had internal bathrooms when they were documented. The other households presumably used outhouses.

Other than rooms with multiple functions, there are only two room functions that are unique to either Zuni vernacular or HUD housing. About 10 percent of the sample (16 vernacular houses) have rooms dedicated to use as workshops, and this function does not occur in HUD houses as designed by non-Zuni architects. HUD houses have a "heating room" where the mechanical appliances (furnaces, water heaters) related to heating are placed. This type of space does not occur in the vernacular houses, where water heaters are commonly not

Table 6.3. Function and Size of Rooms in Zuni Vernacular and HUD Houses

	Zuni Vernacular Houses			HUD Houses		
Room Function	n	%	Mean area (sq. m)	n	%	Mean area (sq. m)
Unknown (?)	75	8	23.54			
Bathroom-Utility (B/U)	1	< 1	17.64			
Bedroom-Workshop (B/W)	11	1	30.26			
Bathroom (BA)	90	9	7.25	14	8	4.31
Bedroom (BR)	298	31	21.69	31	18	12.12
Bedroom-Bathroom (BR/BA)	1	< 1	14.70			
Bedroom-Dining Room (BR/D)	1	< 1	43.07			
Closet (C)	40	4	2.60	54	31	1.16
Dining Room (DR)	16	2	19.65	6	3	9.38
Extra (E)	4	< 1	27.43			
Hall (Ha)	44	5	8.92	23	13	4.19
Heating (H)				9	5	1.58
Kitchen (K)	40	4	19.32	9	5	7.83
Kitchen-Bedroom (K/BR)	2	< 1	36.26			
Kitchen-Dining (K/D)	101	11	26.04			
Kitchen-Living (K/LR)	1	< 1	30.28			
Kitchen-Workshop (K/W)	1	< 1	21.27			
Living-Bedroom (L/B)	1	< 1	27.86			
Living (LR)	126	13	26.93	6	3	20.39
Living-Dining (L/DR)				3	2	38.38
Porch (PO)	20	2	14.62	5	3	9.22
Storage (S)	45	5	16.23	7	4	3.06
Utility (U)	8	1	7.42	10	6	3.15
Unoccupied (UN)	14	1	39.47			
Workshop (W)	16	2	14.40			
Total	956		19.95	177		6.06

NOTE: Percentages are rounded off to integers.

enclosed in their own space but placed within other rooms such as the kitchen or bathroom. Fireplaces and wood stoves provided heating in most vernacular houses, and these features were generally placed in living rooms or kitchens.

To facilitate comparison of the use of space in Zuni vernacular and HUD houses, the categories of room use in Zuni houses were consolidated into primary functions: for example, kitchen-bedrooms were classified as kitchens, bedroom-workshops were classified as bedrooms. Closets and storage rooms were collapsed into a single category. Because so many Zuni houses have kitchen-dining rooms, this category was retained. Rooms with unknown function or which were unoccupied were not included in the tabulation of primary room function summarized in Table 6.4.

Several differences are apparent in the use of space in vernacular houses as compared to HUD houses. In vernacular houses, 68 percent of the partitioned spaces are used for bedrooms, kitchen-dining rooms, and living rooms. In contrast, in HUD houses these room functions account for only 28 percent of the partitioned spaces. These percentages, of course, do not reflect the size of the areas being used for these functions but rather the number of spaces. The most numerous partitions in HUD houses were closets and storage rooms; these relatively small spaces equaled 34 percent of the total number of spaces in HUD houses, compared to 10 percent of the spaces in Zuni vernacular houses. One other major difference between vernacular and HUD houses is the number of hallways. In vernacular houses these transitional spaces constitute only 5 percent of the total number of spaces, whereas in HUD houses they constitute 13 percent. Even without considering the actual dimensions of the partitions, it is clear that HUD houses have a much higher amount of space devoted to functions peripheral to main living activities than do Zuni vernacular houses, including closets, storage rooms, hallways, and heating rooms. In vernacular houses, spatial emphasis is devoted to the main activities of sleeping, living, and eating.

Histograms of room area measured in square meters for vernacular and HUD houses show that vernacular houses have a greater range in the size of rooms and that rooms are larger than in HUD houses (Figs. 6.19, 6.20). The modal room size for vernacular houses is 20 to 25 square meters, whereas the modal room size for HUD houses is less than 10 square meters.

Table 6.4. Primary Function of Rooms in Zuni Vernacular and HUD Houses

Primary Room Function	Zuni Vernacular Houses n	Zuni Vernacular Houses %	HUD Houses n	HUD Houses %
Bathroom	92	11	14	8
Bedroom	310	36	31	18
Closet/Storage	85	10	61	34
Dining Room	16	2	6	3
Hall	44	5	23	13
Heating			9	5
Kitchen/Dining/Other	145	17	9	5
Living	127	15	9	5
Porch	20	2	5	3
Utility	8	1	10	6
Workshop	16	2		
Total	863		177	

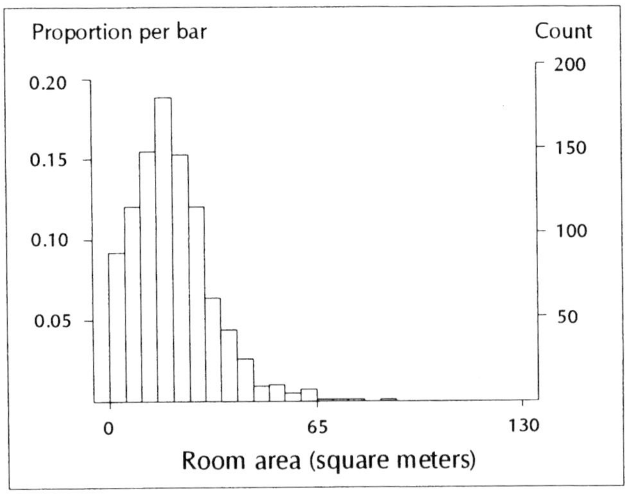

Figure 6.19. Histogram of room area of vernacular houses.

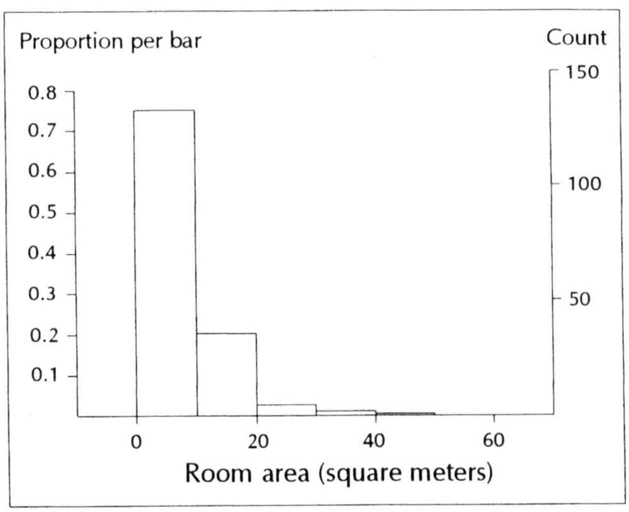

Figure 6.20. Histogram of room area of HUD houses.

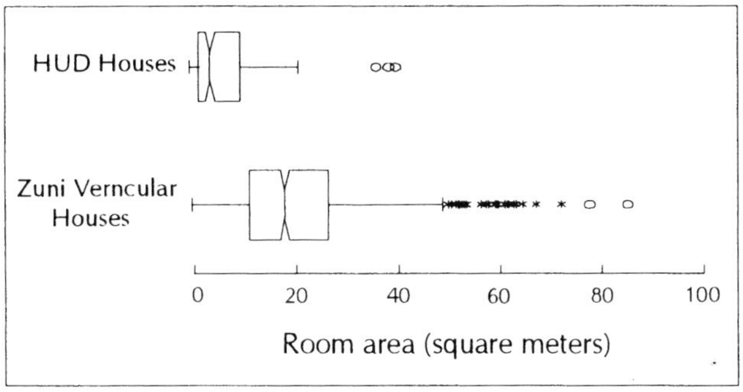

Figure 6.21. Notched box plots of room area of Zuni vernacular and HUD houses.

There is a striking difference in the mean size of rooms between vernacular and HUD houses, as tabulated in Table 6.3. In vernacular houses, the mean room size is 19.95 square meters, and in HUD houses the mean room size is only 6.06 square meters. The difference in mean room size is not only a result of the numerous closets in HUD houses. When closets and heating rooms are deleted from the analysis, the mean room size for vernacular rooms is 20.74 square meters, and the mean size for HUD houses is only 8.74 square meters. Of particular interest with regard to social interaction is that Zuni vernacular houses have kitchen-dining rooms that average 26.04 square meters, whereas HUD kitchens average 7.83 square meters.

The statistical significance of the difference in room area between Zuni vernacular and HUD houses is demonstrated in both notched box plots and an analysis of variance. In the notched box plots (Fig. 6.21), the confidence intervals of the two distributions do not overlap, nor, in fact, do the interquartile ranges. A number of outliers with room sizes that range from 50 to 87 square meters are depicted in the distribution of values for vernacular houses in Figure 6.21. Most of these large rooms are in houses located in the core architecture of Zuni Pueblo. The analysis of variance using the Mann-Whitney U Test statistic verifies that the room size of vernacular houses is indeed different from that of HUD houses (Table 6.5).

Area of Vernacular and HUD Houses

Although Zuni vernacular houses have larger rooms than HUD houses, there is no significant difference in median house size between the two forms of architecture. The notched box plots of house area presented in

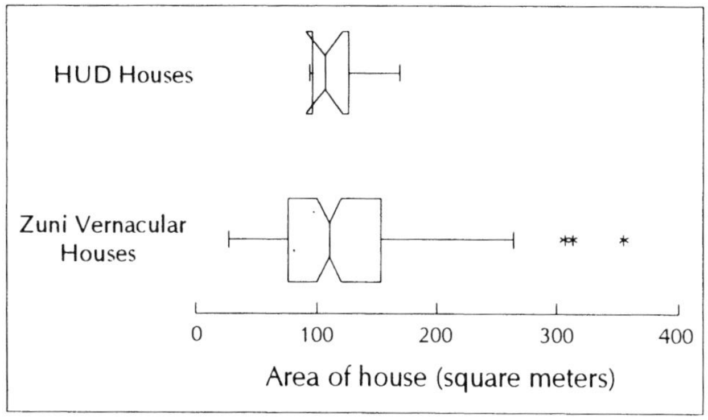

Figure 6.22. Notched box plot of area of Zuni vernacular and HUD houses.

Table 6.5. Analysis of Variance of Room Area and House Area of Zuni Vernacular and HUD Houses

Group	Count	Mann-Whitney U Test Statistic	Probability
Of Room Area			
Zuni Vernacular Houses	955	603377.500	0.000
HUD Houses	177		
Of House Area			
Zuni Vernacular	152	12263.000	0.718
HUD Houses	9		

Figure 6.22 show overlapping confidence intervals in the distribution of house size. The HUD houses have a tighter size range than do the vernacular houses, varying between 96 and 171 square meters. Vernacular houses, in comparison, range from 29 to 357 square meters. The mean size of vernacular and HUD houses, however, are close: 125.35 square meters for vernacular houses and 119.44 square meters for HUD houses. An analysis of variance confirms the box plots and indicates there is no statistical difference between the means of distributions of house size for Zuni vernacular and HUD houses (Table 6.5).

A bivariate plot of the area and number of rooms of Zuni vernacular houses shows only a relatively weak correlation ($R = 0.779$) of these variables (Fig. 6.23). In general, house size increases as the number of rooms in the house increases. However, the occurrence of many vernacular houses with only relatively few but very large rooms weakens the correlation between house size and number of rooms.

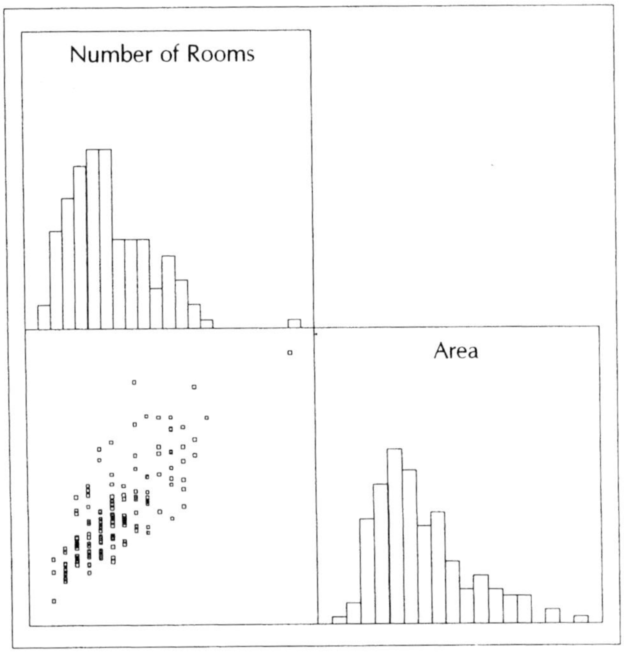

Figure 6.23. Bivariate plot of number of rooms and area of Zuni vernacular houses (in square meters).

Table 6.6. Maximum Syntactic Depth of Zuni Vernacular and HUD Houses

n levels	n Vernacular Houses	n HUD Houses
1	3	
2	33	
3	68	
4	32	4
5	15	2
6	2	3

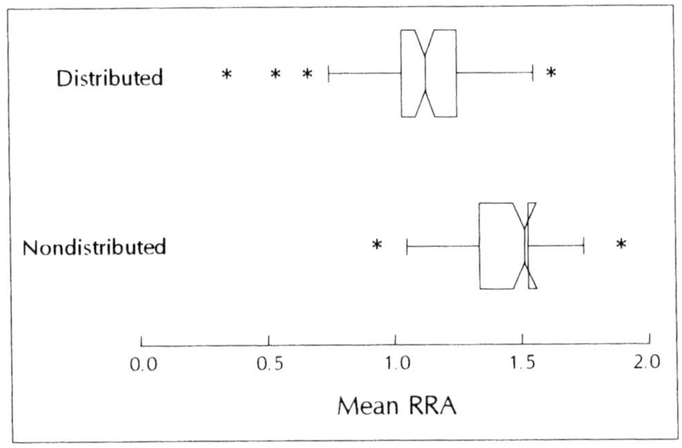

Figure 6.24. Notched box plots of mean RRA of Zuni vernacular houses with distributed and nondistributed spatial structures.

Real Relative Asymmetry of Vernacular and HUD Houses

Relative asymmetry (RA) measures the integration or segregation of rooms within a house by calculating the number of steps separating a particular room space from all other room spaces. Real relative asymmetry (RRA) standardizes RA values to allow comparisons between houses with different numbers of rooms. The mean RRA of all the rooms in a house is used as a measure of the integration within the house as an entity. Low RRA values indicate high integration in spatial structure, and high RRA values indicate low integration or segregation.

In part, RRA is a function of the number of levels in the graph that represents the spatial structure of the house interior. Information about the maximum syntactic depth of Zuni vernacular and HUD houses is summarized in Table 6.6. Vernacular houses are more variable than HUD houses and have syntactic depths that range from one to six levels. HUD houses, in contrast, have depths of from four to six levels. The three vernacular houses with a single level all contain a single room. Not all the houses with two levels have two rooms, however, as the presence of multiple rooms with openings to exterior space will reduce the number of levels in a graph. Other factors affecting RRA include the interconnection of room spaces and the number of nondistributed branches within a graph. The measure of RRA takes all these variables into account and provides a standardized means to compare integration in houses that have differing numbers of rooms and levels.

The mean RRA values of Zuni vernacular houses with distributed and nondistributed spatial structures were investigated to determine if there is any significant difference between these groups. Houses with RRA of zero were deleted from the analysis, that is, all houses with less than five rooms. The notched box plots of the RRA values of distributed and nondistributed vernacular houses do not have overlapping confidence intervals, demonstrating that their medians are statistically different (Fig. 6.24). An analysis of variance confirms this result (Table 6.7). The box plots show that nondistributed Zuni houses have a higher median RRA than distributed houses, indicating the spatial structure of nondistributed houses is significantly more segregated.

Vernacular houses with nondistributed and distributed spatial structures were combined to compare the integration of vernacular houses as a group with that of HUD houses. The notched box plots of the mean RRA values of vernacular and HUD houses reveal that the

Table 6.7. Analysis of Variance of Mean RRA of Zuni Vernacular Houses

Group	Count	Mann-Whitney U Test Statistic	Probability
Nondistributed spatial structures	43	404.000	0.000
Distributed spatial structures	78		

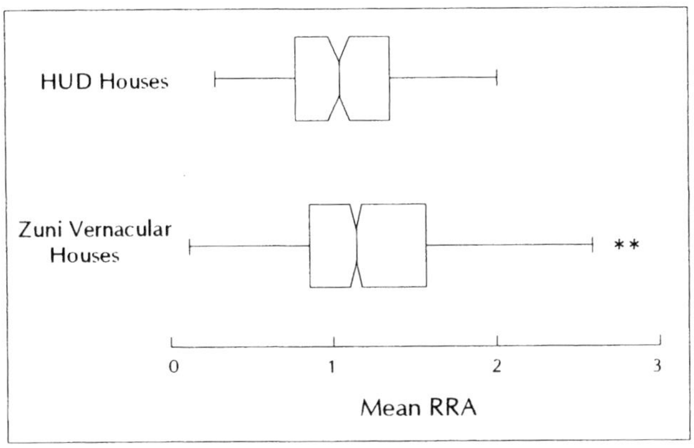

Figure 6.25. Notched box plots of mean RRA of Zuni vernacular and HUD houses.

two distributions do not have overlapping confidence intervals (Fig. 6.25). An analysis of variance provides further support that there is a significant difference between the mean RRA of vernacular and HUD houses (Table 6.8). It is concluded that HUD houses as a group have more integration in their spatial structure than vernacular houses.

In addition to analyzing the mean RRA of houses as entities, it is also instructive to examine the RRA of rooms classified by function. The analysis of the RRA of individual room functions helps to elucidate the similarities and differences in the spatial organization of vernacular and HUD houses (Figs. 6.26, 6.27). The box plots of room functions for vernacular houses do not include those functions with only one case, so many of the compounded room functions are left off the plots. The mean RRA value for vernacular houses is 1.104, and for HUD houses the mean value is 1.071.

Nine room functions in vernacular houses have RRA values below the mean, indicating highly integrated rooms. These room functions include hallways, living rooms, kitchen-dining rooms, porches, extra rooms, dining rooms, rooms of unknown function, bedroom work-

Table 6.8. Analysis of Variance of Mean RRA and of Control Values of Zuni Vernacular and HUD Houses

Group	Count	Mann-Whitney U Test Statistic	Probability
Of Mean RRA			
Zuni Vernacular Houses	1003	106941.000	0.001
HUD Houses	186		
Of Control Values			
Zuni Vernacular Houses	1096	104312.500	0.608
HUD Houses	186		

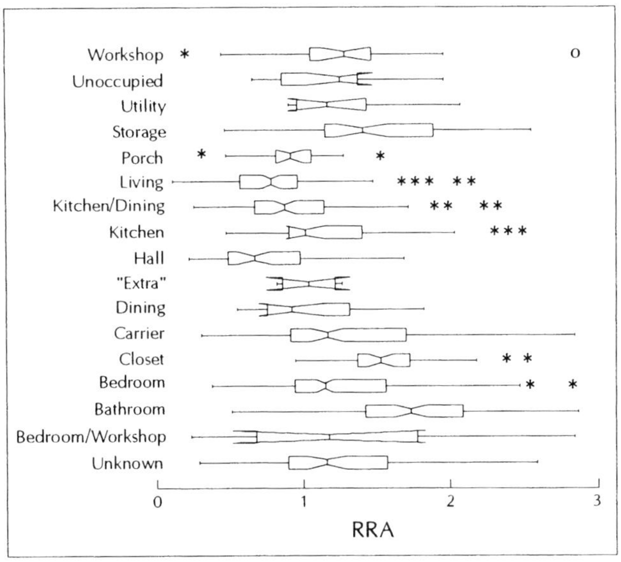

Figure 6.26. Notched box plots of RRA of room function in Zuni vernacular houses.

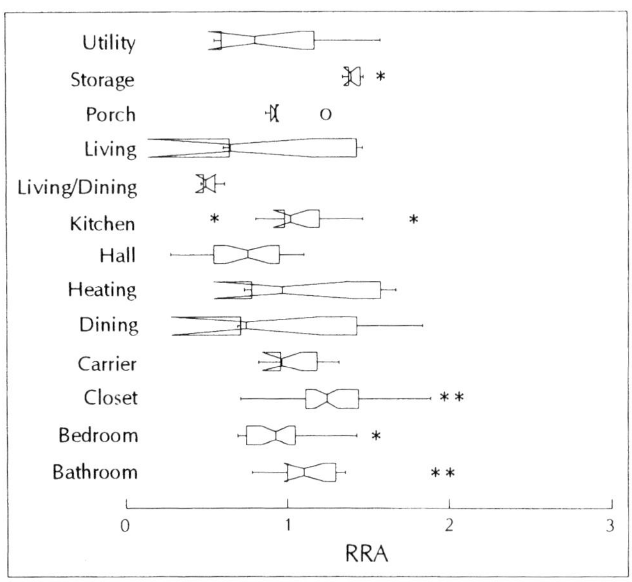

Figure 6.27. Notched box plots of RRA of room function in HUD houses.

shops, and unoccupied rooms. Eight room functions in HUD houses have values below the mean, including living-dining rooms, living rooms, hallways, dining rooms, utility rooms, bedrooms, and porches.

The vernacular and HUD houses are alike in that hallways, living rooms, and dining rooms are among the most integrated spaces. However, the kitchen-dining room is the third most integrated space in vernacular houses, and the kitchen in HUD houses ranks ninth in terms of integration. The kitchens in HUD houses have a mean RRA below that of HUD domiciles, but they are less integrated than many other rooms in HUD houses. The integration of kitchen-dining rooms in vernacular houses is indicative of the importance of food preparation and consumption in Zuni social interaction.

The three most segregated types of rooms with the highest RRA values in both vernacular and HUD houses are bathrooms, closets, and storage rooms. Other segregated rooms in vernacular houses include bedrooms, workshops, and utility rooms. Other segregated rooms in HUD houses include the heating rooms. Although bedrooms in vernacular houses have RRA values above the mean, the 10 rooms with a combined function of bedroom-workshop have values below the mean, indicating they are more integrated. In HUD houses, bedrooms are more integrated into the spatial structure of the house than is the case in vernacular houses.

Control of Room Spaces in Vernacular and HUD Houses

Unlike RRA, which is a global measure comparing a single space to all other spaces in a structure, control is a local syntactic measure that relates how individual spaces regulate access to the spaces that are adjacent to them. Notched box plots (Fig. 6.28) and an analysis of variance (Table 6.8) demonstrate there is no significant difference in the median control values for Zuni vernacular and HUD housing. Houses with control values of zero (the three one-room houses) were excluded from this analysis.

Notched box plots of control values for different room functions in vernacular and HUD houses are presented in Figures 6.29 and 6.30. The mean control value for vernacular houses is 0.867, and the mean value for HUD houses is 0.929. As the box plots illustrate, however, there is a wide range of control values in both vernacular and HUD houses, with values as high as 5.5.

The room function with the most control in both vernacular and HUD houses is the hallway. This obser-

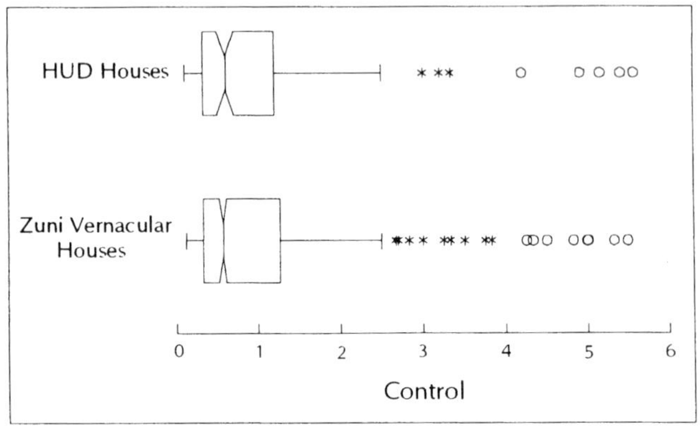

Figure 6.28. Notched box plots of control values of Zuni vernacular and HUD houses.

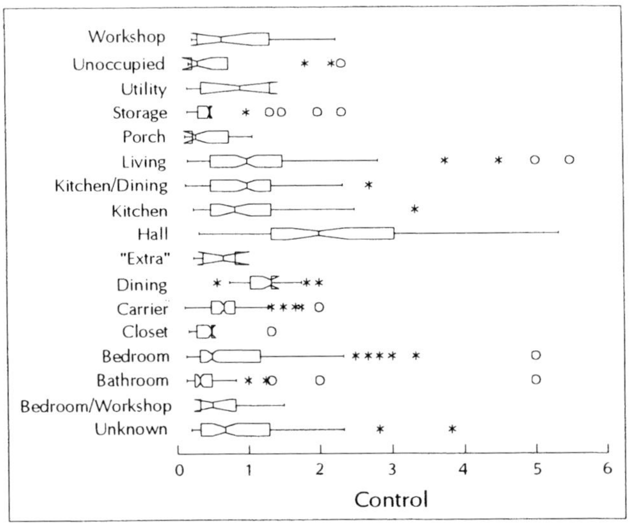

Figure 6.29. Control values of room function in Zuni vernacular houses.

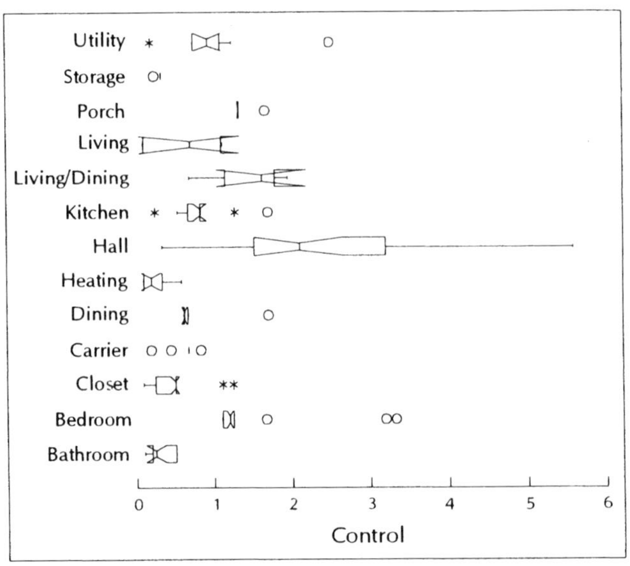

Figure 6.30. Control values of room function in HUD houses.

vation is not surprising because hallways are transitional spaces whose primary purpose is to provide access to other spaces. Living rooms in vernacular houses and living-dining rooms in HUD houses also have high control values, as do dining rooms in both types of houses. The other rooms with control values above the mean vary between vernacular and HUD houses. Kitchens also have high control values in vernacular houses, but not in HUD houses. Porches and bedrooms have control values above the mean in HUD houses, but not in vernacular houses.

The room function with the lowest control in both vernacular and HUD houses is the bathroom. Storage rooms in both forms of houses also have low control values. The other room functions with low control differ between vernacular and HUD houses: in vernacular houses, closets, bedrooms, porches, and unoccupied rooms have low control, and in HUD houses, heating and dining rooms have low control.

Relative Ringiness of Vernacular and HUD Houses

Relative ringiness is a standardized measure that calculates the number of rings or circuits in a spatial structure in relation to the number that is theoretically possible given a particular number of spaces. The measure thus takes into account the number of rings in a house and the total number of rooms. Houses with zero rings have nondistributed spatial structures, represented by 68 vernacular houses (44%) but only one HUD house (11%; Table 6.9). Most vernacular houses with distributed structures have only one or two rings, and most HUD houses with distributed structures have two rings.

Notched box plots of values for relative ringiness (Fig. 6.31) and an analysis of variance (Table 6.10) both indicate that vernacular houses have a significantly higher median relative ringiness than do HUD houses.

Table 6.9. Number of Rings in Zuni Vernacular and HUD Houses

n Rings	n Vernacular Houses	n HUD Houses
0	68	1
1	59	1
2	14	6
3	10	1
4	1	
5	1	

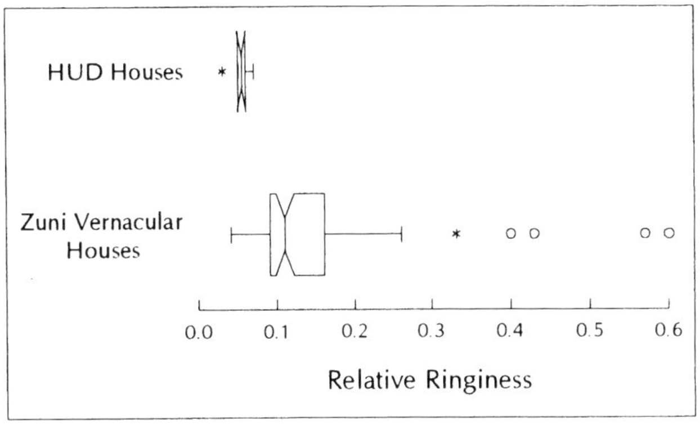

Figure 6.31. Notched box plots of relative ringiness of Zuni vernacular and HUD houses.

Table 6.10. Analysis of Variance of Relative Ringiness of Zuni Vernacular and HUD Houses

Group	Count	Mann-Whitney U Test Statistic	Probability
Zuni Vernacular Houses	85	624	0.000
HUD Houses	8		

HUD houses have lower RRA values, indicating they are more integrated. This interesting finding demonstrates that distributedness is only one way to integrate spatial structure and that the number and depth of nondistributed branches can offset the relative ringiness of spatial structure. The greater number of rooms in HUD houses per ring acts to reduce the value of relative ringiness.

INTERPRETATION

Hillier and Hanson (1984: 144–145) observe that the spaces *within* buildings are unlike the continuous open space *between* buildings because the interior spaces are potentially discontinuous. The arrangement of space within buildings, coupled with strong or weak boundaries, helps reproduce social systems and impart a sense of order to them through analogy with the internal spaces of other houses. Social groups gain identity in part through the structural comparability between the buildings they occupy and the buildings occupied by other similarly organized groups. Hillier and Hanson posit that a transpatial or organic social solidarity will result in a structuring of internal space that emphasizes the discreteness of the occupants by strong control of the boundary. In contrast, a spatial or mechanical solidarity results in buildings with an internal structure organized toward contiguity and encounter, with movement across boundaries facilitated rather than controlled.

The difference in spatial structure between Zuni vernacular and HUD houses is a matter of degree rather than kind. Both vernacular and HUD houses have relatively strong control over the boundary that delineates the interior and exterior of houses. In the Durkheimian terms favored by Hillier and Hanson, all Zuni housing is organized more toward organic than mechanical solidarity. At the most basic level, vernacular and HUD houses both impart structure to the household, the basic unit of Zuni social organization. The spatial structure of HUD houses, however, is oriented primarily toward serving only the household, whereas many Zuni vernacular houses are also oriented toward the spatial realization of larger social groups such as lineages and clans. These larger, transpatial social groups regularly come together in the homes of their clan and lineage matriarchs during feasts and other ritual occasions. In addition, Shalako houses are built annually by clan groups to host religious rituals and subsequently are converted for residential use by individual households. Many Zuni houses thus spatially incorporate, at least episodically or periodically, more social groups than the households that are their primary occupants.

Every Zuni household is realized in space, regardless of the size and complexity of the space they control. Households with one room have a fundamental analogical similarity to households with twenty rooms in that they both have an interior space with a boundary they control with respect to access into the household. The partitioning of the interior space within households introduces additional structural differences between social groups, but all these groups remain households of one type or another. Zuni households are at one and the same time spatial and transpatial groups. Households are spatial in the literal sense of being defined on the basis of sharing hearth and home, but they are also transpatial in the sense that they exemplify a fundamental social category, a lineage segment.

The boundaries of both Zuni vernacular and HUD houses are strongly regulated. Spatially this is evident in the fact that the carrier space that constitutes the threshold of both types of houses is neither highly integrated nor strongly controlling. Much of the space in both vernacular and HUD houses is relatively segregated from the threshold, which strengthens the boundary between the inside and outside. Similarly, the moderate control value for the carrier means that the threshold does not provide access to many other spaces within the house, a spatial arrangement that again strengthens the boundary. HUD houses have a front yard that acts as an additional spatial buffer between the public space of the street system and the private space inside the house. Although many vernacular houses do not have formal front yards in the same sense as do HUD houses, the Zuni custom of driving vehicles to someone's house and honking the horn to get their attention rather than physically approaching the threshold serves to behaviorally regulate the spatial boundary. This social custom allows the occupants of a house to control access to the interior of their homes without being overtly rude. Visitors are kept away from the threshold, thus avoiding having to invite a visitor at the threshold to come inside the house if that is not desired.

Zuni vernacular housing is organized around several different spatial models. There are houses with distributed and nondistributed spatial structures, as well as houses with different levels of ringiness coupled with nondistributed branches. In the absence of ethnographic research, however, social interpretation of these different spatial structures is tenuous, especially considering the wide range in size of Zuni household groups and the number and area of the rooms they occupy. Nonetheless, from the perspective of structuration theory the partitioning of large rooms into smaller rooms as proposed for many of the Zuni houses documented in the Housing Improvement Physical Survey indicates a change was occurring in Zuni social structure in the late 1960s and early 1970s. It is significant that the increased partitioning of space into more and smaller units was designed and implemented by the Zuni for their own self-defined purposes; it was not something imposed on them by commercially oriented non-Zuni architects. There were some highly partitioned Zuni vernacular houses in the late 1960s and unpartitioned Zuni houses were being changed to become more like them.

The relatively few rooms in many Zuni vernacular houses prior to the Home Improvement Program modifications meant there was less differentiation of room function than in the remodeled vernacular houses and in the HUD houses that were subsequently constructed. In many houses, the functionally differentiated space only included a kitchen-dining room, a living room, bedrooms, and, sometimes, a bathroom. Many living activities took place in rooms that had multiple functions: bedrooms were combined with workshops, bathrooms, dining rooms, kitchens, and living rooms. Many vernacular houses lacked appliances and therefore did not have utility rooms or heating rooms where mechanical equipment was installed. Transitional spaces like hallways or entries were relatively rare.

The combination of sleeping functions with so many other activities in vernacular houses is the result of a generalized use of space that is in part cultural and in part a consequence of many large Zuni households occupying domiciles with relatively few rooms. Traditionally, use of interior space within Zuni Pueblo was much more generalized than it is today. People had living rooms, store rooms, and cooking rooms, but most of the household activities took place in one or two living rooms used sequentially for sleeping, food preparation, eating, and other social activities (Stevenson 1904: 349–354).

The generalized use of space typical of Zuni households in earlier periods has become increasingly rare. With relatively high household size and small houses, many activities differentiated in larger and presumably newer vernacular houses were combined in the older and smaller houses. The partitioning of the Zuni vernacular houses undertaken by the Home Improvement Program following the housing survey and the construction of HUD housing represent a change toward the more specialized use of space that is the norm in American society.

The fact that some highly partitioned Zuni vernacular houses had specialized rather than generalized space use in 1967 and 1970 further attests to the changes that were occurring in Zuni society at the time. Although information on household income is not available for Zuni houses with different kinds of residential space use, it is likely that families with less access to the financial resources needed to construct larger, more partitioned houses had more generalized space use.

In comparing Zuni vernacular and HUD houses, the syntactic analysis documents that vernacular houses as a group have a more segregated and a more ringy spatial structure. There was no statistically significant difference in the median control values of room spaces of the vernacular and HUD houses. The real social meaning of the variation in syntactic measures, however, comes less from the comparison of mean values than from an examination of how different types of rooms are integrated into spatial arrangements in the two types of housing.

HUD houses are more spatially integrated than vernacular houses, but this integration derives from the connection of living rooms and bedrooms via the transitional space of hallways. Many vernacular houses have a more fundamental integration of primary use spaces than do HUD houses; that is, there are bedrooms connected only through other bedrooms. The Zuni organization of space structures a social interaction that takes place in rooms occupied by people (in living rooms, kitchen-dining rooms, and bedrooms), and not in hallways and other spaces that are traversed but not occupied. Hallways are not as common in vernacular houses as in HUD houses, but where they occur in vernacular houses, of course, they do serve to integrate and control access to adjacent rooms.

Table 6.11. Room Functions

Zuni Vernacular Houses	HUD Houses
With Low RRA and High Control	
Living room	Living/dining room
Kitchen/dining room	Bedroom
Hall	Hall
Dining room	Porch
	Utility
With High RRA and Low Control	
Bathroom	Bathroom
Storage	Storage
Closet	
Unoccupied	

Table 6.11 lists the room functions of vernacular and HUD houses that have spatial properties that combine high integration (low RRA) with high control. These are key rooms in the spatial structure because they are relatively easy to access, and it is through them that other rooms are accessed. It is significant that in vernacular houses three of the four key rooms have functional uses related to living activities that involve the entire household, and that only one room is a transitional space used for access rather than living activities per se. In contrast, in HUD houses only one of the five key room functions is used by the entire household. A second room function, bedroom, is used primarily by subsets of the household. Two of the key rooms in HUD houses are transitional spaces, hallways and porches. The last key space is the utility room, a specialized space that is not a focus of social interaction. The high integration and control of many of the utility rooms in HUD houses derive in large measure from their location on rings connecting the outside with the kitchen and with other rooms in the house. To a large degree, then, these utility rooms function as a transitional space much like a hallway.

It is clear from the large size and combined functions of kitchen-dining rooms in vernacular houses that there is an emphasis in Zuni social life on the preparation and consumption of food. Most ritual occasions entail feasts shared by large gatherings of family and friends. These ritual occasions include Zuni religious observances like Shalako and secular occasions like Headstart and high school graduations. The social interaction involved during these ritual occasions is a key factor in the integration of the transpatial groups of kin and clan spread between several households.

Spaces oriented toward the preparation and consumption of food in Zuni society are controlled by women. The emphasis of these rooms in the spatial structure of Zuni vernacular houses derives from the role of women in Zuni society as matriarchs who symbolically and physically nurture their families and lineages. Vernacular houses are arranged to facilitate social interaction with the women of the household during the performance of the activities needed to feed and sustain their families. This arrangement can be abstracted to symbolize the importance of women in Zuni society, but the real social meaning of the arrangement is the social interaction that revolves around the hearth or its modern Zuni equivalent, the kitchen-dining room.

The small size of kitchens in HUD houses and their physical separation from dining rooms breaks the Zuni social interaction entailed in food preparation and consumption into different activities. The small areas devoted to kitchens and dining areas in HUD houses also physically constrain traditional forms of social interaction by limiting the number of people who can actually sit together during feasts. Unlike Zuni vernacular houses, where large tables seat many people at a meal, social gatherings in HUD houses are often broken up with subsets of participants occupying different rooms. Some contemporary social functions conducted in HUD houses, like wedding celebrations, may take place in more than one house, because the relatively small living rooms and kitchens limit the maximum number of people that can occupy them.

The asymmetric position of spaces involved with food preparation in HUD houses weakens the social role of women by spatially constraining their social interaction during family gatherings. If the men and other family members not engaged in cooking are situated in other rooms in the house, women have less opportunity to interact socially and less control over the social interaction. The role of women shifts from being the interactional focus of social activity to a role more characteristic of a servant who caters to the needs of other groups of people in the house. The spatial structure of HUD houses is thereby contributing to the reformulation of Zuni society toward the norms of middle-class American families, smaller social groups with less emphasis on the females in the household than there is in traditional Zuni life.

In many instances the breakup of the spatial structure devoted to social activities revolving around the preparation and consumption of food is not critical for the young Zuni who have moved into HUD houses. These young people continue to return to the houses of their mothers and grandmothers for ritual occasions. The real social change inherent in the spatial organization of HUD houses will not become manifest until the young Zuni women who moved into HUD homes become the matriarchs of their lineages. When this occurs, it will become increasingly difficult to maintain traditional Zuni social relations based on sharing food in large groups.

Table 6.11 lists the rooms in Zuni and HUD houses that have spatial structures that combine low integration (high RRA) with low control. These are the rooms that are the most removed from social interaction in the houses. Bathrooms are among the most segregated, least controlling spaces in both vernacular and HUD houses. This arrangement is indicative of the shared cultural values held by both the Zuni who built vernacular houses and the non-Zuni architects who designed HUD houses regarding privacy in activities associated with bodily functions. The spatial structure of vernacular and HUD houses works to isolate these activities as much as possible from social interaction.

Rooms with storage functions are segregated from other rooms in the spatial structure of both vernacular and HUD houses. This arrangement is not surprising because these storage areas are meant to be accessed by the occupants of the household and not by visitors. Closets are segregated in the spatial structure in vernacular houses, but not in HUD houses where most closets occur in association with bedrooms. Bedrooms in HUD houses are well integrated into the spatial structure; most closets are only one syntactic step from the bedrooms, so their relative segregation is less than in vernacular houses.

The unoccupied rooms in vernacular houses are characterized by low integration and low control. When all the rooms in a house are no longer needed, it is the rooms that have the most isolated positions in the spatial arrangement that are relinquished, and living activities are consolidated in the more highly integrated room spaces.

In summary, the phenomenal increase that occurred in Zuni population during the twentieth century created a need for new housing at the same time that economic hardships resulting from the reduction of the Zuni land base made it hard for many Zuni to acquire the resources needed to construct that housing. Rehabilitation of existing housing using the resources of the BIA Home Improvement Program and the construction of new housing sponsored by HUD are two of the ways the Zuni obtained enough housing to shelter all tribal members.

Most of the Zuni houses documented in the 1967 and 1970 Housing Improvement Physical Survey were being modified at the request of the Zuni to include smaller rooms and many of the amenities present in HUD houses. A convergence in the spatial organization of Zuni vernacular housing with the standards typified in HUD housing was underway *prior to* the wholesale introduction of commercially designed housing at Zuni Pueblo.

The Zuni people themselves recognized a need for increased partitioning of interior space in houses and sought to attain it in the spatial structure of their domiciles. Much of the increased partitioning was related to a shift from a generalized to a specialized use of space. In particular, a larger number of bedrooms were constructed to replace living-sleeping rooms, which resulted in increased privacy between household members and in a major shift in the traditional patterns of social interaction within Zuni households.

A comparison of Zuni vernacular and HUD houses indicates that the two types of houses share many spatial properties, but that their overall organization is nonetheless significantly different. Vernacular houses are oriented toward social activities involving the entire household, and especially toward the preparation and consumption of food. The spatial arrangement of vernacular houses is organized to support the social interaction of large groups of people from within and outside the household and to integrate the activities of women when this social interaction occurs. In contrast, the spatial organization of HUD houses is organized more toward individual activities than activities involving the entire household, and the small size of HUD houses does not facilitate the temporary spatial realization of large social groups that transcend the household.

Although the open space structure of HUD subdivisions is similar to that of the vernacular suburbs, the internal organization of space in HUD houses differs from that of Zuni vernacular houses in critically important ways. In many respects, the interior organization of HUD houses does appear to be a "Trojan Horse" (Ferguson and others 1990: 116) in that HUD housing was and still is an attractive solution to the overcrowding in many Zuni houses, but one which may eventually have unforeseen social consequences. The spatial organization of HUD housing is oriented toward small social groups and arranged to undercut the role of women in Zuni society. The constraints this spatial arrangement poses for traditional forms of Zuni social interaction will become increasingly manifest as the women living in HUD houses become matriarchs in their lineages and clans.

This analysis has focused on the syntactic organization of space. These syntactic considerations aside, it is noted in closing that many HUD houses were not built to fulfill Zuni cultural needs. For instance, one set of HUD houses was built without wood stoves or fireplaces, making it impossible to ritually feed deceased ancestors by offering bits of food to a fire. Some Zuni in these HUD houses resolutely maintain their traditions by burning these offerings on their back porch. Other cultural and economic problems with HUD houses come from the high cost of heating commercially designed housing with gas or electricity rather than with wood stoves, the expense of monthly payments, and the relatively low standards of mass produced housing. These factors, along with the structuring of social interaction described above, combine to make HUD houses a poor fit to the needs of Zuni social life.

Many young Zuni families choose HUD housing so they can start new households spatially separate from their relatives. Inasmuch as this shift from matrilocality to neolocality occurs through the occupation of HUD houses, there is also a slow but inexorable change in the social interaction that constitutes Zuni society. The structure of contemporary architecture at Zuni Pueblo is thus both adjusting to and changing Zuni society.

CHAPTER SEVEN

The Structure of Architectural and Social Change

The role of individuals and their relation to society is a central problem in anthropology, because society has no tangible reality apart from its members who share relations of common behavior, culture, and institutional organization. An investigation of social change must therefore incorporate the interaction that occurs between individuals in a society. It is social structure that organizes and enables individuals to carry out the activities that sustain their lives. The rules and resources that constitute social structure are recursively drawn upon and reconstituted in processes of reciprocal social action. Thus social structure is not static, and its persistence depends on the repetition of behavior that can and does change through time.

This research has investigated change in Zuni society by delineating systematic links between the structure of Zuni society and the structure of the architectural forms that house Zuni people. Structure gives form and shape to social life but it is not itself that form or shape. Consequently, the built environment takes a form congruent with social structure and this coherence permits social structure to be inferred from architectural forms. The theory of space syntax used here is that social relations and processes are expressed in space through the internal and external configuration of buildings. Space, and its partitioning within and among the architectural units of the built environment, has a social logic that derives from two relationships: the relations among occupants, and the relations between the occupants and other people. This logic derives from the paradoxical need to maintain continuity in a system of space that is constructed by erecting discontinuities, that is, the walls and buildings that comprise the cells of architectural space. These discontinuities are designed to either constrain or enable social interaction.

Order in space is conceptualized as restrictions on a random process in the production and placement of cells. More complex restrictions result in more complex forms of order. Social interaction is ordered by syntactic arrangements of space that bring members of a society together with other members of the society and with people from outside the society. The spatial order inherent in the rooms of a building, the way interior space is connected to exterior space, and the way the continuous structure of open space that surrounds all the buildings in a settlement is organized are all related to the definition and control of social interaction.

SUBSTANTIVE CONCLUSIONS ABOUT ZUNI ARCHITECTURE AND SOCIETY

The theory of space syntax was applied in an analysis of (1) the open space structure of a series of Zuni settlements occupied between the seventeenth century and today, and (2) the internal residential structure of Zuni vernacular and HUD houses from the 1960s through the 1980s. The analysis of open space within historic Zuni settlements demonstrates there is variation in the syntactic arrangement of buildings and the continuous structure of open space around them, and that this variation changed through time. The open space structure of Zuni Pueblo is different from that of the contemporaneous farming villages. The analysis of residential interiors shows that Zuni vernacular houses have both syntactic similarities and differences with HUD houses. In the analyses of both settlements and buildings, the variation in spatial structure is shown to be a matter of degree rather than kind.

The spatial structure of the early seventeenth-century Zuni villages is similar to the core of Zuni Pueblo. All these settlements are characterized by spatial structures that are highly segregated and more dendritic than circuitous. Plazas at all the settlements provide a strong global organization to the space system. The role that the spatial structure of Zuni Pueblo plays in social integration is well known from ethnographic observations, and the spatial structures of the early seventeenth-century villages are inferred to have operated in much the same way.

The plazas and other noninterchangeable architectural elements (shrines and sacred pathways) at Zuni Pueblo are used in the interaction that integrates the social groups that crosscut the fundamental social unit of the household. It is in the public spaces of Zuni Pueblo that members of different households interact with other members of their own clan and religious organizations, as well as with members of other clans and religious sodalities. The probabilistic social encounters that occur in the public spaces of the pueblo encourage the social interaction that binds together the members of different households. This spatial arrangement is a noncorrespondence system in that it brings together the representatives of clans and religious groups whose membership does not correspond to the spatially defined residential households.

The interface created by the open space within Zuni Pueblo and in the early seventeenth-century villages is thus oriented toward fostering social interaction among the occupants of the village. The strong global organization of these settlements is interpreted as evidence that they housed communities with a strong social structure based on an organic solidarity that bound together the members of different households. The theory of space syntax is not powerful enough to identify the nature of the social groups entailed in the social structure of the early seventeenth-century villages, but there is no reason to think they were anything but the clans, kivas, medicine fraternities, and priesthoods that still constitute the heart of Zuni society. The spatial structure of the early seventeenth-century villages, like Zuni Pueblo, would have facilitated the social interaction these transpatial groups required to perpetuate their existence.

The variation in the way that the Catholic churches constructed at Hawikku, Kechiba:wa, and Zuni Pueblo were integrated into the settlement structure is indicative of the historical imposition of Spanish political and social control. In the seventeenth century, the Spaniards were in the initial stages of coercing Zuni's participation in a state level political and economic system. It is significant that the major institution and symbol of Spanish control at Zuni, the Catholic mission, was not well integrated into the spatial structure of the two seventeenth-century villages studied. At Hawikku, the church and mission were located at the edge of village and not surrounded by highly integrated open space. At Kechiba:wa, the visita was situated in a plaza that was segregated from most of the pueblo. In contrast, during the consolidation of Spanish rule following the Pueblo Revolt of 1680, the Catholic church at Zuni Pueblo came to occupy a central position in the largest plaza of the village. The church at Zuni Pueblo is now surrounded by highly integrated, highly controlling open space. The most public routes of access within Zuni Pueblo direct non-Zunis to the church. The location of the Catholic church in the spatial arrangement of Zuni Pueblo is more than symbolic; the spatial integration of the church facilitated the social interaction that occurred between the Zuni people and the representatives of Spanish rule.

The settlement that the Zuni occupied during the Pueblo Revolt of 1680 has a spatial structure that is vastly different from the villages that were occupied before and after that time. Unlike the highly segregated and nondistributed spatial structure of the early seventeenth-century villages and Zuni Pueblo, the spatial structure of the settlement on Dowa Yalanne is highly integrated and highly distributed. The defensive character of the village comes from its location on top of a mesa, not from the spatial structure that provides relatively open access within and around all parts of the settlement. The diversity in the size and placement of room blocks is interpreted as evidence that the Zuni were experimenting with the composition of the social groups that formed the village. The many small room blocks surrounded by open space indicate a strong tendency toward correspondence in spatial and social groups. At the same time, the occurrence of several larger room blocks suggests there were also elements of a noncorrespondence system.

The settlement on Dowa Yalanne was occupied by the remnants of six or seven semiautonomous villages. It is perhaps not surprising, then, that the spatial structure of the Dowa Yalanne settlement suggests there was a weaker social integration there than in the villages it replaced. Many of the constituent room blocks are spatially equivalent and are not organized into a strong global system oriented around plazas or other noninterchangeable spaces. The orientation of the Dowa Yalanne settlement is not toward ritual spaces used by the whole community, but toward the strongly controlled spaces of individual room blocks set apart from each other. The spatial structure of Zuni Pueblo, where the entire Zuni Tribe consolidated settlement following the Pueblo Revolt, indicates the Zuni people ultimately reintegrated their society into a single village with a social structure presumably much like the one that existed in the early seventeenth-century. The settlement on Dowa Yalanne is a transitional development in the reduction of Zuni settlement from multiple villages into a single pueblo.

Much of the structure of open space in Zuni settlements is understandable in terms of the interface it creates between the occupants of a village and visitors or outsiders. This interface is related to the defensive needs of many historic Zuni settlements. The early seventeenth-century villages, the core of Zuni Pueblo before 1915, the early farming villages, and two of the 1885 farming villages all have spatial structures oriented toward controlling the access of visitors into and within the settlements. The relatively asymmetrical arrangement of axial space, coupled with a relatively few, highly regulated routes into the settlements make these villages defensible from intrusion by unwelcome interlopers. The location of many of these settlements on elevated landforms also contributed to the spatial properties that made them defensible.

The fact that all Zuni settlements underwent a change toward a more integrated and distributed open space structure after Navajo and Apache raids ceased is not simply coincidental. The defensive characteristics of the spatial structure that inhibited intrusion from outsiders also made it more difficult for the occupants of villages to travel around within their settlements. The change in the nature of social interaction with outsiders made it possible to restructure the open space of villages to better facilitate social interaction between residents. As new houses were built and old houses were reconstructed, their spatial arrangement took into account the new patterns of social interaction. Social interaction is the mechanism that generated the new spatial structure.

The spatial structures of Zuni Pueblo and its contemporaneous farming villages in the nineteenth and twentieth centuries are substantially different. Unlike Zuni Pueblo, the farming villages had no fixed architectural spaces used for the public or private performance of rituals. The organization of the farming villages consequently had a local rather than a global structure. The open space within the farming villages was significantly more integrated and more distributed than at Zuni Pueblo. The primary transpatial groups at the farming villages were clans, but the areas in which these clans spatially realized themselves were farm fields rather than architectural cells. The clans formed the basis for communal work parties in the farming villages, but the ritual activities associated with these clans primarily took place in Zuni Pueblo. The kivas, medicine fraternities, and other religious groups did not have a spatial realization in the farming villages as they did in the main pueblo. The primary social group at the farming villages was thus the spatially delineated residential household.

The spatial structures of the farming villages were organized more toward a correspondence rather than a noncorrespondence system. This social structure is incorporated in the highly integrated, more distributed, and more localized spatial structure of the farming villages as compared with Zuni Pueblo. The increase in the integration and distributedness in the spatial structures of the farming villages is associated with a social structure that became increasingly oriented toward individual households rather than toward the village organization as a whole.

Like the farming villages, the open space structure of the core of Zuni Pueblo has changed to become more symmetrical and more distributed through time. Nonetheless, the core of Zuni Pueblo remains the most segregated and nondistributed of all the occupied Zuni settlements. This feature suggests there are factors other than simply defense involved in the segregated and nondistributed spatial properties of Zuni Pueblo. Much of the segregation and nondistributed character of the core of Zuni Pueblo is due to the social interaction associated with the use of open space for rituals that integrate transpatial social groups.

Even as Zuni society changes, the layout of open space defined by the buildings constructed in the past continues to influence present behavior. In this way, history and precedence in architectural design (Rapoport 1990) contribute to continuity in past and present forms of Zuni social behavior. For example, even though motorized vehicles have become the dominant form of transportation within Zuni Pueblo, the central dance plaza and other key sacred areas where people gather to participate or observe ritual performances are still only accessible on foot. This feature of the pueblo helps to sustain the opportunities for the face-to-face social interaction that is essential for integration of the Zuni community.

The spatial structure of the suburbs of Zuni Pueblo is more integrated and distributed than that of the core architecture. Interestingly, the structures of the suburbs in 1915 had a closer approximation to a grid than did the suburbs in 1978. This arrangement resulted in large measure from the nature of Zuni infilling of open space, which until recently was not oriented toward a rectangular transportation grid. The original transportation routes radiated out from the core of Zuni Pueblo like spokes on wheel, and houses were oriented facing the core pueblo instead of facing these transportation spokes. More recently, a rectangular grid of roads has been overlain on this earlier system, creating a more complex pattern of open space. Increasingly, houses are oriented toward access from roads rather than toward the core architecture.

Compared to the core of Zuni Pueblo, the spatial structures of the suburbs in 1915 and 1978 are predicated on a shorter set of restrictions in random growth, coupled with more reproductive events. There are no plazas or other publicly used ritual spaces in the suburbs whose configuration needs to be protected in the global structure of the settlement. The shrines that exist in the suburbs are used in esoteric rather than public rituals, and their structural integrity only requires local protection. Construction in areas that are not adjacent to these shrines is undertaken with no consideration of them. The primary rule governing the production of new houses in the suburbs is that of the "clump syntax," which only specifies that a building has an open space facing it. The suburbs of Zuni Pueblo are thus characterized by spatial structures that have high integration and high distributedness.

The open space structures of Zuni vernacular and HUD subdivisions are similar syntactically. The major difference between Zuni and HUD suburbs is in the density of occupation. There has been more infilling in Zuni vernacular suburbs and they therefore have a greater density. The spacing of houses in HUD subdivisions is much more regular and controlled than in Zuni vernacular suburbs. It has not been determined whether or not the greater density in Zuni suburbs has any impact on social interaction.

The modal structures of interior space in vernacular and HUD houses exhibit a number of similarities and several important differences. Both vernacular and HUD houses have well-defined interiors with well-controlled boundaries. This similarity indicates both vernacular and HUD houses provide a strong spatial definition for the household groups that occupy them. The similar way that vernacular and HUD houses provide structure to the fundamental social unit in Zuni society is one reason the Zuni have been able to adopt HUD housing so readily. Although HUD housing is not isomorphic with vernacular housing, they both provide strong spatial structures for the social interaction that sets Zuni households apart from one another.

Zuni vernacular houses traditionally had a more generalized use of space than is inherent in the more overtly specialized functions of HUD houses. This feature of vernacular houses, however, began to change even before the introduction of HUD housing at Zuni Pueblo. The variation in Zuni vernacular houses, and the changes proposed under the auspices of the BIA's Home Improvement Program, attest to the gradual shift in vernacular houses from a generalized to a more specialized use of space. Rooms combining multiple living activities (living-bedrooms) have been increasingly replaced with rooms dedicated to one major function.

The shift from general to specialized use of space represents a major change toward more privacy in the internal social relations of household groups. This shift in the use of space has been accompanied by a change in the corporate nature of the Zuni household from a relatively large economic group to a smaller kinship unit. The extended families of earlier households at Zuni Pueblo, with close ties in their farming, grazing, and other economic activities, are gradually being replaced by smaller social units such as the nuclear family. Privacy in the use of space has increased as the need to interact in joint economic pursuits has decreased.

There is one important exception in the trend toward more specialized use of space in Zuni vernacular households: the retention of the kitchen-dining room as the focus of social interaction in the household. This space combines food preparation and food consumption activities and is oriented toward social interaction involving the women in a household. Although clan identity in Zuni society is bilateral, it is from women that all Zuni obtain their primary clan affiliation. During most ritual occasions, male and female children return to their mother's household to interact socially during feasts. The large kitchen-dining rooms of vernacular houses are designed to support this critically important integrative activity. Sharing food and interacting socially on a regular basis organizes the transpatial lineage segments of clans with a social identity that is realized spatially in the kitchen-dining rooms of the clan matriarchs.

It is in the organization of spaces associated with food preparation and food consumption that HUD houses differ the most from Zuni vernacular houses. In vernacular houses, the kitchen-dining room is generally one of the most integrating and controlling spaces in the structure of residential space. In HUD houses, food preparation is segregated from food consumption, and both types of spaces are more segregated from the overall structure of the domicile than in vernacular houses. The spatial organization of the kitchens and dining rooms in HUD houses weakens the key role of women in Zuni society. The small size and bifurcated organization of spaces associated with food preparation and consumption in HUD houses makes it difficult to accommodate large social groups and fragments the social interaction that occurs during these ritual occasions.

The continuities in the open space structure of Zuni Pueblo derive from the persisting social activities of transpatial social groups such as kivas, medicine fraternities, and priesthoods. The changes that have occurred in the open space structure of Zuni settlements in the late nineteen and twentieth centuries, however, and the more recent changes in the internal structure of Zuni residential space both suggest that Zuni society is undergoing social change. The more numerous and smaller houses surrounded by open space that have become common at both Zuni Pueblo and the farming villages indicate that the basic household units are becoming smaller and more fragmented. In ethnographic terms, the changing spatial structure of Zuni architecture suggests Zuni society is changing from a strongly unilinear to an increasingly bilateral social system with more neolocality in postmarital residence.

EVALUATION OF THE METHOD AND THEORY OF SPACE SYNTAX AS APPLIED IN ARCHAEOLOGY

One of the objectives of this research was to explore the techniques, method, and theory of space syntax (Hillier and Hanson 1984) to evaluate the usefulness of this approach in archaeological research. Based on the results obtained in the analysis of historic Zuni settlements, this evaluation is mixed.

The techniques of graph analysis are robust in their ability to differentiate and quantify the spatial relationships of architectural structure. The justified graphs depicting the internal structure of buildings clarify spatial relationships of asymmetry and visually distinguish between distributed and nondistributed components. These graphs are amenable to quantification that may be used in a statistical comparison of different house structures. The graphs of the axial and convex space structures of settlements are less intuitively meaningful than the justified permeability graphs of building interiors, but the basic syntactic measures derived from them are valid. The measure of relative asymmetry and its transformed value of real relative asymmetry, and, to a lesser degree, the measure of control, are especially useful. The reduction of open space graphs that are not visually intuitive to statistical measures that make sense is definitely helpful in analysis. The various statistics describing the approximation of open space to a grid (for example, grid convexity, grid axiality, convex articulation) seem to validly describe spatial structure, but have less obvious analytical utility than measures of asymmetry and control.

The analytical techniques derived from graph theory are clearly the strongest aspect of the space syntax approach. They allow spatial structures identified in archaeological sites to be rigorously characterized and quantified in novel and useful ways using formal attributes. The measures of asymmetry and distributedness suspport far more detailed descriptions of architectural space than many of the geometrically derived terms commonly used in Southwestern archaeology, such as "L-shaped" room blocks, "plaza-oriented" pueblos, and similar descriptors.

The method for joining the measurements obtained with graph theoretic analytical techniques to social theory is intellectually derived from the sound premises of structuration theory. This method relates the architectural products derived from individual actions to social structure defined as the recursive use of rules and resources. Such a method is of critical importance in using the tangible archaeological record to study an intangible subject like society.

The descriptive theory of space syntax makes the process of architectural growth understandable. This descriptive theory starts with a random process of adding architectural cells to open space. Different architectural forms are attained through various rules that restrict the random growth process. In this growth process, a global structure can be imparted to settlement form from many individual actions as well as from centralized planning. This descriptive theory adequately describes the growth process that occurred at all the historic Zuni settlements other than HUD subdivisions, which were designed by non-Zuni architects. In and of itself, the descriptive theory of space syntax offers a valuable way to view the genesis and growth of architectural structure. As Hillier and Hanson (1984: 80) observe, however, the rules that can be abstracted to describe settlement growth are limited, because the application of simple generative syntax to increasingly complex spatial arrangements yields increasingly general relational structures and tenuous descriptions. For this reason, Hillier and Hanson developed techniques to quantify the syntactic properties of open space and building interiors.

The descriptive theory of space syntax has only limited explanatory power concerning why the members of different societies would construct buildings and settlements with different spatial arrangements. To address this issue, Hillier and Hanson (1984: 18–22, 96–97, 142) turn to Durkheimian sociology and the concepts of organic and mechanical solidarity. In their formulation, organic solidarity (interdependence through differences in the division of labor) requires a dense, integrated space, and mechanical solidarity (integration through similarities of group belief and structure) requires a segregated and dispersed space. Hillier and Hanson postulate that the syntactic property of asymmetry equates to social segregation and that of symmetry equates to social integration. Similarly, they postulate that distributedness equates to the diffusion of social groups and nondistributedness equates to superordinate control of social interaction. These postulates remain exactly that, assumptions that have not been independently confirmed with empirical findings.

The Durkheimian concepts of organic and mechanical solidarity have a heuristic value. Because all societies exhibit both forms of solidarity in different degrees, however, the concepts have weak explanatory power. The changes in historic Zuni social structure have been relatively gradual and subtle, not catastrophic. Explanation of this social change in terms of organic and mechanical solidarity is difficult at best. Perhaps an archaeological analysis using concepts of Durkheimian solidarity would yield more cogent and satisfying results if Zuni architecture and social structure were compared with those of societies organized very differently, such as Navajo outfits or Ashanti palaces. The fact that differences in the spatial structure of Zuni settlements were found to be a matter of degree rather than kind makes understanding the differences difficult in Durkheimian terms, especially when Zuni society, like all societies, exhibits both forms of solidarity.

An attempt has been made here to apply the techniques of space syntax using the recommended methodology and then "squeeze" as much meaning as possible from the results using the theoretical paradigm. At times, this exercise yielded interesting results, such as the spatial integration of churches in early seventeenth-century villages as related to the history of Spanish colonial rule, the social experimentation inferred to have occurred in the Dowa Yalanne settlement based on architectural forms, and the manner in which HUD houses weaken the traditional role of women in Zuni society. At other times, however, the ideas derived using the explanatory paradigm were less interesting and not always meaningful.

Exactly what the syntactic spatial relationships mean for social structure is often ambiguous. In Hillier and Hanson's (1984) work, and in this research, the results obtained with the graph theoretic measures of space syntax are useful in framing interpretations that are essentially discursive in nature. Applied archaeologically, the results can be used to generate and describe many inductive and hypothetical notions about social structure. The current state of the art of space syntax method and theory, however, is such that its use in a purely deductive-nomological paradigm is more limited.

Statistical comparisons of the syntactic measures were used herein to investigate change in spatial structure through time. This sort of statistical manipulation is underutilized in the work of Hillier and Hanson and their colleagues. Although the syntactic measures of Hillier and Hanson are statistics, these measures have been used essentially for descriptive rather than quantitative purposes. The work of Berg (1987) and the analyses in this study point to ways the methodology of space syntax can be productively extended using statistical procedures to determine whether differences in spatial structures are significant.

The social meaning of the demonstrated variation in syntactic measures, however, was elucidated less by a comparison of mean values and more by a contextual analysis of how different types of open space or room functions were integrated into the overall structural arrangement. This procedure, of course, entails the use of functional attributions of space whose determination is in itself a difficult archaeological problem. Ultimately, then, productive results using the space syntax approach require more than purely formal descriptions of space. In the absence of ethnographic information about room function or about noninterchangeable open spaces like sacred areas and shrines, the space syntax approach generates interesting notions but little secure knowledge.

The use of space syntax in the archaeological investigation of historic Zuni settlements suggests that the method and theory of the social logic of space need further development. At present, Hillier and Hanson's approach works well to explicitly discuss known aspects of social organization in relation to architectural arrangements, but working from the known to the unknown is more problematical. To some degree, Leach's (1978) criticism is correct. Space syntax as *currently* developed cannot fully work unless something is already known of the relevant social structure and the observed patterns of spatial arrangement can be related to known social structure in retrospect. Ultimately, however, this does not need to remain the case. By combining analyses of space syntax with more conventional means of reaching archaeological inferences about social structure, and by building a large set of ethnographic and archaeological case studies to provide benchmarks about congruence in architectural and social structures, the additional method and theory that is needed can be developed so that the approach can reach its potential in archaeological research. This research is offered as a procedural example and as an initial case study toward establishing these benchmarks.

ISSUES FOR FUTURE RESEARCH

This research raises several issues concerning Zuni architecture and society, and the method and theory of space syntax, that merit further investigation. First, the fact that all historic villages have distributed open space structures, whereas several Zuni villages occupied in the period from A.D. 1250 to 1400 have strongly nondistributed open space structures, suggests there was a major change in Zuni social organization in the late prehistoric era. This observation deserves further investigation using the method and theory of space syntax. The resolution of architecture in the site plans of many of the nondistributed prehistoric pueblos seems adequate for a productive application of the techniques of space syntax. Such an analysis may yield results indicating a difference in the kind as well as in the degree of spatial arrangements. Such a fundamental spatial difference may support an inference about a corresponding difference in the predominant form of social integration in late prehistoric Zuni society.

The results of the analysis of residential space in Zuni Pueblo could be augmented and strengthened by several types of ethnographic research. The actual use of rooms in HUD houses occupied by the Zuni should be determined ethnographically. It would be interesting to learn how many living rooms are converted to bedrooms at night and in what spaces home workshops have been installed. Additional ethnographic research is needed to quantify the nature and amount of social interaction in the various rooms of both HUD and Zuni vernacular houses. Detailed behavioral observations would provide an independent means to evaluate the theoretical postulates of the space syntax approach.

Similarly, research to document the frequency and type of social encounters in the open space of Zuni pueblo and its suburbs is needed to independently confirm the results of the space syntax analysis. Are there more encounters and social interaction in highly integrated spaces than in less integrated spaces? Does the density of houses in Zuni vernacular suburbs yield more social interaction than the less dense HUD subdivisions? The answers to these and other questions should be obtained through ethnographically oriented environmental-behavioral research using a rigorous theoretical and methodological foundation like that described by Rapoport (1990).

At Zuni, it would be useful to undertake a syntactic analysis of social structure using kinship terminology to elucidate social relations and then compare the results of this study to a syntactic analysis of the architectural spaces used by particular social groups. Theoretically, a paradigmatic classification of social groups would move ethnography beyond its limited ability to deal with the variation that exists in Zuni family structure. If systematic relationships were documented between social and spatial structures as described syntactically, this approach would provide a significant new way to understand Zuni social organization.

Some means need to be developed to combine a syntactic approach with a distributional approach that incorporates all the buildings on the Zuni Indian Reservation and not simply the village settlements. This kind of application is needed in part because there is a gradual and not always well-defined boundary between the farming villages and the outlying sheep camps on the reservation. The inclusion of all buildings on the reservation in an analysis rather than only the architecture present in the larger settlements would ensure that all aspects of Zuni society are incorporated into the analysis. The early farming villages perhaps represent the initial development of a patrilineal or bilateral settlement component associated with the livestock industry. To investigate this idea further, contemporary sheep camps need to be analyzed and compared to the early farming villages. Investigation of village settlements was a productive point of departure using the space syntax approach, but the next logical development would be to incorporate all buildings and the landscapes in which they are situated.

The techniques of space syntax were only applied to analyze open space at ground level in this study. In retrospect, this limited approach does not adequately capture the real routes of access within a multistoried pueblo where rooftop terraces are used as activity areas. A more sophisticated analysis that incorporates this third dimension is theoretically possible, because people only travel on plane surfaces, accessing higher planes or levels via stairs, ladders, or other bridging devices. The analysis of the two-story HUD apartment buildings demonstrates how multistoried residential architecture can be analyzed using space syntax. Similar conventions could be used in the analysis of rooftop terraces as open space. Determining the routes of access via ladders in Zuni in 1881 would involve careful analysis of historical photographs. The lack of complete photographic coverage, however, and the ease with which ladders were moved around, would present significant impediments to analysis. In this research, the actual technique of counting the distance of each axial space from every other space was done manually. Greatly increasing the number of axial lines by including rooftop terraces would require an automated means of quantifying intersections and syntactic distance; using a computerized geographic information system (GIS) program would be advisable.

An analysis of the contemporaneous use of both internal and external space is needed to fully interpret space syntax. In an application of space syntax at Sand Canyon Pueblo in Colorado, for instance, Bradley (1992: 94–95; 1993: 29–32) determined that the structures that were highly integrated in terms of internal permeability were also in areas of the settlement that were difficult to access, whereas the structures with less internal integration, inferred to be ceremonial in nature, were adjacent to more accessible public space like the plaza.

The methodology of space syntax is proving to be useful, especially when applied to well-preserved archaeological sites with detailed floor plans showing doorways and other means of access. Syntactic analysis of small house sites and Greathouses in Chaco Canyon is promising in this regard (Bustard 1995; Cooper 1995). The work of Wendy Bustard (1995) is especially interesting because it simultaneously analyzes the permeability of internal and external spaces.

In Bustard's analysis of the different types of space contained within the small house sites of Chaco Canyon, she determined that there is a consistent ordering of functional spaces with respect to the measures of integration. She refers to this ordering as a "functional genotype," expressed by identifying which types of spaces are more spatially integrated than others. The genotype for Chacoan small house sites is "plaza > kiva rooftop > mealing room > room with firepit > room with no features > storage." As interpreted by Bustard, this means that plazas are more spatially integrating or accessible than kiva rooftops, which are more integrating than rooms with mealing bins, and so forth. Storage rooms are the least integrating and most inaccessible spaces.

By analytically reducing syntactic measures of integration to a genotype, Bustard is able to systematically compare the small house sites of Chaco Canyon with other prehistoric and historic archaeological settlements. In the analysis of Zuni building interiors, for instance, Zuni vernacular houses have a genotype of "living room > kitchen-dining room > porch > bedroom > utility room > building exterior > workshop > storage space > bathroom," whereas HUD houses have a genotype of "living-dining room > utility room > porch > bedroom > building exterior > kitchen > bathroom > storage space."

Bustard's technique for describing genotypes facilitates the identification of similarities and differences. For instance, storage spaces are systematically the most inaccessible rooms in all forms of housing, including prehistoric and historic Puebloan buildings and HUD housing. Prehistoric Chacoan small house sites and Zuni vernacular houses are similar in that rooms used to prepare food (mealing rooms, kitchens) are among the most integrated interior spaces. This situation is in marked contrast with HUD houses, in which the kitchens are among the least accessible spaces. The spatial isolation of kitchens in the HUD genotype has potentially deleterious implications for Puebloan modes of social interaction.

The spatial integration of rooms used for food preparation in Chacoan small house sites and in Zuni vernacular houses represents a fundamental continuity in the use of space that can be investigated at other Southwestern archaeological sites. The application of space syntax to a wider range of prehistoric and historic archaeological settlements will also enable archaeologists to systematically compare architecture from different periods and geographical areas. The underlying spatial structure of buildings and settlements can be analyzed independently of the particular combination of construction materials and architectural styles that characterize regional architecture through time and space. As the work of Berg (1987) and Bustard (1995) demonstrates, space syntax is particularly useful when it is used to investigate different room functions or categories of spaces.

Ultimately, with respect to space syntax as a theoretical approach, a better bridge is needed between ethnographic and archaeological views of society. One way to build this bridge is through an ethnoarchaeological investigation of space syntax at Zuni Pueblo. Such a study would enable the structural relationships between settlement layout and social interaction to be independently measured and evaluated in terms of the theoretical sociology of space syntax. This important ethnographic information could then be used to strengthen the theoretical application of space syntax to the archaeological record. Space-behavior correlations demonstrated with ethnoarchaeological data could then be applied in a purely archaeological application of the method to the archaeological record.

Ethnographic and archaeological (structural) views of Zuni society will not and do not need to be isomorphic, but each perspective needs to make sense in terms of the other. We can state unequivocally that Zuni Pueblo has a higher mean RRA than its contemporaneous farming villages, but what this more segregated spatial structure really means in terms that are understandable either to the Zuni or to anthropologists is not yet entirely clear. The goal should not be to end a syntactic analysis with a return to an ethnographic perspective, but to create new structural views of social organization in terms of the archaeological record. Although it makes sense to explicate this new structural view in terms of ethnographic benchmarks, the archaeological study of society has the potential to create new forms of knowledge that broaden sociocultural anthropology. The space syntax approach offers an intriguing and useful beginning in this endeavor.

In conclusion, the techniques of space syntax provide useful ways to analyze space, but the theoretical foundation of space syntax needs more development. There is no reason why the techniques and methods of space syntax have to remain wedded to Durkheimian concepts of social solidarity. Hillier and Hanson have described the rudiments of an innovative approach that can be highly productive in the archaeological study of architecture. It is exciting to realize that as archaeologists we can adapt this approach to the exigencies of the archaeological record and build an anthropological theory that makes appropriate and beneficial use of space syntax.

References

ABERLE, DAVID F.

1970 Comments. In *Reconstructing Prehistoric Pueblo Societies*, edited by William A. Longacre, pp. 214–223. Albuquerque: University of New Mexico Press.

ADAMS, E. CHARLES

1978 Synthesis of Hopi Prehistory and History. MS on file, Museum of Northern Arizona, Flagstaff.

1983 The Architectural Analogue to Hopi Social Organization and Room Use, and Implications for Prehistoric Northern Southwestern Culture. *American Antiquity* 48(1): 44–61.

AGORSAH, EMMANUEL KOFI

1988 Evaluating Spatial Behavior Patterns of Prehistoric Societies. *Journal of Anthropological Archaeology* 7: 231–247.

1993 Archaeological Considerations on Social Dynamics and Spatial Pattern Development of Traditional Settlements. In "Spatial Boundaries and Social Dynamics, Case Studies from Food-Producing Societies," edited by Augustin Holl and Thomas E. Levy, pp. 7–24. *International Monographs in Prehistory, Ethnological Series* 2. Ann Arbor, Michigan.

ALEXANDER, CHRISTOPHER

1966 A City is Not a Tree. *Design Magazine* 206: 46–55.

ALEXANDER, CHRISTOPHER, HAJO NEIS, ARTEMIS ANNINOU, AND INGRID KING

1987 *A New Theory of Urban Design*. New York: Oxford University Press.

ALEXANDER, CHRISTOPHER, SARA ISHIKWA, MURRAY SILVERSTEIN, MAX JACOBSON, INGRID FIKSDAHL-KING, AND SHLOMO ANGEL

1977 *A Pattern Language*. New York: Oxford University Press.

ALLEN, WILLIAM L., AND JAMES B. RICHARDSON

1971 The Reconstruction of Kinship from Archaeological Data: The Concepts, the Methods, and the Feasibility. *American Antiquity* 36(1): 41–53.

ALTMAN, IRWIN, AND MARTIN M. CHEMERS

1980 *Culture and Environment*. Monterey, California: Brooks/Cole.

ANKERL, GUY

1981 *Experimental Sociology of Architecture*. The Hague: Mouton.

ANYON, ROGER

1992 The Late Prehistoric and Early Historic Periods in the Zuni-Cibola Area, A.D. 1400–1680. In *Current Research on the Late Prehistory and Early History of New Mexico*, edited by Bradley J. Vierra, pp. 75–83. Albuquerque: New Mexico Archaeological Council.

ANYON, ROGER, AND T. J. FERGUSON

1983 Settlement Patterns and Changing Adaptations in the Zuni Area after A.D. 1000. Paper presented at the Anasazi Symposium, San Juan Museum Research Center, Bloomfield, New Mexico.

ANYON, ROGER, AND BEN ROBERTSON

1983 Site Descriptions. In "Archaeological Investigations between Manuelito Canyon and Whitewater Arroyo, Northwest New Mexico," Vol. 1, edited by Roger Anyon, Susan M. Collins, and Kathyrn H. Bennett, pp. 83–435. *Zuni Archaeology Program Report* 185. Pueblo of Zuni, New Mexico.

BAGLIVO, JENNY A., AND JACK E. GRAVER

1983 *Incidence and Symmetry in Design and Architecture*. Cambridge: Cambridge University Press.

BANDELIER, ADOLPH F.

1890a Final Report of Investigations among the Indians of the Southwestern United States, Carried on Mainly in the Years from 1880 to 1885, Part 1. *Papers of the Archaeological Institute of America, American Series* 3. Cambridge: John Wilson and Son, University Press.

1890b Hemenway Southwestern Archaeological Expedition Contributions to the History of the Southwestern Portion of the United States. *Papers of the Archaeological Institute of America, American Series* 5. Cambridge: John Wilson and Son.

1892a Hemenway Southwestern Archaeological Expedition 1, An Outline of the Documentary History of the Zuñi Tribe. *Journal of American Ethnology and Archaeology* 3(1): 1–115.

1892b Final Report of Investigations among the Indians of the Southwestern United States, Carried on Mainly

BANDELIER, ADOLPH F. (*continued*)
in the Years from 1880 to 1885, Part 2. *Papers of the Archaeological Institute of America, American Series* 4. Cambridge: John Wilson and Son, University Press.

BANNISTER, BRYANT, JOHN W. HANNAH, AND WILLIAM J. ROBINSON
1970 *Tree-ring Dates from New Mexico M-N, S, Z, Southwestern New Mexico Area.* Tucson: Laboratory of Tree-Ring Research, University of Arizona.

BATKIN, JONATHAN
1987 *Pottery of the Pueblos of New Mexico.* Colorado Springs: Taylor Museum of the Colorado Springs Fine Arts Center.

BATTY, MICHAEL
1989 Review of *Social Logic of Space*, by Bill Hillier and Julienne Hanson. *Sociology* 19: 161–162.

BAUM, ANDREW, AND STUART VALINS
1977 *Architecture and Social Behavior: Psychological Studies of Social Density.* New York: John Wiley.

BAYBARS, I., AND C. M. EASTMAN
1980 Enumerating Architectural Arrangements by Generating their Underlying Graphs. *Environment and Planning B* 7: 239–310.

BELL, WILLIAM A.
1870 *New Tracks in North America, A Journal of Travel and Adventure Whilst Engaged in the Survey for a Southern Railroad to the Pacific Ocean during 1867–8.* London: Chapman and Hall.

BENDER, NORMAN J.
1984 *Missionaries, Outlaws, and Indians; Taylor F. Ealy at Lincoln and Zuni, 1878–1881.* Albuquerque: University of New Mexico Press.

BERG, MARJANNA
1987 *Spatial Aspects of Social Organization: A Study of Buildings for Daycare.* Göteborg: Department of Urban Design and Planning, Chalmers University of Technology.

BIEBER, RALPH P.
1974 *Marching with the Army of the West, 1846–1848, by Abraham Robinson Johnston, Marcellus Ball Edwards, and Philip Gooch Ferguson.* Philadelphia: Porcupine Press.

BIGELOW, GEORGE T.
Map Map of Ruins of Old Zuñi, Tâ Ai Yälane or Thunder Mountain. Map on file, Culin Archival Collection, Cushing Sketches (6.3.029). Brooklyn: Brooklyn Museum Archives.

BINFORD, LEWIS R.
1968 Archaeological Perspectives. In *New Perspectives in Archaeology*, edited by Sally R. Binford and Lewis R. Binford, pp. 5–32. Chicago: Aldine.

BINFORD, LEWIS R., AND JEREMY SABLOFF
1982 Paradigms, Systematics, and Archaeology. *Journal of Anthropological Research* 38(2): 137–153.

BOCK, PHILIP K.
1964 Social Structure and Language Structure. *Southwestern Journal of Anthropology* 20: 393–407.

BOLTON, HERBERT E.
1949 *Coronado on the Turquoise Trail: Knight of Pueblos and Plains.* Albuquerque: University of New Mexico Press.

BORCHERS, PERRY
1972 The Central and Original Portion of the Pueblo of Zuni, Zuni Reservation, McKinley County, New Mexico, U.S.A. Prepared at the School of Architecture, Ohio State University, Columbus, Ohio, under the direction of the National Park Service, United States Department of the Interior. Drawing on file, Historic American Buildings Survey, Washington.
1979a Ojo Caliente, Farming Village of the Pueblo of Zuni, Zuni Indian Reservation, Valencia County, New Mexico. Drawing on file, Zuni Archaeology Program, Pueblo of Zuni.
1979b Upper Nutria, Farming Village of the Pueblo of Zuni, Zuni Indian Reservation, McKinley County, New Mexico. Drawing on file, Zuni Archaeology Program, Pueblo of Zuni.
1979c Lower Nutria, Farming Village of the Pueblo of Zuni, Zuni Indian Reservation, McKinley County, New Mexico. Drawing on file, Zuni Archaeology Program, Pueblo of Zuni.

BRADLEY, BRUCE
1992 Excavations at Sand Canyon Pueblo. In "The Sand Canyon Archaeological Project," edited by William D. Lipe, pp. 79–91. *Occasional Paper* 2. Cortez, Colorado: Crow Canyon Archaeological Center.
1993 Planning, Growth, and Functional Differentiation at a Prehistoric Pueblo: A Case Study from SW Colorado. *Journal of Field Archaeology* 20: 23–42.

BREW, JOHN O.
1979 Hopi Prehistory and History to 1850. *Handbook of North American Indians*, William C. Sturtevant, General Editor, Vol. 9, *Southwest*, edited by Alfonso Ortiz, pp. 514–523. Washington: Smithsonian Institution.

BUNTING, BAINBRIDGE
1976 *Early Architecture in New Mexico.* Albuquerque: University of New Mexico Press.

BUNZEL, RUTH L.
1932 Introduction to Zuni Ceremonialism. *Forty-seventh Annual Report of the Bureau of American Ethnology for the Years 1929–1930*, pp. 467–544. Washington.

BUSHNELL, G. H. S.
1955 Some Pueblo IV Pottery Types from Kechipaun, New Mexico, U.S.A. *Anais do 31 Congresso Internacional de Americanistas, São Paulo* 2: 657–665. Sao Paulo: Editora Anhembi.

BUSTARD, WENDY

1995 Genotypes of Space: A Spatial Analysis of Domestic Structures in Chaco Canyon. Paper presented at the 60th Annual Meeting of the Society for American Archaeology, Minneapolis.

CAMERON, CATHERINE M.

1992 An Analysis of Residential Patterns and the Oraibi Split. *Journal of Anthropological Archaeology* 11(2): 173–186.

CAMP, CHARLES L., Editor

1966 *George C. Yount and His Chronicles of the West Comprising Extracts from his "Memoir" and from the Orange Clark "Narrative."* Denver: Old West Publishing.

CAYWOOD, LOUIS R.

1972 *The Restored Mission of Nuestra Señora de Guadalupe de Zuni, Zuni, New Mexico.* St. Michael's, Arizona: St. Michael's Press.

CHIPPENDALE, CHRISTOPHER

1986 Archaeology, Design Theory, and the Reconstruction of Prehistoric Design Systems. *Environment and Planning B, Planning and Design* 13: 445–485.

COHEN, IRA

1990 Structuration Theory and Social Order: Five Issues in Brief. In *Anthony Giddens, Consensus and Controversy*, pp. 33–45. London: Falmer Press.

COLLINS, RANDALL

1988 The Durkheimian Tradition in Conflict Sociology. In *Durkheimian Sociology: Cultural Studies*, edited by Jeffrey C. Alexander, pp. 107–128. Cambridge: Cambridge University Press.

CONNELLEY, WILLIAM E.

1907 *Doniphan's Expedition and the Conquest of New Mexico and California.* Kansas City: Bryant and Douglas Book and Stationary.

COOK, SHERBURNE F.

1972 Prehistoric Demography. *Addison-Wesley Module* 16. Reading: Addison-Wesley.

COOPER, LAUREL M.

1995 *Space Syntax Analysis of Chacoan Great Houses.* Doctoral dissertation, University of Arizona, Tucson. Ann Arbor: University Microfilms.

COZZENS, SAMUEL WOODWORTH

1876 *The Marvellous Country*. Boston: Lee and Shepard.

CULIN, STEWART

1903 Report on a Collecting Expedition among the Indians of New Mexico and Arizona, April–September, 1903. Expedition Notes. MS on file, Culin Collection, Brooklyn Museum Archives, New York.

1907 Expedition Report, Zuni Notes, Vol. 1. MS on file, Culin Collection, Brooklyn Museum Archives, New York.

CURTIS, EDWARD S.

1926 *The North American Indian*, Vol. 17. Norwood, Massachusetts: Plimpton Press.

CURTIS, WILLIAM E.

1883 *Children of the Sun.* Chicago: Inter-Ocean Publishing.

CUSHING, FRANK HAMILTON

Item 36 Biography of Pedro Pino. MS on file, Hodge-Cushing Collection, Southwest Museum, Los Angeles.

Item 155 Corrected Copy of Outline Report on the Origin, Working Hypothesis and Preliminary Researches of the Hemenway Southwestern Archaeological Expedition. MS on file, Hodge-Cushing Collection, Southwest Museum, Los Angeles.

1882 The Zuni Social, Mythic, and Religious Systems. *Popular Science Monthly*, June, pp. 186-192.

1890 Preliminary Notes on the Origin, Working Hypotheses, and Primary Researches of the Hemenway Southwestern Archaeological Expedition. *Proceedings of the Seventh International Congress of Americanists*, pp. 151-194. Berlin.

1896 Outlines of Zuni Creation Myths. In *Thirteenth Annual Report of the Bureau of American Ethnology for the Years 1891-1892*, pp. 321–447. Washington.

1901 *Zuñi Folk Tales*. New York: G. P. Putnam's Sons. (Reprinted 1931, Alfred A. Knopf, New York.)

1920 Zuñi Breadstuff. *Indian Notes and Monographs* 8. New York: Museum of the American Indian.

DEAN, JEFFREY S.

1969 Chronological Analysis of Tsegi Phase Sites in Northeastern Arizona. *Papers of the Laboratory of Tree-Ring Research* 3. Tucson: University of Arizona.

1970 Aspects of Tsegi Phase Social Organization: A Trial Reconstruction. In *Reconstructing Prehistoric Pueblo Societies,* edited by William A. Longacre, pp. 140–174. Albuquerque: University of New Mexico Press.

DEDERICH, DEVON

1978a Settlement in Zuni, 1978. Map on file, National Park Service, Southwest Region, Santa Fe, New Mexico.

1978b Change and Continuity in the Settlement Pattern in Zuni. National Park Service, Division of Remote Sensing. MS on file, Zuni Archaeology Program, Pueblo of Zuni.

DEETZ, JAMES F.

1982 Households, A Structural Key to Archaeological Explanation. *American Behavioral Scientist* 25(6): 717–724.

DILLON, RICHARD H., Editor

1970 *Journal of Private Josiah M. Rice, 1851: A Cannoneer in Navajo Country*. Denver: Old West Publishing.

DOHM, KAREN

1990 Effect of Population Nucleation on House Size for

DOHM, KAREN (*continued*)
Pueblos in the American Southwest. *Journal of Field Archaeology* 9: 210–239.
1992 Architecture and Privacy in Pueblo Housing. *Visual Anthropology* 5: 1–15.

DOZIER, EDWARD P.
1970 Making Inferences from the Present to the Past. In *Reconstructing Prehistoric Pueblo Societies*, edited by William A. Longacre, pp. 202–213. Albuquerque: University of New Mexico Press.

DUBLIN, SUSAN A., AND NAN A. ROTHSCHILD
1994 Deep Trash: A Tale of Two Middens. In "Exploring Social, Political, and Economic Organization in the Zuni Region," edited by Todd L. Howell and Tammy Stone, pp. 91–102. *Anthropological Research Papers* 46. Tempe: Arizona State University.

DURKHEIM, EMILE
1964 [1893] *The Division of Labour in Society*. New York: Free Press.
1965 [1915] *The Elementary Forms of the Religious Life*. New York: Free Press.

EARL, C. F.
1980 Rectangular Shapes. *Environment and Planning B* 7: 311–342.

EGGAN, FRED
1950 *Social Organization of the Western Pueblos*. Chicago: University of Chicago Press.

EGGAN, FRED, AND T. N. PANDEY
1979 Zuni History, 1850–1970. In *Handbook of North American Indians*, General Editor, William C. Sturtevant, Vol. 9, *Southwest*, edited by Alfonso Ortiz, pp. 474–481. Washington: Smithsonian Institution.

FERGUSON, T. J.
1980 Zuni Settlement and Land Use. Expert testimony submitted to the United States Claims Court as evidence in the case *Zuni Indians* v. *United States*, Docket 161–79L (Ct. Cl., filed April 27, 1979).
1981a Rebuttal Report. Expert testimony submitted to the United States Claims Court as evidence in the case *Zuni Indians* v. *United States*, Docket 161-79L (Ct. Cl., filed April 27, 1979).
1981b The Emergence of Zuni Culture and Society, A Summary of Zuni Tribal History, A.D. 1450 to 1700. In "The Protohistoric Period in the North American Southwest," edited by David R. Wilcox and W. Bruce Masse. *Anthropological Research Papers* 25: 336–353. Tempe: Arizona State University.
1985 Patterns of Land Use and Environmental Change on the Zuni Indian Reservation, 1846–1985. Expert testimony submitted to the United States Claims Court as evidence in the case *Zuni Indians* v. *United States*, Docket 327–81L (Ct. Cl., filed May 27, 1981).
1989 The Impact of Federal Policy on Zuni Land Use. In "Seasons of the Kachina: Proceedings of the California State University Hayward Conferences on the Western Pueblos, 1987–1988," edited by Lowell John Bean. *Anthropological Papers* 34: 85–131. Hayward, California: Ballena Press.
1992 Zuni Settlement Patterns during the Pueblo Revolt. In *Current Research on the Late Prehistory and Early History of New Mexico*, edited by Bradley J. Vierra, pp. 85–92. Albuquerque: New Mexico Archaeological Council.
1995 An Anthropological Perspective on Zuni Land Use. In *Zuni and the Courts*, edited by E. Richard Hart, pp. 103–120. Lawrence: University Press of Kansas.

FERGUSON, T. J., AND E. RICHARD HART
1985 *A Zuni Atlas*. Norman: University of Oklahoma Press.

FERGUSON, T. J., AND BARBARA J. MILLS
1982 Archaeological Investigations at Zuni Pueblo: 1977–1980. *Zuni Archaeology Program Report* 183. Pueblo of Zuni, New Mexico.
1987 Settlement and Growth of Zuni Pueblo: An Architectural History. *The Kiva* 52(4): 243–266.
1988 Wood Reuse in Puebloan Architecture: Evidence from Historic Zuni Settlements. Paper presented at the 53rd Annual Meeting of the Society for American Archaeology, Phoenix.

FERGUSON, T. J., E. RICHARD HART, AND CALBERT SECIWA
1988 Twentieth Century Zuni Political and Economic Development in Relation to Federal Indian Policy. In "Public Policy Impacts on American Indian Economic Development," edited by C. Matthew Snipp, pp. 113–144. *Institute for Native American Development, Development Series* 4. Albuquerque: Native American Studies, University of New Mexico.

FERGUSON, T. J., BARBARA J. MILLS, AND WILLIAM A. DODGE
1977 Archaeological Investigations at Kyaki:ma, Zuni Indian Reservation, McKinley County, New Mexico. *Zuni Archaeology Program Report* 37. Pueblo of Zuni, New Mexico.

FERGUSON, T. J., BARBARA J. MILLS, AND CALBERT SECIWA
1990 Contemporary Zuni Architecture and Society. In *Pueblo Style and Regional Architecture*, edited by Nicholas C. Markovitch, Wolfgang E. F. Preiser, and Fred G. Sturm, pp. 103–121. New York: Van Nostrand Reinhold.

FEWKES, JESSE WALTER
1891 Reconnoissance of Ruins In or Near the Zuni Reservation. *A Journal of American Ethnology and Archaeology* 1(3): 93–133.

FIRTH, RAYMOND
1963 *Elements of Social Organization*. Boston: Beacon.

FOREMAN, GRANT A.
1941 *A Pathfinder in the Southwest: The Itinerary of Lieutenant A. W. Whipple during his Explorations for a Railway from Fort Smith to Los Angeles in the Years 1853 & 1854.* Norman: University of Oklahoma Press.

FOUCAULT, MICHEL
1979 *Discipline and Punish.* Harmondsworth, England: Penguin.

FRIEDMAN, YONA
1975 *Toward a Scientific Architecture.* Translated by Cynthia Land. Cambridge: MIT Press.

GARCIA-MASON, VELMA
1979 Acoma Pueblo. In *Handbook of North American Indians*, General Editor, William C. Sturtevant, Vol. 9, *Southwest*, edited by Alfonso Ortiz, pp. 450–468. Washington: Smithsonian Institution.

GIDDENS, ANTHONY
1979a *Central Problems in Social Theory.* London: Macmillan.
1979b *Emile Durkheim.* New York: Viking Press.
1984 *The Constitution of Society, Outline of the Theory of Structuration.* Berkeley: University of California Press.
1989 A Reply to My Critics. In *Social Theory of Modern Societies: Anthony Giddens and His Critics*, edited by David Held and John B. Thompson, pp. 249–301. Cambridge: Cambridge University Press.
1990 Structuration Theory and Sociological Analysis. In *Anthony Giddens, Consensus and Controversy*, edited by Jon Clark, Celia Modgil, and Sohan Modgil, pp. 297–315. London: Falmer Press.

GLASSIE, HENRY
1975 *Folk Housing in Middle Virginia, A Structural Analysis of Historic Artifacts.* Knoxville: University of Tennessee Press.

GLOAG, JOHN
1975 *The Architectural Interpretation of History.* New York: St. Martins.

GOODY, JACK
1971 The Developmental Cycle in Domestic Groups. *Cambridge Papers in Social Anthropology* 1. Cambridge: Cambridge University Press.

GREEN, JESSE, Editor
1990 *Cushing at Zuni, The Correspondence and Journals of Frank Hamilton Cushing, 1879–1884.* Albuquerque: University of New Mexico Press.

HACKETT, CHARLES W., Editor
1942a *Revolt of the Pueblo Indians of New Mexico and Otermín's Attempted Reconquest, 1680–1682.* Vol. 1, translated by Charmion C. Shelby. Albuquerque: University of New Mexico Press.
1942b *Revolt of the Pueblo Indians of New Mexico and Otermín's Attempted Reconquest, 1680–1682.* Vol. 2, translated by Charmion C. Shelby. Albuquerque: University of New Mexico Press.

HALL, EDWARD T.
1966 *The Hidden Dimension.* New York: Doubleday.

HALL, THOMAS D.
1989 *Social Change in the Southwest, 1350–1880.* Lawrence: University Press of Kansas.

HAMMOND, GEORGE P., AND AGAPITO REY, Editors
1940 *Coronado Cuarto Centennial Publications, 1540–1940.* Vol. 2, *Narratives of the Coronado Expedition, 1540–1542.* Albuquerque: University of New Mexico Press.
1953 *Coronado Cuarto Centennial Publications, 1540–1940.* Vol. 5, *Don Juan de Oñate, Colonizer of New Mexico, 1595–1628.* Albuquerque: University of New Mexico Press.
1966 *Coronado Cuarto Centennial Publications, 1540–1940*, Vol. 3, *The Rediscovery of New Mexico, 1580–1594.* Albuquerque: University of New Mexico Press.

HANSON, JULIENNE
1989 Order and Structure in Urban Design: The Plans for Rebuilding London after the Great Fire of 1666. *Ekistics* 334/335: 22–42.

HANSON, JULIENNE, AND BILL HILLIER
1982 Domestic Space Organization. *Architecture & Comportment/Architecture & Behavior* 2: 5–25.

HARRIS, MARVIN
1968 *The Rise of Anthropological Theory.* New York: Crowell.

HART, E. RICHARD
1980 Boundaries of Zuni Land: With Emphasis on Details Relating to Incidents Occurring 1846–1946. Expert testimony submitted to the United States Claims Court as evidence in the case *Zuni Indians* v. *United States*, Docket 161–79L (Ct. Cl., filed April 27, 1979).
1985 Damage to Zuni Trust Lands. Expert testimony submitted to the United States Claims Court as evidence in the case *Zuni Indians* v. *United States*, Docket 161–79L (Ct. Cl., filed April 27, 1979).
1988 The Zuni Mountains: Chronology of an Environmental Disaster. Expert testimony submitted to the United States Claims Court in *Zuni Tribe* v. *United States*, Dockets 327–81L and 224–84L.
1991a Appendix I, Zuni Population, 1539–1989. In "A History of Zuni Water Use," by E. Richard Hart. Expert testimony submitted to the Department of Justice in behalf of the Zuni Indian Tribe in *City of Gallup* v. *USA*, No. Civ. 84–0164, District Court, McKinley County, New Mexico. MS on file, Institute of the NorthAmerican West, Seattle.
1991b A History of Zuni Water Use. Expert testimony submitted to the Department of Justice in behalf of the Zuni Indian Tribe in *City of Gallup* v. *USA*, No. Civ. 84–0164, District Court, McKinley Coun-

HART, E. RICHARD (*continued*)
ty, New Mexico. MS on file, Institute of the North-American West, Seattle.

HASSAN, FERKI
1981 *Demographic Archaeology*. New York: Academic Press.

HIEB, LOUIS A.
1990 The Metaphors of Hopi Architectural Experience in Comparative Perspective. In *Pueblo Style and Regional Architecture*, edited by Nicholas C. Markovitch, Wolfgang E. F. Preiser, and Fred G. Sturm, pp. 122-132. New York: Van Nostrand Reinhold.

HILL, JAMES N.
1970a Broken K Pueblo, Prehistoric Social Organization in the American Southwest. *Anthropological Papers of the University of Arizona* 18. Tucson: University of Arizona Press.
1970b Prehistoric Social Organization in the American Southwest: Theory and Method. In *Reconstructing Prehistoric Pueblo Societies*, edited by William A. Longacre, pp. 11-58. Albuquerque: University of New Mexico Press.

HILLIER, BILL
1985 The Nature of the Artificial: The Contingent and the Necessary in Spatial Form in Architecture. *Geoforum* 16: 163-178.
1989 The Architecture of the Urban Object. *Ekistics* 334/335: 5-21.

HILLIER, BILL, AND JULIENNE HANSON
1984 *The Social Logic of Space*. Cambridge: Cambridge University Press.

HILLIER, BILL, AND ADRIAN LEAMAN
1973 The Man-Environment Paradigm and its Pardoxes. *Architectural Design* 43: 507-511.
1976 Architecture as a Discipline. *Journal of Architectural Research* 5(1): 28-32.

HILLIER, BILL, AND ALAN PENN
1992 Dense Civilizations: The Shape of Cities in the 21st Century. *Applied Energy* 43: 41-66.

HILLIER, BILL, JULIENNE HANSON, AND H. GRAHAM
1987 Ideas are in Things: An Application of the Space Syntax Method to Discovering House Genotypes. *Environment and Planning B: Planning and Design* 14: 363-385.

HILLIER, BILL, ADRIAN LEAMAN, P. STANSALL, AND M. BEDFORD
1976 Space Syntax. *Environment and Planning B* 3: 147-185.

HODGE, FREDERICK WEBB
1907 [Editor] Handbook of American Indians North of Mexico. *Bureau of American Ethnology, Bulletin* 30. Washington: Smithsonian Institution
1918 Excavations at the Zuni Pueblo of Hawikuh in 1917. *Art and Archaeology* 7(9): 367-379.
1937 History of Hawikuh, New Mexico: One of the So-called Cities of Cibola. *Frederick Webb Hodge Anniversary Publication Fund* 1. Southwest Museum. Los Angeles: Ward Ritchie Press.
1939 A Square Kiva at Hawikuh. In *So Live the Works of Men*, edited by Donald D. Brand and Fred E. Harvey, pp. 195-214. Albuquerque: University of New Mexico Press.
1954 *Tówayálane, A Mesa with a History*. Privately printed, Los Angeles.
1966 Ceremonial Deposits in the Hawikuh Cemetery. In "The Excavation of Hawikuh by Frederick Webb Hodge," by Watson Smith, Richard B. Woodbury, and Natalie F. S. Woodbury, pp. 279-293. *Contributions from the Museum of the American Indian* 20. New York: Heye Fondation.

HOLL, AUGUSTIN
1993 Introductory Note to Spatial Boundaries and Social Dynamics: Rounds, Recycling, and the Buildup of an Upward Spiral. In "Spatial Boundaries and Social Dynamics, Case Studies from Food-Producing Societies," edited by Augustin Holl and Thomas E. Levy. *International Monographs in Prehistory, Ethnological Series* 2: 1-6.

HOLMES, BARBARA E.
1983 The Cushing Census and the Zuni Household. Paper presented at the Annual Meeting of the American Society for Ethnohistory, Albuquerque.

HOLMES, BARBARA E., AND ANDREW P. FOWLER
1980 The Alternate Dams Survey: An Archaeological Sample Survey and Evaluation of the Burned Timber and Coalmine Dams. *Zuni Archaeology Program Report* 65. Pueblo of Zuni, New Mexico.

HOPKINS, M. R.
1987 Network Analysis of the Plans of Some Teotihuacán Apartment Compounds. *Environment and Planning B* 14: 387-406.

HOWELL, TODD L.
1992 The Decision-Making Structure of Protohistoric Zuni Society. Paper presented at the 57th Annual Meeting of the Society for American Archaeology, Pittsburgh.
1994 The Decision-Making Structure of Protohistoric Zuni Society. In "Exploring Social, Political, and Economic Organization in the Zuni Region," edited by Todd L. Howell and Tammy Stone, pp. 61-90. *Anthropological Research Paper* 46. Tempe: Arizona State University.

HUANG, SHIJUN
1985 *Meaning in Environmental and Cultural Change, A Case Study of Two Pueblos*. Unpublished Master's thesis, School of Architecture and Urban Design, University of Kansas.

HUNTER-ANDERSON, ROSALIND L.
1977 A Theoretical Approach to the Study of House Form. In *For Theory Building in Archaeology*,

edited by Lewis R. Binford, pp. 287-315. New York: Academic Press.

JOJOLA, THEODORE

1993 Prepublication manuscript of "Pueblo Indian and Spanish Town Planning in New Mexico: The Pueblo of Isleta." In *Proceedings: The Mesa Verde Symposium on Anasazi Architecture and American Design, May 17-19, 1991*, edited by Baker H. Morrow and Vincent B. Price. Publication expected 1996 by University of New Mexico Press, Albuquerque.

JONES, ROBERT ALUN

1986 Emile Durkheim, An Introduction to Four Major Works. *Masters of Social Science* 2. Beverly Hills: Sage Publications.

KARP, IVAN

1983 Agency and Social Theory: A Review of Anthony Giddens. *Ethnologist* 3: 131-137.

KING, ANTHONY D., Editor

1980 *Buildings and Society, Essays on the Social Development of the Built Environment.* London: Routledge and Kegan Paul.

KINTIGH, KEITH

1985 Settlement, Subsistence, and Society in Late Zuni Prehistory. *Anthropological Papers of the University of Arizona* 44. Tucson: University of Arizona Press.

1990 Protohistoric Transitions in the Western Pueblo Area. In *Perspectives on Southwestern Prehistory*, edited by Paul E. Minnis and Charles L. Redman, pp. 258-275. Boulder: Westview Press.

1991 The Cibola Region in the Post-Chacoan Era. MS on file, Department of Anthropology, Arizona State University, Tempe.

KLETT, FRANCIS

1874 The Zuni Indians of New Mexico. *The Popular Science Monthly*, May-October, pp. 580-581.

KRAMER, CAROL

1982 *Village Ethnoarchaeology, Rural Iran in Archaeological Perspective.* New York: Academic Press.

KROEBER, ALFRED L.

1916 Zuñi Potsherds. *Anthropological Papers* 18(1): 1-37. New York: American Museum of Natural History.

1917 Zuni Kin and Clan. *Anthropological Papers* 18(2): 39-205. New York: American Museum of Natural History.

KRUGER, M. J. T.

1979a An Approach to Built-form Connectivity at an Urban Scale: System Description and its Representation. *Environment and Planning B* 6: 67-88.

1979b An Approach to Built-form Connectivity at an Urban Scale: Relationships between Built-form Connectivity, Adjacency Measures, and Urban Spatial Structure. *Environment and Planning B* 6: 163-194.

1979c An Approach to Built-form Connectivity at an Urban Scale: Variations of Connectivity and Adjacency Measures Amongst Zones and Other Related Topics. *Environment and Planning B* 6: 305-320.

1981a An Approach to Built-form Connectivity at an Urban Scale: Modeling the Distribution of Partitions and Built-Form Arrays. *Environment and Planning B* 8: 41-56.

1981b An Approach to Built-Form Connectivity at an Urban Scale: Modeling the Distribution of Partitions and Built-form Arrays. *Environment and Planning B* 8: 57-72.

LADD, EDMUND J.

1979a Zuni Social and Political Organization. In *Handbook of North American Indians*, General Editor, William C. Sturtevant, Vol 9, *Southwest*, edited by Alfonso Ortiz, pp. 482-491. Washington: Smithsonian Institution.

1979b Zuni Economy. In *Handbook of North American Indians*, General Editor, William C. Sturtevant, Vol 9, *Southwest*, edited by Alfonso Ortiz, pp. 492-498. Washington: Smithsonian Institution.

LANG, JON

1987 *Creating Architectural Theory, The Role of the Behavioral Sciences in Environmental Design.* New York: Van Nostrand Reinhold.

LANGE, CHARLES H., AND CARROLL L. RILEY, Editors

1970 *The Southwestern Journals of Adolph F. Bandelier, 1883-1884.* Albuquerque: University of New Mexico Press.

LANGE, CHARLES H., CARROLL L. RILEY, AND ELIZABETH M. LANGE, Editors

1975 *The Southwestern Journals of Adolph F. Bandelier, 1885-1888.* Albuquerque: University of New Mexico Press.

LAWRENCE, DENISE L., AND SETHA M. LOWE

1990 The Built Environment and Spatial Form. *Annual Review of Anthropology* 19: 453-505.

LAWRENCE, RODERICK J.

1986 Review of *The Social Logic of Space*, by Bill Hillier and Julienne Hanson. *Anthropos* 81: 331.

1987 *Housing, Dwellings and Homes; Design Theory, Research and Practice.* Chichester, England: John Wiley.

LEACH, EDMUND R.

1978 Does Space Syntax Really 'Constitute the Social'? In "Social Organization and Settlement: Contributions from Anthropology," edited by David R. Green, Colin Haselgrove, and Matthew Spriggs, pp. 385-401. *British Archaeological Reports, International Series* 471. Oxford.

1983 The Gatekeepers of Heaven: Anthropological Aspects of Grandiose Architecture. *Journal of Anthropological Research* 39(3): 243-264.

LEBLANC, STEVEN A.

1971 An Addition to Naroll's Suggested Floor Area and Settlement Population Relationship. *American Antiquity* 36(2): 210–211.

1978 Settlement Patterns in the El Morro Valley, New Mexico. In *Investigations of the Southwestern Anthropological Research Group: An Experiment in Archaeological Cooperation*, edited by Robert C. Euler and George J. Gumerman, pp. 45-51. Flagstaff: Museum of Northern Arizona.

LEONARD, ROBERT D.

1991 The Change from Small Villages to Large Pueblos after A.D. 1275. In *Zuni History, Victories in the 1990s*, edited by E. Richard Hart and T. J. Ferguson, Section II, p. 26. Seattle: Institute of the NorthAmerican West, Seattle.

LESLEY, LEWIS BURT, Editor

1929 *Uncle Sam's Camels: The Journal of May Humphreys Stacey Supplemented by the Report of Edward Fitzgerald Beale (1857-1858)*. Cambridge: Harvard University Press.

LEVY, JERROLD E.

1992 *Orayvi Revisited, Social Stratification in an "Egalitarian" Society*. Santa Fe: School of American Research Press.

LIPE, WILLIAM D.

1970 Anasazi Communities in the Red Rock Plateau, Southeastern Utah. In *Reconstructing Prehistoric Pueblo Societies*, edited by William A. Longacre, pp. 84–139. Albuquerque: University of New Mexico Press.

LONGACRE, WILLIAM A.

1966 Changing Patterns of Social Integration: A Prehistoric Example from the American Southwest. *American Anthropologist* 68(1): 94–102.

LOTHROP, SAMUEL K.

1919–1923 Kechipauan: Excavation Notes and Diary. MS on file, Museum of Archaeology and Ethnology, Cambridge, England.

LOWIE, ROBERT H.

1929 Notes on Hopi Clans. *Anthropological Papers* 30(6): 303–360. New York: American Museum of Natural History.

1948 *Social Organization*. New York: Rinehart.

LYNCH, KEVIN

1981 *A Theory of Good City Form*. Cambridge: MIT Press.

MARCH, LIONEL, AND PHILIP STEADMAN

1971 *The Geometry of Environment*. London: RIBA Publications.

MARKUS, T. A.

1987 Buildings as Classifying Devices. *Environment and Planning B: Planning and Design* 14: 467–484.

MCGUIRE, RANDALL H., AND MICHAEL B. SCHIFFER

1983 A Theory of Architectural Design. *Journal of Anthropological Archaeology* 2: 277–303.

MCNITT, FRANK, Editor

1964 *Navajo Expedition: Journal of a Military Reconnaissance from Santa Fe, New Mexico to the Navajo Country Made in 1849 by Lieutenant James H. Simpson*. Norman: University of Oklahoma Press.

MERRILL, WILLIAM L.

1988 *Rarámuri Souls*. Washington: Smithsonian Institution Press.

MILLS, BARBARA J.

1991 Zuni Ceramic Production and Distribution during the 15th through 17th Centuries. In "*Zuni History, Victories in the 1990s*," edited by E. Richard Hart and T. J. Ferguson, Section II, p. 27. Seattle: Institute of the NorthAmerican West, Seattle.

1995 The Organization of Protohistoric Zuni Ceramic Production. In *Ceramic Production in the American Southwest*, edited by Barbara J. Mills and Patricia L. Crown, pp. 200–230. Tucson: University of Arizona Press.

MILLS, BARBARA J., AND T. J. FERGUSON

1980 Processes of Architectural Change: Examples from the Historic Zuni Farming Villages. Paper presented at the 45th Annual Meeting of the Society for American Archaeology, Philadelphia.

MILLS, BARBARA J., BARBARA E. HOLMES, AND T. J. FERGUSON

1982 Performance Report for an Architectural and Historical Study of the Zuni Farming Villages. MS on file at the Zuni Archaeology Program, Pueblo of Zuni, New Mexico.

MILLS, GLENN

1989 Space and Power in South Africa: The Township as a Mechanism of Control. *Ekistics* 334/335: 65–74.

MINDELEFF, COSMOS

1900 Localization of Tusayan Clans. In *Nineteenth Annual Report of the Bureau of American Ethnology for the Years 1897–1898*, Part 2, pp. 635–653. Washington.

MINDELEFF, VICTOR

1891 A Study of Pueblo Architecture in Tusayan and Cibola. In *Eighth Annual Report of the Bureau of American Ethnology for the Years 1886–1887*, pp. 3–228. Washington.

MINDELEFF, VICTOR, AND COSMOS MINDELEFF

Item 2621 Field plans and diagrams on inhabited pueblos and pueblo ruins of Arizona and New Mexico, ca. 1881–1886. MS on file, National Anthropological Archives, Smithsonian Institution, Washington.

MINGE, WARD ALAN

1980 Zuni in Spanish and Mexican History. Expert testimony submitted to the United States Claims Court as evidence in the case *Zuni Indians* v. *United States*, Docket 161–79L (Ct. Cl., filed April 27, 1979).

MITCHELL, WILLIAM J.
1990 *The Logic of Architecture: Design, Computation, and Cognition.* Cambridge: MIT Press.

MOLLHAUSEN, BALDWIN
1858 *Diary of a Journey from the Mississippi to the Coasts of the Pacific, with a United States Government Expedition.* Vol. 1, translated by Mrs. Percy Sinnett. London: Longman, Brown, Green, Longmans, and Roberts.

MURDOCK, GEORGE PETER
1949 *Social Structure.* New York: Macmillan.

NAROLL, RAOUL
1962 Floor Area and Settlement Population. *American Antiquity* 27(4): 587–589.

ORTNER, SHERRY B.
1984 Theory in Anthropology since the Sixties. *Comparative Studies in Society and History* 26(1): 126–166.

PANDEY, TRILOKI NATH
1977 Images of Power in a Southwestern Pueblo. In *Anthropology of Power: Ethnographic Studies from Asia, Oceania, and the New World,* edited by Raymond D. Fogelson and Richard N. Adams, pp. 195–215. New York: Academic Press.

PARSONS, ELSIE CLEWS
1918 War God Shrines of the Laguna and Zuni. *American Anthropologist* 20(4): 381–405.
1924 The Scalp Ceremonial of Zuni. *Memoirs of the American Anthropological Association* 31.
1933 Hopi and Zuni Ceremonialism. *Memoirs of the American Anthropological Association* 39.
1939 *Pueblo Indian Religion.* 2 vols. Chicago: University of Chicago Press.

PEPONIS, J. E. HADJINIKOLAOU, C. LIVIERATOA, AND D. A. FATOUROS
1989 The Spatial Core of Urban Culture. *Ekistics* 334/335: 43–55.

PLIMPTON, C. L., AND F. A. HASSAN
1987 Social Space: A Determinant of House Architecture. *Planning and Environment B* 7: 439–449.

PREZIOSI, DONALD
1979 *The Semiotics of the Built Environment, An Introduction to Architectonic Analysis.* Bloomington: Indiana University Press.

RAPOPORT, AMOS
1980 Vernacular Architecture and the Cultural Determinants of Form. In *Buildings and Society,* edited by Anthony D. King, pp. 283–305. London: Routledge and Kegan Paul.
1990 *History and Precedence in Environmental Design.* New York: Plenum Press.

REDMAN, CHARLES L., EDWARD CURTIN, NINA VERSAGGI, AND JEFFREY WANSER
1978 Social Archeology: The Future of the Past. In *Social Archeology, Beyond Subsistence and Dating,* edited by Charles L. Redman, Mary Jane Berman, Edward V. Curtin, William T. Langhorne, Jr., Nina M. Versaggi, and Jeffrey C. Wanser, pp. 1–17. New York: Academic Press.

REID, J. JEFFERSON, AND IZUMI SHIMADA
1982 Pueblo Growth at Grasshopper: Methods and Models. In "Multidisciplinary Research at Grasshopper Pueblo, Arizona," edited by William A. Longacre, Sally J. Holbrook, and Michael W. Graves, pp. 12–18. *Anthropological Papers of the University of Arizona* 40. Tucson: University of Arizona Press.

REID, J. JEFFERSON, AND STEPHANIE M. WHITTLESEY
1982 Households at Grasshopper Pueblo. *American Behavioral Scientist* 25(6): 687–703.

RILEY, CARROLL L.
1975 The Road to Hawikuh: Trade and Trade Routes to Cibola–Zuni during Late Prehistoric and Early Historic Times. *The Kiva* 41(2): 137–159.

ROBERTS, FRANK H. H., JR.
1931 The Ruins at Kiatuthlanna, Eastern Arizona. *Bureau of American Ethnology Bulletin* 100. Washington.
1932 The Village of the Great Kivas on the Zuñi Reservation, New Mexico. *Bureau of American Ethnology Bulletin* 111. Washington.
1939 Archaeological Remains in the Whitewater District, Eastern Arizona, Part 1, House Types. *Bureau of American Ethnology Bulletin* 121. Washington.

ROCK, JAMES T.
1974 The Use of Social Models in Archaeological Interpretation. *The Kiva* 40(1–2): 81–91.

ROHN, ARTHUR H.
1971 Mug House, Mesa Verde National Park, Colorado. *Archaeological Research Series* 7–D. Washington: National Park Service.

ROTHSCHILD, NAN A.
1991 Incorporating the Outdoors as Living Space, Ethnoarchaeology at Zuni Pueblo, New Mexico. *Expedition* 31(1): 24–32.

ROTHSCHILD, NAN A., AND SUSAN A. DUBLIN
1995 The Zuni Farming Village Study and Excavations at Lower Pescado Village: A Report on the Columbia/Barnard Archaeological Field School, 1989–1991. MS on file at the Zuni Heritage and Historic Preservation Office, Pueblo of Zuni, New Mexico.

ROTHSCHILD, NAN, BARBARA J. MILLS, T. J. FERGUSON, AND SUSAN DUBLIN
1993 Abandonment at Zuni Farming Villages. In *The Abandonment of Settlements and Regions,* edited by Catherine M. Cameron and Steven Tomka. Cambridge: Cambridge University Press.

RUESCHEMEYER, DIETRICH
1982 On Durkheim's Explanation of Division of Labor. *American Journal of Sociology* 88(3): 579–589.

SAILE, DAVID G.
1982 Community at the Middle Place: Zuni Systems of Integration. MS on file, Center for Humanistic Studies, University of Kansas, Lawrence.

SAUNDERS, PETER
1989 Space, Urbanism and the Created Environment. In *Social Theory of Modern Societies: Anthony Giddens and His Critics*, edited by David Held and John B. Thompson, pp. 215-234. Cambridge: Cambridge University Press.

SCOTT, ALLEN J.
1971 *Combinatorial Programming, Spatial Analysis and Planning*. London: Methuen.

SEARS, WILLIAM H.
1961 The Study of Social and Religious Systems in North American Archaeology. *Current Anthropology* 2: 223–231.

SECRETARY OF THE INTERIOR
1875 *Annual Report of the Secretary of the Interior, 875*. 44th Congress, 1st Session, House Executive Document. Washington.

SITGREAVES, LORENZO
1962 [1853] *Report of an Expedition down the Zuni and Colorado Rivers*. U. S. Senate, Executive Document 59, 32nd Congress, 2nd Session. Chicago: Rio Grand Press.

SMALL, DAVID B.
1987 Toward a Competent Structuralist Archaeology: A Contribution from Historical Studies. *Journal of Anthropological Archaeology* 6: 105-121.

SMITH, WATSON, RICHARD B. WOODBURY, AND NATALIE F. S. WOODBURY
1966 The Excavation of Hawikuh by Frederick Webb Hodge. *Museum of the American Indian, Contributions* 20. New York: Heye Foundation.

SPIER, LESLIE
1917 An Outline for a Chronology of Zuñi Ruins. *Anthropological Papers* 18(3): 207–331. New York: American Museum of Natural History.

ST. LOUIS GLOBE-DEMOCRAT, MAGAZINE SECTION
1911 A Missourian after Whom a Town, A Mountain, and a River are Named. As told by Jesus Rupert Valdez Archuleta, The Mexican Centarian who was a friend to Bill Williams. December 24, pp. 5-6.

STEA, DAVID
1987 Foreword. In *Housing, Dwellings and Homes; Design Theory, Research and Practice*, by Roderick J. Lawrence, pp. ix-xiv. Chichester, England: John Wiley and Sons.

STEADMAN, J. P.
1976 Graph-theoretic Representation of Architectural Arrangement. In *The Architecture of Form*, edited by Lionel March, pp. 94–115. Cambridge: Cambridge University Press.
1983 *Architectural Morphology*. London: Pion.

STEVENSON, MATILDA COXE
1881 *Zuni and the Zunians*. Privately printed, Washington.
1887 The Religious Life of the Zuñi Child. In *Fifth Annual Report of the Bureau of American Ethnology for the Years 1883–1884*, pp. 533–555. Washington.
1904 The Zuñi Indians, Their Mythology, Esoteric Fraternities, and Ceremonies. In *Twenty-third Annual Report of the Bureau of American Ethnology for the Years 1901–1902*, pp. 3-634. Washington.

STINY, G.
1980a Introduction to Shape and Shape Grammars. *Environment and Planning B* 7: 343–351.
1980b Kindergarten Grammars: Designing with Froebel's Building Gifts. *Environment and Planning B* 7: 409–462.

STINY, G., AND J. GIPS
1978 *Algorithmic Aesthetics*. Berkeley: University of California Press.

STINY, G., AND W. J. MITCHELL
1980 The Grammar of Paradise: On the Generation of Mughul Gardens. *Environment and Planning B* 7: 209–226.

STORPER, M.
1985 The Spatial and Temporal Constitution of Social Action: A Critical Reading of Giddens. *Environment and Planning D* 3: 407–424.

STUBBS, STANLEY A.
1950 *Bird's-eye View of the Pueblos*. Norman: University of Oklahoma Press.

SUMNER, W. M.
1979 Estimating Population by Analogy: An Example. In *Ethnoarchaeology: Implications of Ethnography for Archaeology*, edited by Carol Kramer, pp. 164-174. New York: Columbia University Press.

TABOR, PHILIP
1976 Analyzing Route Patterns. In *The Architecture of Form*, edited by Lionel March, pp. 352–378. Cambridge: Cambridge University Press.

TAFURI, MANFREDO
1980 *Theories and History of Architecture*. New York: Harper and Rowe.

TEDLOCK, DENNIS
1979 Zuni Religion and World View. In *Handbook of North American Indians*, General Editor, William C. Sturtevant, Vol. 9, *Southwest*, edited by Alfonso Ortiz, pp. 499–508. Washington: Smithsonian Institution.

TENNEY, AMON
1876 Entry for May 2, 1876 in Journal of 1875–1876. MS on file at Archives, Historical Department, Latter Day Saints Church, Salt Lake City, Utah.

THRIFT, N. J.
1983 On the Determination of Social Action in Space and

Time. *Environment and Planning D* 1: 23–57.

1987 No Perfect Symmetry. *Environment and Planning D* 5: 400–407.

UPHAM, STEADMAN

1982 *Polities and Power: A History of the Western Pueblo*. New York: Academic Press.

URRY, J.

1987 Survey 12: Society, Space, and Locality. *Environment and Planning D* 5: 435–444.

U.S. SENATE

1854 Reports of Explorations and Surveys to Ascertain the Most Practicable and Economical Route for a Railroad from the Mississippi River to the Pacific Ocean, 1853–1854. *33rd Congress, 2d Session, Executive Document* 78, Vol. 3. Washington.

VARGAS, ZAPATA LUJAN PONCE DE LEON, DIEGO DE

1914 The Re-conquest of New Mexico, 1692: Extracts from the Journal of General Don Diego de Vargas Zapata Lujan Ponce de Leon. *Old Santa Fe Magazine* 1: 288–307.

VARIEN, MARK

1990 Excavations at Three Prehistoric Sites along Pia Mesa Road, Zuni Indian Reservation, McKinley County, New Mexico. *Zuni Archaeology Program Report* 233, *Research Series* 4. Pueblo of Zuni, New Mexico.

VIVIAN, R. GWINN

1990 *The Chacoan Prehistory of the San Juan Basin*. San Diego: Academic Press.

VOELKER, FREDERICK E.

1971 William Sherley (Old Bill) Williams. In *Mountain Men and Fur Traders*, edited by Leroy R. Hafen, Vol. 3. Glendale, California: Arthur H. Clark.

WATSON, PATTY JO, STEVEN A. LEBLANC, AND CHARLES L. REDMAN

1980 Aspects of Zuni Prehistory: Preliminary Report on Excavations and Survey in the El Morro Valley of New Mexico. *Journal of Field Archaeology* 7: 201–218.

WHEELER, GEORGE M.

1889 *Report Upon United States Geographical Surveys West of the One Hundredth Meridian*, Vol. 1, *Geographical Report*. Washington.

WHIPPLE, AMIEL W.

1856 Itinerary, Explorations, and Surveys for a Railroad Route from the Mississippi River to the Pacific Ocean. Route Near the Thirty-fifth Parallel Under the Command of Lieut. A. W. Whipple, Topographical Engineers in 1853 and 1854. Reports of Explorations and Surveys, to Ascertain the Most Practicable and Economical Route for a Railroad from the Mississippi River to the Pacific Ocean. Vol. 3. *33rd Congress, 2d session, Executive Document No. 78 (Serial No. 760)*. Washington: Beverley Tucker.

WHITELEY, PETER M.

1985 Unpacking Hopi "Clans": Another Vintage Model Out of Africa? *Journal of Anthropological Research* 41: 359–374.

1986 Unpacking Hopi "Clans," 2: Further Questions about Hopi Descent Groups. *Journal of Anthropological Research* 42: 69–79.

WILCOX, DAVID R.

1975 A Strategy for Perceiving Social Groups in Puebloan Sites. In "Chapters in the Prehistory of Eastern Arizona," 4, by Paul S. Martin, Ezra B. W. Zubrow, Daniel C. Bowman, David A. Gregory, John A. Hanson, Michael B. Schiffer, and David R. Wilcox. *Fieldiana: Anthropology* 65: 120–159.

WILKINSON, LELAND

1990 SYGRAPH: The System for Graphics. Evanston, Illinois: SYSTAT.

WOODBURY, RICHARD B.

1956 The Antecedents of Zuni Culture. *Transactions of the New York Academy of Sciences*, 2d Series, 18(6): 557–563.

1959 A Reconsideration of Pueblo Warfare in the Southwestern United States. *Actas del 33 Congreso Internacional de Americanistas* 2: 124–133. San Jose, Costa Rica.

1979 Zuni Prehistory and History to 1850. In *Handbook of North American Indians*, General Editor, William C. Sturtevant, Vol. 9, *Southwest*, edited by Alfonso Ortiz, pp. 467–473. Washington: Smithsonian Institution.

ZEISEL, JOHN

1975 Sociology and Architectural Design. *Social Science Frontiers* 6. New York: Russell Sage Foundation.

Index

Abstract

The historic architecture and settlements of the Zuni Indian Tribe in western New Mexico provide an opportunity to investigate change in Zuni society through an archaeological application of space syntax. The development of historic Zuni society is analyzed by delineating systematic links between the structure of Zuni society and the structure of the architectural forms that the Zuni people built to facilitate their activities.

This structural approach is applied to Zuni villages occupied in the historic period: three villages dating to the early seventeenth century; Dowa Yalanne, a settlement occupied during the Pueblo Revolt of 1680–1692; Zuni Pueblo in 1881, 1915, and 1972; four seasonal farming settlements of the eighteenth and nineteenth centuries; and four seasonal farming villages documented in 1885 and 1979. The suburbs of Zuni Pueblo are analyzed in addition to its core architecture. The interior structure of residential architecture is investigated using a sample of 155 Zuni vernacular houses described in 1967 and 1970. Zuni vernacular architecture is compared to nine house prototypes designed by commercial architects in federally subsidized housing programs in the 1970s and 1980s.

Social structure is a product of the recursive allocation of resources during social interaction. Social structure is thus not static and its persistence depends on the repetition of behavior that can and does change through time. A structural theory of space syntax is used that explains social relations and processes in terms of how they are expressed in space through the internal and external configuration of buildings. The partitioning of space within and between the architectural units of the built environment has a social logic that derives from two relationships: the relations among occupants and the relations between the occupants and other people.

Settlement plans and building interiors are reduced to graphs whose spatial properties are quantified for comparative analysis. Statistical measures derived from graphs characterize how easy or difficult it is to gain access into a settlement and to move around once access is gained. These statistical measures are also applied to building interiors to understand how space controls the social interaction of the occupants and their visitors. Change in social structure is inferred from change in the structure of architectural space.

Resumen

La arquitectura y asentamientos históricos de la Tribu India Zuni en Nuevo México occidental brindan una oportunidad para investigar cambios en la sociedad Zuni a través de la aplicación arqueológica de sintaxis espacial. Para analizar el desarrollo de la sociedad Zuni en tiempos históricos, se delínean lazos sistemáticos entre la estructura de esta sociedad y la estructura de formas arquitectónicas que los Indios Zuni construyeron para facilitar sus actividades.

Esta aproximación estructural se aplica a pueblos Zuni ocupados durante el periodo histórico: tres pueblos que datan del siglo diecisiete; Dowa Yalanne, un asentamiento ocupado durante la Revuelta de los Indios Pueblo entre 1680 y 1692; Zuni Pueblo en 1881, 1915, y 1972; cuatro ranchos estacionales que datan de los siglos dieciocho y diecinueve; y cuatro pueblos agrícolas estacionales documentados en 1885 y 1979. Además, se analizan los suburbios de Zuni Pueblo. Se describe la estructura interior de la arquitectura residencial utilizando una muestra de 155 casas vernáculas Zuni que fueron documentadas en 1967 y 1970. La arquitectura vernácula Zuni se compara con nueve casas prototípicas diseñadas por arquitectos comerciales en projectos subsidiados por el gobierno federal en las décadas de 1970 y 1980.

La estructura social es producto de una asignación reiterada de recursos durante la interacción social. La estructura social no es, por lo tanto, estática y su persistencia depende de la repetición de conducta que puede cambiar y de hecho cambia a través del tiempo. Se utiliza una teoría estructural de sintaxis espacial que explica las relaciones y procesos sociales en cuanto a la manera en que éstos son expresados en el espacio a través de la configuración interna y externa de edificios. La partición de espacio dentro y entre unidades arquitectónicas del medio ambiente construido tiene una lógica social que se deriva de dos tipos de relación: relaciones existentes entre los ocupantes mísmos y aquéllas establecidas entre ocupantes y otra gente.

Los planos de asentamientos e interiores de edificios son reducidos a gráficos cuyas propiedades espaciales se cuantifican y analizan comparativamente. Medidas estadísticas derivadas de estos gráficos ilustran cuán asequible es un asentamiento y cuán fácil o difícil es el moverse dentro del asentamiento una vez que éste ha

The research demonstrated that the early seventeenth-century pueblos had an open space structure that was highly segregated and nondistributed, making access into and within these settlements difficult for outsiders. In contrast, the spatial structure of Dowa Yalanne, where the Zuni people coalesced during the Pueblo Revolt of 1680–1692, was highly integrated and highly distributed. Access into the village on Dowa Yalanne was made difficult for outsiders by its location on top of a steep-sided mesa rather than by the structure of its open space.

After the Pueblo Revolt, the Zuni people reintegrated their society into a single village at Zuni Pueblo, with a spatial structure similar to the seventeenth-century villages. The highly segregated and nondistributed structure of Zuni Pueblo funneled outsiders to the Catholic church in the middle of the village, but access to the rest of the village was difficult. The seasonally used farming villages occupied in the eighteenth-century had a spatial structure similar to that of Zuni Pueblo, and this helped reinforce their defensive character. The farming villages occupied in the nineteenth- and twentieth-centuries, however, had a more integrated and distributed spatial organization that facilitated movement into and within the settlements.

The comparison of Zuni vernacular housing with newer HUD housing documented a change in the integration of spaces associated with food preparation and food consumption that weakens the key role of Zuni women in Zuni society. The organization of space in HUD houses segregates Zuni matriarchs from social interaction with other members of their households and lineages. In ethnographic terms, Zuni architecture is linked to a shift from a matrilineal social organization to an increasingly bilateral social system with more neolocality in postmarital residence. The volume concludes with an evaluation of space syntax and suggestions on how this approach can be usefully applied in future archaeological research.

sido penetrado. Estas medidas estadísticas también son aplicadas al interior de edificios para comprender cómo el espacio controla la interacción social de los ocupantes y sus visitantes. Se infiere un cambio en la estructura social a partir del cambio en la estructura del espacio arquitectónico.

Esta investigación demuestra que los pueblos de principios del siglo diecisiete tuvieron una estructura de espacio abierto sumamente segregada y no-distribuida, dificultando la entrada de forasteros en estos asentamientos. En contraste, la estructura espacial de Dowa Yalanne, donde los Indios Zuni convivieron durante la Revuelta de los Indios Pueblo, entre 1680 y 1692, es altamente integrada y distribuida. El acceso de forasteros al pueblo en Dowa Yalanne era difícil, no por su estructura de espacio abierto sino más bien por su localización en la cumbre de una meseta rodeada de precipicios. Después de la Revuelta, los Indios Zuni reintegraron su sociedad en un único asentamiento, Zuni Pueblo, con una estructura espacial similar a los asentamientos del siglo diecisiete. La estructura altamente segregada y no-distribuida de Zuni Pueblo permitió el fácil acceso de estranjeros a la capilla Católica en el centro del pueblo, pero no al resto del asentamiento. Los ranchos ocupados en el siglo dieciocho tuvieron una estructura espacial similar a la de Zuni Pueblo; esto ayudó a reforzar su caracter defensivo. En contraste, los pueblos agrícolas de los siglos diecinueve y veinte tuvieron una organización espacial más integrada y distribuida, lo que facilitó el acceso y la circulación de gente dentro de ellos.

La comparación entre arquitectura vernácula doméstica en Zuni y las lotizaciones modernas de HUD documenta un cambio en la integración de espacios asociados con la preparación y consumo de alimentos, el cual debilita el rol crucial de la mujer en la sociedad Zuni. La organización del espacio en casas HUD separa a las matriarcas Zuni de la interacción social con otros miembros de su familia y linaje. En términos etnográficos, la arquitectura Zuni está atada a la transformación de una organización social matrilineal en un sistema social cada vez más bilateral, con frequente residencia posmarital neolocal. Este estudio concluye con una evaluación de sintaxis espacial y varias sugerencias para la aplicación de este método en la investigación arqueologíca.

ANTHROPOLOGICAL PAPERS OF THE UNIVERSITY OF ARIZONA

1. **Excavations at Nantack Village, Point of Pines, Arizona.** David A. Breternitz. 1959.
2. **Yaqui Myths and Legends.** Ruth W. Giddings. 1959. *Now in book form.*
3. **Marobavi: A Study of an Assimilated Group in Northern Sonora.** Roger C. Owen. 1959. (O.P.)
4. **A Survey of Indian Assimilation in Eastern Sonora.** Thomas B. Hinton. 1959. (O.P.)
5. **The Phonology of Arizona Yaqui.** Lynn S. Crumrine. 1961. (O.P.)
6. **The Maricopas: An Identification from Documentary Sources.** Paul H. Ezell. 1963. (O.P.)
7. **The San Carlos Indian Cattle Industry.** Harry T. Getty. 1964. (O.P.)
8. **The House Cross of the Mayo Indians of Sonora, Mexico.** N. Ross Crumrine. 1964. (O.P.)
9. **Salvage Archaeology in Painted Rocks Reservoir, Western Arizona.** William W. Wasley and Alfred E. Johnson. 1956.
10. **An Appraisal of Tree-Ring Dated Pottery in the Southwest.** David A. Breternitz. 1966. (O.P.)
11. **The Albuquerque Navajos.** William H. Hodge. 1969. (O.P.)
12. **Papago Indians at Work.** Jack O. Waddell. 1969.
13. **Culture Change and Shifting Populations in Central Northern Mexico.** William B. Griffen. 1969.
14. **Ceremonial Exchange as a Mechanism in Tribal Integration Among the Mayos of Northwest Mexico.** Lynn S. Crumrine. 1969. (O.P.)
15. **Western Apache Witchcraft.** Keith H. Basso. 1969. (O.P.)
16. **Lithic Analysis and Cultural Inference: A Paleo-Indian Case.** Edwin N. Wilmsen. 1970. (O.P.)
17. **Archaeology as Anthropology: A Case Study.** William A. Longacre. 1970.
18. **Broken K Pueblo: Prehistoric Social Organization in the American Southwest.** James N. Hill. 1970.
19. **White Mountain Redware: A Pottery Tradition of East-Central Arizona and Western New Mexico.** Roy L. Carlson. 1970. (O.P.)
20. **Mexican Macaws: Comparative Osteology.** Lyndon L. Hargrave. 1970.
21. **Apachean Culture History and Ethnology.** Keith H. Basso and Morris E. Opler, eds. 1971.
22. **Social Functions of Language in a Mexican-American Community.** George C. Barker. 1972.
23. **The Indians of Point of Pines, Arizona: A Comparative Study of Their Physical Characteristics.** Kenneth A. Bennett. 1973. (O.P.)
24. **Population, Contact, and Climate in the New Mexico Pueblos.** Ezra B. W. Zubrow. 1974. (O.P.)
25. **Irrigation's Impact on Society.** Theodore E. Downing and McGuire Gibson, eds. 1974.
26. **Excavations at Punta de Agua in the Santa Cruz River Basin, Southeastern Arizona.** J. Cameron Greenleaf. 1975.
27. **Seri Prehistory: The Archaeology of the Central Coast of Sonora, Mexico.** Thomas Bowen. 1976.
28. **Carib-Speaking Indians: Culture, Society, and Language.** Ellen B. Basso, ed. 1977. (O.P.)
29. **Cocopa Ethnography.** William H. Kelly. 1977.
30. **The Hodges Ruin: A Hohokam Community in the Tucson Basin.** Isabel Kelly, James E. Officer, and Emil W. Haury, collaborators; edited by Gayle H. Hartmann. 1978.
31. **Fort Bowie Material Culture.** Robert M. Herskovitz. 1978.
32. **Artifacts from Chaco Canyon, New Mexico: The Chetro Ketl Collection.** R. Gwinn Vivian, Dulce N. Dodgen, and Gayle H. Hartmann. 1978.
33. **Indian Assimilation in the Franciscan Area of Nueva Vizcaya.** William B. Griffen. 1979.
34. **The Durango South Project: Archaeological Salvage of Two Late Basketmaker III Sites in the Durango District.** John D. Gooding. 1980.
35. **Basketmaker Caves in the Prayer Rock District, Northeastern Arizona.** Elizabeth Ann Morris. 1980.
36. **Archaeological Explorations in Caves of the Point of Pines Region, Arizona.** James C. Gifford. 1980.
37. **Ceramic Sequences in Colima: Capacha, an Early Phase.** Isabel Kelly. 1980.
38. **Themes of Indigenous Acculturation in Northwest Mexico.** Thomas B. Hinton and Phil C. Weigand, eds. 1981.
39. **Sixteenth Century Maiolica Pottery in the Valley of Mexico.** Florence C. Lister and Robert H. Lister. 1982.
40. **Multidisciplinary Research at Grasshopper Pueblo, Arizona.** William A. Longacre, Sally J. Holbrook, and Michael W. Graves, eds. 1982.
41. **The Asturian of Cantabria: Early Holocene Hunter-Gatherers in Northern Spain.** Geoffrey A. Clark. 1983.
42. **The Cochise Cultural Sequence in Southeastern Arizona.** E. B. Sayles. 1983.
43. **Cultural and Environmental History of Cienega Valley, Southeastern Arizona.** Frank W. Eddy and Maurice E. Cooley. 1983.

44. **Settlement, Subsistence, and Society in Late Zuni Prehistory.** Keith W. Kintigh. 1985.

45. **The Geoarchaeology of Whitewater Draw, Arizona.** Michael R. Waters. 1986.

46. **Ejidos and Regions of Refuge in Northwestern Mexico.** N. Ross Crumrine and Phil C. Weigand, eds. 1987.

47. **Preclassic Maya Pottery at Cuello, Belize.** Laura J. Kosakowsky. 1987.

48. **Pre-Hispanic Occupance in the Valley of Sonora, Mexico.** William E. Doolittle. 1988.

49. **Mortuary Practices and Social Differentiation at Casas Grandes, Chihuahua, Mexico.** John C. Ravesloot. 1988.

50. **Point of Pines, Arizona: A History of the University of Arizona Archaeological Field School.** Emil W. Haury. 1989.

51. **Patarata Pottery: Classic Period Ceramics of the South-central Gulf Coast, Veracruz, Mexico.** Barbara L. Stark. 1989.

52. **The Chinese of Early Tucson: Historic Archaeology from the Tucson Urban Renewal Project.** Florence C. Lister and Robert H. Lister. 1989.

53. **Mimbres Archaeology of the Upper Gila, New Mexico.** Stephen H. Lekson. 1990.

54. **Prehistoric Households at Turkey Creek Pueblo, Arizona.** Julie C. Lowell. 1991.

55. **Homol'ovi II: Archaeology of an Ancestral Hopi Village, Arizona.** E. Charles Adams and Kelley Ann Hays, eds. 1991.

56. **The Marana Community in the Hohokam World.** Suzanne K. Fish, Paul R. Fish, and John H. Madsen, eds. 1992.

57. **Between Desert and River: Hohokam Settlement and Land Use in the Los Robles Community.** Christian E. Downum. 1993.

58. **Sourcing Prehistoric Ceramics at Chodistaas Pueblo, Arizona.** María Nieves Zedeño. 1994.

59. **Of Marshes and Maize: Preceramic Agricultural Settlements in the Cienega Valley, Southeastern Arizona.** Bruce B. Huckell. 1995.

60. **Historic Zuni Architecture and Society: An Archaeological Application of Space Syntax.** T. J. Ferguson. 1996.